Rating Global
Economic Freedom

D1252841

Rating Global
Economic Freedom

Edited by

Stephen T. Easton
and
Michael A. Walker

The Fraser Institute
Vancouver, British Columbia, Canada

The authors in this book have worked independently and opinions expressed by them, therefore, are their own, and do not necessarily reflect the op͙͙͙͙ ͙ ͙members or the trustees of The Fraser Institute.

HB
95
.R38
1992

Canadian Cataloguing in Publication Data

Rating global economic freedom

Includes bibliographical references.
ISBN 0-88975-145-5

1. Free enterprise. 2. International economic relations.
I. Easton, Stephen T. II. Walker, Michael, 1945-
III. Fraser Institute (Vancouver, B.C.).
HB95.E27 1992   330.12′2   C92-091452-7

Printed in Canada.

Contents

Topics in the Measure of Economic Freedom

†Presented at the Third Liberty Fund-Fraser Institute Conference on Rating Economic Freedom, Banff, Alberta, 1989.
 *Presented at the Fourth Liberty Fund-Fraser Institute Conference on Rating Economic Freedom, Sea Ranch, California, 1990.

About the Authors and Symposium Participants

James C.W. Ahiakpor is Associate Professor of economics at the California State University, Hayward, on leave from Saint Mary's University, Halifax, Nova Scotia, since September 1991. Born in Ghana in 1945, he received his B.Sc. and M.Sc. in economics from the University of Ghana, Legon, in 1971 and 1974 respectively, and taught economics at the same university from 1973 to 1976. He received his M.A. in economics from the University of British Columbia in 1977 and Ph.D. from the University of Toronto in 1981, specializing in monetary theory and development economics. He is author of two books, numerous journal articles, commentaries and book reviews.

Juan F. Bendfeldt, Guatemalan architect and developer, is Executive Director of The Center for Economic and Social Studies (CEES), an educational and research institution devoted to the advancement of freedom, founded in Guatemala in 1959. Bendfeldt is also Professor of Economics and Social Ethics at Francisco Marroquin University of Guatemala, where he is a Trustee and a member of the Board of Directors. He is also a member of the Leonard E. Read Society, and of the Foundation for Economic Education —FEE—of New York. He is founder of the Center for Research on National Economics, CIEN, of Guatemala and Director of Studies of the Guatemalan Development Foundation, FUNDESA. Juan Bendfeldt also serves as Trustee and Director of the Guatemalan Educational Foundation.

Walter E. Block is professor of Economics at the College of the Holy Cross, Worcester, Massachusetts and Adjunct Scholar at the Fraser Institute in Vancouver, British Columbia. He received his B.A. from Brooklyn College and Ph.D. from Columbia University. He has worked in various research capacities for the *National Bureau of Economic Research, the Tax Foundation,* and *Business Week.*

The author of more than 30 scholarly articles, he is also the editor of 15 books. Most recent are *Economics and the Environment: A Reconciliation, Economic Freedom Toward a Theory of Measurement: Proceedings of an International Symposium* and *Breaking the Schackles: Deregulating Canadian Industry.* He writes a syndicated column for Sterling Newspapers and lectures widely on public policy issues to university students, service, professional and religious organizations.

Jack L. Carr was born in Toronto in 1944 and graduated from the University of Toronto in 1965 before taking his Ph.D. at the University of Chicago in 1971. In 1968 he joined the Department of Political Economy in the University of Toronto and became Associate Professor in 1973 and Full Professor in 1978. Professor Carr is also a Research Associate of the Institute for Policy Analysis at the University of Toronto.

Professor Carr's publications include: *The Money Supply and the Rate of Inflation,* a study prepared for the Prices and Incomes Commission in 1972; *Cents and Nonsense* (Holt, Rinehart and Winston), a book of popular essays on economic policy, and numerous contributions to scholarly journals. His study *The Day Care Dilemma,* was published by the Fraser Institute in 1987.

John F. Chant was educated at the University of British Columbia and Duke University where he received his Ph.D. He has taught at University of Edinburgh, Duke University, Queen's University and Carleton University. He currently is Professor and Chair of the Department of Economics at Simon Fraser University. Professor Chant's research interests are in the area of monetary economics and, in particular, the regulation of financial institutions. He has been Director of the Financial Markets Group at the Economic Council of Canada, and has served as a consultant to the Bank of Canada, several federal and provincial government departments and Harvard Institute of International Development. He is the co-author of *The Economics of the Canadian Financial System: Theory, Policy and Institutions,* as well as several other books and numerous articles on aspects of monetary economics and financial markets and policy.

Edward H. Crane is president and founder of the Cato Institute. He is the coeditor of *An American Vision: Policies for the '90s* and *Beyond the Status Quo*, and the author of numerous articles for such publications as the *Wall Street Journal*, and *Washington Post*, and the *Chicago Tribune*. He is the publisher of *Regulation* magazine and former publisher of *Inquiry* magazine. Crane is also a Chartered Financial Analyst and was previously employed by the investment management firms of Scudder, Stevens, Clark and Alliance Capital Management Corporation, where he was vice president. He holds degrees from the University of California at Berkeley and the University of Southern California Graduate School of Business Administration. Crane serves on the boards of directors of Americans to Limit Congressional Terms and the Institute for Research on the Economics of Taxation, and is a member of the Mont Pelerin Society.

Arthur T. Denzau is a Professor of Economics at Washington University (St. Louis), and Fellow of the Center for Political Economy. Born in Brooklyn, New York, in 1947, he received a B.S. in Mathematics at Arizona State University in 1969, and a Ph.D. in Economics from Washington University in 1973. He worked at Virginia Polytechnic Institute and State University (VPI) and the Public Choice Center from 1973 to 1975, and then went to the University of Arizona. In 1976-77, he visited the Hoover Institute as a National Fellow, and then returned to VPI in 1979. After two years, he returned to Washington University where he has helped many graduate students get their careers started. His publications include 6 books, over 20 academic articles and a dozen policy publications at the Center for the Study of American Business. His research focuses on endogenizing government decisions in political economic models.

Thomas J. DiLorenzo holds the Scott L. Probasco, Jr. Chair of Free Enterprise at the University of Tennessee at Chattanooga. He received his Ph.D. in Economics from Virginia Polytechnic Institute and State University in 1979; his fields of specialization are Public Finance, Public Choice, Industrial Organization, and Labor Economics. He has published over 50 articles in such academic journals as the *American Economic Review, Economic In-*

quiry, Southern Economic Journal, and *Public Choice,* and is the author or co-author of five books. He has also published in popular journals such as *Readers Digest* and the *Wall Street Journal.* Dr. DiLorenzo has held faculty positions at George Mason University, State University of New York at Buffalo, Washington University in St. Louis, and Wittenberg University. He is an adjunct scholar of the Cato Institute, an adjunct fellow of the Center for Study of American Business at Washington University, and is a member of the Mont Pelerin Society.

Stephen T. Easton is a professor of economics at Simon Fraser University. In addition to his book, *Education in Canada* (Fraser Institute, 1988), he has published extensively in international economics and economic history. Among his more recent journal contributions are articles in the *Journal of International Economics* and *Explorations in Economic History.* An analysis of the duration of political regimes in parliamentary democracies is the subject of an article in the *American Journal of Political Science,* and there are several contributions to both journals and books on the subject of economic integration in North America and Europe.

Milton Friedman is a Senior Research Fellow at the Hoover Institution, Stanford University; and Professor Emeritus of Economics, University of Chicago, where he taught from 1946 to 1976. Born in Brooklyn, New York in 1912, he received a B.A. in 1932 from Rutgers University, an M.A. in 1933 from the University of Chicago, and a Ph.D. in 1946 from Columbia University. In addition to numerous scientific books and articles, Professor Friedman has written extensively on public policy, always with primary emphasis on the preservation and extension of individual freedom. He is past president of the American Economic Association, the Western Economic Association, and the Mont Pelerin Society, and is a member of the American Philosophical Society and the National Academy of Sciences. He has been awarded honorary degrees by universities in the United States, Japan, Israel, and Guatemala, and is the recipient of the Nobel Prize in Economic Science (1976), the Presidential Medal of Freedom (1988), and the National Medal of Science (1988).

John C. Goodman is president of the National Center for Policy Analysis, a Dallas-based think tank founded in February, 1983. Dr. Goodman has a

Ph.D. in economics from Columbia University and has been engaged in teaching and/or research at seven colleges and universities, including Columbia University, Stanford University, Sarah Lawrence College, Dartmouth College and Southern Methodist University.

He is author of six books and numerous articles published in professional journals. In 1988, he won the prestigious Duncan Black award for the best scholarly article on public choice economics.

James D. Gwartney is a Professor of Economics and Policy Sciences at Florida State University. He received a B.A. degree from Ottawa University in 1962 and a Ph.D. in Economics from the University of Washington in 1969. He is the coauthor (with Richard Stroup) of *Economics: Private and Public Choice*, a widely-used principles of economics text published by Harcourt Brace Jovanovich. He has published in the leading journals of professional economics, including the *American Economic Review, Journal of Political Economy, Industrial and Labor Relations Review, Cato Journal*, and *Southern Economic Journal*. His popular writings on economic topics have appeared in many newspapers including the *New York Times* and *The Wall Street Journal*. He is an adjunct scholar of the Cato Institute and the James Madison Institute, a vice president of the Southern Economic Association, and a member of The Mont Pèlerin Society.

Edward Lee Hudgins is Deputy Director, Economic Policy Studies, The Heritage Foundation. He is recognized as one of Washington's leading international economists, specializing in trade, development, and monetary issues.

A former research fellow at the Institute on Strategic Trade, Hudgins has degrees from American University, the University of Maryland, and a Ph.D. from Catholic University.

Hudgins' writings have appeared in leading newspapers and economic journals in the United States and overseas. He is a frequent lecturer and has also taught at the University of Maryland, both at its College Park campus and at its overseas extension in Munich, Germany.

Ronald W. Jones is currently Xerox Professor of International Economics at the University of Rochester. He received his A.B. from Swarthmore College in 1952 and his Ph.D. from the Massachusetts Institute of Technology in

1956. He has been at the University of Rochester since 1958, holding visiting positions as well at the London School of Economics, Stanford, Berkeley, Simon Fraser University, Queens University and the University of Stockholm. He is a Fellow of the Econometric Society and the American Academy of Arts and Sciences and holds an honorary doctorate from the University of Geneva. He is the author of over eighty articles on the theory of international trade as well as a co-author of the textbook *World Trade and Payments*.

Robert A. Lawson (M.S. Florida State University; B.S., Ohio University) expects to complete his Ph.D. requirements at Florida State in 1992. His fields are public finance, public choice, and labor economics. His dissertation, "The Limits of Leviathan: Governments in Competition," analyses the effects of federalism and fiscal decentralization on the size of government.

Richard McKenzie is Walter B. Gerken Professor of Enterprise and Society in the Graduate School of Management at the University of California, Irvine and John M. Olin Adjunct Fellow at the Center for the Study of American Business at Washington University in St. Louis. He specializes in policy analysis from a public choice perspective, having recently completed studies on "The Retreat of the Elderly Welfare State," "The Mandated-Benefit Mirage," and "The 'Fortunate Fifth' Fallacy." His most recent book is with Dwight Lee and is *Quicksilver Capital: How the Rapid Movement of Wealth Has Changed the World*. He is currently completing the book *Reality is Tricky: The Exorbitant Claims that Have Misguided Public Policy Debates*.

Joanna F. Miyake is presently a researcher at The Fraser Institute and an economic graduate student at Simon Fraser University. Her current area of research interest is the economics of health care.

Charles Murray is the Bradley Fellow at the American Enterprise Institute. Born and raised in Iowa, Murray obtained a B.A. in history from Harvard in 1965 and a Ph.D. in political science from the Massachusetts Institute of Technology in 1974. He began his career in Thailand, where he spent six years working in rural development. Subsequently he was a senior scientist at the American Institutes for Research (AIR), eventually rising to the position of Chief Scientist. From 1981 to 1989, he was a Senior Fellow at the Manhattan Institute, where he wrote *Losing Ground: American Social Policy*

1950-1980, and *In Pursuit: Of Happiness and Good Government*. In addition to his books, Murray has written extensively in *The Public Interest, Commentary, The Atlantic, The New Republic, Political Science Quarterly, National Review, The Wall Street Journal, Washington Post*, and *The New York Times*. He is currently at work on a new book in collaboration with Professor Richard Herrnstein of Harvard University.

Alvin Rabushka is a Senior Fellow at the Hoover Institution of Stanford University. Born in St. Louis in 1940, he received his B.A., M.A., and Ph.D. degrees from Washington University in St. Louis. From 1968 to 1976, he taught in the Department of Political Science at the University of Rochester. Dr. Rabushka is the author or co-author of 18 books and dozens of articles on the subjects of race and ethnic relations, aging and housing policy, tax policy in both the United States and developing nations, constitutional limits on government, economic development (especially East Asia), and Israel. He is a frequent contributor to such newspapers as *The Wall Street Journal* and *The New York Times*. He is a member of the Mont Pelerin and Philadelphia Societies and serves on advisory boards or as adjunct scholar to numerous research institutions.

Richard W. Rahn is President of Novecon Corporation. Previously, he served as the vice president and chief economist of the U.S. Chamber of Commerce, and also served as executive vice president of the Nation Chamber Foundation. Dr. Rahn has directed or participated in economic growth projects, seminars and studies in a number of countries, including Brazil, Estonia, Hungary, Mexico, the Philippines, and Thailand, and served as the U.S. co-chairman of the Bulgarian Economic Growth and Transition Project. He also served as the editor-in-chief of the *Journal of Economic Growth*. Prior to joining the Chamber, Dr. Rahn was executive director of the American Council for Capital Formation. He taught economics and business at the Polytechnic University, Florida State University, Rutgers University, George Washington University, and George Mason University. Dr. Rahn is a member of The Mont Pelerin Society. He served as an economic advisor to President Bush during the 1988 Presidential campaign. Dr. Rahn is a frequent guest commentator on tax and economic issues on national radio and television. He has been published in newspapers, such as the *Wall Street Journal* and *The New York Times*, as well as in numerous magazines and professional journals and has testified before the U.S. Congress more than fifty times. He earned his B.A. in economics at the University of South Florida, an M.B.A. at Florida State University and his Ph.D. in business economics at Columbia University.

Alan Reynolds is Director of Economic Research at the Hudson Institute in Indianapolis, and economic consultant to Wall Street firms through Keane Securities. He is a regular columnist with *Forbes* magazine, and frequent contributor to *The Wall Street Journal*, *National Review* and *Detroit News*, as well as professional publications. Mr. Reynolds was previously Chief Economist at Polyconomics, Inc., a consulting firm in New Jersey, and before that was a Vice President with The First National Bank of Chicago. His undergraduate and graduate studies in economics were at U.C.L.A. and Sacramento State College. He has served as an adviser in tax and monetary policy to the U.S. Office of Management and Budget, the U.S. Central Intelligence Agency, the Canadian Finance Ministry, and to public and private economic organizations in Mexico, Turkey, Greece, Australia and Europe.

Laurie Rubiner is a Legislative Assistant to U.S. Senator John H. Chafee of Rhode Island. Born in Detroit, Michigan in 1962, she received her B.A. from Barnard College/Columbia University in 1985. She has previously served on the staffs of U.S. Senator Connie Mack and U.S. Senator Robert Dole.

Gerald W. Scully is Professor of Economics at the University of Texas at Dallas. Born in New York City in 1941, he received his Ph.D. in economics from Rutgers University in 1968. He has taught at Ohio University, Southern Illinois University, and Southern Methodist University. He is the author of five books and fifty journal articles. His most recent book is *Constitutional Environments and Economic Growth*, Princeton University Press. He is a senior fellow of the National Center for Policy Analysis and the Foundation for Research on Economics and the Environment, and a member of the Mont Pelerin Society.

Bernard H. Siegan is distinguished professor of law at the University of San Diego School of Law, and the author or editor of eight books. He is a member of the National Commission on the Bicentennial of the Constitution, and has served as a member of President Reagan's Commission on Housing and as a Consultant to the U.S. Department of Justice, the Department of Housing and Urban Development, and the Federal Trade Commission. He was a member of the U.S. Advisory Team on Bulgarian Growth and Transition and authored its recommendations for a proposed Bulgarian Constitution.

Zane A. Spindler is a professor of economics at Simon Fraser University. He has published numerous scholarly articles on public policy issues such as, privatization, tax reform, economic sanctions, insurance-induced unemployment, pension-induced single parenthood, proprietary squatting, and constitutional design. He has travelled and lectured world-wide, and has held visiting positions at the universities of Adelaide, Cape Town, Essex, Helsinki, Paris, Singapore and Stellenbosch.

Alan C. Stockman is Professor of Economics at the University of Rochester, Research Associate at the National Bureau of Economic Research, and Consulting Economist at the Federal Reserve Bank of Richmond and Cleveland. Born in Cleveland in 1951, he received his B.A. summa cum laude at Ohio State University and his Ph.D. at the University of Chicago in 1978. Professor Stockman has received numerous research grants and has published more than 50 research papers in leading professional journals. He has presented over 60 talks at universities and professional conferences in the last 5 years, made over 50 television and radio appearances, and has supervised Ph.D. dissertations by 21 economists who now teach at top universities (including Stanford, UCLA, the Universities of Pennsylvania, Maryland, and California at Santa Barbara) in 7 countries. He has also taught at UCLA, the Graduate Institute for International Studies in Geneva, Switzerland, and other institutions, and he serves on editorial boards of three professional journals. His textbook, *Introduction to Economics*, will be published by Dryden Press in 1992.

Richard L. Stroup is a Professor of Economics at Montana State University and a Senior Associate of the Political Economy Research Center in Bozeman, Montana. He was born in Sunnyside, Washington, in 1943 and received his B.A., M.A., and Ph.D from the University of Washington. From

1982-1984, he was Director of the Office of Policy Analysis at the Interior Department.

Dr. Stroup is a widely published author on natural resources and environmental issues and has also written on tax policy and labor economics. His work has been a major force in the development of the approach to resource problems known as the New Resource Economics. He is co-author, with James D. Gwartney, of a leading economics principles textbook, *Economics: Private and Public Choice* (Harcourt Brace Jovanovich, 1990) now in its fifth edition. Other books include *Natural Resources: Bureaucratic Myths and Environmental Management* (Ballinger Publishing Co. 1983), written with John Baden, and *Bureaucracy vs. the Environment: The Environmental Cost of Bureaucratic Governance* (University of Michigan Press, 1981), edited with John Baden. Dr. Stroup's recent research has focused on alternative institutional arrangements for dealing with hazardous waste, global warming, and other environmental risk.

Dr. Stroup is a Cato Adjunct Scholar, a member of the Mont Pelerin Society, and a former member of the executive committee of the Western Economics Association.

Melaine S. Tammen directs the Cato Institute's Project on Global Economic Liberty, which examines bilateral and multilateral aid programs, including those of the World Bank and IMF, as well as trade, debt, other issues related to U.S. policies toward the developing world and the nations of the former Eastern bloc. From 1988 to 1990, Tammen worked at the Competitive Enterprise Institute, also in Washington, D.C. directing a research and outreach effort on the critical role of the U.S. federal deposit insurance system in demise of America's depository institutions. From 1987 to 1988, she worked as a research associate with The Heritage Foundation; and during 1986 she served as a researcher in the World Bank's Agriculture Department. Her articles have appeared in *The Wall Street Journal, Chicago Tribune, Institutional Investor, Reason, The Journal of Law and Politics* (University of Virginia), *Cato Journal,* and other publications. She has a B.A. in International Relations from Rollins College in Winter Park, Florida and an M.A. in Middle East Studies from Georgetown University's School of Foreign Service.

Michael A. Walker is Executive Director of The Fraser Institute. Born in Newfoundland in 1945, he received his B.A. (summa) at St. Francis Xavier University in 1966 and his Ph.D. in economics at the University of Western Ontario in 1969. From 1969 to 1973, he worked in various research capacitites at the Bank of Canada, Ottawa. Dr. Walker has taught monetary economics and statistics at the University of Western Ontario and Carleton University. He is a syndicated columnist and radio broadcaster. His publications include 10 books as author and 15 as editor-contributor. He is a member of Statistics Canada's Advisory Committee on the Service Sector, the International Trade Advisory Committee to the Government of Canada, the Mont Pelerin Society, and the Canadian and American Economic Associations.

Introduction

THIS VOLUME IS THE THIRD in a series of books reporting on a program of research and discussion in The Fraser Institute Rating Economic Freedom project. The project has emerged out of a series of symposia which are part of the program of the Liberty Fund Inc. and which are designed to explore the relationships among civil, economic and political freedom, and to devise methods of theoretically isolating these concepts and providing measurements of them.

Four such symposia have been held. The first held in the Napa Valley, California was prompted by Milton and Rose Friedman's comment in the book *Capitalism and Freedom* that "historical experience speaks with a single voice on the relation between political freedom and a free market. I know of no example in time or place of a society that has been marked by a large measure of political freedom, and that has not also used something comparable to a free market to organize the bulk of economic activity." One of the obvious questions that occupied the first colloquium was whether or not political freedom in the sense of freedom to elect one's political representatives is a necessary condition for maintenance of a competitive markets approach to economic organization. This became clearer in the first symposium and the ones that followed.

The idea of economic freedom is a difficult one to articulate. This is particularly the case as economists are wont to be precise, and there is as yet no unambiguous, clear conceptual definition of economic freedom to which most people are willing to subscribe. The Liberty Fund-Fraser Institute conferences on economic freedom have followed this issue along two distinct paths. The first is theoretical, and the second is empirical. Most of the authors have proposed one definition or another of economic liberty, or at least impediments to it. In designing empirical measures to correspond to their notions, they have frequently come face to face with both the limitations of their characterization of economic freedom, and the adequacy with which they could measure it.

But unlike other efforts of pure philosophy, our authors have made the effort to draw the relevant evidence to the theory wherever possible. It is worth reminding the reader that these papers have been drawn from two conferences hosted by the Liberty Fund and The Fraser Institute. The authors were working from relatively specific guidelines at both conferences, but these differed as the second built upon the contributions of the first. At the first conference, authors were asked to assess economic freedom in sectors of the economy for a number of different countries. At the second, some were asked to provide a candidate index for future research in comparing countries. In both cases there were many measures proposed and many issues developed that will serve as guides for future research.

The book has been divided into three sections corresponding to emphasis since most papers deal in some measure with both theory and empirics. The first section develops characterizations of economic freedom which range from philosophical to empirical. The four papers in this section share the general characteristic of delving into the problem of what kinds of restrictions should be measured as reducing economic freedom. The first paper, by Jones and Stockman, is primarily theoretical although it does sketch an agenda for empirical research. Easton's two papers rely on a definition of impediments to economic freedom that allows him to make measurements consistent with those made for consumer surplus. He calculates a number of indexes of economic freedom in the international sector, the first paper, and for a number of different countries in the second. Jack Carr considers an output based measure of impediments to economic freedom in his paper on capital markets. The second section stresses the development of indexes for a wide range of countries. Gwartney, Block and Lawson provide a consistent index for four different time periods for nearly eighty countries. Spindler and Miyake develop indexes consistent with suggestions made at previous conferences, while Scully and Slottje introduce factor analysis to collapse many variables into a few specific measures of economic freedom. Included, too, in this section is a survey or experiment conducted by Milton and Rose Friedman using the (Sea Ranch) participants as the sample. In their experiment, they tried to assess the ability of the group to rank eleven relatively well known countries according to their relative levels of economic freedom. The third section provides a look at particular problems. Denzau considers why particular prices are so politicized while DiLorenzo tackles the labour market and its distortions. Reynolds rounds out this section by reporting on particular expenditure and tax distortions in several Latin American countries.

Section I

Ronald W. Jones and Alan C. Stockman explore the consequences of defining the loss of economic freedom as the consumer and producer losses associated with third party constraints on transactions. Constraints include both prohibited and mandated behaviour. Their illustrations include the appropriate calculation of the losses associated with transfers, taxes, minimum consumption requirements, and both quantity and price coercion. Their framework is broad and exciting. They introduce the notion of "bundling" to pose the question of whether government restrictions on freedom should be treated individually and their costs computed, or whether the whole package of restrictions should be treated as one bundle. Such a distinction is important if we think of Peter being required to transfer one dollar to Paul and then Paul being forced to transfer one dollar back to Peter. If these are lump-sum transactions so that there is no distortion, on a bundled basis neither is worse off. On a transaction by transaction basis, both are worse off. In addition to providing a formal proof of the freedom reducing character of an "optimal" tariff, they raise a host of important conceptual problems with what we think we mean when we discuss economic freedom. Their framework, however, allows for the calculation of many of the costs of impediments to freedom and is an extension in both the theoretical and empirical literature on economic freedom.

Stephen Easton in exploring economic freedom in the international markets develops a quantitative measure of the loss in economic freedom as an extension to consumer surplus related measures. In particular he asserts that any distortion that impedes free exchange is a loss in freedom. Thus the value of the loss in freedom is the value of the distortion. Unlike the consumer surplus triangle, however, the direct loss in freedom includes both the rectangle (the tax revenue, for example) plus the triangle. In the case of international trade taxes the loss in freedom is complicated by the domestic production of importable goods. The imposition of a trade tax reallocates rent to domestic producers, and Easton includes this as an indirect loss in economic freedom. He shows that even though an "optimal tariff" will raise income, it will result in a loss in economic freedom.

In his second paper in this volume, Easton develops his measures of economic freedom for a variety of different countries. To this end he uses two gross indexes—the ratio of government expenditure to national income and the number of government employees relative to population. The former is a measure of direct government intervention by way of the tax "rectangle" distortion while the latter is an attempt to measure the impediments to freedom posed by government regulation. Each government worker is (heroically) assumed to impede economic freedom by the same amount. Easton aggregates the two measures by estimating the relative price in terms of income of each government employee and then summing the two measures. This he does through an immigration function. The level of immigration from country A to country B is written as a function of government expenditure and government employees per head and per capita income. The amount of income it would take to induce an additional person to immigrate (per change in the number of government employees) provides the implicit price of the regulatory environment. Thus his approach allows for an explicit pricing of the implied cost of regulation although his measure only considers immigration to the United States or Canada.

In examining capital markets, Jack Carr takes the stance that economic freedom is not an end in itself, and thus does not include it as a separate argument in the utility function. Anything that impedes free exchange will impinge on economic freedom, and this, he suggests reduces economic welfare. The notion of a definition of economic freedom, he argues, is like the definition of money. It is not independent of the uses to which it will be put. He proposes a measure that would be one of many factors of production in the aggregate output function. Economic freedom is seen as being the index that best helps predict aggregate output. His paper finds that deregulation of financial markets has increased freedom over the past twenty years in several of the more developed countries. To measure economic freedom in this sector he considers such features as the regulation of the central bank, the regulation of commercial banks, the regulation of capital flows and the regulation of the stock market. Among the group of six countries considered, West Germany was the least impeded, followed by Canada, the United Kingdom and the United States, while France was the most impeded of the group.

Section II

The second section explores a number of empirical measures of economic freedom typically involving a wide range of countries and the consideration of many possible contributors to an index. The first by Gwartney, Block and Lawson rates 79 countries along dimensions such as price stability, the size of government, discriminatory taxes, and restraint of international trade. Their index is devised for four periods, 1975, 1980, 1985 and 1988. It shows Hong Kong as the economically most free and permits an extensive ranking of the rest of the countries in the sample. Further analysis suggests that countries with high indexes of economic freedom tend to have grown more rapidly than those with poorer levels of economic freedom. Their extensive data set has been reproduced in the Appendix to the paper and is also available on diskette.

Gerald W. Scully and Daniel J. Slottje used 15 attributes (from foreign exchange regimes and freedom to travel, to the rule of law and conscription) combined into indexes weighted by the ranks of the attributes, the principle components of the attributes and a hedonic representation of the attributes. Based on these indexes Scully and Slottje provide an overall index that combines the component rankings into a final assessment.

Zane Spindler and Joanna Miyake provide a number of rankings for different countries by integrating several measures of economic freedom that were suggested at a previous conference. (Hence their use of the title the "homework" measures.)

Milton and Rose Friedman took the opportunity to survey the assembled group. Their point was that while we have different indexes available, we need some mechanism to test whether they conform to our own notions of usefulness. In particular, they argued, we must be sure that whatever ratified combination of objective factors we observe, they conform in some measure to our general sense of which countries are more economically free than others. By surveying the audience, they found considerable consistency of view (over the dozen countries they listed), but were not convinced that the other indexes which had been constructed reflected the general consensus too well.

Section III

Arthur Denzau argues that a critical feature of the restriction to economic freedom derives from the state's politicization of prices. Rather than being free to buy and sell, firms must first meet various political tests before they are allowed to buy and sell. Such added costs to the pricing mechanism reduced economic efficiency, but also formed the basis for the argument that the microenvironment is the critical location from which we should measure impediments to economic freedom. Detailed questionnaires form the basis for current research into the kinds of impediments present in the Peruvian economy.

Labour market freedom was assessed by Tom DiLorenzo for four major countries: the U.S., Canada, England, and Japan on the basis of some thirty categories. These categories included whether there was compulsory collective bargaining, agency shop, taxes on immigration, and temporary work permits to mention a few. Rather than construct a weighted index, Di Lorenzo ranks each of the thirty categories from zero to ten and sums them for each country. Although he finds England the most free and Japan the least in this small group, a number of categories could not be assessed, and he is reluctant to view these rankings as final.

Alan Reynolds considers the tax and expenditure policies of a number of countries. His paper reports in some detail on tax rates in a small group of Latin American countries in which the taxes (income tax, sales tax, social security tax, wealth tax and investor tax) are used to construct an overall rating of different tax regimes. In the final analysis, Bolivia scores relatively well (even when measures of the deficit are included) followed by El Salvador and Brazil, then Mexico and Argentina.

Concluding Remarks

These papers have devised many measures of economic freedom. Progress has taken place over the past several years. The ideas we have now of economic freedom are substantially advanced over those that we explored at the first conference. Although there is anything but universal agreement about which measures are the most appropriate, we have identified a number of useful ways in which to think about economic freedom conceptually, and a number of good candidates for indexes to correspond to those conceptualizations. To drive home the point that the ideas and measures are still in development, we have included a synopsis of some of the main features of the discussion that followed each paper. Although many of the remarks may at times appear pointed, they serve the purpose of sharpening the issues that need to be further discussed. In this context, however, it is worth recalling that the papers were presented at two conferences (the first taking place at Banff, Alberta and the second at Sea Ranch, California) and are incorporated in the current volume as a function of their content, not their chronological development. As a result some of the issues may appear slightly redundant in light of papers developed "earlier" in the volume, some of the papers have been revised to reflect particular comments, and some commentators are conspicuous by their absence in some of the commentaries — they may have only attended the "other" conference. But on the whole we believe that the wide-ranging discussion serves to enliven, enlighten and elaborate the text.

Notes

[1] From the first conference the selected papers are by Carr, Di Lorenzo, Easton, Reynolds, Scully and Slottje, and from the second, Denzau, Easton, Gwartney, Block and Lawson; Jones and Stockman.

[2] The earlier conferences are chronicled in Michael Walker, ed. *Freedom, Democracy and Economic Welfare*, Vancouver: The Fraser Institute, 1988, and Walter Block, ed., *Economic Freedom: Toward a Theory of Measurement*, Vancouver: The Fraser Institute, 1991.

[3] The Table of Contents identifies at which conference the paper was given. The Banff conference was held a year before the Sea Ranch conference.

The Concept of Economic Freedom

On the Concept of Economic Freedom

Ronald W. Jones and Alan C. Stockman
University of Rochester

Introduction

E CONOMIC FREEDOM IS A CONCEPT yet to make its way formally into the economics vocabulary. Although there are many discussions of economic freedom, writers usually use the term in a vague way. Precisely what does economic freedom mean and why is the concept important? Few writers have tried to define the term, and we have found almost no attempts to relate the concept of economic freedom to the analytic framework of economics.[1]

The general concept of freedom is subject to considerable confusion, with different writers using the term in completely different ways. Without disputing the importance of inner peace, security, absence of fear or hunger, or psychic well-being unencumbered by certain undesirable emotional or mental states, we will use the term freedom to mean, roughly, the absence of coercion. This is the meaning of freedom that many people (including previous writers) have in mind when they discuss these issues. The present paper explores concepts of economic freedom that are consistent with this view, connects those concepts with the usual analytic framework of economics, and provides a theoretical foundation for measurement of economic freedom. We propose a tentative definition of restrictions on economic freedom and explore the properties of this definition. After examining many of the issues that arise in formulating an adequate definition, we discuss some alternative definitions that are consistent with our general approach to the concept of economic freedom. Each definition suggests a way to measure restrictions on economic freedom, though the appropriate measurement may not be easy in practice.[2]

In one of the few papers on the meaning of economic freedom, Stigler (1978) argued that economic freedom is synonymous with wealth or utility.[3] We disagree with this position. While definitions are arbitrary, some are more useful than others. Our approach is intended to emphasize some important distinctions. With our concept of economic freedom, government actions that restrict economic freedom need not reduce wealth; they could raise it. Our concept allows us to consider the possibility of a tradeoff between economic freedom and other values. People may, in some cases, choose to sacrifice economic freedom for other values, or other values for economic freedom.[4]

We will not attempt to define economic freedom itself. Instead, we will define *losses* in economic freedom. We follow Hayek (1960, pp. 11-22), Friedman (1962), and others in identifying losses in economic freedom with the results of man-made coercion inhibiting voluntary economic transactions or requiring certain transactions. We believe people with widely differing opinions on the proper role of government in society should be able to agree on the meaning of (losses in) economic freedom, and recognize that some of their disagreements may involve disputes over the connections between economic freedom and other desirable ends, and the relative importance of each. People ought to agree, for example, that an excise tax on alcohol and a prohibition on growing marijuana in one's own garden (even for one's own consumption) reduce economic freedom, whatever their value may be in promoting other ends. After we propose a definition of losses in economic freedom in the next section, we will explore examples to discuss the implications of that definition and to clarify it. We will then discuss certain fundamental issues that arise in defining losses in economic freedom and, at the end, make some remarks on why people do or should care about economic freedom and so why the distinctions our definition makes are important.

It is hard to imagine meaningful research to *measure* economic freedom prior to a decision on the meaning of the term. Any attempt to measure economic freedom (or its loss) empirically presupposes some concept of it, whether or not that concept is made explicit. As this paper will indicate, the concept of economic freedom raises intricate issues without obvious resolutions.

Restrictions on Economic Freedom

A Tentative Definition

We will explore the following definition of restrictions on economic freedom.

> Consider a constraint imposed by a third party on voluntary transactions among other people. The **loss in economic freedom** to those people from this constraint is the sum of the losses in consumer and producer surplus in those constrained transactions. If the constraint requires a person to take a specific action, the **loss in economic freedom** includes the cost to that person of that constrained action.

The term "transactions" refers as well to those a person conducts with himself. Thus a law preventing a person from growing and consuming a crop is a violation of his economic freedom. Notice that this definition automatically distinguishes and weights more and less important restrictions on economic freedom. We will clarify later the way we use the term "cost."

Constraints imposed by people versus those imposed by nature

We consider only constraints imposed by people. We want to distinguish these from constraints imposed by nature. One reason for this distinction is that the actions we would take to try to change those constraints are different. Economic freedom is not the same as technology, or wealth or utility. This does not mean that one set of constraints is more or less important or severe than the other. It merely suggests that for some purposes it is worth making this distinction.

Governments or third parties?

The most common source of man-made constraints is government. But we need not limit ourselves to constraints imposed by official governments: other people who try to prevent, control, or tax voluntary transactions also restrict economic freedom. When an entrepreneur must pay off thugs or gangs to operate a business (or suffer physical harm to himself and his business), the effects on the entrepreneur are the same whether we regard those thugs or the "official" government as the actual government. But once we admit this, there is no limit to how many governments may restrict a person's economic freedom or who they may be. We could, of course, discuss the loss in economic freedom caused by a particular party, such as an official government. Or we could discuss the loss in economic freedom imposed by all governments and thugs on particular people.

Two types of constraints

As our tentative definition makes clear, there are two types of restrictions that a third party can place on economic freedom. The tentative definition simply defines and then adds the losses from each type of restriction. We might instead place different weights on these losses or consider losses in economic freedom to be multidimensional. We will return to these issues when we consider some alternative definitions.

Basic Examples of Restrictions on Economic Freedom

We will begin exploring the consequences of our tentative definition by considering very simple cases, and proceed to more complicated situations in which some difficult issues arise. We will initially assume that there is general agreement about the distribution of property rights among people in an economy,[5] that property rights are complete (universal, exclusive, and transferable), with no transactions costs, and that the government owns no property. We also assume there is a legal system defining and enforcing those property rights. We will consider initially a *single* restriction on economic freedom, and leave for later problems that arise with multiple restrictions.

Transfers

Transfers between agents imposed by government represent a clear loss of economic freedom to those making the payments. Suppose the government taxes Peter $100 to pay Paul $100. Then Peter's wealth *and* economic freedom have been reduced by $100. Paul is a recipient, and his wealth rises by $100, but this transfer does not raise his economic freedom. Clearly, our use of the term economic freedom is at odds with Stigler (1978), who identified liberty or freedom with wealth or utility and would describe Paul's economic freedom as having risen. We certainly agree that Paul is now "free" to expand his consumption set, but we do not believe this represents an increase in economic freedom. Economic freedom is something an individual possesses until deprived of it by government or third parties. One advantage of thinking about *losses* in economic freedom rather than economic freedom itself is that it emphasizes this point: the transfer to Paul does not mitigate in any way Paul's loss of economic freedom from other restrictions.

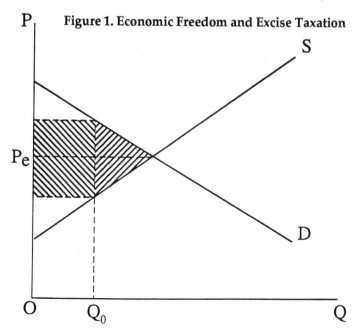

Figure 1. Economic Freedom and Excise Taxation

An Excise Tax

We can obtain more insight into our definition of a loss in economic freedom by considering a simple excise tax on a commodity in which market forces are depicted in Figure 1. The tax restricts sales to level Q_0, and the height of the shaded area represents the level of the tax. The tax causes producers and consumers to restrict their economic exchanges with each other; the shaded triangle shows the loss in producer and consumer surplus on these foregone transactions. On the sales of Q_0 that remain, the shaded rectangle shows the sum of the losses in consumer and producer surplus, so the entire shaded area captures the loss in economic freedom from the tax. The shaded rectangle also represents tax payments to the government, which it can disburse in any number of ways. Thus there may be other recipients of this tax revenue, but this does not increase the economic freedom of those recipients, although it increases their wealth. Later, in discussing tariffs, we consider the case in which the tax income is redistributed to the *same* people who have been deprived of economic freedom.[6]

Minimum Consumption Requirements

Consider a government restriction that requires people to buy *at least* X units of a good. The amount X may be more or less than people would have chosen voluntarily. The loss in economic freedom from this restriction is the cost of minimal compliance with the restriction. If the government requires people to buy at least 25 units of the good, the loss in economic freedom is area A+B+D+E in Figure 2. If the government requires people to buy at least 20 units of the good (the amount they would have bought anyway), their loss in economic freedom is area D+E in Figure 2. If the government requires them to buy at least 15 units of the good (less than they would have bought anyway), their loss in economic freedom is area E in Figure 2. If the supply curve were upward-sloping when they are required to buy at least 15 units of the good, the loss in economic freedom is area E in Figure 3. In this case, the loss of economic freedom is *less* than the actual cost of buying those 15 units of the good: the fact that the price is higher is a result not of the constraint but of consumers' voluntary choices to buy more than 15 units.

Figure 2. Economic Freedom and Mandated Consumption:
Constant Costs

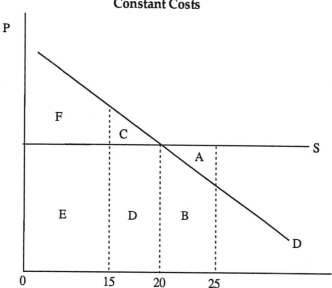

Notice one consequence of this definition of economic freedom: the loss in economic freedom from a government minimal-purchase requirement that costs $100 to comply with is the same as the loss in economic freedom from a lump-sum $100 tax in which the government destroys the (real) tax revenue, even though people get valuable goods in return in the first case and not in the second case. This highlights one distinction between economic freedom and utility or wealth.

Maximum Consumption Requirements

Suppose instead the government requires people to buy *no more* than X units of a good. The amount X may again be more or less than people would have chosen voluntarily. If this restriction is binding, as if X is 15 units in Figure 2, then the loss in economic freedom is the loss in consumer and producer surplus, which is area C in Figure 2 (with a horizontal supply curve) or area C+G+H in Figure 3 (with an upward-sloping supply curve). If the restriction is *not* binding—if X equals or exceeds the amount of the good that people would have bought voluntarily, then there is *no loss* in economic freedom from this restriction.[7]

Government Quantity Coercion

Suppose the government requires people to consume *exactly X units* of a good. We will initially consider the case in which X is *precisely* the amount people would have consumed without the constraint: 20 units in Figure 2.[8] Our definition implies that this constraint imposes a loss in economic freedom, even though the constraint imposes *no* loss in utility.[9] The loss in economic freedom is the cost of consuming X units of the good: the sum of areas D and E in Figure 2. Although people would have chosen this quantity

Figure 3. Economic Freedom and Mandated Consumption:
Upward Sloping Supply

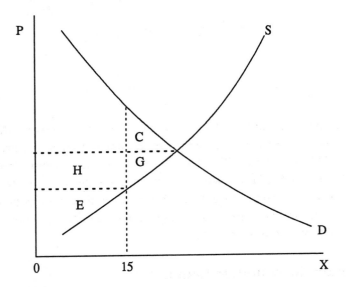

freely without the constraint, they lose economic freedom because they are no longer free to *choose* to do so; they are *forced* instead. Although our example concerns consumers, analogous arguments apply to constraints on firms, as when the government requires firms to provide a certain amount of health insurance or parental leave. (The following discussions of minimum and maximum consumption requirements also apply to production requirements or other constraints on firms.)

Suppose the government requires people to consume *more* than they would have consumed voluntarily without the constraint, such as 25 units when they would have bought 20. The loss in economic freedom is the cost of this required action: the area A+B+D+E in Figure 2.[10]

Suppose instead the government requires people to consume *less* of the good than they would have chosen without the constraint, such as 15 units rather than 20. Then the loss in economic freedom is area E+C in Figure 2. Area E represents the loss in economic freedom from being required to buy

Figure 4. Economic Freedom and Tax Revenue

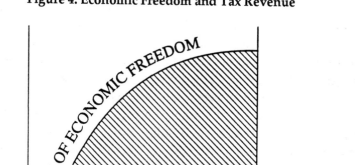

no less than the quantity 15. Area C represents the loss in economic freedom from being required to buy *no more* than the quantity 15. Figure 3 shows the result with an upward-sloping supply curve: the loss in economic freedom from a constraint that requires people to consume exactly 15 units (no more, no less) is area C+G+H+E in Figure 3. The area E shows the loss in economic freedom from being required to buy no less than 15 units of the good. The area H shows a loss in economic freedom from a loss in producer surplus that equals a gain in consumer surplus; this gain in consumer surplus is an increase in consumers' wealth but *not* in their economic freedom. The areas C and G represent losses in consumer and producer surplus that are also losses in wealth.

A Note on Economic Freedom and Utility

When the government requires people to consume *exactly* X units of a good, where X is the amount they would have chosen voluntarily without the constraint, the loss in economic freedom is shown by areas such as D+E in Figure 2. Now suppose the government reduces X. This clearly lowers utility as consumers are pushed away from their most desired consumption bundle. But it (initially) *raises* economic freedom, or, in our language, *reduces the loss* in economic freedom. For example, suppose X=15 in Figure 2. The loss in economic freedom is area E+C, which is smaller than E+D because C<D. This may appear to be a strange result—that people who are *required* to consume *precisely* the amount they would have chosen voluntarily could be *less free* than people who are required to consume less of the good. But this result appears strange only when one forgets the distinction between economic freedom and utility. While utility falls, there are *two* forces operating on economic freedom. The requirement that a person buy *exactly* X units of a good is a composite of two requirements: that he buy no *less* than X, and that he buy no *more* than X. When the government reduces X, economic freedom tends to rise because the loss in economic freedom from the *minimum*-consumption constraint falls: that minimum-consumption constraint becomes less severe. This is the gain in economic freedom of D in Figure 2. On the other hand, economic freedom tends to fall when the government reduces X because the *maximum*-consumption requirement becomes *more* severe. This is the loss in economic freedom of C in Figure 2. Whether a reduction in government-mandated consumption of a good lowers or raises economic freedom at the margin depends on the shapes of the demand and supply curves. However, a small reduction in the restriction, from a position where the mandated consumption exactly matches the unrestricted bundle, always reduces the loss in economic freedom.

Restrictions on Asset Transactions

Suppose the government imposes a restriction that prevents you from holding some financial asset. We can derive a demand curve for that financial asset using standard optimal-portfolio analysis. The loss in economic freedom from this restriction is analogous to the consumer-surplus loss from a prohibition on buying some good. If another asset that is a perfect substitute (in your view) is available, there is no loss of consumer surplus or economic freedom. Otherwise, the loss in economic freedom corresponds to the foregone interest or foregone value of a portfolio with better risk properties.

Should the analogy with consumer markets carry over to asset markets when the government requires you to hold a certain security? Suppose the government forces you to buy a bond issued by some private corporation. If its rate of return is lower than market alternatives, then you have lost economic freedom. Suppose, however, that the interest rate on this asset equals the market equilibrium interest rate. If you were already holding these bonds (or equivalent assets), then we *could* say there is a loss in economic freedom equal to the cost of buying (or not selling) the bonds, in analogy with requirements that you consume certain products. Alternatively, if there is no loss in the value of the portfolio, one could say there is no loss in economic freedom. At this stage of our argument, this alternative looks unattractive. However, issues will arise later in this paper that suggest consideration of this alternative definition (see Section 6 on bundling, particularly the withholding tax example).

Tax Payments and Economic Freedom

Some people have argued that government tax receipts serve as a useful proxy for the loss of economic freedom. Suppose the excise tax illustrated in Figure 1 represents the only interference on voluntary transactions. Figure 4 illustrates that at low tax rates the identification of tax revenues and loss of economic freedom is entirely appropriate. However, as tax rates increase, the gap between the two concepts widens. Indeed, for tax rates sufficiently high that receipts are falling, the two measures go in opposite directions. Tax revenue is zero at the prohibitive tax rate, whereas this is the rate that maximizes the loss in economic freedom.

To fill in details, let t denote a specific excise tax in this market and R represent tax revenue. Thus

$$dR/dt = Q + t \, dQ/dt,$$

with the second term negative. As for the loss in economic freedom, a small increase in the tax rate raises price to consumers by dp^D, so that the loss in consumer surplus reflected by this price increase is the "terms-of-trade" effect, Qdp^D. Producers see their price decreased by the tax, eventuating in a "terms-of-trade" loss for them of $-Qdp^S$. Adding these effects, the total increment to the loss in economic freedom, L, is

$$dL/dt = Q,$$

where dt equals the sum of dp^D and $-dp^S$. Thus the two curves in Figure 4 are tangent to each other at the origin, and at the prohibitive tax rate the "loss in economic freedom" curve becomes horizontal. Economists are prone to dismiss welfare triangles as being relatively unimportant compared with rectangles. This, we submit, leads to gross error if tax rates are high or if government regulations prohibit certain types of economic transactions. A prohibition of market activity in Figure 1 leads to a loss of economic welfare (freedom) that is captured *entirely* by a triangle.

Economic Freedom Is Not Economic Efficiency

Expand the setting, now, to include a variety of private transactions in which the government has levied excise taxes, including taxes and other restrictions in factor markets that create gaps between returns paid to factors across industries. These restrictions create inefficiencies corresponding to an inward shrinkage of the transformation schedule and inequality between the slopes of indifference curves and transformation schedules. The loss in efficiency due to these government restrictions and taxes, however, differs from the loss in economic freedom from those government actions. Recall the simple case in which the government taxes Peter to pay Paul, and suppose Peter pays a lump-sum (poll) tax. That case involves a loss of economic freedom without any change in aggregate production or consumption. With widespread taxes and subsidies, economic inefficiency nets out the gainers and losers, but losses in economic freedom do *not* net out. Peter's loss in wealth is Paul's gain, but Peter's loss in economic freedom is not offset by any increase in economic freedom for Paul. In the case of excise taxes, the loss in economic freedom is reflected in dead-weight welfare losses to society (triangles of the type shown in Figure 1) *and* the tax payments (the rectangle in the figure). While the government may redistribute those tax payments to other people, those payments nevertheless represent losses in economic freedom.

Restrictions on Economic Freedom Affect Other Markets

While measures involving total tax collections, on the one hand, or total net efficiency losses, on the other, underestimate the loss of economic freedom represented by a government activity, we can contemplate a measure that would typically overestimate the loss in economic freedom. Consider any government activity such as a tax, expenditure, or regulation. In an interconnected economy each such activity disturbs many commodity and factor markets, changing many relative prices. For each such price change there are gainers and losers: net suppliers and net demanders of goods whose relative prices change. One *could* add all these losses (and ignore the gains) when measuring the loss in economic freedom from the governmental activity.[11] But that is not what our definition says to do. Our definition tells us to include only the losses from transactions that are directly constrained. A government restriction on buying good X may change other relative prices and, through this route, alter real incomes of net buyers and sellers of other goods. While those changes in real income result from the government action, they are not restrictions on economic freedom: no one is restricting transactions involving those goods. This implies again that freedom and welfare are fundamentally different.

Some General Equilibrium Considerations

The earlier discussion of a single excise tax illustrated the loss of economic freedom reflected in losses in consumer and producer surplus in the market being taxed. In this section we sketch out a scenario to analyze some general-equilibrium ramifications of government restrictions.

Pears, Peaches and Cream

Consider an economy producing and consuming three commodities: pears, peaches, and cream. Peaches and pears are substitutes to consumers, whereas peaches and cream are complements. (We assume away any connections on the supply side.) From an initial undistorted equilibrium, suppose the government levies an excise tax on peaches. This imposes losses in economic freedom of the type illustrated by the shaded areas in

Figure 1. Here, though, the rise in the price of peaches to consumers affects the pear and cream markets. The demand for pears shifts to the right, and the demand for cream shifts to the left. The price of pears rises. Although net demanders of pears lose wealth from this price rise, they do not lose economic freedom. Focus on someone who is a net buyer of peaches; this person lost economic freedom from the tax on peaches. If this person is a large net seller of pears, she will *gain* wealth on net from the tax on peaches since her terms of trade improve. If we included this change in the terms of trade in our measure of the loss of economic freedom, this person would not have suffered any loss in freedom despite the imposition of the tax. This example shows why one should ignore such terms-of-trade changes in measuring the loss in economic freedom from the tax on peaches, although they properly belong in a calculation of changes in economic welfare.

Now suppose the tax on peaches remains fixed and a tax is levied on pears. There is a loss in economic freedom to transactors in the pear market. But there is a further calculation now that needs to be made, to take account of the greater demand for peaches, since they are substitutes for pears. This shift in demand, due to the tax on pears, alters the loss in economic freedom from the tax on peaches. This is akin to a "volume-of-trade" effect, as in international markets. However, the sign of the change in economic freedom is precisely *opposite* to the effect typically considered for economic welfare. In standard welfare analysis an increase in consumption of an item that is taxed (peaches) at a given rate *increases* economic welfare because the item is worth more at the margin to consumers than the marginal cost of production. This very same change, however, is an increase in the volume of activity in a market that restricts economic freedom.

Again retain a fixed tax on peaches and suppose that (instead of a tax on pears) the government imposes an excise tax on cream. Since peaches and cream are complements, the direct loss in economic freedom from the tax on cream is accompanied by a reduction in the loss in economic freedom from the tax on peaches. The change in the peach market might even outweigh that in the cream market. This is akin to the "second-best" phenomenon in welfare analysis—here an increase in one restriction (the tax on cream) deflects demand from a market that is already taxed (peaches), with the possibility that the loss in economic freedom reflected in the entire tax system will have been mitigated.

The examples discussed above clarify our definition of economic freedom: the *change* in economic freedom from adding a new constraint is the sum of losses in consumer and producer surplus associated with the newly-constrained transactions *plus* the altered losses of economic freedom from constraints on *other* voluntary transactions.

International Transactions

To the extent that a country's residents are involved in international transactions, governmental restrictions on voluntary transactions affect the economic freedom of foreign as well as home residents. In principle a measure could be conceived of the loss in economic freedom imposed on *home* residents by the totality of all restrictions, whether imposed by home third parties or government, or alien ones. Instead, we concentrate on the concept of the loss of economic freedom entailed by restrictions imposed by home third parties or government, thus facilitating a comparison of the restrictive policies adopted by different nations.

A Ban on Foreign Goods

Our first simple scenario involving international transactions presupposes that we are entirely dependent on foreign sources for some commodity. Figure 5 illustrates a free trade equilibrium at point F, with the total of our demand (D) and foreign demand (D*) matching total supply, all of it foreign (S*). If our government had banned all imports of this commodity, the equilibrium abroad would be shown by point A. Potential home consumers look enviously at price 0B, and would demand quantity BC at that price. However, triangle EBC overestimates the loss in home consumer surplus as a result of the ban on imports. If there were no government interference, the price would be 0G, so that the ban wipes out home consumer surplus by the triangle EGI.

Figure 5 also indicates the shaded area, BGFA of relevance to foreign producers. The home country's ban on imports from abroad would represent a restriction on the economic freedom of two groups: home consumers lose area EGI, and foreign producers lose BGFA. The import ban admittedly favors one group: foreign consumers gain area GHAB. In calculating the loss in economic freedom to home residents and foreigners, should this gain to foreign consumers be netted out of the losses to home consumers and foreign producers? We have argued against this procedure. In discussing government taxation of Peter to pay Paul, we emphasized the loss of economic freedom to Peter; the gain to Paul is an increase in his welfare, but not in his economic freedom. The present situation is analogous, but slightly different in that the ban on trade results in a loss of freedom (and welfare) to home consumers and foreign producers which outweighs the gain in welfare (but not in freedom) to foreign consumers. This discrepancy is the deadweight loss from preventing mutually profitable trade.

Figure 5. Economic Freedom and International Trade

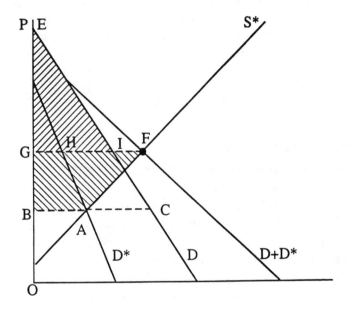

A Tariff Hike

Turning now from a complete ban on imports to a situation in which they are allowed, subject to a (specific) rate of duty, we analyze the effect on economic freedom of a small tariff hike, and contrast this with the effect of such an increase in duties on real income or welfare in the home country.

We suppose that tariff rates are lower than the "optimal" rate, so that a small increase would, via standard analysis, raise home real incomes and tariff revenue. This presupposes that changes in our rate are sufficient to force changes in foreign supply price (the "large-country" case). We assume (for simplicity) that foreign producers have no local market, but we now include a set of home producers who share the home market with imports. The change in real income at home (dy) can be broken down into a terms-of-trade effect and a volume-of-trade effect:

$$dy = -Mdp^* + tdM,$$

where M represents the volume of imports, t the specific tariff rate, and p^* the foreign price of importables (our terms of trade). We have assumed dy to be positive for a small rise in t from low levels. This net gain is made up of three parts: (i) the government's tariff revenue increases by d(tM); (ii) home suppliers have an increase in producer surplus given by xdp, where x denotes home production and p is the domestic price behind the tariff wall; and (iii) home consumers lose real income by an amount Ddp, where D is total home demand. The change in real income abroad is captured only by the terms-of-trade effect:

$$dy^* = Mdp^*$$

As for the loss in economic freedom produced by the tariff hike, home consumers have lost Ddp. Any subsequent redistribution of tariff proceeds may help to compensate consumers, but if the amount of such redistribution received by any consumer is independent of his purchases, the restriction on economic freedom is not thereby lessened. The change in real income and the change in economic freedom are separate concepts. Abroad the loss in economic freedom is $-Mdp^*$, so that the home government's increase in the tariff rate has resulted in a total loss of economic freedom of:[12]

$$(x + M)dp - Mdp^* = xdp + Mdt.$$

One final calculation is instructive. The home government might claim that its action has raised home real incomes by imposing a loss in economic freedom. How do these two aggregates compare? The loss in economic freedom exceeds the gain in the home country's real income; this excess is shown by:

$$\{Ddp - Mdp^*\} - \{-Mdp^* + tdM\} = Ddp - tdM$$

That is, the loss in economic freedom exceeds the gain in home real incomes by the sum of the loss in consumer surplus and the deadweight loss to the world of the tariff hike, the latter captured by the tax spread times the reduction in imports.

Bundling Constraints on Voluntary Transactions

A Fundamental Problem in Measuring Economic Freedom

Governments impose many constraints on voluntary actions. People are often beneficiaries of some government programs and losers from others. In a typical welfare state, the government may take $X from an average person and return $Y worth of transfer payments and goods (both public goods and government-provided private goods); typically we have $X > $Y.[13] Any attempt to measure economic freedom in a country like this must come to grips with a fundamental issue: roughly, does the loss in economic freedom refer to the *gross* take of the government $X or the *net* take of the government $X-$Y? We will refer to this as the *bundling issue*. The question is whether various government actions should be bundled together and considered as a group, so that a person's loss in economic freedom from the bundle of actions refers to his *net* (consumer and producer) surplus loss from this bundle of government actions, or whether each government action should be considered separately, so that a person's loss in economic freedom from *each* separate government constraint is his (consumer or producer) surplus loss from *that* constraint, and his total loss in economic freedom from all the government actions is the sum of these separate losses in economic freedom.[14] These two ways of measuring economic freedom would give vastly different answers in any real-life situation, particularly in societies with high taxes and a large government sector. We will argue below that the answer to the bundling problem is not at all clear — a good case can be made for (and against) two alternative answers with quite different empirical consequences. Any attempt to measure economic freedom and compare it over time or across countries must implicitly assume some answer to this fundamental bundling question. Yet the following sections suggest that doing so is fraught with difficulties.

We do not believe there is a clear answer to the bundling problem: we believe that there are *several alternative notions of economic freedom* which answer the bundling question in different ways, and that no single measure captures all the features of economic freedom that most people have in mind when they use that term. We now present several short, highly stylized examples in which we think there is room for disagreement about the best answer to the bundling problem.

(1) Pass the Buck (the Circle Game)

Suppose the government forces people to sit in a circle and to give a dollar to the person on one's left. Each person, therefore, does two things: gives a dollar and collects a dollar.[15] The government's requirements do not reduce anyone's wealth. The question is whether it reduces economic freedom.

One answer is to consider the requirement to participate in the circle as the constraint on people, which means bundling together the required payment with the left hand and receipt with the right hand. Then we would say there is no loss in economic freedom. The other answer is not to bundle these constraints: to separate the requirement that one must pay a dollar from the fact that the government's circle program also provides each person with a dollar. Then we would say each person loses one dollar in economic freedom from the requirement to participate in the circle, though no one loses wealth (or, perhaps, utility). The unbundling solution makes a clear distinction between constraints that lessen economic freedom and changes in wealth.

Suppose the government taxes Peter $100 to pay Paul $100, and taxes Paul $100 to pay Peter $100. To focus on the key question, suppose these are lump-sum taxes. If we bundle the two constraints together, we would say the loss in economic freedom is zero (and equal to the loss in wealth).

If we unbundle the two constraints, the loss in economic freedom is $200 ($100 to each person).

(2) A Withholding Tax

Suppose the government does *two* things if you work an additional hour: out of each additional dollar earned, (1) it takes 40 cents as withholding tax, and (2) it refunds 10 cents the following May. If we bundle the government activities, we would say the loss in economic freedom is 30 cents (plus several months' interest on the 40 cents) per extra dollar earned. If we unbundle them, we would say the loss in economic freedom is 40 cents (the amount people were forced to pay). We might want to bundle, however, when the government does several things if people undertake some voluntary transaction. We could say these several government actions *jointly* form a constraint on the transaction. The loss in economic freedom from this constraint would then be the *net* sum of the losses in consumer and producer surplus in those constrained transactions: we would bundle together these government actions before calculating the loss in economic freedom.

A withholding tax is an example of a forced loan to the government, to which we return below in the subsection on perceptions.

(3) A Sales Tax with a Lump-sum Transfer to Consumers

Suppose the government levies an excise tax on consumption of a good and uses the tax revenue to finance lump-sum transfers to the group of (identical) people who happen to buy the good. (We will suppose that the subsidy is lump-sum, so it does not depend on the decision to buy or how much to buy.) If we bundle the tax and the transfer, the loss in economic freedom is the shaded triangle in Figure 1. If we unbundle, the loss in economic freedom is the entire shaded area in Figure 1.

(4) A Maximum-consumption Constraint with an Offsetting Lump-sum Transfer from Consumers to Producers

Look back at Figure 3. Suppose the government requires that people consume *no more* than 15 units of a good. We argued earlier that the loss in economic freedom from this constraint is H+C+G. Now suppose the government combines this constraint with a lump-sum tax on consumers equal to H and a lump-sum transfer to producers equal to H. If we bundle these government actions together, we would say the loss in economic freedom is C+G, which also equals the efficiency loss from the maximum-consumption constraint. If we unbundle, then we say the tax/transfer program is like taxing Peter to pay Paul: it causes a loss in economic freedom equal to H. And since we are unbundling, we add this loss in economic freedom to the original loss H+C+G. Then we would say the total loss in economic freedom is 2H+C+G.

(5) A Sales Tax and a Production Subsidy

Suppose the government levies a $10-per-unit tax on consumption of a good and subsidizes producers of the good $10 per unit. The tax *alone*, aside from the disposition of the tax revenue, causes a loss in economic freedom equal to the shaded area in Figure 1. The subsidy alone, aside from the taxes to finance it, causes no loss in economic freedom. If we *un*bundle, the loss in economic freedom is then the shaded area in Figure 1. If we bundle, there is *no* loss in economic freedom.

(6) Prohibitions on Sales to Particular Groups

Suppose the government prohibits females from buying goods and that this prohibition is effective.[16] Figure 6 shows the supply, the demand by males, and the total demand by males and females. The loss in economic freedom from an effective prohibition on female customers is area B+C+D. The fall in demand lowers the price, so male customers gain wealth. Area D is part of the loss in producer surplus from the restraint preventing sales to females, the part that is a gain to males.

Now suppose the government *adds* the constraint that males cannot buy the good. Given the prohibition on females, this prohibition on males reduces economic freedom by the amount A+D+E. So if we unbundle these two constraints, the loss in economic freedom would be A+B+C+2D+E, while if we bundle them the loss in economic freedom would be A+B+C+D+E. The problem is that the male group gains utility when females are banned. Although this gain is not counted as a positive incre-

Figure 6. Economic Freedom and Selective Prohibitions

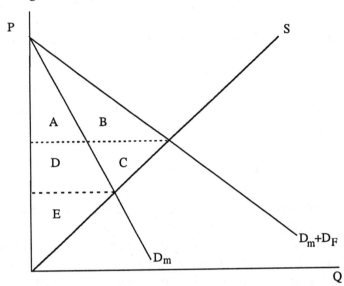

ment to economic freedom, the subsequent loss of this gain *is* counted when the government prohibitions are not bundled. Since any restraint on a group of people can be reinterpreted as a constraint on each member of the group, or each subset of the group (such as males and females), it appears we must bundle the constraints in this case. In general, it appears that whenever a constraint on a *single* good[17] applies to *many* people, we should bundle the constraints.

Perceptions

One possible solution to the bundling problem aside from complete bundling or complete unbundling involves bundling in cases where people *perceive* government actions to be bundled. If people *think* two or more government programs or constraints are linked, then we would bundle them. Otherwise we would unbundle them. But this solution introduces a new "expectations" feature that creates difficulties for measurement of economic freedom. And it also creates other new problems, such as how to deal with situations in which people differ in their perceptions about how government programs are linked, how to deal with cases in which people have never thought about the issue, and how to deal with situations in which people think programs are *weakly* linked.

Nevertheless, differences in perceptions appear to matter. Suppose the government requires Peter to pay $100 to Paul in year 1, and requires Paul to pay $110 to Peter in year 2. Moreover, suppose the market interest rate is 10 percent per year. There are at least two ways to calculate the loss in economic freedom.

(1) We can view this as two separate tax/transfer schemes (see "pass the buck" above). Then the loss in economic freedom in year 1 is $100, and the loss in economic freedom in year 2 is $110. The discounted present value of the loss in economic freedom is $200.

(2) Alternatively, we can view this as a forced loan. Then the loss in economic freedom is $10 (in one of the years).

Which of these views should we adopt? The answer perhaps depends on the *perceptions* of the people involved. If Peter views this constraint as a tax rather than a loan, then view (1) seems appropriate. But if Peter views the constraint as a forced loan, view (2) seems appropriate.

A Suggested Guide to Bundling

A general principle concerning bundling might be the following: ask whether the candidates for bundling are all consequences of a single voluntary (individual) choice; if so, bundle the constraints; if not, do not bundle. In the withholding-tax example, this principle implies the loss in economic freedom would be 30 cents per dollar earned (plus the foregone interest), i.e., the tax.[18] On the other hand, this principle implies we should *not* bundle a sales tax and a lump-sum transfer to the people who happen to buy the good.

Some Other Issues

Government Ownership and the System of Property Rights

Our concept of economic freedom presupposes some allocation of property rights. Property rights are like bundles of sticks, with each stick representing the right to use property in a particular way. One way to define economic freedom is relative to an *arbitrary* allocation of property rights. Given any arbitrary initial distribution of property rights, *restrictions on economic freedom* occur if the government changes, violates, or refuses to enforce those property rights. A problem with this way of viewing economic freedom is illustrated by a 50-percent income tax. One could say the government owns half of all labor services. Then when someone sells labor services, a 50% income tax would not reduce economic freedom. It would not be a tax at all; it would be merely a recovery of the government's property.

An alternative way to define economic freedom is relative to a *particular* allocation of property rights, or a particular set of allocations. Then allocations of property rights outside this set are *per se* violations of economic freedom. For example, one could argue that if the government owns any valuable resource, this constitutes a loss in economic freedom. This is a natural extension of the notion that a tax on sales of a good (such as labor services) results in a loss in economic freedom of the tax payment plus the deadweight social loss from the tax. A tax of **k** percent is equivalent to the government saying it owns k percent of the good (and is just collecting its revenue from the sale). If k is 10 percent, 50 percent, or 90 percent, we say there is a loss in economic freedom equal to the shaded area in Figure 1. Now suppose **k** is 100 percent, in which case the government owns the property. The loss in economic freedom is the entire area above the supply curve and below the demand curve. So, by the analogy with a tax, government ownership of any good or asset reduces economic freedom.

Our tentative definition of losses in economic freedom does not attempt to specify an allocation of property rights (or set of allocations) to which the definition applies. This is consistent with the view that violations of economic freedom can be defined relative to any fixed initial allocation of property rights, and that while some initial allocations of property rights may be better than others from a standpoint of equity or some other criterion (such as promoting economic growth), such judgements on the merits of alternative systems of property rights are separate from the positive task of measuring restrictions on economic freedom within a society with some particular set of property rights. On the other hand, we do not feel comfortable concluding that *any* arbitrary allocation of property rights, such as an allocation in which the government owns all the resources, is an equally good benchmark from which to measure restrictions on economic freedom. Any attempt to measure restrictions on economic freedom and compare these restrictions across countries must take a stand on this issue.

Capital Gains and Losses

A puzzle

Restrictions on voluntary exchanges often impose capital losses on owners of assets. Suppose Smith owns an apartment building. The government puts rent controls on the building. This reduces Smith's wealth by the discounted present value of the loss in rents. Should we say Smith loses this discounted present value in economic freedom at the date the rent controls appear? Or should we say Smith suffers a loss of economic freedom each year equal to the difference between the free-market and price-controlled rent?

Now suppose Hume buys Smith's building at the equilibrium price, which reflects the rent controls. Hume does not lose wealth when he buys the building; he pays the market price. But when Hume owns the building, he is coerced by the government not to engage in certain voluntary exchanges (renting the apartment at a price above the controlled price). This constraint applies each year Hume owns the building. According to our definition, Hume suffers a loss in economic freedom each year. Smith clearly suffers a loss of wealth equal to the fall in the price of the building he sold Hume. Does Smith lose economic freedom?

The solution

Each period, the owner of the building suffers a loss in economic freedom equal to the difference between market and controlled rents. But the government does not impose any constraints on sales of buildings. We noted near the end of section 3 that restrictions on economic freedom affect other markets. As we explained there and in the example of peaches and cream, losses of wealth in those other markets are not losses in economic freedom. So Smith's capital loss is not a loss of his economic freedom, though it equals the present value of expected future losses in economic freedom.

Alterations in Market Structure

Suppose the government restricts entry into a market and thereby allows the market structure to change from competition to monopoly or some variant of oligopoly. For example, the government may prevent a newly-arrived, foreign-trained doctor from practicing medicine although he may be willing to charge less than a local doctor who has been certified for practice by state boards issuing certifications. This causes a loss in economic freedom much like those discussed earlier.

Alternatively, suppose the government forces producers in an industry to restrict production, and the price rises enough that each producer gains, i.e., the government forces producers to cartelize. (Crop restrictions provide an example.) Then the loss in economic freedom is the consumer surplus loss to buyers: the shaded area above P_e in Figure 1.[19]

Sometimes a government restriction that appears to be ineffective causes a loss in economic freedom. We argued earlier that a government restriction saying people could *not buy more* than X units of some good causes no loss in economic freedom if X equals or exceeds the amount they would buy anyway. This conclusion changes if the restriction alters market structure. For example, suppose a local firm competes with a number of foreign firms in a competitive industry. With free trade, the local firm is a price taker. We assume there is a law preventing other local firms from entering the industry. But this law prevents them from doing something they would not do anyway, so it does not reduce economic freedom. Now suppose the government imposes an import quota equal to the amount that people would import anyway. This changes the demand conditions facing the local firm and (with the laws against entry by other local firms) gives it a degree of monopoly power. The local firm raises its price. The combination of these two restrictions (neither of which reduces economic freedom individually) causes a loss in economic freedom.

Externalities

Suppose a person's actions impose negative externalities on other people. Does this create a loss in their economic freedom? Would a government restriction that prevents the externality-causing action increase economic freedom? We suggest the following approach to this problem.

Figure 7. Budget Set Definitions of Economic Freedom

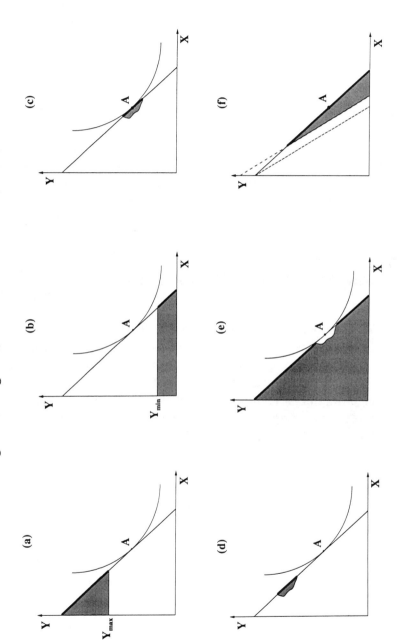

Consider a world with complete property rights but with transactions costs.[20] Bentham imposes an externality on Blackstone (perhaps polluting the air on Blackstone's property while producing a product). Blackstone has legal recourse for a remedy, but the transactions costs are high enough that Blackstone chooses not to seek that remedy. Suppose the resulting allocation would *not* be efficient in the absence of transactions costs. Our definition implies that Bentham's actions restrict Blackstone's economic freedom. If the government restricts the extent to which Bentham can engage in the actions that harm Bentham (or taxes production or sales of Bentham's product), then the government restricts Bentham's economic freedom. The same government action that restricts Bentham's economic freedom can reduce the restriction on Blackstone's economic freedom.[21] In situations like this, it is impossible to have *zero* restrictions on economic freedom.

Some Alternative Definitions

The concept of losses in economic freedom that we have suggested in this paper is consistent with more than the one particular definition we have tentatively selected. There are several alternative approaches. One involves only a minor change: rather than adding the losses in economic freedom from constraints on voluntary transactions to the losses from mandates that require certain specific actions, one can define the loss in economic freedom as a vector with two components. This makes explicit the notion that a constraint is a qualitatively different kind of loss in freedom (perhaps with a different effect on welfare as well) than a mandate requiring individuals do something that they may have done anyway.

Another approach focuses on the budget constraints and defines the loss in economic freedom as the (absolute or proportional) reduction in the size of the opportunity set due to restrictions imposed by a third party on voluntary trades. This reduction could be measured either by the lost area within the budget set or by the lost area on the frontier (i.e., on the budget line, in two dimensions). Figure 7 illustrates this idea. Panel (a) shows a budget constraint, an indifference curve, and a person's choice of consumption of goods X and Y, with the optimal selection at point A. If the government imposes a restriction that prevents the person from consuming more than Y_{max} units of good Y, the shaded area is removed from the budget set, and the thick line segment is removed from its frontier. One could use either measure to define the loss in economic freedom from this restriction; we will refer to these as the budget-set definitions of losses in economic freedom.

These budget-set definitions differ from the tentative definition discussed earlier. According to the earlier definition, economic freedom is unaffected by the nonbinding restriction illustrated in panel (a) of Figure 7. In contrast, the budget-set definitions imply a loss in economic freedom from that restriction. Panel (b) of Figure 7 illustrates a mandate to consume at least Y_{min} units of good Y. The budget-set definitions, like our earlier definition, imply that there is a loss in economic freedom from this nonbinding requirement. The quantitative measure of the loss, however, differs across definitions.

The properties of the budget-set definitions of economic freedom differ from the properties of our earlier definition. The loss in economic freedom, according to the budget-set definitions, is unrelated to the size of consumer and producer surplus losses from a restriction.[22] For example, Panels (c) and (d) of Figure 7 show losses in economic freedom that are equivalent in size according to the budget-set definitions, but differ in size according to our earlier definition. Similarly, the loss in economic freedom is larger, according to the budget-set definitions, in Panel (e) than in Panel (c), though the surplus loss is zero in panel (e) and positive in Panel (c).

The budget-set definitions imply a solution to the bundling problem. If the loss in economic freedom is a measure of the reduction in the budget set or its frontier, then all restrictions that contribute to that reduction are automatically bundled. In the circle game, for example, the net receipt of transfers would automatically be bundled with required payments, leading to a zero loss of economic freedom. Aside from foregone interest, the withholding tax and subsequent subsidy would be bundled in the example considered earlier (where the appropriate budget set involves intertemporal elements). Similarly, a sales tax and production subsidy would be bundled.

The budget-set definitions are less appealing in some situations than in others. Consider a sales tax with a lump-sum transfer to consumers, as we discussed earlier. This rotates a consumer's budget line as in panel (f) of Figure 7, reducing the size of the budget set by the shaded area but also *adding* area to each individual's budget set because of the lump-sum transfer. Similarly, the frontier of the budget set changes position and may become larger or smaller. Neither budget-set definition gives an appealing measure of the loss in economic freedom from restrictions like this.[23] Despite these problems, the budget-set definitions of losses in economic freedom are alternatives with some attractive features. Like our earlier tentative definition, they distinguish economic freedom from wealth or utility, measure the results of coercion, and are consistent with our general concept of economic freedom.

Conclusions

Our definitions of economic freedom differ from Stigler's (1978). Stigler argued that the reason for a limitation on choice—whether it is due to poverty or actions of other people—"is elusive" (p140), and that a person suffers in either case.[24] While Stigler is right that people suffer in either case, that fact does not make the distinction unimportant. The distinction is important because it identifies the source of limitations on choices and can help us design a remedy for these limitations and the associated suffering.[25]

There is another, more important reason to distinguish economic freedom from utility or wealth. We have, throughout the paper, discussed the *utility* effects of government restrictions as if utility depended only on consumption of goods and services. While this is a standard assumption in economics (and is perfectly adequate for most purposes), we think it is a mistake when thinking about economic freedom. Economic freedom should enter as a separate argument, *in addition to consumption of goods*, in the utility function.[26] We think it is clear from introspection and casual observation of people that people prefer to make their own choices than to be coerced *even when* they would voluntarily make the same choice as the coercer.[27] In addition to getting utility directly from their *own* economic freedom, people may get utility from living in a society which *generally* permits economic freedom.[28] Economic freedom may also be an *input* into the production of wealth (we think it is), but that is not its only value to people.

We have proposed and explored a concept and several definitions of losses in economic freedom. The concept corresponds closely with the common meaning of this term. The definitions to which the concept leads are explicit enough to express with standard economic tools. They are also explicit and precise enough to guide the measurement of losses in economic freedom for comparisons over time and across countries. On the other hand, there are certain fundamental issues, such as those involving bundling and initial allocations of property rights, that raise difficult questions. These fundamental issues *must* be addressed, explicitly or implicitly, in any attempt to measure economic freedom. For example, any choice of how to use data on government spending, taxes, and transfers to help measure losses in economic freedom implicitly takes a stand on the definition of losses in economic freedom and on the bundling and property-rights issues. While we do not claim to have resolved those intricate issues in this paper, we hope to have clarified them and contributed to their ultimate resolution.

Notes

[1] Two exceptions are Stigler (1978) and Easton (1989), a revised version of which is "Rating Economic Freedom: International Trade and Financial Arrangements," this volume.

[2] Our discussion can also help indicate which (of many) possible definitions a writer must implicitly have in mind if he chooses certain ways to *measure* restrictions on economic freedom.

[3] Stigler says "the distinction between wealth and liberty is not easily drawn, and in fact has not been undertaken in convincing explicitness."

[4] Economic freedom would often promote these other values, however.

[5] Thus we dispense with problems caused by private groups (e.g. Indian tribes) claiming that they have been dispossessed of rightful ownership in the past so that, say, physical occupation of land currently claimed by other parties would not (by them) be considered a loss of anyone else's economic freedom.

[6] This raises a fundamental issue that we discuss in the section below on "bundling."

[7] Of course, if demand rises, the restriction would become binding and would then reduce economic freedom.

[8] Throughout this discussion, we assume that everyone affected by the restriction is alike. This simplifies matters by making the constraint the same on all people. It is not hard to generalize to cases of heterogeneity. The quantities in all examples and figures refer to *per capita* quantities.

[9] At this stage of the argument, we assume there is no utility from economic freedom *per se*. We think this is not true (see the concluding section below), but it is a standard assumption in economics.

[10] If the supply curve were upward sloping, this area would be even larger because the constraint (which is applied to all demanders) would raise the equilibrium price.

[11] It also raises another important question that we defer until later: should such a calculation be made separately for each and every activity of government, or should some or all of these activities be "bundled," so that only net losses in consumer and producer surplus (net of any gains) represent a loss in economic freedom? We postpone our discussion of this very important issue of bundling until section 6.

[12] If there is a local market abroad, so that D>0, the loss in producer surplus abroad equals $-(D^*+M)dp^*$. Of this, only $-Mdp^*$ is a loss in economic freedom to foreigners because their own sales to their own consumers are not taxed.

[13] $Y represents the typical person's valuation of the transfers and goods the government provides rather than the cost of those goods and transfers to the government.

[14] As in the transfer example above, we never aggregate effects on consumer and producer surplus *across people* before calculating the loss in economic freedom.

[15] The receipt of a dollar from the person on one's right could be optional: one could perhaps refuse to take it, but there is no reason in this setup for anyone to refuse to do so.

[16] Sweden once differentially restricted sales of liquor to females. An effective restriction means that males cannot buy liquor for resale to females.

[17] Here the question of what is a single good is *not* semantics: the answer is whatever the government considers to be the good for purposes of enforcing the constraint.

[18] A similar principle applies to requirements that a person hold certain financial assets.

[19] If producers are heterogeneous and some lose income from this restriction (e.g. it applies differentially across sellers), then those income losses add to the loss in economic freedom.

[20] In an economy with a complete (universal, exclusive, and transferable) set of property rights and zero transactions costs, there would be no externalities.

[21] It might appear that there is a better approach to this problem. One might say that Bentham's actions do not restrict Blackstone's economic freedom, because Blackstone's property rights confer not an absolute right to unpolluted air but the right to seek a legal remedy (at some cost) in case someone such as Bentham pollutes it. When Blackstone purchases the property, he knows that the costs of seeking a remedy are high enough that in certain cases he would choose not to do so. Then Bentham's actions would not violate Blackstone's economic freedom because Blackstone never owned the right to completely unpolluted property: he owned *only* the right to seek legal remedy for violations, which he chose not to do. This approach has some appeal because it distinguishes the amount of economic freedom from the extent to which government provides a certain public good, viz. an efficient system of liability rules and procedures for seeking remedies. Whether the law specifies an efficient standard contract for certain transactions (to minimize transactions costs) is a different issue than whether the government restricts economic freedom. For example, a government may establish inefficient liability standards for tort cases, but that does not in itself restrict economic freedom. Despite this appeal, this approach to economic freedom in the presence of externalities is very unsatisfactory. If someone knows he may be robbed (perhaps by the government), we want to say that the robbery (as well as the threat of robbery) reduces the victim's economic freedom. But there is no general principle to distinguish between these cases of robbery and pollution. So we conslude that Bentham's action violates Blackstone's economic freedom.

[22] In this sense, the budget-set definitions do not weight restrictions according to their "importance" as our earlier tentative definition did. One might view this as an advantage of the budget-set definitions: they distinguish the quantitative size of the restricitons that create losses in freedom from the importance of those losses. One must be careful, however, to

distinguish between the importance of a restriction for creating a loss in freedom and the importance of freedom for something else, such as utility.

[23] One could, however, define the loss in economic freedom in this case as the lost area in the budget set or on its frontier and *ignore* the added area, much as we earlier counted losses but not gains in wealth from government-imposed income redistributions as losses in economic freedom.

[24] Stigler says, "Whether the state forbids me...to use more than ten gallons of gasoline a week, or whether I am prevented from doing so by its high price (not including taxes) is of little direct significance to me: in either case my driving is limited by decisions (to ration or to buy gasoline) of my fellow citizens." We think that the distinction is important—at least because it affects what that person might want to do to change the situation.

[25] Stigler's second argument is that it is impossible to distinguish between limitations on choice by coercion and by voluntary actions of others. Stigler gives several examples. First, he assumes there is little demand in a community for a symphony, and this prevents it from occurring and so prevents Stigler from attending. Stigler argues that this reduces his utility, which he identifies with freedom. The key point for Stigler is that he is affected (via market prices) by the behaviour of others. People may prefer for others to act differently, but this (for us) has little to do with freedom.

Stigler's second example concerns a high price for symphonies, caused by a high income tax which reduces demand for symphonies. He considers a case in which the income tax was not *intended* to reduce the demand for symphonies, but has that effect. Our definition implies that a loss of consumer or producer surplus in the symphony market is not a loss in economic freedom because no one is coerced to buy or not to buy symphony services, though people lose economic freedom directly from the labour income tax.

Stigler's third example involves user fees for the court system and the distinction between a fine for a parking violation and a rental fee for the parking space. These issues involve government property (the courts, the parking space), which we have argued may violate economic freedom. But this does not provide a complete answer to Stigler's question. Governments may charge a fee for use of the legal system to define or enforce property rights. We have not addressed the issue of whether these fees reduce economic freedom, and we are not sure of the answer.

[26] Suppose a person could be wealthier by moving to Albania, where the government may (for some reason) provide him with substantial material goods. He may choose not to move there, nevertheless, because it is less free. Or he may choose to move there, raising his utility despite the loss of freedom. Freedom differs both from wealth and utility. We think people value freedom and wealth (among other things), and make decisions based on tradeoffs among these ends.

[27] People (of all ages) often say things like, "I'll do it anyway, I just don't want to be told to." This suggests that people get direct utility from their own economic freedom. But it also suggests a shortcoming of our tentative definition. That definition says there is no loss in economic freedom from a government restriction that prevents you from buying more of a good than you would have bought anyway. The obvious problem is that people may believe their economic freedom is limited by such a restriction (and not just potentially limited if they tried to buy more in the future). They may say, for example, "I *won't* do it anyway, I just don't want to be told *not* to."

[28] Landsburg (1991) has recently analyzed the consequences of the assumption that people care directly about the philosophical rules governing the society (as expressed in a fictional social planner's objective function).

References

Stephen Easton, "Rating Economic Freedom: International Trade and Financial Arrangements," (this volume).

Milton Friedman, *Capitalism and Freedom*, Chicago: University of Chicago Press, 1962.

Friedrich A. Hayek, *The Constitution of Liberty*, Chicago: University of Chicago Press, 1960.

Steven E. Landsburg, "Normative Economics: A Positive Approach," unpublished paper, Department of Mathematics, Colorado State University, 1991.

George J. Stigler, "Wealth and Possibly Liberty," *Journal of Legal Studies 7*, no. 2 (1978): 213-17, reprinted in George J. Stigler, *The Intellectual and the Marketplace,* enlarged edition, Cambridge, Massachusetts: Harvard University Press, 1984.

Discussion

Zane Spindler commented that some of the measures of freedom that characterize quantity restrictions (in Figure 2) are really on the supply side rather than the demand side and are ignoring the marginal change in coercion. Instead the measure focuses on the total amount of coercion. Further, the consumer is restricted, not the supplier, and "D" and "E" should not be included. Spindler also wondered if, from a rational expectations perspective, there can be a restriction on freedom if we live in a rent-seeking environment in which anticipated rents are dissipated. Any particular restriction, he suggested, can be seen as already anticipated as a consequence of the basic constitution and rent-seeking behaviour. Jones responded that in the case of the government order that you **must** consume 25 units, it is a loss in economic freedom whether or not you wanted to consume them. I.e. even if it is not a loss in utility, it is a loss in freedom. Arthur Denzau responded that rational expectations are not the same as perfect foresight. Spindler replied that we would distinguish anticipated from unanticipated restrictions.

John Goodman argued that even if we can call this a loss in freedom, we cannot measure it by counting 20 units times the price. This would lead to the conclusion that if we required they take 15 units (less than the 20 units they wanted), then the loss in economic freedom is less than would be the case if the government required that they take the (desired) 20 units. Suppose that the government required that people take 25 units. How do we measure this? John Chant suggested that we tend to confuse two distinct concepts: (i) the consequences of the restrictions of economic freedom; (ii) the extent of the restrictions we face. For example, corresponding to the first concept there are lists of regulations that potentially impede transactions—"Is it illegal to mistreat an oyster?" whether one ever intends to do so or not; while the second approach provides a greater sense of the magnitude of the restrictions. How far can we go? Perhaps we want a framework in which, for a given technology, we stand behind a veil of ignorance, and our concept of economic freedom carves out our opportunity set before we introduce our tastes. We do not talk about marginal restrictions because we have no starting point—all our restrictions are of the same sort.

James Ahiakpor felt that the measure of freedom and utility appear to be the same thing. Jones responded that even though changes in utility and changes in economic freedom are measured in the same currency, they are **not** the same thing. They can go in different directions. The Jones/Stockman paper does not add or subtract measures of freedom and utility because that depends upon what a restriction on your economic freedom means to you.

Edward Hudgins stressed that if the government forces you to consume that which you want to consume, you lose the opportunity to change your mind. Milton Friedman pointed out that to restrict your freedom does not mean that you are worse-off. It arises from a utility function that has both freedom and wealth as arguments. People may even be willing to pay to restrict their freedom as they do with Christmas clubs. James Gwartney felt that the option to consume more or less than the mandated amounts should be valued. Walter Block had trouble with the idea that a Christmas club was in any way a restriction on economic freedom since it was completely voluntary. He argued that the way to capture the value of the impediment is to ask what people would be willing to pay to rescind it. Richard Stroup suggested that even if we increase our economic freedom by actively participating in some voluntary arrangement, the difference is between a total and a partial effect. The total effect is that we have chosen to do it. The partial effect is that it reduces our freedom to do it even though we have not had to restrict ourselves. Had it been possible to restrict others we would not have suffered the loss in freedom. Milton Friedman argued that there is a more subtle issue here: the ability to agree to restrict your economic freedom is part of economic freedom. This raises several difficulties. If government is involved, then the issue may turn on whether by accepting a loss in economic freedom you are not preventing some larger loss of freedom. Richard Rahn emphasized that if the government required you to have polio shots and therefore polio is wiped-out, then you would be willing to pay to have government do what you would already wish to do.

Stephen Easton suggested that the option value should be taken more seriously and wondered if the rectangle was the appropriate way to characterize that valuation. Further, dealing with the rectangle evaluation of losses in Figures 2 and 3, if rent-seeking dissipates the rectangle profits arising from restrictions, then measuring the rectangle is a way to approximate the amount people are willing to pay to remove the restrictions—or get the restrictions for themselves. John Chant felt that the best way to express the problem associated with measuring economic freedom was to look at the rectangle loss which is the dollar consumer loss and insist that this is the loss in wealth. Then he suggested we can rename the loss in economic freedom as units of freedom which we will, for simplicity, identify with the dollar losses even though they are different units—one of "freedom(s)," and one of dollars. We should have identified $100 of wealth losses and $100 in freedom losses—which may be freedom units. Ronald Jones indicated that we do not add these two dollar losses together since both enter separately into utility.

James Gwartney elaborated on the idea that the impediment value of the restriction which mandates you to do what you would have done in any case, is what you would be willing to pay to have it removed. He noted that this is complicated by the recognition that different people would be willing to pay different amounts depending on how they value the option to do things differently. Alan Stockman wanted to face the issue directly: Do you lose economic freedom when you are required to do what you would have done in any case? He pointed out that the paper attempts to define this by the minimum cost of compliance with the restriction. If we agree that this is a restriction on our freedom, then there is the question of how to measure it. What are the alternatives to the Jones-Stockman measure? He did not see any relevance of the option approach. It still confuses wealth and economic freedom. By being required to consume that which would have been consumed anyway, there is no loss from the utility of consumption part of the utility function, but there is a loss in the utility of economic freedom part of the utility function. The restriction that requires consumption of 15 units is two losses. The first is the restriction that requires consumption of at least 15 units—which is measured as the cost of compliance. The second is the surplus loss associated with the restriction that no more than 15 units may be consumed. Stockman used the following example: Suppose public and private schools are perfect substitutes. Then by measuring all public expenditures as a loss in economic freedom, there is an implicit assumption that you would have consumed it (the same schooling) anyway. Alternatively, you wouldn't want to count raw government expenditure.

Milton Friedman contrasted two approaches: the definitions suggested by Jones and Stockman, and the approach that asks: How much would you pay to get rid of it? Consider driving on the left hand side of the road. In this case there is undoubtedly a loss in economic freedom. How much would you pay to get rid of it? Surely, nothing. The Jones-Stockman approach goes a long way toward reconciling very difficult conceptions of economic freedom into a single index.

Rating Economic Freedom: International Trade and Financial Arrangements

Stephen T. Easton,
Simon Fraser University

Introduction

THIS IS A CHARACTERIZATION OF economic freedom in a number of countries with respect to their international exchanges. The measures developed are relentlessly additive. This means that in comparison with earlier work, the characterization of economic freedom may appear narrow.[1] The advantage to this strategy is that additional research may always add (literally) to what is extant without any reweighting or complex indexing. Tables in the text illustrate the measures developed, and a summary table at the end highlights the dollar values of the reduction in economic freedoms as I see it.

Two issues have arisen in conjunction with the development of my measures. First, identifying economic freedom sector by sector is awkward as the measures in one sector may overlap with those of another sector and lead to double counting. I.e., suppose a study of the domestic economy uses taxation as a measure of freedom's reduction. Since one of my measures of freedom's reduction in the international sector is related to expenditure, unrequited official transfers, we may not wish to count both revenue and expenditure as distinct reductions in economic freedom. Reconciliation of the national freedom accounts will have to take place.

Second, by choosing to focus on an additive characterization of economic freedom, the indexes devised have emphasized the trade accounts which are relatively easy to measure, to the virtual exclusion of the loss in freedom associated with the flows of factors, which are comparatively difficult to measure. Even though, as I will argue below, the conceptual measures of freedom are the same, more extensive research is required to continue with the same systematic characterization of economic freedom as has been accomplished for the trade accounts.

A Working Definition of Freedom

As we can see from the discussions at the two previous conferences related to rating economic freedom (Walker, 1988; Block, 1991), a conception of economic freedom is difficult to define in a clear and unambiguous fashion. In the absence of consensus, perhaps the measure that serves best is the most simple. Economic freedom is the voluntary allocation of resources. Now in the extreme such a definition may not serve. "Your money or your life!" presents an opportunity for "voluntary" exchange which most of us would agree is not appropriate.

One would like a definition that says that economic freedom is the voluntary allocation of resources subject to as few constraints as possible — other than those imposed by nature, and those imposed by voluntary, non-coercive associations of others. But as a definition, this is a quagmire. There will be divergent views on what is voluntary, what is the state of "nature," and what is "non-coercive." Rather than attempt a definitive statement, or even one that caters successfully to most peoples' views, the task at this point emphasizes identifying, enumerating and elaborating what I take to be the relevant constraints. Other conceptions of freedom may involve additional or even very different sets of constraints on voluntary exchange.

In the context of international trade and finance, the relevant dimensions are comparatively simple. Individuals of different countries are more free if they have the opportunity to allocate their own resources. For these purposes, the government is *not* just another individual. It is instead a direct impediment, through its powers of taxation and reallocation, to the exercise of economic freedom. We need to be careful here. This does *not* imply that there is no role for government. It does suggest, however, that the rule of law, and the provision of all the other goods and services government provides, should be seen as trading-off with individual freedom and viewed with healthy suspicion in consequence.

Freedom in the Context of International Exchange

From the international trade perspective, the ability to allocate one's own resources takes several forms. If you, in your own country cannot trade at the prices available to individuals in another country (net of "natural" costs such as transportation, insurance, and the like), then some distortion exists. I will take it as obvious that by far the most significant distortions in this regard are those created by government fiat. Impediments to both goods and factor trade abound. Tariffs and non-tariff barriers, prohibitions on immigration and emigration are rife. Exchange controls and controlled exchanges are far more common than genuinely flexible exchange rates. In all of these cases, the ability to engage in free exchange is compromised.

How we identify and quantify this diminution in our freedom is the task of this paper. It is a search along one dimension. As a result, some of the issues which are characterized as diminishing our freedom may nonetheless lead to a higher level of national income. In this respect we part company with traditional economic analysis which tends to take income maximization as the objective function. In contrast, our analysis pays little heed to the consequences of government spending — for "good" or "ill" — but characterizes the act of taxation as freedom reducing as it stands between the individual's resources and the individual's allocation of those resources.

Appropriate Categorizations

Once we decide upon constraints that need to be measured, there are several ways in which we may classify aspects of economic freedom. We may choose categorical, ordinal, or cardinal measures.

Categorical measures are those that can be answered with a "yes" or a "no," a "present" or "absent," etc. For example, we might ask, "Does a country require a permit to emigrate or immigrate?" or "Is the exchange rate freely floating?" The most information that can be gleaned from these measures is whether they exist, or have they changed from previous observations. Categories are useful, but are of limited value in the long run. Although categorization requires less information (than ordinal or cardinal measures) at some level of abstraction, they require strong criteria for deciding whether the variable is "on" or "off" which may obscure important nuances. Categorization does not readily permit consistent aggregation over sub categories. This means that sub categories are unlikely to be very useful in terms of constructing broad indexes reflecting economic freedom. Since the information requirements necessitated by such measures are less stringent than for ordinal or cardinal measures, categories of economic freedom are likely to be with us for some time. Spindler and Still (1991) have provided an extensive list of categories identifying dimensions of economic freedom.

There are two kinds of ordinal rankings which are usefully distinguished. The first is of the kind, "Is what I am measuring significantly different than in some previous (base) period?" This is the kind of question familiar to economists who are interested in inflation, and indexes in general. In this case, price comparisons can be made between periods even though the value of the index itself is entirely arbitrary. It would make no sense to compare a price index in one country with the level of some price index in another country. But comparisons of rates of change of these price indexes, the rates of inflation, across countries is often revealing.

A second ordinal measure asks simply whether something is greater or less than something else. For example, "Are trade taxes greater in one country than another?" In this case we have a comparison that is without reference to some base period — the measures are intrinsically meaningful.[2]

For our purposes, a cardinal measure means that measurements are additive. For example, taxes are additive: tax A gathers $10 and tax B gathers $25 so that the total tax burden is $35. A cardinal measure is most useful as it can do at least what the other rankings can accomplish. In the present context it is particularly fruitful because it is both easily interpretable and open-ended. These are virtues insofar as it will undoubtedly take many iterations to establish a satisfactory or consensus set of dimensions for measuring freedom. If the total value of freedom's loss is $100 using the measures available today, additional research may provide an additional measure that suggests the loss is another $25. Rather than create a new, improved index that embodies some relatively arbitrary reweighting of old and new categories which makes the index difficult to compare with past efforts, the new costs may be added to the old. An additive index which gives the opportunity to cumulate is particularly well suited for the ongoing development of characterizations of economic freedom. Of course additive measures also impose the most stringent information requirements. Our discussion of economic freedom develops almost exclusively cardinal, additive measures of freedom.

The Measure of Freedom

The notion of economic freedom I will use is based on the idea that the individual has the "right" to allocate the resources that he or she owns without impediment. In the context of international trade this means that tariffs, quotas, voluntary export restraints (VERs), and other nontariff barriers (NTBs), which diminish the individual's ability to trade at international prices reduce freedom. Similarly, interference with factor flows which reduces the opportunity for the equalization of factor returns also diminish freedom.

As a working hypothesis, I will assume that the measure of economic freedom (in a negative sense) is the dollar value of the impediments to free exchange and allocation. This is not the same as saying that the measure of economic freedom is the dollar *cost* of the impediment.

To illustrate this difference consider the case of an idealized excise tax. The usual definition of the cost is the "welfare cost" associated with the tariff. Figure 1 is drawn for linear demand, DD', and constant marginal cost which, in the absence of tariffs or other impediments, is equal to the domestic price, p_0. The usual "welfare cost" associated with the tax, T, is the triangle, *ABC*. This represents the loss in value of the quantities Q_0Q_1 foregone due to the tax. The revenue from the tax, area P_0P_1AB is usually assumed to be returned to the domestic consumer in some lump-sum, non-distorting, fashion.

My (first) measure of the loss in freedom is exactly this revenue rectangle. This is the value of resources over which the individual has lost control. They may be returned or they may not be returned, but the essential feature for our purposes is that the individual consumer does not have the freedom to allocate these resources.[3]

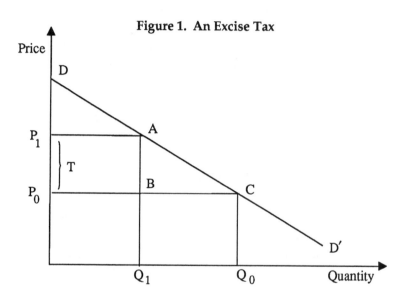

Figure 1. An Excise Tax

Economic Freedom and Income Maximization

The issue in the context of international trade is a little more subtle. This characterization of freedom may actually put real income maximization at odds with what we described as a more free society. That is, income maximization may lead to a loss of freedom!

To illustrate this point recall that an import tariff distorts domestic choice and thereby reduces freedom by raising the domestic price above the international price. The effect of the distortion on domestic income is related to the volume of goods affected, the change in the quantity of imports induced by the tariff, and the effect on the terms of trade. A tariff may raise the level of domestic income if the home country is able to affect world prices. A tariff may reduce domestic demand, and if the home country is "large," lower the world price sufficiently so as to leave the domestic economy better-off once tariff revenues are returned to the populace. This is the traditional argument for an "optimal tariff."[4]

But any suggestion that because (an optimal) tariff raises domestic income, it enhances economic freedom should be rejected for several reasons. First, although it is not the focus of this paper, it is worth remarking that even though domestic income rises by the imposition of (an optimal) tariff, world income, the sum of domestic and foreign incomes is reduced since world trade is distorted. Second, domestic residents are denied the opportunity to trade at world prices. Third, domestic residents are now dependent upon the government to redistribute the tariff revenue in some fashion across the general populace. And fourth, the government has redistributed income throughout the economy as a result of changing relative prices.

Direct and Indirect Measures of Economic Freedom's Loss

It is these last three characteristics that I will use as a foundation for measuring the loss of freedom for each country. The revenue from the tariff is the direct measure of the loss of command over resources suffered by the populace, and the change in economic rents induced by the tariff are the indirect losses associated with the distorted prices. Were we to use a measure of price distortion alone, i.e. the difference between world and domestic prices, we would have to weight each distortion by its importance unless we were satisfied with a mere catalogue of goods taxed. The revenue raised by the tax aptly describes the command over resources lost to the private sector.

But using tariff revenue as a characterization of freedom's loss is not sufficient.[5] A tariff may be sufficiently high so as to be prohibitive, and we do not want to allow this state of affairs to be confused with no diminution in freedom which would be the case if the tariff were zero. Indeed as tariff rates rise, at some point revenue must be reduced.[6]

To avoid this problem and capture the distortion taking place in resource allocation, two dimensions of our characterization of economic

Figure 2. Direct and Indirect Costs

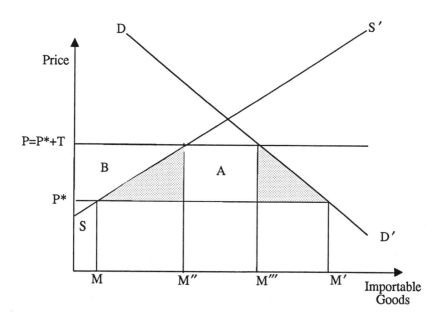

freedom can be distinguished: direct and indirect diminutions in economic freedom. The direct effects are those reallocations of resources that are spent by the government. The indirect effects are those reallocations that are caused by government policy but spent by private individuals.

Figure 2 is a traditional, partial equilibrium representation of the effect of a tariff in a small country. The (linear) demand curve for the importable good is DD' and the (linear) domestic supply schedule is SS'. The world price is p^*, and without tariffs the home country imports MM'. With the imposition of a tariff, T, the domestic price rises to $p=p^*+T$, and the quantity of imports falls to $M''M'''$. The area, A, is the tariff revenue, as it is the tariff rate times the quantity of imports. This I have called the direct effect of the tariff in reducing economic freedom. Tariff revenue is both taken away from the private sector and spent in ways that differ from the private owner's allocation.

The second effect is the indirect effect a tariff has in reducing economic freedom. It is represented as (trapezoid) B in Figure 2. The indirect effect of the tariff arises from the reallocation of resources in the domestic industry that produces the importable good. Output of the importable good rises as the price received by the producer at home increases in proportion to the tariff. The increase in price draws additional resources into the industry and provides an increase in economic rents to (fixed) factors already employed in the industry.[7] This is a reduction in economic freedom because it represents an effect of government policy that stands between the producer and the undistorted value of the resources that are owned. I term it indirect because even though the government policy has changed the allocation of resources to particular individuals, the resources are not spent by the government directly, but by private citizens.[8] Which of these measures is most important? Obviously if there is no domestic production, the indirect losses are nonexistent. Just as obviously the indirect costs are likely to be vastly greater than the direct costs if domestic production is large relative to excess demand — imports.

How does this measure deal with the problems of a prohibitive tariff?[9] If the tariff is prohibitive, then the (indirect) loss is the value of domestic production, which is the same as domestic consumption, times the tariff rate — again, ignoring the second order welfare costs, the shaded areas under both the demand and supply schedules.[10]

Extending the Measure to Non-tariff Barriers

The effect of *non-tariff* barriers can be assessed in the same framework. A quota has a tariff equivalent, voluntary export restrictions, VERs, have effects similar to a quota, variable import levies, VILs, have effects similar to those of tariffs, non-automatic import authorizations, NAIAs, may be thought of as a form of quota, and even government purchasing can be seen as a device reallocating domestic rents.

Calculating the Loss of Freedom

Distortions in the international sector are divided into those affecting trade in goods and services and distortions affecting the flows of factors of production — labour and capital. Among the activities we can catalogue which lead to a decrease in freedom in the goods component of the international sector are tariffs and NTBs: quotas, VERs, and various specific arrangements.

Tariffs

As we have discussed, there are several elements of tariffs that can reduce the ability to allocate resources without distortion. First there is the tariff rate itself. As a first approximation, a 10% ad valorem tariff adds 10% to the private individual's cost of the good.[11] The direct effect of the tariff is to raise revenue for the government. This constitutes resources no longer available to be allocated by private individuals. The indirect effects are those that arise from the increase in price as rents on factors already employed in the industry are created and new resources are brought into production. To measure the rents created requires knowledge of the amount of domestic production. For example, if the tariff is 10% and domestic production before the tariff is imposed amounts to 100 units each of which is worth $1 on the international market, then roughly $10 of indirect rent reallocation is created by the tariff (for the factors already employed).[12]

Our description of the tariff is based on the direct and indirect costs to freedom. In particular we can observe the revenue generated by the outstanding tariff structures around the world. Table 1 provides such a listing for twenty-seven countries. Each country is described by the level of trade taxes in column 3, the value of imports in column 4, and gross domestic product in column 5. All are measured in domestic currency. Columns 6 and 7 suggest a basis for comparing the loss of freedom induced by such taxes. In column 6 we have the percentage of imports that the taxes reflect, and in column 7 the taxes are expressed as a percentage of gross domestic product.

In terms of our categories, all countries obtain some revenue from tariffs, but the figures in the last two columns enable us to rank countries in terms of the relative amounts trade is distorted by taxation (scaled for convenience by imports), and the fraction of total income affected by these taxes. Yugoslavia is the least free in this regard, and the less developed countries are generally more actively involved in the reallocation of resources as a share of their national incomes than the developed countries. Italy, for reasons that are unclear, and Luxembourg appear to be the least distorted by tariffs.

Table 1: Revenue Generating Taxes Associated With International Transactions

Country	Date	Taxes	Imports	GDP	Tax to Import (%)	Tax to GDP (%)
		(Billions of Local Currency)				
United States	1987	14.75	484	4497	3.0	0.33
United Kingdom	1985	1.425	98.94	353.72	1.44	0.40
Austria	1986	6.92	514.6	1432.5	1.3	0.48
Belgium	1984	31	3276	4534	0.94	0.68
Denmark	1986	1.69	215.61	667.14	0.78	0.25
France	1985	9.2	1093	4695	0.84	0.20
Germany	1986	6.18	523.7	1931.2	1.18	0.32
Italy	1986	98	16367	90224	0.06	0.01
Luxembourg	1984	0.086	186.59	221.53	0.04	0.04
Netherlands	1986	2.39	214.65	429.88	1.1	0.56
Norway	1986	1.348	213.04	513.72	0.60	0.26
Sweden	1986	1.81	277.05	931.78	0.60	0.19
Switzerland	1985	3.449	88.1	228	3.9	1.50
Canada	1985	4.316	123.4	478.77	3.4	0.90
Japan	1985	668	40163	31611	1.6	0.21
Finland	1985	0.802	94.89	336.82	0.8	0.24
Greece	1984	12.36	1139.1	3804.7	1.1	0.32
Iceland	1985	4.487	49.051	119.17	9.1	3.87
Ireland	1984	0.503	9.815	16.483	5.1	3.05
Malta	1985	0.0341	0.4205	0.476	8.1	7.1
Portugal	1985	34.407	1439.5	3536.3	2.4	0.9
Spain	1984	265.6	5360	25121	5.0	1.1
Turkey	1986	465.2	7561	39168.	6.1	1.2
Yugoslavia	1983	117.65	951.6	4083.5	12.4	2.9
Australia	1986	3.408	46.22	246.74	7.3	1.4
New Zealand	1985	0.587	15.093	44.861	3.9	1.3
South Africa	1984	0.661	25.931	105.22	2.5	0.63

Source: International Monetary Fund, *International Financial Statistics*.
Column 3 is 81F.H or (.5); column 4, 98c; column 5, 99b.

Table 2. International Transaction Taxes Compared

Country	Date	Population (Millions)	Taxes (Billions of $US)	Full Cost	$US/ Capita
United States	1987	243.77	14.75	97.82	98
United Kingdom	1985	56.62	2.06	4.15	73
Austria	1986	7.56	0.50	1.44	190
Belgium	1984	9.86	0.50	0.69	70
Denmark	1986	5.12	0.23	0.70	137
France	1985	55.17	1.22	2.44	44
Germany	1986	61.05	3.18	7.35	120
Italy	1986	57.22	0.07	0.25	5
Luxembourg	1984	9.4	0.00	0.0	0
Netherlands	1986	14.56	1.09	2.18	150
Norway	1986	4.17	0.18	0.48	113
Sweden	1986	8.37	0.27	0.68	81
Switzerland	1985	6.47	1.66	2.87	443
Canada	1985	25.36	3.09	7.72	304
Japan	1985	120.75	3.33	3.30	27
Finland	1985	4.9	0.15	0.50	101
Greece	1984	9.9	0.10	0.31	31
Iceland	1985	0.24	0.11	0.28	1164
Ireland	1984	3.54	0.55	1.16	327
Malta	1985	0.34	0.07	0.13	376
Portugal	1985	10.16	0.22	0.58	56
Spain	1984	38.34	1.53	6.32	164
Turkey	1986	50.3	0.61	2.73	54
Yugoslavia	1983	22.8	0.94	3.61	158
Australia	1986	15.97	2.29	6.35	397
New Zealand	1985	3.25	0.29	0.87	268
South Africa	1984	30.9	0.46	1.70	55
Total of Above		876.09	39.45	201.16	229.61

Notes: Column 4 is expressed in billions of US dollars converted at end of year rate. Column 6 is based on the penetration ratio for each country or the world average when the individual country information is not available.

Source: International Monetary Fund, *International Financial Statistics*.

Column 3 is from 99z, taxes are from Table 1, and the penetration ratio is from Pearson and Ellyne (1985).

These categorical and ordinal measures of freer trade are the most traditional of the measures that we can construct. They are based on a comparison of countries each of which is considered an entity in its own right whose trade is obstructed relative to others. Can we say that a country is twice as free (in this dimension) as another? Probably we can, although deflating taxation by domestic product which includes government expenditures evaluated at cost must be at best a second best deflator.

The relative measures do not permit us to aggregate across categories of trade taxes. If we are to generate a ranking with quotas, it is surely possible that a country will rank first in terms of one measure and last in terms of the other. Further the ranking generated in Table 1 does not emphasize the distinction between the direct loss of freedom and the indirect measure. These points are developed more fully in Table 2.

The Direct and Indirect Costs of Tariffs

In Table 2 the "cost" of the tariff reflects more than the direct trade costs —the tariff revenue. In constructing column 5, we assume that prices of all traded goods increase by the (trade) tax rate. The penetration ratio, the ratio of imports to total domestic consumption, is used to obtain the fraction of traded goods produced for each country.[13] Added to the direct costs of the tariff, the tariff revenue, this yields an approximation to the total cost—direct and indirect of the outstanding taxes on trade. Column 6 expresses the total U.S. dollar cost on a per capita basis for each country. A per capita valuation seems appropriate as it emphasizes the loss in freedom per individual.[14]

In Table 2 it is clear that Icelanders suffer the greatest loss in freedom to acquire goods at world prices and that their government is most deeply involved in reallocating resources with costs amounting to over $1,000 a head. Switzerland, Australia, Portugal, Malta, Canada and New Zealand comprise the next most affected countries with freedom diminished by $300-$400 per capita. There is a gap until roughly $150 per head. And the costs diminish steadily thereafter.

Non-tariff Barriers

But unlike tariffs which are relatively easy to quantify, the cost of non-tariff barriers is difficult to measure. Further, unlike tariffs which have been diminished in significance through past rounds of the GATT negotiations, the formation of freer trade areas in both Europe and North America, and the antipodes, NTBs have been increasing in importance over the years. Table 3 provides a rough idea of the "coverage" of imported goods that are subject to quota in a number of developed countries.[15] Columns 2 and 3 report the non-tariff coverage ratios in 1981 and 1986. From column 4, which reports the difference between the two years, it is clear that more goods are covered by quotas now than in 1981. This is an issue that is likely to be of increasing importance.

Table 4 indicates the kinds of NTBs that are present in the countries of the OECD in 1986.[16] The second column indicates the share of imports facing quotas, the third, the share facing voluntary export restraints, the forth, restrictions under the Multifibre Arrangement; the fifth, non-automatic import authorizations; and the sixth, variable import levies. From Table 4 it would seem that quotas, voluntary export restrictions and non-automatic import authorizations are the most extensive devices to limit freedom, while both the Multifiber Arrangements and variable import levies are of less significance.[17]

It is striking how much certain countries favour one device over another. New Zealand and Japan prefer quotas and NAIA, while the U.S. chooses VERs, notably autos, and the Multifiber Arrangement. Italy, which appears to have very low tariff revenue, does a more thorough job with quotas and other restrictions. In broad terms it appears that quotas, NAIAs, and VERs have become roughly equal participants in the barriers affecting world trade.

To get a handle on measuring the effects on resource allocation of a quota, in principle it can be treated as a tariff at a particular level. However, unlike the tariff, the quota generates no revenue directly. Rents are created since the domestic price will rise as supply from abroad is restricted. Most analysis of quotas is spent identifying the magnitude of the the welfare losses generated and who benefits from the rents generated — although this is not our task here. In contrast we are concerned with the magnitude of the rents created as it is they that are a measure of the indirect loss of freedom in the nomenclature devised above. They are losses as they change the allocation of resources, and they are indirect as they are spent by private individuals rather than by governments directly.

Table 3. Non Tariff Barriers			
	Trade Coverage Ratios		
	1981	1986	Difference
Belgium-Luxembourg	12.6	14.3	1.7
Denmark	6.7	7.9	1.2
Germany	11.8	15.4	3.6
France	15.7	18.6	2.9
Greece	16.2	20.1	3.9
United Kingdom	11.2	12.8	1.6
Ireland	8.2	9.7	1.5
Italy	17.2	18.2	1.0
Netherlands	19.9	21.4	1.5
EC(10)	13.4	15.8	2.4
Switzerland	19.5	19.6	0.1
Finland	7.9	8.0	0.1
Japan	24.4	24.3	-0.1
Norway	15.2	14.2	-1.0
New Zealand	46.4	32.4	-14.0
United States	11.4	17.3	5.9
All the Above	15.1	17.7	2.6

Source: Cletus C. Coughlin and Geoffrey E. Wood, "An Introduction to Non-Tariff Barriers to Trade" *Review the Federal Reserve Bank of St. Louis*, Vol. 71 No.1, (1989): 35.

But obtaining the tariff equivalent is easier said than done. Wood and Coughlin (1989) note that there is no tariff equivalent available for the aggregates they have generated.[18] But can we assume that a coverage rate of 12% means a greater loss of freedom than a coverage rate of 6%? Certainly that is possible, but until a detailed study of each country identifies the prices available for each product, we have little recourse but to approximate.

Table 4. Types of Non-Tariff Barriers: 1986
Shares of Imports Facing Each Type of Non-Tariff Barrier

	Quotas	VER	MFA	NAIA	VIL
			(All measured in percent)		
Belgium-Luxembourg	1.3	7.3	1.2	5.7	5.2
Denmark	0.4	3.8	2.2	1.1	1.4
Germany	0.9	5.0	4.3	3.0	2.0
France	7.4	3.0	1.8	7.1	2.2
Greece	8.6	9.2	1.2	3.9	3.8
United Kingdom	1.3	4.6	2.9	5.1	4.4
Ireland	0.2	6.1	1.3	2.2	2.2
Italy	8.1	2.0	1.7	7.0	6.6
Netherlands	2.9	5.6	2.8	14.0	6.3
EC(10)	3.1	4.4	2.8	5.6	3.7
Switzerland	2.5	0.0	0.4	2.8	0.5
Finland	0.9	0.0	0.3	6.7	1.8
Japan	14.3	0.0	0.0	7.7	1.8
Norway	4.7	0.0	0.0	3.3	0.0
New Zealand	26.9	0.0	0.0	16.8	0.0
United States	2.0	11.3	3.2	0.0	1.4
All the Above	4.7	5.3	2.2	4.1	2.6

Source: From Cletus C. Coughlin and Geoffrey E. Wood, "An Introduction to Non-Tariff Barriers to Trade" *Review the Federal Reserve Bank of St. Louis*, Vol. 71 No.1, p.37. (31-46.)

	Price Increase Due to			Per Capita US$ Quota Cost
Table 5. Tariff and Non-Tariff Barriers				
	Tariff	Quota Coverage	Total	
Belgium-Luxembourg	0.9	1.4	2.3	27
Denmark	0.8	0.8	1.6	33
Germany	1.2	1.5	2.7	77
France	0.8	1.9	2.7	49
Greece	1.1	2.0	3.1	20
Great Britain	1.4	1.3	2.7	33
Ireland	5.1	1.0	6.1	30
Italy	0.1	1.8	1.9	66
Netherlands	1.1	2.1	3.2	176
Switzerland	3.9	2.0	5.9	112
Finland	0.8	0.8	1.6	34
Japan	1.6	2.4	4.0	20
Norway	0.6	1.4	2.0	77
New Zealand	3.9	3.2	7.1	73
United States	3.0	1.7	4.7	27

Sources: Tables 1, 3 and Department of Finance, 1988.

One approximation strategy is to use the information we have on one country in which we know the details of both the coverage ratio and the price effects of the quota. In the case of the United States while the effect of the quotas is to have the effect of increasing prices by 1.7% as opposed to the 2.8% identified as the effect of tariffs (Department of Finance, 1988 pp. 58-60), the "coverage ratio" of Table 3 is some 17%.[19] If this rough ratio of 10% were to be true in the rest of the world as well, a truly heroic assumption, then the effects of the non-tariffs barriers can be calculated in the manner of Table 2.[20] Table 5 gives the results.

In Table 5, column 2 gives the tariff induced price changes, column 3 the calculated induced price changes and column 4 the total effect on relative prices. The inclusion of the quota/non-tariff barriers in many cases more than doubles the effects on prices induced by tariffs. This means that the values associated with the "full cost" calculations would also more than double. The implied full cost per capita caused by the NTBs — the rent reallocation—is included as column 5 in the table.

International Factor Flows

There are many dimensions along which restrictions can be measured. In principle, the problem is the same as before. We plot the demand or marginal product of capital or labour, then the loss of freedom associated with the international immobility or interference with free exchange is the economic rent created by the discrepancy between real wage rates (or real rates or return on capital) measured in each country compared with the "world" wage or rate of return net of appropriate transportation costs. The impediments to factor mobility create a wedge between the world opportunity cost and the rewards at home. What we have called freedom is ability to move owned factors to their desired location at world prices.

Labour Mobility and Freedom

None of the countries in the above tables have a prohibition against emigration, and all have some restrictions on immigration. The actual restrictions are difficult to identify. In particular, a survey of documents depicting the restrictions on labour migration around the world is not presently available. This, as I was told by both U.S. and Canadian research divisions of the respective immigration authorities, would be an extremely useful but academic study which they themselves would like to read but would be reluctant to commission as it would be of no particular consequence to domestic policy.

In principle, the way to assess the impact of factor mobility is to estimate a demand for labour schedule and then assess the wage paid now relative to the equilibrium world wage, i.e. the wage that would be paid to labour if it were free to flow to the location of greatest remuneration. Some adjustment has to be made for differences in accumulated human capital, and each country has a different demand for various types of labour, but in principle the task could be done. The stock of labour in any country is likely to be quantity constrained, so differences in wages times the amount of labour indicates the distortion imposed by an immigration policy. Although there are many issues related to immigration and national advantage, from the perspective of economic freedom, the lack of mobility is reflected in wage differentials on comparable labour in different countries.

Capital Mobility and Freedom

The difference between labour and capital is primarily that capital is far more mobile internationally than labour. In the jargon of economics, capital is in perfectly elastic supply at a world real rate of return. A country can impose restrictions on capital that will generally speaking reduce the quantity of capital at home, but not the real rate of return that is available to foreigners, and hence domestic residents. The cost, therefore, of restrictions on the flow of capital are borne by domestic residents, not through different rates of return at the margin, but through a lower stock of capital than would otherwise exist.

Thus unlike the case of labour, it is unlikely that a careful study of restrictions on capital flows will identify a differential between the returns in one country relative to another in a systematic fashion. In terms of defining economic freedom, the shift in the marginal product of capital schedule needed to identify the consequences of capital restrictions are particularly difficult to characterize in the absence of a returns differential.

But there are some issues related to capital and financial issues that can be identified. Table 6 indicates that not all exchange rates are free to float.[22] As categorical variables, it is not immediately useful in quantifying the degree of distortion that the different policies create.

In contrast, Table 7 points to international exchange reserve accumulation as one source of the diminution of economic freedom. Recall that our definition is that an individual has the right to allocate his or her own resources. If a national government accumulates international reserves, then that act potentially separates the exchange rate from the decisions of the private sector. Decumulation has the effect of reducing demand for foreign exchange on international markets and accumulation has the effect of increasing the demand for foreign exchange. The price of one currency vis-a-vis another is different when there are reserve accumulations and decumulations.[23]

Table 6: Categories of Exchange Rate Freedom

Country	Degree of Distortion
United States	F
United Kingdom	F
Austria	P
Belgium	wa;Z
Denmark	Z
France	Z
Germany	Z
Italy	Z
Luxembourg	Z
Netherlands	Z
Norway	P
Sweden	P
Switzerland	F
Canada	F
Japan	F
Finland	P
Greece	MF
Iceland	P
Ireland	rh;Z
Malta	rh;MF
Portugal	MF
Spain	F
Turkey	MF
Yugoslavia	MF
Australia	rh
New Zealand	rh
South Africa	rh(mult.)

Notes: Exchange Regime is reported as F=flexible; P=pegged; MF=managed float; Z=member of European Monetary System; other codes refer to IFS line numbers for specifically distorted rates.

Source: International Monetary Fund, *International Financial Statistics*, 8 June 1989.

Table 7: Foreign Exchange Rates, Reserves and Accumulation: 1987-88

COUNTRY	1987		1988		CHANGES		
	FOREIGN CURRENCY		FOREIGN CURRENCY		% Reserve Change Due to Accum.	$ Value of Reserve Accum.	% Change in the Exchange Rate
	Reserves ($US)	Exchange Rate (-/$)	Reserves ($US)	Exchange Rate (-/$)			
Canada	6.218	1.2998	13.517	1.1927	85	6.19	-8
France	29.634	5.34	22.359	6.059	59	-4.26	13
Germany	72.893	1.5815	53.324	1.7803	66	-12.87	13
Greece	2.5819	125.93	3.5234	148.1	166	1.56	18
Great Britain	38.56	41.12	0.53433	0.552636	155	3.97	3
Ireland	4.431	1.675	4.725	1.507	-61	-0.18	-10
Italy	27.81	1658.9	32.5	1757.2	141	6.61	6
Japan	75.657	175.2	90.514	169.36	80	11.8	-3
Finland	5.989	3.946	5.874	4.169	-189	0.22	-6
New Zealand	3.258	0.4635	2.824	0.4669	95	-0.41	1
Norway	3.128	6.2375	2.173	6.57	88	-0.84	5
Switzerland	27.162	1.813	24.045	2.0239	10	-0.32	12
Netherlands	14.174	1.7775	14.542	1.9995	594	2.18	12
United States	13.09		17.36				

*All Reserves and Changes in Reserves in Billions of US Dollars

Source: Lines 1d.d and ag from International Monetary Fund, *International Financial Statistics*, June 1989.

Table 8: The Value of Foreign Exchange Accumulation or Decumulation (1987)		
	Absolute Dollar Value of Reserve Accumulation (Billions)	Per Capita Value of Accumulation
Australia	2.86	179
Austria	0.72	95
Belgium	0.99	100
Canada	6.19	244
Denmark	1.94	380
Finland	0.22	44
France	4.26	77
Germany	12.87	211
Greece	1.56	158
Iceland	0.07	292
Ireland	0.18	51
Italy	6.61	115
Japan	11.84	98
Malta	0.40	118
Netherlands	2.18	150
New Zealand	0.41	127
Norway	0.84	201
Portugal	2.52	248
South Africa	0.32	10
Spain	7.56	197
Sweden	0.69	82
Switzerland	0.32	49
Turkey	2.36	47
United States	3.27	13
United Kingdom	3.97	70
Yugoslavia	8.93	392

Sources: Table 6 and Table 2.

In Table 7, column 7 identifies the U.S. dollar value of the reserve accumulation net of currency revaluation.[24] Column 8 reports the change in exchange rates. There is clear evidence that the major currencies are managed as depreciations in local currencies. Positive values of the percentage change in exchange rates, are associated with decreases in foreign reserve holdings as central banks try to "lean against the wind" and slow the adjustment to market demands and supplies. Table 8 identifies these costs on a per capita basis at the national level.[25]

But there are more international costs to government activity than those associated with the exchange rate. Table 9 points to transfers made at the international level from one government to another. The amount of *official* development assistance is a clear example of resources extracted from one country to give to another. There is little question that this reduces freedom at home as there is no quid pro quo at the margin, nor any hint that private transfers would take place in such orders of magnitude. Column 4 reports the transfers on a per capita basis.

There are also transfers made by governments measured by the balance of payments. In some sense this is a less revealing measure than the direct government to government transfer for assistance explored in Table 9, as it nets out many transfers that are into a country as well as from a country. These transfers are reported in Table 10.

Summing Up

Table 11 provides a summary of the impingements on individual freedom from the international perspective. It is incomplete as I have been at pains to indicate, but it is useful as a starting point that can be extended by future analysis. To the extent that further research is additive, we can add a column to the table and apply the calculations directly.

What emerges from the table is that a group of countries (of those that are complete in the table) for which the diminution in freedom amounts to $600-700 per capita with tariffs and foreign exchange transactions playing a dominant role, and then the United States, Japan and Britain which have costs of freedom at a distinctly lower level of roughly $200 per capita. Part of the reason for this is that the United States and Japan are relatively large economies in which international distortions play less of a role than in smaller economies. It is also true that the levels of distortion are lower.

Table 9: Sources of International Official Development Aid: 1985

Country	Population (Millions)	Official Development Assistance (Billions of $US)	$US/Capita
United States	243.77	9.55	39
United Kingdom	56.62	1.49	26
Austria	7.56	0.25	33
Belgium	9.86	0.43	44
Denmark	5.12	0.44	86
France	55.17	4.02	73
Germany	61.05	2.97	46
Italy	57.22	1.10	19
Netherlands	14.56	1.1772	77
Norway	4.17	0.56	134
Sweden	8.37	0.84	100
Switzerland	6.47	0.30	46
Canada	25.36	1.64	65
Japan	120.75	3.80	31
Finland	4.9	0.21	43
Australia	15.97	0.75	47
New Zealand	3.25	0.05	15

Sources: Table 2 and World Bank, *World Development Report* (New York: Oxford University Press, 1986) 218-219.

Table 10. Official Unrequited Transfers, 1988

Country	Population (Millions)	Official Unrequited Transfers (Billions of $US)	US$/Capita
United States	243.77	12.57	52
United Kingdom	56.62	5.894	10
Austria*	7.56	0.071	9
Belgium*	9.86	1.283	130
Denmark*	5.12	0.131	26
France*	55.17	3.114	56
Germany	61.05	11.82	194
Italy*	57.22	2.30	40
Netherlands	14.56	1.149	79
Norway*	4.17	0.778	187
Sweden*	8.37	1.014	121
Switzerland*	6.47	-0.046	-7
Canada	25.36	0.319	13
Japan	120.75	3.05	25
Finland	4.9	0.405	83
Australia	15.97	0.158	10
New Zealand	3.25	0.063	19

Sources: Table 2 and International Monetary Fund, *International Financial Statistics,* row 77agd.

Note: * is for transfers in 1987.

Table 11. Economic Freedom Rating Per Capita Costs Measured in U.S. Dollars

Country	Per Capita Costs of Economic Freedom in U.S. Dollars					
	Tariff	Non-Tariff Barriers	Foreign Exchange	Official Aid Transfer	Official Unrequited Transfer	Total
United States	98	27	13	39	52	229
United Kingdom	73	33	70	26	10	212
Austria	190		95	33	9	327
Belgium	70	27	100	44	130	371
Denmark	137	33	380	86	26	662
France	44	49	77	73	56	229
Germany	120	77	211	46	194	640
Italy	5	66	115	19	40	245
Luxembourg	0	27	0			27
Netherlands	150	176	150	77	79	632
Norway	113	77	201	134	187	646
Sweden	81		82	100	121	384
Switzerland	443	112	49	46	7	657
Canada	304	94	244	65	13	720
Japan	27	20	98	31	25	201
Finland	101	34	44	43	83	305
Greece	31	20				51
Iceland	1164		292			1456
Ireland	327	30	51			408
Malta	376		118			494
Portugal	56		248			304
Spain	164		197			361
Turkey	54		47			101
Yugoslavia	158		392			550
Australia	397		179	47	10	633
New Zealand	268	73	127	15	19	502
South Africa	55		10			65

Sources: Previous tables. Quota data for Canada are drawn from Department of Finance, 1988, pp. 58-60.

Notes

[1] Spindler and Still (1991) discuss previous efforts to characterize economic freedom and provide a number of dimensions along which it may be measured.

[2] Strictly speaking we could interpret one set of taxes as the base period with which to compare the other, but the point is that we do not have to have comparisons only between *changes* in taxes in one country with changes in taxes in another country. We can compare the *level* of taxation at home with the level of taxation abroad.

[3] Although attributable to the tax, the triangle losses are of a "second order" of small in comparison with the "first order" rectangle losses. It is the latter that are stressed here for practical reasons. To calculate the welfare losses we need to know more information about the underlying demand and supply schedules—the relevant elasticities of demand and supply. As a matter of theory, the welfare losses are generally an order of magnitude smaller than the first order redistribution effects which are relevant to our discussion of freedom, but in principle there is no reason why they would not qualify as yet another component of freedom lost.

[4] The appropriate calculation is that the change in income, dy, equals the level of imports, M, times the (negative of) change in world prices for domestic importables, dp^*, plus the difference between the distorted value of domestic goods, p, and the world price, p^*, all multiplied by the change in domestic goods, p, and the world price, p^*, all multiplied by the change in domestic imports induced by the tariff: $dy = -Mdp^* + (p-p^*)dM$. The traditional *optimal tariff* is one that balances the gain in the terms of trade induced by the tariff, a fall in p^*, with the loss in income associated with the fall in imports.

If the home country is small in world markets, then a tariff induces no change in world prices, $dp^*=0$, and the domestic country loses in proportion to the distortion, $(p-p^*)$, which is positive as one tariff imposes a wedge between domestic and world prices, and the change in the quantity of imorts, dM, which is negative, as higher prices serve to reduce domestic imports. The effect is to reduce domestic income.

[5] The tariff will stand for general tax distortions in the following discussion. This is to simplify the exposition and retain the international flavour of the analysis.

[6] Since tariff revenue starts at zero tariff rate and ends at zero with a prohibitive tariff, there will be a region in which increases in the tariff rate increases tariff revenue, some point of maximum revenue, and a region in which increases in the tariff rate decreases tariff revenue—ultimately to zero. In the macroeconomic setting this is familiar to the popular press as the "Laffer Curve."

[7] Economic theories of rent-seeking focus on the gains, B, as the source of political pressure by interest groups, the producers of the importable who own some of the "fixed" factors, which lead to tariff creation.

[8] In passing it is important to remember that we are reversing the importance economists usually assign to the distortions induced by tariffs. Typically tariff revenue is assumed to be redistributed to the general population in a "lump-sum" or (at the margin) nondistorting redistribution of the tariff revenue. This is more an analytical convenience than a serious statement about the behaviour of governments. The usual notions of a tariff's distortion lies in the two shaded triangles of Figure 2. They represent the resource loss to society induced by the tariff. This is an important but very different issue than the one we are addressing here. A more detailed analysis would include both triangles as they indicate losses. As explained above, however, including them requires much more information about the details of the economy and the loss in an order of magnitude smaller than those already detailed.

[9] By analogy any other tax that chokes-off exchange.

[10] Where the measure fails to allow simple application is the case in which there is a prohibitive tariff and no domestic production. Without insight into the demand curve, there is little we can say other than to report the nominal tariff schedule.

[11] We will assume that the countries under consideration are small: they do not have the ability to affect the world price. Although no doubt an oversimplification in some situations, a great deal more information at every level of generalization—e.g. the elasticities of excess demand—is required to go much further.

[12] More precisely the rent created depends on the elasticity of supply, ε, and comes to $\$10+(1/2)t^2 Q_0 \varepsilon$ in the linear case, where Q_0 is the level of

domestic production prior to the imposition of the tariff. Should foregone benefits be taken into account on the demand side, we would add another triangle proportional to the square of the tariff rate, the level of domestic consumption, and the elasticity of demand.

A more complete conception of economic freedom which requires even more information would take account of the repercussions in other domestic markets. These markets may be distorted. This leads to additional revenue gathered through other taxes, and rents redistributed because of the relative price changes. Although a theoretically attractive stance, it is not a practical alternative for the present paper.

[13] Where possible the import penetration ratio is issued as reported in Pearson and Ellyne (1985, p. 404-405). Where it is not available, the world average is employed—0.33 of GDP. This is then multiplied by two under the assumption that trade is roughly balanced to obtain the direct effects on traded goods.

[14] An alternative such as costs relative to per capita domestic product would scale each individual's loss by the average level of domestic income. But the implicit assumption of such a scaling is to say that a dollar's loss in freedom in one country is different than a dollar's loss in another country.

[15] Coverage refers to the share (in value) of products restricted relative to total imports. Restricted products include "core" NTBs: variable import levies, quotas, non-automatic import authorizations (voluntary export restraints, restrictive import licensing, and trade covered by the Multifiber Arrangement).

[16] Australia, Canada, and Sweden were exluded because of problems associated with obtaining adequate measures of the NTBs (Coughlin and Wood, p. 35).

[17] This is in terms of their significance to developed countries. Their effects on exporting, poorer, less developed countries is not assessed here.

[18] Their study is drawn from an unpublished manuscript by Laird and Yeats, *Quantitative Analysis for Trade Barrier Analysis* (Macmillan, forthcoming) which appears to be the last word on the subject. In an aerlier study Roningen and Yeats conclude that there is no relation between simple coverage of a sort and relative price differences. They attribute this phenomenon to a masking of the effect of the coverage by other domestic government interferences (Vernon Roningen and Alexander Yeats, "Nontariff Distortions of International trade: Some Preliminary Empirical Evi-

dence," in Hans Singer, Neelamber Hatti, and Rameshwar Tandon, *New Protectionism and Restructuring* (New Delhi: Ashish Publishing House): 317-332.

[19] Note that this is the quota rate in the U.S. but the coverage rate refers to the core NTBs.

[20] No coverage ratios were available on a comparable basis for Canada, nor were the detailed effects of the entire quota structure readily available for any of the other countries. Detailed studies on the structure of imports and exports have been done for European countries so that potentially there are more data available.

[21] Another difficulty is that the wage rate does not capture the full return to labour in most economies. There is to a greater or lesser extent a pro-rata splitting of publicly provided services. Thus wage alone does not capture the full value of the gain to mobility.

[22] As before our definition of freedom may conflict with income maximization. A country may not be an optimum currency area and may choose to fix its exchange rate with another country. This may increase income. But from the point of view of individual freedom within a country, it seems more reasonable to insist that an individual be free to exchange whatever currency he or she is paid for whatever other currencies are available without interference by the national authority. This begs the question, however, of competitive currency creation since it assumes the current extant units of exchange as the only alternatives.

[23] Here we ignore the issue of the loss in freedom from the initial state of reserve accumulations and look only at the implications of the changes in the stock.

[24] This is a bit ticklish. If the foreign currency depreciates against the U.S. dollar by 10%, I treat foreign holdings of a constant stock of U.S. dollars as no changes in accumulation.

[25] There are obviously more dimensions to international financial arrangements than those described here. The security of assets in Switzerland and Luxembourg is not captured by these measures, nor are the effects of multiple exchange rates in, for example, Belgium and South Africa, let alone Yugoslavia.

References:

Block, Walter, ed., *Economic Freedom: Toward a Theory of Measurement* (Vancouver, B.C.: The Fraser Institute, 1991).

Coughlin, C.C. and G.E. Wood, "An Introduction to Non-Tariff Barriers, to Trade" *Review the Federal Reserve Bank of St. Louis*, Vol. 71, No.1: 31-46.

Department of Finance Fiscal Policy and Economic Assessment Branch, *The Canada-U.S. Free Trade Agreement: An Economic Assessment* (Ottawa: Canadian Government Publishing Centre, 1988)

International Monetary Fund, *International Financial Statistics* (Washington, D.C., 1989)

Pearson, C. and M. Ellyne, "Surges of Imports: Perceptions versus Evidence," *The World Economy* (1985) reprinted in H. Singer, N. Hatti and R. Tandon. *New Protectionism and Restructuring* (New Delhi: Ashish Publishing House, 1988):, 397-420.

Spindler, Z. and L. Still, "Economic Freedom Ratings," in Walter Block, ed., *Economic Freedom: Toward a Theory of Measurement* (Vancouver, B.C.: The Fraser Institute, 1991).

Walker, Michael A., ed., *Freedom, Democracy and Economic Welfare: Proceedings of an International Symposium* (Vancouver, B.C.: The Fraser Institute, 1988)

World Bank, *World Development Report* (New York: Oxford University Press, 1986) 218-219.

Discussion

Milton Friedman liked the general approach to valuing economic freedom with a dollar measure as it goes beyond the internal calculus. The problem with this approach arises from the presence of transactions costs. There are tradeoffs to be made: national defense and tariffs, for example. A tax may be the least costly way to preserve economic freedom by preventing long-run domination by a foreign power.

Richard McKenzie remarked that what is here is an index of government impediments. But with the advent of new technologies, fewer governmental institutions are needed. Thus we are freer regardless of the state of tariffs. A well-known New York insurance company ships data (for entry into a company data base) to Ireland and then ships it back to New York each day. Newer technologies may lead to more economic freedom in and of themselves.

Tom DiLorenzo made two points. First, the costly, rent-seeking behaviour of lobby groups is manifestly obvious as one sees the many companies springing-up around Washington. Second, foreign aid has two costs. The first is the cost in economic freedom to the country giving the aid (as resources are allocated by the government), and the second is the cost to the people in the foreign country as the aid attempts to prop-up governments that reduce economic freedom.

Clifford Lewis suggested that nominal restrictions and actual restrictions on economic freedom were not always the same. In many LDC's there are prohibitive tariffs, but everything is smuggled and available. AID conducted some price surveys of certain computer products and found that they were cheaper (than in the United States) in some countries that nominally prohibited their entry. The reason is that the added cost to smuggled goods is a function of weight, and software does not weigh very much.

Jack Carr suggested that more thought be given to the points raised in the paper that tax revenue falls with the higher tax rate beyond some point, and amplified the issue that once some government is taken as needed, we must have some tax revenue. Thus to evaluate economic freedom, one needs the whole picture of a society.

James Gwartney remarked that trade taxes understate the degree of loss in economic freedom to the extent that customs inspectors have discretion about what rates to charge. The bribes to bring merchandise into a country "tax-free" should be counted against economic freedom as they add to the excess burden.

Easton replied that his measure is not a measure of excess losses but a measure of first-order losses. In particular, it measures extant price distortions that diminish economic freedom through rent reallocation as well as, in principle, the second order losses. The whole picture is not at issue, he argued, as this measure of the loss in economic freedom is a measure along a single dimension—the economic freedom dimension, not an effort to measure the highest level of income, or even contingent freedom in the future. Thus economic freedom can be traded-off against alternatives, but this is a different issue than that of measurement and quantification.

Alvin Rabushka argued that identifying fixed exchange rates with losses in freedom is wrong. For example, Hong Kong benefitted enormously from fixed rates. Flexible rates are not intrinsic to the notion of freedom. Protection of the standard of value is what needs to be protected. Easton replied that freedom and income do not necessarily coincide, and to the extent that the foreign exchange authority is involved, resources are allocated by someone other than the individual who earned the money. Walter Block suggested that the gold standard period was one of free exchange. Milton Friedman responded that this was not the case as governments were intimately involved in the gold standard from the beginning. It was a pegged price for gold. If the market had chosen, it probably would have chosen silver. Further there was a confusion between pegged exchange rates and a unified currency. Hong Kong went to a unified currency with the United States dollar and did not prohibit the use of other currencies. The right indicator is whether there is a central bank, and in Hong Kong's case, there was no central bank. It would not improve economic freedom if California started to issue California dollars.

Walter Block argued that there was a contradiction in Easton's measure. Easton says that a government can increase income through an optimal tariff, but then tries to use income as a measure of economic freedom. How can this be if they go in opposite directions? Easton replied that we can distinguish full income and measured income. Economic freedom is part of full income. We need a marginal valuation of economic freedom to aggregate it with measured income. One possible way would be to use immigration among countries with measured economic circumstances as similar as possible. We could then "price" a measure of economic freedom in terms of immigration flows.

Milton Friedman was concerned with the use of the exchange rate to add-up losses in economic freedom across countries. He felt that some kind of purchasing power exchange rate should be used to compare countries. Is a dollar in the U.S. as relevant as a dollar in Italy? The issue is that the income used should be potential, not actual, income. If a country loses $5, then it is more serious if the potential income in that country is $50 rather than $500. India has a potential income far greater than current income. We do not get a good measure of the scale of the economy by using current income. Easton replied than an ideal measure would be with "one world." Friedman agreed saying that the utopian level of income would be the levels of national incomes associated with freely flowing factors of production as well.

Alan Reynolds suggested that some revenue needed to be raised through tariffs. Milton Friedman responded that we use the difference between the tariff and domestic excise taxation to measure protection. Walter Block argued we need to count all current restrictions regardless of the reasons. He didn't care why there was a draft, just that it exists. Friedman replied that you may need a short-run loss in freedom to protect economic freedom in the long-run. The draft is a good example. It may be necessary in Israel or even Switzerland. In the short-run it may be impossible to satisfy the need for soldiers without some kind of forced service. It is certainly a restriction on economic freedom.

James Gwartney was concerned with Easton's measure of economic freedom that did not normalize for the size of the country. It would lead to a situation that a large country would have larger losses in freedom just because it was large. Easton replied that a dollar loss was a dollar loss and that the issue went back to that raised earlier about the purchasing power prices and potential income versus measured income.

Measures of Economic Freedom

Stephen T. Easton,
Simon Fraser University

Introduction

DURING THE LAST RATING OF Freedom Conference I proposed a measure of economic freedom that seemed to offer some hope that a cardinal measure of economic freedom could be devised. In this paper I propose to elaborate that measure and suggest some ways in which it can be implemented.

Conceptual Measures of Economic Freedom

Although there is no generally accepted definition of economic freedom, I will define it as the allocation of one's own resources at one's own behest.[1] Two possible approaches to measuring economic freedom might be characterized as the "constructive" approach and the "impediments" approach.

At first blush, the constructive approach is the most natural to an economist. Economic freedom is conceived of as a separate argument of the utility
function. An increase in "F" has exactly the same impact on utility as an
increase in consumption of any other good or service. What remains to be
decided is what constitutes the measure of "F." The second notion of
freedom is based on impediments. The essence of this conception is that
economic freedom is associated with the ability to trade at prices set by
individual agents without impediment. Any artificial wedge between the
price demanded and received reduces the freedom of individual economic
agents. The most relevant ingredient of the artificial wedge is the application of governmental authority through taxation and regulation. The reduction in economic freedom is identified as the value of the impediments.[2]

What should a definition or a measure of freedom do? A definition
should correspond to a common understanding of what economic freedom
means. But whose understanding? I will take those who share the view that
the (market) economy functions best with a minimum of government
interference, the philosophy of economic liberalism, as the appropriate
audience at least initially.[3]

A definition should pass some test of usefulness. It should be possible
to use the definition to develop frameworks that answer questions we wish
to pose. In this case we wish to rank countries as to the amount of economic
freedom they permit. I see two competing approaches to the definition of
economic freedom which are characterized in the next two sections.

The Constructive Approach

If we define freedom constructively, we need a characteristic or good or
service that can be identified with economic freedom. It may be associated
with a variant of a particular set of economic activities. For example, our
notion of economic freedom may be that higher income yields command
over more resources and makes people "freer." Alternatively, more choice
or a more equal distribution of income may be what we wish to use as a
definition of more freedom. In this way we can produce an index of any
number of "goods" to represent economic freedom. Regardless of what is
chosen, however, the constructive definition allows economic freedom to
be "traded-off" against other arguments of the utility function and will

imply that there is a demand for economic freedom to which the usual economic calculus applies.

Although these are congenial terms to economists, the difficulty with this conception is that no single construction has emerged to claim the mantle of "freedom." Until such a "good" is identified, the constructivist approach is empty. To date the most promising approaches have identified many categories of activities which contribute to economic freedom (Spindler and Still (1991), Scully and Slottje (this volume) and Spindler and Miyake (this volume)). A review of past Symposia, however, provides little grounds for complacency that "something will turn up" as a common core of goods and services to identify as the set of activites constituting economic freedom.

The Impediments Approach

Unlike the constructive approach, the impediments approach to a definition of economic freedom stresses interference with free exchange as reducing freedom. This approach flows from the assumption that the demand price reflects the individual's marginal benefit from consumption and the supply price reflects the marginal value of resources brought into production. Since both are the result of an "individual" optimization, any interference reduces utility. But this is awkward. As pointed out in Easton (this volume, previous chapter), an optimal tariff raises income (and, if you will, utility) of those imposing the tax. Yet, I think we are in general agreement that the tariff reduces economic freedom, i.e., if we think of economic freedom as reflecting the individual's right to the fruits of his or her own labor (or, more generally, one's own resources), then the interference in the pricing of a transaction reallocates economic rents, and that reallocation is a reduction in economic freedom—the right to allocate one's own product.[4] If the amount of one's own economic reward allocated freely could be measured directly, and valued explicitly, perhaps we would have an ideal measure. But failing this, the impediments viewpoint focusses on measuring the amount of economic rent being reallocated by government action.[5]

To see what is being defined as a loss in freedom, consider Figure 1 in which equilibrium is initially at point **A**, the intersection of the downward sloping demand schedule, **P*D**, and the (horizontal) supply schedule, **PS**, for some good. Equilibrium prices and quantitites are at **P** and **Q**. Now imagine the imposition of a tax that increases price to **P+T**, from **P**. As is well-known, the value of the consumption foregone is approximated by the "triangle" losses in region **W** in Figure 1.[6] The loss in economic freedom, however, is something more. All transactions that were taking place at point **A** have been impeded. The impediment to these transactions is in two parts. The losses associated with foregone consumption in region **W**, plus the impediment to every transaction that is made—the rate of tax times the volume of transactions, i.e., the value of the tax, region **R**.

Figure 1. Economic Freedom and Economic Welfare Measurement

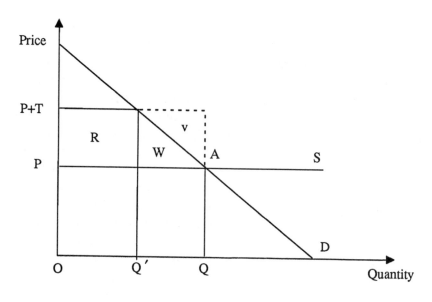

Notice what is being defined in this characterization of economic freedom. We are not defining a loss in economic freedom as the loss in economic welfare associated with a distortion. We are, instead, defining the loss of economic freedom as the (marginal) value of the distortion weighted by the number of transactions both undertaken and foregone. The triangle loss is part of the loss in freedom, but only insofar as it reflects the weight of foregone transactions rather than realized transactions. We could approximate the loss in freedom as the quantity that would have transacted without the tax, **Q**, times the distortion, in which case the rectangle,

R+W+V, would provide one measure of the loss in freedom. The transaction weight with which we choose to aggregate the distortion is unimportant for small changes, but it becomes of crucial importance if we are considering distortions that are prohibitive in a market. The greater the number of foregone transactions, the more important the distinction. If we have enough information about a particular market, then we can calculate the loss in freedom as the area between the demand and supply schedules foregone.

Some Complications

This conception of economic freedom deals with rent reallocation, but there are a number of complications. In the (first) case of the simple tax described in Figure 1, the appropriate measure is the value of the tax itself, **R**, plus the triangle, **W**. In the (second) case of a prohibitive tax, then rent reallocation is approximated either at the price at which the demand schedule hits the axis, **P***, times the number of foregone equilibrium transactions, **Q**, or with sufficient information, the triangle loss itself—**P*AP**. It would be grossly inappropriate to use the actual (zero) transaction weights. In the (third) case of traded goods there are two possible measures of the loss of economic freedom.[7] These are displayed in Figure 2. We have the losses associated with the tariff revenue, **R**, and the triangle welfare losses, **W** and **W***, and in addition we include the reallocation of rent that takes place as a result of the higher prices. Area **Z** is being reallocated from consumer to producer and as a result, economic freedom is being reduced. In Easton (previous chapter) I referred to the latter as an indirect loss. This led to the observation that the loss in economic freedom in a traded-goods setting is (approximately) proportional to the volume of consumption times the value of the tariff rather than merely the value of tariff revenue plus the triangles of welfare loss.

If rent reallocation is our characterization of a reduction in economic freedom, then we need to establish some principles by which we can measure the various countries of the world. The first principle is that we can sum the measured distortions in each market to reach a total. That is, we do not have to worry about the effect that a change in a distortion in one market has on the value of the distortion in any other. Consider two

Figure 2. Economic Freedom and Traded Goods

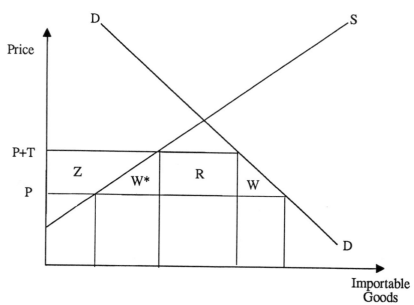

markets in which the goods are substitutes. If we introduce a distortion in the first market, we can calculate the rent reallocation exactly as described in Figure 1. In the second market, the demand schedule will shift. To the extent that there is already an existing distortion in that market, the increase in demand will raise additional revenue and be captured fully when we measure the distortion in the second market.[8]

Thus the sum of the tax revenues plus the triangle losses in each market is a measure of the loss in (direct) economic freedom. These are losses in the sense that the government reallocates the resources directly in the case of taxation, and by forcing individuals to forego transactions in the case of the triangle losses. We saw from Figure 2 that indirect losses accumulate when goods are traded and that these losses are (roughly) proportional to the value of domestic production. Indirect losses in freedom also occur when demand shifts cause prices to change in secondary markets. Unfortunately these are less easy to measure and result from an adjustment on the part of individuals to the new configuration of demands and supplies induced by government policies.

The second principle is that for purposes of measurement, all distortions can be conceptualized as relative price distortions.[9] If there are quantity restrictions, or there are prohibitive restrictions, then, in principle, knowledge of the relevant demand and supply schedules would allow measurment of the direct losses. Figure 1 remains appropriate with only a slight change in emphasis. Let Q' be the restricted quantity. The "tax revenue" becomes a reallocated rent and is now measured as an **indirect** loss of freedom. The rent accrues to whichever group has the property rights to the restricted supply, and the rest of the analysis is the same. With a prohibitive tax, knowledge of the equilibrium quantity and the highest price that could be charged would allow us to identify one measure of lost freedom—rectangle P^*Q in Figure 1, the product of the price and the equilibrium quantity. However, if we know the demand and supply schedules, then we can either calculate the area under the demand schdule, P^*PQ, measure of the loss in freedom as well. Although conceptually possible, calculations of this sort are commonly done with respect to the impact of non-tariff barriers and are notoriously laborious.

Directions

What then are the lessons for a set of calculations based on this methodology? In the first instance, the level of total taxation (relative to income) gives a rough measure of the direct loss in freedom through government reallocation of rents. This includes revenue taken from all levels of government.[10] These kinds of data are comparatively easy to obtain. What about the more difficult measures of impediments? In study after study (Spindler and Still (1991), Spindler and Miyake (this volume)) we see examples of the myriad ways in which governments restrict choice. There is no magic formula here. The "correct" way to do the job is to estimate the distortions in each and every market.[11]

But this is an enormous undertaking. One alternative is to consider only certain "sectors" of the economy. The rationale underlying an index is that the transaction is the unit of account. The distortion of transactions is what leads to the loss of economic freedom. Our problem is to identify a significant proportion of transactions to assure ourselves that we have a robust measure of the loss in economic freedom. But how have transactions based theories proceeded in the past? Recall the discussion underlying the early quantity theory (Friedman, 1968). Fisher wrote the quantity equation as

MV=PT where the measures of velocity and prices referred to **all** transactions. What transpired in part was that it was difficult to measure all transactions, and, gradually, **final** transactions, national income, was substituted as an available measure.[12] Although the theory looked the same mechanically, $MV_y=P_yy$, the subscripts remind us that it refers to a different level of economic activity.

Another alternative is to construct a computable general equilibrium model of the economy and identify the major distortions. Such a framework is popular in many trade and tax policy contexts but requires a decision about which sectors are most important. Finally we may wish to move to an instrumental level and try to identify a measure that we think may be associated with some of the less easily measured forms of taxation. Having chosen such a measure, we then try to find a "test" of the measure in some dimensions. This is the tack chosen in the remainder of this paper.

Indexes of Economic Freedom

In this section of the paper I illustrate a method by which two (highly imperfect) measures of economic freedom can be devised. The principle behind both measures is that the loss in economic freedom arises from two sources: the overt taxation by government, and by the regulations that the government imposes. One natural measure of the direct taxation by government is the level of government expenditures: the real withdrawal resources from the economy for reallocation.[13] No such simple tool exists for measuring the levels of regulation and the attendant loss of economic freedom. This is the major problem confronting the measurment of economic freedom in this framework.

Let us assume for the moment that we have such an appropriate indicator. If we have such a measure we could add it to the direct costs and be finished. Difficulties arise from two sources. First, if we are unable to identify the actual losses associated with the unmeasured impediments to exchange, and are forced to choose a proxy measure, how do we link this to the better identified government spending measure in a consistent fashion? Second, we want the indirect losses to be comparable to the direct losses., i.e., with total revenue (or expenditure) we have a measure of all government taxation which is gathered throughout the economy. We are not concerned that a little further study will add a new unidentified amount of explicit revenue and hence cause a dramatic change in the measured loss in freedom from this source. With the measure of indirect costs, however, the more we study any particular economy, the more we are likely to discover regulatory impediments to free exchange. As a result there will be a tendency to identify higher costs with more closely scrutinized environments. This is likely to engender a spuriously high measure of loss for economically developed countries.[14]

Weights and Measures

Let us consider a particular proxy for regulatory cost and develop a methodology for integrating the direct and indirect costs when the latter are measured by proxy. Suppose that regulations are developed and deployed by governments in proportion to the number of government employees. Thus a greater number of government employees per capita means a greater degree of regulatory activity. Assume further that the distortion in prices caused by regulatory activity is the same in each country. We have an overall loss index that looks like (1):

$$\text{(1)} \qquad \qquad \text{Loss} = F(G,E)$$

in which the Loss is equal to some function of government spending (in levels or more likely relative to national income) and the number of employees (either in levels or per capita). If we wish to generate an index of costs, then we can do so by providing a weighted average of government spending and employment. What weights should we use in the index?

Here I think the answer is clear. The weights must derive from the universe of transactions from which they were collected. For example, suppose that government revenue arises primarily from revenue collected by a tax on income. Suppose further that impediments to exchange are primarily located in final goods and services (as distinct from intermediate goods and services). In this case the value of trade in each market relative to the sum of the value of trades in both markets would be a reasonable weight. In the example of the Loss Index of equation 1, the weights might be specified as in equation 2,

(2) $Loss=G^{\Theta}E^{1-\Theta}$,   where $\Theta = [WL/(Y+WL)]$

where the Y is national income, WL, is labor income and Θ is the share of labor income (transactions) in the value of all transactions under consideration.

Index F1

The first index I have constructed is a simple one. It relates the loss in freedom to the share of government expenditures in national income and the proportion of the population that works for the government. In this case the weights are equal since the transactions cover the same ground—the entire economy. Both government revenues and impediments to exchange introduced by government employees are present at all levels of exchange in the economy. So that a doubling of the inputs amounts to a doubling of the loss in freedom, I have taken the square root of both percentages:

(3) $F1= (G/Y)^{0.5} (EMPL)^{0.5}$,

where (G/Y) is the proportion of all government spending relative to national income, and (EMPL) is the per capita employment of all government workers—national, "state" and local.[15]

Column 1 of Table 1 lists the countries in order of their loss in economic freedom—the index, F1, which is reported in column 2. The index itself runs between zero and unity with a higher score suggesting more impediments. To see how our sample is distributed, Figure 3 displays a plot of the distribution of the values of Index F1 with a few of the developed countries identified. The ranking of the countries calls attention to the limitations of the construction. It raises the question whether Senegal is really more free economically than Canada or whether Japan is more free than the U.S. What may be highlighted here is that the amount of bureaucratic obstruction per bureaucrat is different in the different countries. The presence of a number of African countries not known for their economic liberalism raises the same question although perhaps we might also need to ask if transactions are more free than our casual empiricism suggests. Perhaps there are a large number of transactions that take place outside the range of the government's interference. Among the developed countries, however, there is some correspondence with casual observation.

Figure 3. Impediments to Freedom: Index F1

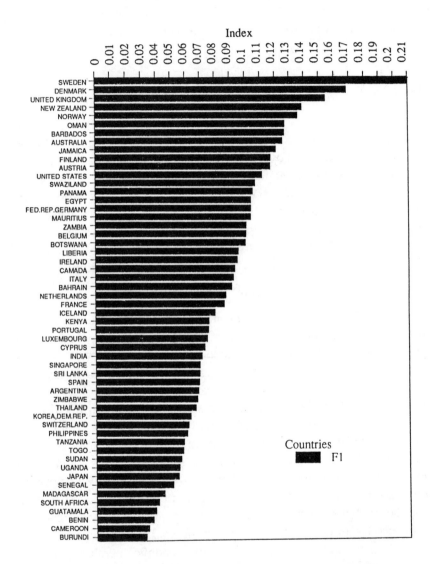

Country	F1	F2	F2(G)	F2(E)	F2/ PGDP	Country
					(1987 U.S. Dollars) Per Capita	
Sweden	0.21	287	280	7	0.40	Zambia
Denmark	0.17	271	264	7	0.39	Liberia
United Kingdom	0.15	2286	2183	103	0.39	Oman
New Zealand	0.14	4942	4134	808	0.36	Sweden
Norway	0.14	244	235	9	0.35	Swaziland
Oman	0.13	854	824	30	0.34	Botswana
Barbados	0.13	801	752	49	0.32	Jamaica
Australia	0.13	1224	1163	61	0.31	Panama
Jamaica	0.12	4466	3780	686	0.30	Denmark
Finland	0.12	314	310	4	0.29	Senegal
Austria	0.12	3537	3068	470	0.29	United Kingdom
United States	0.11	302	295	8	0.29	India
Swaziland	0.11	388	366	22	0.29	Egypt
Panama	0.11	214	206	7	0.27	Kenya
Egypt, Arab Rep.	0.10	2778	2424	353	0.26	New Zealand
Germany, Fed.Rep.	0.10	305	296	9	0.26	Zimbabwe
Mauritius	0.10	100	97	2	0.25	Tanzania
Zambia	0.10	3908	3347	561	0.25	Norway
Belgium	0.10	1290	1231	58	0.23	Portugal
Botswana	0.10	152	147	4	0.23	Togo
Liberia	0.10	115	112	3	0.23	Uganda
Ireland	0.09	1867	1713	154	0.22	Ireland
Canada	0.09	95	95	1	0.21	Burundi
Italy	0.09	155	150	5	0.21	Sudan
Bahrain	0.09	3005	2651	354	0.20	Germany
Netherlands	0.09	534	471	63	0.20	Mauritius
France	0.09	2590	2175	415	0.20	Finland
Iceland	0.08	2505	2106	399	0.20	Austria
Kenya	0.08	2348	1885	463	0.20	Australia
Portugal	0.08	123	120	3	0.19	Madagascar

Table 1. Economic Freedom Ratings
(Least free shows highest impediment score)

Table 1. Economic Freedom Ratings (Least free shows highest impediment score)						
Country	F1	F2	F2(G)	F2(E)	F2/ PGDP (1987 U.S. Dollars) Per Capita	Country
Luxemburg	0.07	1529	1189	340	0.19	Barbados
Cyprus	0.07	3366	2818	547	0.19	United States
India	0.07	354	338	15	0.19	Philippines
Singapore	0.07	915	897	19	0.18	South Africa
Sri Lanka	0.07	252	249	4	0.18	Cameroon
Spain	0.07	1937	1709	228	0.18	Italy
Argentina	0.07	2326	1971	355	0.18	Belgium
Zimbabwe	0.07	1371	1266	106	0.17	Cyprus
Thailand	0.07	353	328	25	0.17	Sri Lanka
Korea,Dem. Rep.	0.06	2700	2293	407	0.16	Canada
Switzerland	0.06	109	106	2	0.16	Benin
Philippines	0.06	417	386	31	0.16	Thailand
Tanzania	0.06	2049	1773	277	0.16	Netherlands
Togo	0.06	1733	1448	285	0.16	Bahrain
Sudan	0.06	2135	1815	320	0.15	France
Uganda	0.06	688	628	60	0.14	Korea
Japan	0.05	2115	1830	285	0.14	Luxemburg
Senegal	0.05	1223	1079	144	0.14	Spain
Madagascar	0.05	1675	1332	342	0.13	Iceland
South Africa	0.04	552	465	88	0.12	Argentina
Guatemala	0.04	1427	1151	276	0.11	Singapore
Benin	0.04	1526	1232	293	0.10	Switzerland
Cameroon	0.03	190	176	13	0.10	Guatemala
Burundi	0.03	1248	1051	197	0.09	Japan

Sources: Construction as explained in text.

A Second Index

The first Index is just that. It is an index without any real dimensionality of its own. Until we can identify some way to test it for consistency and stability, there is little to be said for it other than that it picks up some variables that we might reasonably think are associated with economic freedom. The second index is more in the spirit of the cardinal measures that I have advocated. The attractiveness of using government spending as a measure of the distortion is enhanced if we set ourselves to calculating the per capita loss in income associated with government interference. In this case we compute government expenditure per head, displayed in the column labelled F2(G) in Table 1, and add it to the value we attach to the loss in economic freedom associated with the number of government employees, the column headed F2(E). The crux of the matter is to provide a sensible basis on which to evaluate the cost in economic freedom imposed by each government employee.

An approach to this pricing problem is to find some tradeoff between the utility diminishing properties of government employees and other aspects of life. To this end I have estimated an immigration function for the United States. In principle, immigration depends upon any number of economic factors and constraints.[16] My framework is to regress the rate of immigration from each country to the U.S. on the proportion of income spent by the government and the per capita number of government employees and several other variables including per capita income and whether the country imposed emmigration restrictions. This is written as equation 4:

(4) $\quad IMM = \alpha_0 + \alpha_1(G/Y) + \alpha_2 EMPL + \alpha_3 \log(GNP) + \alpha_i X_i$

where IMM is the amount of immigration into the U.S. from each country (1981-87) relative to the population of that country, (G/Y) is the share of all government spending in national income, EMPL is the per capita number of government workers, and $\log(GNP)$ is the logarithm of per capita GDP.[17] Among the variables included, the vector, X_i, in equation (4), were several different measures of emmigration restrictions and political and civil liberty indexes familiar to those who have followed this literature. Once the regression results have been calculated, ask the following question: What is the trade-off between income and the number of government employ-ees?[18] This question can be answered by looking at the tradeoff between real income and the number of employees of government. A given level of immigration can be obtained by having either more government employees per capita or a lower level of domestic income. This means that we can attach a value to the number of employees of government—in this case the ratio between the estimated values of α_2/α_3.

A Regression Digression

The results of various regressions for the United States are presented in Table 2. The first regression shows that there is a negative relation between the rate of emigration to the U.S. and each government's spending although this is not of particular importance to our analysis.[19] At the same time, there is a positive relationship between the number of government employees per capita and emigration to the U.S. I have highlighted this result because the same pattern persists in all the regressions (both for the U.S. and Canada). The units of the dependent variable are per thousand of popula-tion. Thus an increase in government spending from 10% of national income to 20% of national income will lower the rate of immigration to the U.S. by 3 per thousand (from the immigrant's country.) Similarly, an increase in government employment per capita from 1 to 11—the extremes of the range, will be associated with an increase of roughly 13 per thou-sand.[20] As is to be expected, the R^2 is low and the standard error of the estimate is large relative to the mean of the dependent variable.

Table 2: Rates of Immigration to the U.S., 1981-87
Dependent Variable is IMM (35 Observations)

Regression 1:

VARIABLE	COEFFICIENT	T-STAT.,
C	6.03	1.31
(G/Y)	-0.27	-2.01
EMPL	1.27	2.38

R-squared 0.16, Mean of dependent var, 2.36
Adjusted R-squared 0.11,
S.E. of regression 7.9

Regression 2:

VARIABLE	COEFFICIENT	T-STAT.,
C	42.49	2.14
(G/Y)	-0.37	-1.68
EMPL	1.75	2.76
LPGDP	-4.28	-1.92
EM1	-7.21	-2.34

R-squared 0.29, Mean of dependent var, 2.36
Adjusted R-squared 0.20
S.E. of regression 7.54,

Regression 3:

Number of observations: 53,

VARIABLE	COEFFICIENT	T-STAT.
C	21.45	1.57
(G'/Y)	-0.15	-0.98
EMPL	1.10	2.20
LPGDP	-2.14	-1.41
POLIT	-2.12	-0.72
EM1	-4.06	-1.84

R-squared 0.20, Mean of dependent var, 1.57
Adjusted R-squared 0.11
S.E. of regression 6.51

Sources: IMM, Table 7 (Department of Commerce); G, and raw data for EM1 (Spindler and Miyake, HF4 and HF6); EMPL (Heller and Tait, Table 21); G',(Wright, various countries); POLIT, (Gastil and Wright); PGDP, and population (AID, Table I).

The second regression in the table, a more complete specification, indicates that although the t-values are marginal by traditional statistical standards, nonetheless the effect of per capita income and EM1, a dummy variable that identifies whether the country has any form of emigration restriction, are consistent with our expectations.[21] Higher income abroad reduces emigration to the U.S. A country with 10 percent higher income will reduce immigration to the U.S. by roughly 4 per thousand. Emigration restrictions imposed by foreign countries reduce it as well.

The third regression in the table shows the consequences of including Gastil and Wright's (1988) measure of political freedom. A similar pattern of results obtained when their measure of civil liberties was used as well—a result not reported. Unlike Friedman's (1988) finding that civil liberties predicted growth rates better than political freedom, I found both to be insignificant in predicting emigration to the U.S.[22] The third regression is also illustrative of several efforts to extend the analysis. The expenditure measure is different. In order to expand the sample it is limited to central government expenditures. A number of other experiments were tried with different measures of political freedom and dummy variables for regions and the like. Except for reducing the significance levels of all the variables, the signs and magnitudes remained as reported in Table 2.

A similar approach was taken to the Canadian immigration rate. These results are listed in the Appendix as Table A. Only four years (1984-87) of data are used and there is some indication that the influence of Canadian immigration restrictions changed during the period. Although the signs are consistently the same as those obtained for the U.S., the significance levels are lower. There are also fewer immigrants in comparison to the U.S.

There is a final observation to support the notion that something useful is being identified by the regression. I regressed the difference (suitably normalized to reflect the different sample size) of the rate of immigration from each country to Canada less the rate of immigration to the U.S., **DIF**, on the measure of each country's government expenditure and government employment. This is reported in Table 3. Since both countries are politically stable and share many attitudes and values, I was curious as to the effect of our two measures. As is apparent from the positive sign on (G/Y), those who come from countries which have relatively more government spending come to Canada, and from the negative sign of EMP, those who come from countries that have more government employees per head come to the U.S. This would be consistent with the casual observation that emigrants are selecting on the basis of whether they prefer relatively fewer impediments to the market or more government expenditure. During this period, Canadian policy has not been designed to admit the most economically able.

Constructing the Index

With the estimates of the coefficients on EMPL and log(PGDP) from which we form the ratio, α_2/α_3, we can develop our additive index. The weight on EMPL is roughly 0.4 x Y.23 This sub-index, which gives the value of EMPL in promoting emigration to the U.S., is reported in Table 2(E). The sum of the two sub-indexes, F2(G) and F2(E) is reported as F2. In addition, the final numerical column of Table 1 is a normalized score—the index F2 relative to per capita GDP. It is this magnitude that is reflected in the ranking of the final column. Figure 4 displays the plot of these per capita scores. It is interesting that among the developed nations the rank remains relatively similar to that devised in the first index. Unlike the first index, however, index F2 reflects the dollar value of the impediments.

Table 3. The Difference Between Per Capita Immigration to Canada and Per Capita Immigration to the United States
Dependent variable is DIF
(34 observations)

VARIABLE	COEFFICIENT	T-STAT.,
C	-5.38	-1.34
EMPL	-1.07	-2.32
(G/Y)	0.24	2.04

R-squared 0.17,   Mean of dependent var, -1.93
Adjusted R-squared 0.11,
S.E. of regression 6.91

Sources: See Table 2 and Table A.

Figure 4. Impediments to Freedom: Index F2

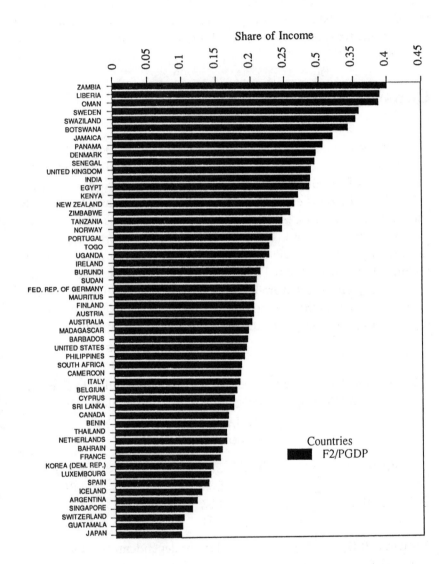

Some Reflections

Although the indexes above are imperfect instruments, it seems to me that this technique for constructing a cardinal measure of freedom's loss has potential. A more useful approach would be to identify all the emmigrants from a country and evaluate their destinations in a simultaneous matrix. With some recognition of the barriers to emmigration and immigration, the evaluation placed by movers on the non-monetary economic characteristics of freedom may be identifiable. This is not the only way to measure the implicit characteristics of economic freedom, but it is one way.

A second extension is to identify bureaucrats engaged in the act of regulation and try to measure the losses they cause within one or another country in specific well defined situations. This could serve to sharpen the cost estimates directly.

A third problem is to tackle the losses in freedom imposed by particular regimes that effectively stymie certain kinds of economic transactions. Communist regimes need to be assessed differently than Western regimes—at least at this point. Likewise dictatorships may also need a different set of variables.

Finally, the estimates in Table 1 may be too generous. We undervalue the costs of freedom of government. Both revenue and expenditure distort. If resources are the vector, R, to which factor rewards, w, pertain, and outputs are denoted by the vector, Y, to which prices, p, are relevant, then it is not double counting to measure the losses in freedom as the sum of both sides of the equation: $(w'-w)R(w')=(p'-p)Y(p')$ where the " $'$ " indicates a distortion from the free market price.

Appendix
Table A. Rates of Immigration into Canada, 1984-87
Dependent Variable is IMM
(35 observations)

1. VARIABLE	COEFFICIENT	T-STAT.
C	0.34	0.85
(G/Y)	-0.02	-1.52
EMPL	0.10	2.29

R-squared 0.14,   Mean of dependent var 0.24
Adjusted R-squared 0.089
S.E. of regression 0.68

2. VARIABLE	COEFFICIENT	T-STAT.
C	1.30	1.05
(G/Y)	-0.01	-0.79
EMPL	0.12	2.25
LPGDP	-0.12	-0.73
EM1	-0.45	-1.50

R-squared 0.22,   Mean of dependent var 0.24
Adjusted R-squared 0.11,
S.E. of regression 0.68

3. VARIABLE	COEFFICIENT	T-STAT.
C	3.21	1.84
(G/Y)	-0.02	-1.29
EMPL	0.10	1.94
LPGDP	-0.26	-1.41
EM1	-0.50	-1.70
POLIT	-0.58	-1.52

R-squared 0.27,   Mean of dependent var 0.23
Adjusted R-squared 0.15
S.E. of regression 0.67, Sum of squared resid, 12.85

Sources: IMM, Table 2.39 (Statistics Canada); G, and raw data for EM1 (Spindler and Miyake, HF4 and HF6); EMPL (Heller and Tait, Table 21); G',(Wright, various countries); POLIT, (Gastil and Wright); PGDP, and population (AID, Table I).

Notes

[1] Finding a definition with which we may all agree is not an easy matter in any discipline. Bertrand Russell (1956) points out that "The question 'What is a number?' is one which has been often asked, but has only been correctly answered in our own time." In Easton (previous chapter, this volume) I identify what I take to be some of the limitations of this definition of economic freedom.

[2] We are characterizing one dimension of choice, economic freedom. We may choose to impose a tax or other distortion, but this tradeoff among economic freedom and other "goods" is a separate issue.

[3] Clearly someone with a philosophy that there is something intrinsically good about a government allocating resources rather than the individual allocating resources will be dissatisfied by my characterization of economic freedom.

[4] Here is where a (constructive) definition of freedom as an argument of the utility function becomes most attractive. There would be no paradox in saying that the commonly calculated "optimal" tariff raises income and yet reduces utility. In the traditional calculation only income matters for reaching the "optimum." Once "F" is in the utility function directly, it is part of full income and consequently a full partner in the optimization calculus.

[5] In a different context Harberger (1964) has referred to "the economics of the nth best." As a practical matter, rather than search for some kind of global optimum, we are constrained to consider the effects of relatively small changes in various impediments.

[6] There are a number of theoretical reasons why this definition of changes in economic welfare is less than fully satisfactory (Silverberg, 1978) although for our purposes, the approach is adequate.

[7] These are explored in Easton (previous chapter, this volume).

[8] This is true if the supply schedule is horizontal. If it has a non-zero slope then in the second market there is going to be an indirect rent reallocation in addition to the direct effect captured in the higher tax.

[9] Although tariffs and quotas have equivalence as far as rent transfer is concerned (although different people may receive the rent), their properties differ in other contexts, e.g. stability of equilibrium is affected by the choice of one or the other. Other measures such as content requirements,

"health" restrictions and the like are difficult to assess, but ultimately can be converted into price increases.

[10] As a matter of practice, government expenditures are probably a better measure than revenue since they include implicit taxes are well as currently identified taxes. One might also choose to double the tax burden as whatever is received distorts one margin, and then does so again as it is spent. We are ignoring the "triangle" losses by simply using spending, too.

[11] I have not chosen to develop various "ordinal" measures of economic freedom. In addition to having difficulty deciding what numerical values to place on particular characteristics, I have been unable to decide on a metric with which to aggregate the various categories. This is not the same thing as saying that the ordinal measures devised are not useful. Those by Spindler and Still (1988), and Spindler and Miayake (1990), for example, are both interesting and useful as they call attention to many features in various economies that are distorted.

[12] In addition, of course, the theory itself evolved.

[13] This ignores the issues raised in Easton (previous chapter, this volume) about the indirect losses in economic freedom associated with traded goods.

[14] I have had to ignore (what were!) the Communist countries because information on "budgets" is so very different from that reported in the West.

[15] A more sophisticated measure would identify direct revenue per employee and develop a sense of the number of "obstructive" bureaucrats.

[16] Determinants of immigration are notoriously cranky with simple measures like per capita GDP in one country relative to another generating "wrong signs" in the regression and the like. The results of the regressions should be judged in this context.

[17] The ratio (G/Y) is included to control for the revenue function of some government employees. This given the amount of revenue raised, the measure EMPL is linked to immigration.

[18] More formally, immigration will take place only if there is some utility gain to emmigration (to the U.S.). If the change in immigration is zero, then the gain in utility is zero as well. Thus set $dI=0$ so that if utility (associated with the act of immigration) is held constant, $(\delta U/\delta E)/(\delta U/\delta Y) \,|\, U = (\alpha_2/\alpha_3)$ which is the relative price of government employees., i.e., it is the tradeoff in terms of real income of those who are emmigrating (to the U.S. or Canada.)

[19] The rate of immigration (per thousand) to the U.S. from each country is the seven year total from 1981-87 divided by the 1986 population.

[20] Of course these are estimated as a cross-section and as a result speak to extant levels of spending and employment, not to changes in a particular country. A more careful look at the time series would be appropriate.

[21] This latter measure is derived from Spindler and Miyake (1990) where those with any restriction, their values 2-5 received a score of 1, and unimpeded emmigration received a 0.

[22] It may be that they are more effective in predicting the total immigration from their respective countries, but this hypothesis I did not test.

[23] That is, $dI=\alpha_2 dEMPL+\alpha_3(dY/Y)$ and for $dI=0$,
$(\alpha_2/\alpha_3).Y. dEMPL=dY$

References

Agency for International Development. *Development and the National Interest:* U.S. Economic Assistance into the 21st Century. A Report by the Administrator of AID (1989). (no printing details)

Friedman, Milton. "The Quantity Theory" *International Encyclopedia of the Social Sciences* Volume X. Macmillan and Free Press (1968).

Friedman, Milton, "A Statistical Note on the Gastil-Wright Survey of Freedom" in Walker, Michael A., ed. *Freedom, Democracy and Economic Welfare: Proceedings of an International Symposium.* The Fraser Institute (1988).

Gastil, Raymond D. and Lindsay M. Wright, "The State of the World Political and Economic Freedom" in Walker, Michael A., ed. *Freedom, Democracy and Economic Welfare: Proceedings of an International Symposium.* The Fraser Institute (1988).

Harberger, Arnold C. "The Measurement of Waste" *American Economic Review* (May 1964): 58-76.

Heller, Peter S. and Alan A. Tait. *Government Employment and Pay: Some International Comparisons* International Monetary Fund Occasional Paper 24 (1983).

Russell, Bertrand. "Definition of Number" in James R. Newman, ed., *The World of Mathematics* Vol I. Simon and Schuster (1956) pp. 537-43.

Silverberg, Gene. *The Structure of Economics.* McGraw-Hill, (1978).

Spindler, Z. A. and L. Still. "Economic Freedom Rating: An Interim Report," in Walter Block, ed. *Economic Freedom: Toward a Theory of Measurement* Vancouver: The Fraser Institute, 1991.

Statistics Canada, *Canada Yearbook 1990* (1989).

United States Department of Commerce, Bureau of the Census, *Statistical Abstract of the United States 1990*, (1989).

Wright, John M, ed. *The Universal Almanac 1990.* Andrews and McMeel: Kansas City (1989).

Discussion

Milton Friedman wanted clarification of Table 1. Easton explained that column 1, Index F1, was separate from the total dollar index of Index F2, column 2, which was in turn composed of the two subindexes (in the next two columns). The per capita measures which were suggested (as an alternative to the gross dollar measures) at the previous conference were the final column of figures and provided the ordering for the countries along the right-hand side. Friedman felt that we should look at the components and see which performed better relative to peoples' judgment rather than rely exclusively on the aggregate index. Easton agreed that some measure of the usefulness of the measure is necessary, but none was developed in this paper.

Zane Spindler made two points about the assumption that government employees perform in the same obstructive ways. He suggested that the reason that India does not rank the way one would think is because an Indian government employee imposes a restriction in a very different way than a government employee in the U.S. Often the Indian government employee will sell the restriction. Second, with respect to immigration, a country may restrict immigration or emigration as a way of capturing the market for its regulation. Thus regulation would be correlated with immigration or emigration.

Juan Bendfeldt wondered whether there was a problem with the regression to the extent that there may be a correlation between government expenditures and government employees per capita. What does the government do with tax revenue? They hire employees. Easton responded that he had run the estimation as a two-stage least squares and although the significance level dropped, there was little change in the coefficients from such a correction. Zane Spindler pointed out that from his tables, although there is such a correlation, it is far from perfect suggesting that some governments are more effective in there use of employees.

Juan Bendfeldt felt that the use of emigration was a useful way of capturing the loss of freedom but that illegal immigration makes these data most unreliable. For example, outside of Guatemala city with 2 million people, the next four cities of Central America with the greatest population are in the United States! They send money back, and so we can see roughly how many people there are abroad. Further, government employment is difficult to measure. There are non-government institutions that function only for the government, and contracting-out is another way to evade responsibility in the official budget but still obtain additional services. Easton did not have any specific information on either of these issues other than the data sources referred to in the paper. Easton remarked that there were no migration data comparable to the International Monetary Fund's, Direction of Trade.

Alan Stockman wondered how U.S. immigration quotas from different countries, would affect the measures Easton used. Second, since government spending is already in the regression equation, is it necessary to aggregate the measures in F2? Finally, thinking of the measures of F2(G) and F2(E) as related to the "bundling issue" in the Jones/Stockman paper (this volume), is this classification an "E" component or a "G" component: a theoretical categorization or one of convenience, and might they not serve to offset or ameliorate one another? Easton argued that his measures were for conceptual reasons as government expenditures crudely capture tax revenue reallocation issues, while the number of government employees were meant to correlate with the degree of regulatory interference with the economy. Perhaps they offset one another to some extent, he maintained, but then the regression is simply picking-up a net effect. As far as the effect of specific U.S. quotas, even though the U.S. had a different system than Canada during this period (Canada used a point count over certain specific characteristics), the similarity of the results for the two countries suggested that it was a useful indicator and gave some confidence in the results.

James Ahiakpor wondered if using both the wage bill and national income in the weights of equation 2 reflected double counting. Easton argued that you need to double count since each is a separate source of distortion. What the double counting in the weights does (in equation 2) is to allow the aggregation of both sources of the distortions. The weights themselves sum to unity. This is not really double counting, but it is a way of assuring that many layers of distortion can be analyzed in a consistent fashion.

Milton Friedman commented that the regressions (1 and 2) show that the higher the percent of income spent by government, the lower the level of emigration. This may reflect the inadequacy of measured income. It is disturbing from the point of view of relying on the ratio of government spending to income. Juan Bendfeldt pointed out that the measure of government's take may be nonlinear. A 13% take from a developing country may be more important than a taking of 40% in a developed country. He found in Guatemala that every time revenue went above 7.7%, the government ran into trouble with decreased national growth. Perhaps there is a "neutral" point of smallest damage, he suggested. Alan Stockman pointed out that the (negative) correlation between the government share of income and emigration means that government spending provides benefits as well as tax losses. The loss of economic freedom should be "added" to welfare. For the measure of economic freedom, however, they should not be netted out. Easton agreed saying the sign of the relationship does not matter since (we agree) that government spending reduces economic freedom which is what it is being calculated. What the regression serves to do is to price government employees. Where this would lead to trouble is if government employees were seen as handing out goodies and thus were valued not for their role as obstructing but for their role in providing benefits. Recall Table 3 takes the relative amounts of immigration between Canada and the U.S. Milton Friedman agreed that high government spending brings benefits as well as costs, but argued that it may also reflect the inability of governments to spend in low income countries in the same way they can in high income countries.

James Ahiakpor was unclear why the optimum tariff didn't lead to a proper measure of welfare. Easton responded that it would if we had the appropriate valuation of economic freedom—that is the tariff maximized a full, freedom inclusive measure of welfare, but then it would balance out the gain in income with that of the loss of economic freedom imposed by the tax.

Alan Stockman wondered if we can get black market data on the right way to emigrate. In Hong Kong they sell a magazine called "Emigrate." Juan Bendfeldt answered that there are such data. In Guatamala there are tours advertized in which they guarantee that they will get you into the Unites States. With the new immigration laws, the cost went up to $7,000. Immigrants expect to repay it within two years. Many Chinese have paid $15,000 to get a Guatemalan passport. The data are available strictly from the newspaper. Alan Stockman suggested that The Liberty Fund could fund a project to gather these kinds of data.

Rating Economic Freedom: Capital Market Controls and Money

**Jack Carr,
University of Toronto**

Introduction

W HEN I WAS ASKED BY the Fraser Institute to examine the degree of economic freedom in domestic capital markets I thought this was a very interesting and feasible research project. I quickly agreed to undertake this research. I made my decision without having attended or read the output from the first two conferences on economic freedom. I have since corrected that deficiency and have given considerable thought to the question. I am now much more humble about the nature of progress that can be made on this research topic.

Before proceeding to analyze economic freedom in domestic financial markets there are a number of important issues to discuss. These issues have been addressed in the first two conferences, but there was no clear consensus on a number of these issues. A resolution of these issues is absolutely vital before any empirical examination can take place. I will try to avoid repetition of the earlier discussion but I feel it is imperative to clarify these issues and state my position on these matters.

Is Economic Freedom a Means or an End?

In the second conference Milton Friedman (my most respected teacher) stated that for him economic freedom (as well as political freedom) is an end by itself. There is a problem in making economic freedom one of the arguments in an objective function. By doing so one arbitrarily decides the issue of whether economic freedom is a good thing. For a number of us, this is an inherently obvious point. However there will be those who do not hold this view. They may have other objective functions. They may believe that income equality or income security should be ends and hence should be arguments in an objective function. Different individuals may posit different objective functions. This being the case it is near impossible to conduct a rational debate among individuals with different points of view. Each individual will posit their own objective function and there will be no way to choose among competing functions. Hence there would be no objective way to decide on various public policies.

This issue is very much like the issue of the role of tastes and preferences in explaining economic behaviour. A number of economic facts can be explained by adoption of a particular utility function. In addition, changes in the data can almost always be explained by resorting to changes in the utility function (i.e. changes in tastes and preferences). My methodological bias is to try to explain as much as possible without resorting to specific utility functions. Similarly, I propose to start with a very general objective function. In this objective function economic freedom will not appear (it will be a means not an end).

Consider a general individual utility function (for which one can get almost universal support)

(1) $$U_i = f(X)$$

where U_i is the utility of the ith individual and X is a vector of goods and services (including leisure).

All economists, whether free marketers or not should have no objections to the utility function in (1). In this utility function, economic freedom does not appear as an argument. An increase in economic freedom (holding X constant) does not lead to an increase in utility.

Although economic freedom does not appear as an argument in (1); nevertheless, traditional economic theory would yield an important utility enhancing role to economic freedom.

Figure 1. Economic Freedom and Utility

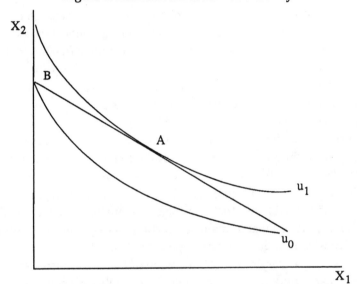

Consider the case where an individual consumes 2 goods, X_1 and X_2, has a fixed income, and faces fixed prices. In a world with complete economic freedom, equilibrium A in Figure 1 will represent the point of maximum utility for this particular individual. Now suppose the state imposes a restriction on the operation of free markets; the state forbids the production or sale of X_1. The constrained equilibrium in this case is B. Clearly at B the individual is at a lower level of utility than A. Restrictions on the freedom to freely choose those commodities which maximize utility will result in a lowering of utility. In this example, less economic freedom always leads to a loss of utility. Economic freedom is a means of allowing individuals to reach maximum satisfaction. It should be noted that similar examples could be constructed on the production side of the economy.

This proposition concerning free markets is an example of what is perhaps the most famous and (perhaps most important) proposition in all of economics and that is the proposition of gains from trade. Free exchange maximizes the gains from trade. Any restriction on free exchange will eliminate profitable opportunities of gains from trade and hence will reduce the overall level of welfare.

The methodology adopted in this paper will be to assume a generalized utility function where economic freedom is not an end. We will then examine economic theory to see how economic freedom affects the operation of the economy. A complete research strategy should test these propositions concerning economic freedom. (These tests are not carried out in this paper.)

Definition of Economic Freedom

If there was one question that was not resolved in either of the first two conferences it was the definition of economic freedom. Everyone agreed that economic freedom was multi-dimensional and a nebulous concept at best. As a student of Milton Friedman I will adopt his methodology that "you cannot define a measure without knowing what the purpose of the measure is" (p. 15, draft of second conference). For one purpose you may adopt one definition and for another purpose you may adopt another definition.

One should note that the problem of finding an empirical counterpart to a theoretical concept is almost universal in economics. Consider an example from monetary economics. The concept of money is crucial in monetary economics. However there has been considerable debate over the exact definition of money. There is a large continuum of financial assets. Where you draw the line and call one set money and the other non-money financial assets is a very difficult problem. Economic theory offers little guidance. What one has to ask is for what purpose one is defining money. For this, economic theory is a necessity. If one has an economic theory that says that the money supply is a prime determinant of the price level, then one can adopt a definition of the money supply which best predicts the price level.[1]

It is this approach that I propose to adopt with respect to the definition of economic freedom. In the previous section we have argued that economic freedom leads to increased levels of utility. One can define economic freedom as that index which best predicts levels of utility. However such a definition is inoperable because utility is not measurable. In addition we desire a definition of economic freedom which is applicable to a country as a whole and not to each individual. With a lot of hand-waving we can use some definition of income as a proxy for utility. To arrive at an aggregate measure, we would add up individual income and obtain national income.

Now we would define economic freedom as that index which best predicts levels of national income.[2] In this sense, the index of economic freedom would be like the index of leading economic indicators. Both are multidimensional and both are meant to predict national income. It is important to note that national income by itself cannot be used as a measure of economic freedom. Economic freedom is only one of a number of factors determining national income. One needs a complete theory of income and economic growth in order to define economic freedom. It should be noted that economists have no good answer to the fundamental question of why some countries are rich and some are poor and why some countries grow at a fast pace and others grow slowly. For simplicity assume a neoclassical production function

(2) $$Y = f(K,L,A,EF)$$

where Y is national income, K is capital, L is labour, A is land including national resources, and EF is an index of economic freedom.

Clearly there can be two countries with the same amount of economic freedom but different levels of national income because there are different levels of the other factors of production. Similarly there can be two countries with the same factors of production but different levels of income. One country may have free markets and the other country may have restrictions which prevent factors moving to where they can contribute most to national income.

In summary, I propose to define economic freedom as that index which adds the greatest explaining power (i.e. has the largest partial correlation coefficient or equivalently the largest "t" value) to the national income equation, given all the other factors determining national income.

One data set would be used to define economic freedom. Clearly one would need other data set to test the propositions that economic freedom is an important determinant of national income.

There are important policy reasons why the proposition of the influence of economic freedom on national well-being should be tested. If restrictions on economic freedom can be shown to lower income levels, a strong case can be made to eliminate these restrictions. Hence one wants to define economic freedom in order to better understand its role in influencing national well-being. Once it can be demonstrated that economic freedom is welfare enhancing, there is a stronger possibility of convincing governments to allow greater degrees of economic freedom.

Difficulty in Applying Any Definition of Economic Freedom

From a theoretical point of view the methodology outlined in the previous section seems simple enough. However, this methodology is very difficult to implement in the real world. The example illustrated in Figure 1 is a clear example of a government restriction that reduces economic well-being. Unfortunately there are a large number of government actions which are not as clear-cut. The government undertakes a large number of actions. The question is which of these actions are restrictions on economic freedom and as a consequence welfare reducing. In an initial examination of government actions it is not obvious which actions should be placed in the freedom reduction category. (In fact, I will argue that in the absence of a well defined economic theory, it is impossible to classify government actions.) Consider the following examples from financial markets.

(a) A number of researchers (see White (1984)) have claimed that the period 1795-1845 in Scottish banking could be characterized as a free banking period. This period would be characterized as one with no restrictions on banking. This view has been challenged by Carr and Mathewson (1988).[3] We argued that three Scottish banks enjoyed the privileges of limited liability granted by the Scottish Parliament. All other banks had to accept unlimited liability. Entry was free but not on the same terms as the three limited liability banks. Is this restriction of unlimited liability a relevant restriction on economic freedom? One cannot answer this question in the absence of some economic theory explaining the importance of the liability rule. The accepted wisdom of the time was that the unlimited liability restriction for new entrants was in the public interest. It protected depositors and protected the integrity of the banking system. Mathewson and I argued that this restriction was in the private interest of the three limited liability banks. Competition was allowed but the playing field was not level. I would argue that this restriction reduced economic freedom and lowered national income. The restriction did raise the income of the owners of the three limited liability banks (assuming that the entire income was not dissipated in rent seeking activities). One cannot characterize government actions unless one understands the effects of these actions and the rationale for these actions. As the above example illustrates, this is not an easy matter to do.

(b) In 1934 in the United States and in 1967 in Canada, deposit insurance was enacted. Did this action reduce economic freedom? Friedman and Schwartz (1963) argued that deposit insurance was necessary to eliminate the contagion effect inherent in bank runs. Carr and Mathewson (1989) present a private interest explanation of deposit insurance. We argue that this scheme subsidized small banks (typically new entrants) at the expense of large incumbent banks. If Friedman and Schwartz are correct deposit insurance would increase national income. According to this interpretation deposit insurance would be desired by all banks as it would improve depositor confidence in the banking system. This view would argue for government rules mandating deposit insurance. These rules could not be interpreted as reducing freedom as they would be desired by all economic agents. On the other hand I would argue that such schemes would reduce national income. Large banks would oppose such rules and small banks would desire them. Clearly a resolution of this issue is needed for a correct definition of economic freedom. Clearly such a resolution is not a simple matter.

(c) Most countries impose restrictions on both the asset and liability side of a number of financial intermediaries. In Canada, the asset portfolio of insurance companies is restricted. Are these restrictions reductions in freedom? Or are these restrictions the result of the most efficient way for insurance companies to post bonds. The liabilities of insurance companies are very long-term. Insurance companies can sell insurance policies to policyholders promising them a particular investment policy. After funds are collected insurance companies could change the investment policy to the detriment of policyholders. Both parties know about the possibility of such opportunistic behaviour. The problem for the insurance company is to find the most efficient way to post bonds which guarantee no change in the riskiness of its portfolio after an insurance policy is purchased. Regulation may be the optimal form of bonding. If such is the case all economic agents desire such regulation and it cannot be viewed as freedom reducing. In addition such restrictions, according to this theory, would not reduce national income.

These are but three of many examples of the difficulty of defining which governmental actions reduce economic freedom. In addition to these difficulties, there are the difficulties of knowing which restrictions on economic freedom are binding? Which restrictions do economic agents easily get around? Faced with these difficulties researchers may throw up their hands and argue that it is impossible to define economic freedom. However I have taken to heart one of the prime messages of the first conference that 'anything worth doing is worth doing imperfectly.' It is hoped through conferences like these one can slowly converge on the optimal definition of economic freedom.

The above discussion indicates that a *detailed* knowledge of *each* country examined is needed to even begin to define economic freedom. At the outset I must admit that I do not possess this knowledge. I know most about financial markets in Canada. Next I know about the U.S. situation. However the farther geographically I get from Canada the less detailed knowledge I possess. Hopefully the conference will correct some of these defects. For future research, given the knowledge required for this research, I would suggest collaborative efforts by scholars chosen from the various countries to be examined.

Rating Economic Freedom in the Money and Capital Market Sectors

Financial Deregulation in the Seventies and Eighties

The purpose of this paper is to rate the level of economic freedom that currently exists in the financial sectors of a number of countries. The countries I propose to examine are Canada, the United States, the United Kingdom, Japan, West Germany and France. If this exercise were done twenty years ago for these same six countries I am convinced that the level of economic freedom in this sector of the economy for all six countries would be substantially less than it is today. In the '70s and '80s financial deregulation has played a significant role in raising the level of economic freedom. Before I embark on the empirical task of rating economic freedom I would like to address the question of why there has been an almost universal movement to freer financial markets.

One hypothesis would be that governments value economic freedom higher today than they did twenty years ago. Unfortunately I do not think there is any evidence to support this hypothesis. The hypothesis I propose to explain worldwide financial deregulation is consistent with the private interest theory of regulation I described in the previous section. I believe financial regulation was adopted, to a large extent, to protect local monopolies. This regulation was in the private interest of the owners of the local monopolies (or the cartels). This regulation was not in the general public interest. In the '70s and '80s financial innovation led to the development of close substitutes for these monopoly services.[4] With the elimination of the monopoly, it was no longer in the interest of the former monopolists to maintain the economic restrictions. As a consequence, these economic restrictions were abandoned. Consider the following three examples.

(a) Since 1933 commercial banks in the United States had been prohibited from paying interest on demand deposits. In addition the Fed through Regulation Q limited the interest rate that commercial banks could pay on time deposits. One interpretation of these interest rate restrictions is that they were put in place to eliminate commercial bank competition for deposit funds. These interest rate restrictions in essence enforced a commercial bank cartel. In the late '60s and '70s inflation in the United States became both high and volatile. This led to high and volatile interest rates which increased the cost to depositors of keeping funds in commercial banks. High and volatile interest rates led to financial innovation. (As the returns to innovation increase, one would expect an increase in innovation). Brokers developed money market mutual funds which were essentially a way to pay interest on demand deposit. With the development of this substitute for a bank deposit, it was no longer in the interest of banks to have the government maintain interest rate restrictions. In 1980 the Depository Institutions Deregulation and Monetary Control Act (DIDMCA) was passed and in 1982 the Garn-St. Germain Act was passed which had the effect (among other things) of removing interest rate controls on money.[5] It should be noted that this example is consistent with the private interest theory of regulation. It is difficult to argue that these interest rate restrictions were in the public interest from 1930 to 1980 (presumably to prevent destructive competition in the banking system leading to a complete collapse of the system) and they were no longer in the public interest in the 1980s (when bank failures continued at a significant rate).

(b) Regulations in the province of Ontario essentially prevented foreign securities firms from entering the Canadian market. Although some people argued that it was in the public interest to have the securities industry controlled by Canadians clearly such protection was in the private interest of Canadian securities firms. In July 1987 the Canadian securities market experienced what became known as the Little Bang.[6] One of the provisions of this deregulation was to allow foreign securities firms into the Canadian market. What is the explanation for this deregulation? I don't believe that this deregulation was due to the Canadian authorities finally seeing the light. This deregulation was forced on the Canadian authorities. Canadian firms in the 1980s were finding that they had alternatives to raising funds other than the use of the Canadian capital market. With deregulation in other countries, Canadian firms could more easily raise funds on world capital markets and bypass the local securities firms. The Canadian firms needed international linkages in order to compete. As such Canadian firms now found it in their interest to have the government allow foreign firms into the Canadian capital market.[7] Again this example supports the private interest theory of regulation.

(c) On October 27, 1986 substantial deregulation occurred for financial institutions operating in the City of London (this deregulation was known as the Big Bang). On this date the practice of fixed minimum commissions for trading securities on the London stock exchange was eliminated. This change was forced on the LSE by the British government. Why did the British government bring about such a change. Again I would argue that fixed minimum commissions prevented broker competition and hence was in the private interest of stock brokers. However since the mid-1970s broker commissions were being deregulated on world stock exchanges. Investors could trade stock on a number of world exchanges. Deregulation in New York and other markets forced deregulation in London.[8] Again this example supports the private interest theory of regulation.[9]

Empirical Rating of Economic Freedom in Money and Capital Markets

As instructed I will assign for each category in each country an integer on a scale of zero to ten. Ten will represent the highest freedom rating and zero will represent the lowest. It will be obvious that such rating schemes are highly judgemental. However their main purpose will be in comparing one country relative to another. Table 2 presents the ratings of each category for each country.

(a) Regulation of the Central Bank

(i) Is the power of the central bank to print money restricted?

The question of the existence of a central bank should be dealt with before examining the powers of the central bank. A standard proposition in monetary theory has been the necessity of government (either acting on its own or through a central bank) to control the money supply. Almost all monetary authorities today monopolize the issue of banknotes. The economic rationalization for this monopoly has been that the issue of banknotes is a natural monopoly. Banknote issue is considered a public good. Recently this view has been attacked primarily by proponents of free banking.[10] Free banking advocates recommend abolishing central banks and allowing for competition among private producers in the issuing of currency.

I could spend considerable time discussing this issue but unfortunately for the empirical purposes at hand the issue is moot. All the countries I examine in this study have active central banks and there is little likelihood that this situation will change. If the main purpose of an index of economic freedom is comparative (either comparing different countries at one point in time or one country at different points in time) then for present purposes one does not have to resolve the debate over competitive note issue. Again this is another example of an issue which is still hotly debated in economics. It is not an easy matter to decide whether restrictions on private note issue are in fact restrictions on economic freedom which led to a reduction in national income.

The following are the salient points on central banks in the six countries examined.[11]

Canada

The Bank of Canada is wholly owned by the government of Canada. In fact the Minister of Finance holds all Bank of Canada shares. Technically the Bank is responsible to its sole shareholder, the Minister of Finance. The Bank of Canada has a statutory duty to maintain the domestic value of the currency, to control the external value of the currency and to maintain full employment. The government has the power to issue directives to the Bank. In practice, the Bank cannot follow a monetary policy different from that desired by the government and no directives have ever been issued. The Governor of the Bank of Canada is appointed for a 7 year term and the Bank is accountable to Parliament.

United States

The Federal Reserve System is a federal government agency consisting of 12 banks whose stock is owned by commercial bank members. The Federal Reserve has a statutory duty to supervise the banking system. The Federal Reserve is responsible to Congress; it must report twice a year on its policies. This report is to Congress and not to the President or Executive. The Federal Reserve is formally independent of government; however, as a practical matter the Fed is in continuous discussions with the Executive branch. The Chairman of the Federal Reserve System is designated by the President for a four year term (which is renewable).

United Kingdom

Since 1946 the Bank of England has been 100% owned by the government. The Bank has a statutory duty to supervise the banking system. The Bank of England is not independent of the government. The Bank is subject to the directions of Treasury, although in practice decisions over monetary policy are reached jointly. On a few rare occasions disagreements between the Bank and Treasury have been publicized. The Bank of England is not accountable to Parliament although as a matter of courtesy files its annual report with Parliament. The Governor is appointed by the government for five years (term is renewable).

Japan

The Bank of Japan is 55% government owned and 45% privately owned. The Bank has a statutory duty to maintain the domestic value of the currency and to control credit expansion. Actions such as changes in banks' reserve ratios require the approval of the Minister of Finance. Open market operations and discount rate changes do not require government approval. The Bank is accountable to the Japanese Diet. The Governor is appointed by cabinet for a 5-year term (renewable).

West Germany

The Bundesbank is 100% owned by the government. It has statutory duties to maintain the domestic value of the currency, to supervise the banking system and to facilitate the clearing of cheques. The government has separate powers to fix exchange rates and regulate the inflow of foreign capital. The Bundesbank is independent of parliament and is independent of the federal government. The federal government may ask for decisions to be deferred to a maximum of two weeks. The Bundesbank has an obligation to support the economic policy of the government but the important point to note is that this obligation is limited by the statutory duty of the Bundesbank to safeguard the currency. Conflicts between the Bank and the government have occurred but have not been of great significance. The Governor is appointed by the President on the nomination of the federal government for an 8 year term.

France

The Bank of France is wholly owned by the government. The Bank has a statutory duty to control credit expansion and to supervise the banking system. The Ministry of Economics fully controls Bank policy. This control extends even to the day-to-day operation. There is no accountability of the Bank to the French Parliament. The Governor of the Bank is appointed by the President on the advice of cabinet for an indefinite term. The President can dismiss the Governor at any time.

As the above descriptions of the central banks show, no central bank is restricted by some external rule in its control of the money supply. A Gold Standard rule would greatly reduce the discretionary powers of the central bank. A Gold Standard will not guarantee short-run price level stability but such a standard would guarantee long-run price level stability. However, it is unlikely that any country will relinquish control over its money supply and adopt some sort of commodity standard. A monetary growth rule as proposed by Milton Friedman would also restrict the arbitrary power of the central bank. Again none of the six central banks have such restrictions.

Statutory restrictions seem the greatest for the Bundesbank. Although the Bundesbank is required to support the economic policy of the government; this support is tempered by its obligation to safeguard the domestic value of its currency. Because of this obligation I will give the Bundesbank a rating of 6. The Federal Reserve is technically independent of the executive branch and I will give it a rating of 5. I give the central banks of Canada, U.K. and Japan a somewhat lower rating of 4. My reasons are as follows. All three of these central banks are subject to significant control from the government of the day. In Canada and the U.K., the Bank is subject to government directives. In Japan the Minister of Finance has been noted for announcing by himself discount rate policy.

In addition these central banks all engage in "moral suasion" in their conduct of monetary policy. In Canada, the Bank of Canada has made requests of chartered banks for which they have no legal authority. In the past the Bank of Canada has requested that the chartered banks limit their loans to sales finance companies. Also the Bank of Canada asked the chartered banks to voluntarily agree to a "secondary reserve ratio" (this was before a change in the Bank Act which gave such a power to the Bank of Canada). The implied threat had been that through changes in reserve requirements (which the Bank has no power to make anymore) or open market operations or some other Bank action that banks could be punished for non-compliance. This use of moral suasion is a fundamental violation to the rule of law. Fortunately for Canada, as the number of banks have increased, the use of moral suasion has diminished for obvious reasons.

In the U.K., the Bank of England works through conventions and understandings with the banks.[12] The actions of the Bank of England have been described as conducting business through informal and friendly conversations as if the Governor was a senior partner in the banking firm dealing with junior partners (the banks).

In Japan moral suasion is known as 'window guidance.' The Bank of Japan determines each bank's reserve requirements and informally negotiates each bank's quarterly lending ceiling. As such it is difficult to expect individual banks to resist a request from the Bank of Japan to refrain from selling U.S. dollars.[13] Again such actions are contrary to the basic principle of the rule of law.

The Bank of France is completely controlled by the government. There is no restraint on the government's ability to use the printing presses to finance government expenditures. As such I gave the Bank of France the lowest rating for economic freedom; a rating of 3.

(ii) Has the central bank succeeded in providing a stable monetary environment?

The major goal of any monetary system is to provide for a stable currency so that private contracts can be made with the minimum amount of uncertainty. In such an environment where the freedom to engage in exchanges of all kind is maximized, national income will be maximized. This question can clearly be evaluated more objectively than the previous question.

Table 1 presents the inflation rates for our six countries for the last five years. In terms of average inflation rates Japan and West Germany experienced the lowest inflation rates whereas the U.K. and France experienced the highest inflation rates. Inflation is a source of government revenue. The higher the inflation rate the higher is the tax on cash balances. In addition for tax systems which are not fully indexed, higher inflation rates in effect mean higher average income tax rates. (These increases in tax rates are particularly pernicious since they occur without any specific act of parliament or congress). Finally if inflation is unexpected, this unexpected inflation reduces the real cost of government debt (i.e. this unexpected inflation is in effect a partial repudiation of the debt).

	Canada	U.S.	U.K.	Japan	West Germany	France
1984	4.3	4.3	5.1	2.3	2.4	7.4
1985	4.0	3.6	6.1	2.0	2.2	5.8
1986	4.2	2.0	3.4	0.6	-0.2	2.5
1987	4.4	3.6	4.2	0.0	0.3	3.3
1988	4.0	4.0	4.9	0.7	1.2	2.7
Mean	4.2	3.5	4.7	1.1	1.2	4.3
Standard Deviation	0.3	0.8	1.0	1.0	1.3	4.7

Table 1. Inflation Rates 1984-1988*

*Inflation is measured by the Consumer Price Index. Data is taken from *International Financial Statistics* published by the International Monetary Fund.

Economists are concerned not only with average inflation but also the volatility of inflation. The more volatile inflation, the more unexpected inflation one will observe. The more volatile inflation the more difficult it is to negotiate long-term contracts. In the late '70s the high and volatile inflation rate made it very difficult (and costly) to issue long-term debt.

Hence both high and variable inflation rates are harmful to the economy and harmful to overall economic freedom. In giving rankings to the performance of various countries one should note that standards change over time. After the double digit inflation of the '70s, Canada's inflation rate of 4% is considered low by most economic observers. However when inflation reached 4% in the late 1960s this was deemed to be a national emergency and a Royal Commission was appointed to investigate the causes of the inflation problem.

Since Japan and West Germany have the lowest inflation rate and relatively low inflation volatility they receive a rating of 9. Canada has a slightly higher inflation rate than the U.S. but it has a more stable inflation rate. I awarded the U.S. and Canada a rating of 7. France has a slightly lower inflation rate than the U.K. but the volatility is much greater. I awarded France a rating of 5 and the U.K. a rating of 6.

(b) Regulation of the commercial banks

(i) Is there free entry into the commercial banking business?

This again is one of those questions for which there is no easy answer. Take the example of Canada. Up until the Bank Act of 1981 it was almost impossible for foreigners to set up a bank in Canada and it was extremely difficult for new domestic firms to enter the field. (A separate act of Parliament was required to set up a Bank.) Although new banks were rare, there were many new entrants into financial institutions which were providing services which were close substitutes to those provided by banks (e.g. trust companies, mortgage loan companies, savings and loans, credit unions, caisse populaires and suitcase banks).

The key question is how effective was the restriction on bank entry? Although non-bank financial intermediaries could enter, it is important to note that the banks had a monopoly on the clearing mechanism. Hence these substitute banks could compete effectively in the provision of time deposits but couldn't compete effectively in the demand deposit market. After 1981 in Canada, a separate act of Parliament was no longer needed to incorporate a bank, entry of foreign banks were permitted,[14] and the chartered banks' monopoly of the clearing system was eliminated. Currently, competition in the banking industry is very healthy in Canada. As such I give Canada an 8 in ease of entry.

In the U.S., banks can be incorporated nationally or at the state level. All national banks have to belong to the Federal Reserve system and state banks have the option of joining the Federal Reserve system. One advantage of belonging to the Fed is obtaining the cheque clearing services provided by the Fed. The large number of U.S. banks would be an indication that entry into the banking field in the U.S. is relatively easy. However the large number of U.S. banks is partially due to the restrictions on branching that exist in the U.S. In some cities (e.g. Chicago) banks are only allowed one branch. In some states banks can branch within the city but not outside the city. Branching across state lines is forbidden. There are those who contend that loopholes in the statutes (i.e. the use of bank holding companies) can be found that do in fact allow for more branching than would at first appear to be the case. However, it seems clear that the anti-branching provisions of the federal and state governments severely limit competition in the U.S. market. Because of these anti-competitive restrictions I would rate the U.S. banking system a 6 on freedom of entry.

In the U.K., London is a large international banking centre. Foreign entry is relatively easy although there are some restrictions (the U.K. has certain reciprocity requirements). In the U.K. the Bank of England has the authority to deny a banking licence. A rating of 8 is given to the U.K.

Japan has substantial barriers to foreign banks. There are large administrative barriers to foreign banks. In addition, domestic banks are granted more favourable capital-asset ratios. Because of these barriers Japan is given a 4.

West Germany has a large number of banks (in 1988 there existed 4,438 banks). There are 58 foreign bank branches. In West Germany, there are a number of conditions to be met in order to obtain a banking licence. Once these conditions are met, the banks have a right in law to be granted a licence. One possible measure of the increasing competition in the banking market is the falling interest rate margins for German banks.[15] A score of 8 is given to West Germany.

In France banking has a large degree of government involvement. Three of the four largest retail banks still belong to the state. Because of the large involvement of government run banks, a score of 2 was given on freedom of entry into the French banking market.

(ii) Are deposits insured by a government agency?

In the introduction I argued that deposit insurance is one of those issues where the effects on economic freedom are very contentious. The conventional wisdom is that government mandated deposit insurance is in the public interest protecting against bank runs. This argument depends critically on the belief that bank depositors face sufficiently high marginal costs of information that they are unable to distinguish between firm-specific shocks and industry wide shocks. I reject this argument. I argue that deposit insurance is in the private interest of smaller banks and is a restriction on economic freedom. (As such it is very much like the anti-branching provisions in the U.S.). Deposit insurance encourages more risk taking of the banks and results in more bankruptcies.[16]

Deposit insurance was first started in Canada in 1967. De jure, the current limit is $60,000 Canadian but de facto there seems to be no limit. In the U.S. deposit insurance was initiated in 1934 and the current limit is $100,000 U.S. Both systems are non-risk rated. A rating of 5 is given to both Canada and the U.S. In the United Kingdom government run deposit insurance only came into force in 1982.[17] The insurance covers 75% of the first £20,000 of bank deposits.[18] The British system of co-insurance tends to minimize the moral hazard problem of the insurance scheme. Depositors still have an interest in monitoring the riskiness of the bank's portfolio. A rating of 6 is given to the U.K.

Japan has a government run system of deposit insurance that insured deposits in 1986 to a maximum of 3 million yen. This limit was expected to increase to 10 million yen. Japan gets a score of 5. West Germany has no compulsory deposit insurance scheme. Private banks set up their own Deposit Protection fund in 1976. Given the voluntary nature of the German scheme, a score of 8 is given.

No evidence of any deposit insurance scheme could be discovered for France. However, given the fact that three of the four largest banks are publicly owned the government in effect guarantees bank deposit. A score of 5 is awarded for France.

(iii) Are there reserve requirements on the banks?

There is an argument in monetary economics that fractional reserve banking is inherently unstable. One aspect of this argument is that because of fractional reserves, that in times of banking panics, even very solid and safe banks will experience runs. This argument depends for its validity on the same assumptions needed to favour government imposed deposit insurance. It requires an inability of depositors to distinguish between firm-secific and industry wide shocks. In such a world only a bank with a 100% reserve will be spared a run. If one believes in free banking then there is no need to have any imposed legal reserve requirement.[19] Banks will have their own optimal reserve ratio and depositors will know what reserves each bank maintains.

Hence this is another one of those contentious issues. One school of thought would argue for 100% reserves. Another would argue that any formal reserve requirement is an undue regulation on banks. Such reserve requirements act as a tax on banks (a tax that other financial institutions do not have to bear and hence impairs the competitiveness of the banks). In addition these legal reserves perform no economic function. These reserves cannot be called upon by the bank in times of financial crises.[20]

It should be noted that even among economists who favour 100% required reserves, there would be no agreement that a 30% reserve ratio is superior to a 20% reserve ratio because there would be no reason to believe that banks subject to a 30% ratio would have less risky portfolios than banks subject to a 20% ratio. Clearly 100% is better than either 30% or 20% but it is not clear that 30% is superior to 20%.

No country in our sample has 100% reserve requirements. All these countries have a fractional reserve banking system. From 1960 to 1984 the average reserve requirement on bank deposits was 6% for Canada, 8% for the U.S., 7% for the U.K., 3% for Japan, 11% for West Germany and 4% for France.[21] There is too small a variation to award any difference in scores. All countries are awarded a 5.

(iv) Are there interest rate ceilings on what the banks can pay on deposits?

Usury laws are perhaps one of the earliest forms of restriction on economic freedom. Usury laws have been very common in the banking field. Currently there are no effective restrictions on what banks can pay on deposits in both Canada and the United States. In the U.S. interest is not allowed on demand deposits. However the use of NOW and Super NOW accounts effectively gets around this restriction. Also DIDMCA has gotten rid of the Regulation Q ceiling on time deposits. Due to this relatively free environment I will give both Canada and the U.S. a score of 9.

I could find no evidence of effective interest rate restrictions for the U.K. and West Germany. Both of these countries get a rating of 9.

In France there are no interest bearing current accounts (as is allowed for in most European countries). In addition, for term deposits below 100,000 francs the maximum rate of interest is 5.5%. Because of these restrictions on the ability of banks to freely raise deposit funds France gets a rating of 3.

In Japan interest rates on deposits with commercial and other banks are limited by ceilings under the Temporary Interest Rates Adjustment Law and guidelines set by the Bank of Japan. No interest has been allowed on current accounts since 1944. It is estimated that almost two thirds of Japanese savings deposits remain under interest rate constraints. The Ministry of Finance sets maximum interest rates for money market certificates $69,000 or lower. Overall, about one third of deposits are under interest rate controls. This represents a subsidy to Japanese banks. The total value of these subsidies to Japanese banks has been estimated at about 3.7 trillion yen or 1% of GNP.[22] Because of these substantial interest rate restrictions, Japan gets a rating of 3.

(v) Can banks enter the security business?

Banks, almost everywhere, have restrictions on the product lines they can offer.[23] One important restriction is on the ability of banks to enter the security business. Firms can borrow either from banks or from capital markets. Restrictions on the ability of banks to enter the security business greatly hamper the ability of banks to compete on the asset side of their balance sheet. I would interpret such restrictions as one impairing economic freedom and enacted primarily to protect the private interest of security dealers. However there is a public interest argument which is advanced to support this restriction. Suppose a bank owns stock of a certain corporation. This bank would have a conflict of interest if it decides to make a loan to this corporation. Because of this potential conflict the government enacts conflict of interest and self dealing provisions to protect bank depositors (and possibly certain classes of bank shareholders). Separation of banks and security dealers is one way to avoid conflict of interest.[24]

The important point to note is that conflicts of interest arise very frequently in economic exchange (this is essentially what economists call the principle-agent problem). Whenever a broker advises a client to buy or sell a stock the broker is in a potential conflict (because he earns commission on the transaction). Either through bond posting or reputational effect the conflict will be solved or in the absence of a solution, the acts of advice giving and stock trading will be separated. If conflicts are so severe, then the market will by itself separate out the activities which are in conflict. There is no need for artificial government separation of the activities.

In July 1987 the Little Bang in Canada resulted in brokers and banks no longer being kept apart. As a result of this deregulation, five of Canada's six largest banks rushed to buy brokerage and security firms. Because of this relative free environment, I will give a 9 to Canada.

The Glass-Steagall Act has kept banks and stockbrokers apart in the U.S. since 1933. Although the years have seen some erosion of Glass-Steagall, essentially U.S. banks have been unable to underwrite corporate securities as many European banks do. Through bank holding companies there has also been erosion of Glass-Steagall. The U.S. Congress is currently considering changes to Glass-Steagall.[25] In addition, at the beginning of this year the Fed decided to allow bank holding companies to underwrite corporate debt and to consider allowing them to underwrite corporate equities within a year. As of now there are still substantial restrictions on the ability of banks to underwrite corporate securities. A rating of 4 is given to the U.S.

The Big Bang in the U.K. in October, 1986 opened up the possibility of full membership on the London Stock Exchange to domestic depository and other financial intermediaries. Prior to the Big Bang there was a traditional division in the U.K. between banks and brokers. Now all large British and foreign banks have entered the security business either through merger or starting up new firms. A score of 9 is given to the U.K.

Japanese law allows Japanese banks to own no more than 5% of a securities firm.[26] However there is a substanital loophole in the law. The law does not stop a bank's associates from having holdings in securities firms. In effect Japanese banks do own securities firms. Japanese banks are allowed to trade in everything but equities and they trade in these through the security companies they control. It should be noted that new products introduced by Japanese banks require approval by the Minister of Finance. Since it would appear that U.S. and Japanese restrictions are similar but the Japanese restrictions are not as effective. A rating of 6 is given to Japan.

In West Germany, the German universal banks act as brokers, there is no separate profession of stock broker. A score of 10 is given to West Germany.

Stockbroking firms in France had until 1988[27] a monopoly on securities trading. Last year the capital in France's 61 stockbrokers was opened up. Now banks, insurance companies and other financial institutions are allowed equity ownership in the 'agents de change,' the small number of companies which essentially run the Bourse.[28] Since last year, 30 of the 45 brokers operating in Paris had been bought and major French banks have been the largest investors. A score of 8 is given to France.

(c) Regulation of Capital Flow

(i) Are there exchange controls?

Canada has no exchange controls. A rating of 10 is given to Canada.

Although the U.S. has no exchange controls, there are certain restrictions for security reasons. Receipts of funds from Cuba, the People's Republic of Kampuchea, the Democratic People's Republic of Korea and the Socialist Republic of Vietnam are generally prohibited, in addition to certain types of payments from the Socialist People's Libyan Arab Jamahiriya. Also there are certain reporting requirements. Travellers entering or leaving the United States carrying more than $10,000 U.S. in cash or negotiable instruments must report this or face confiscation of the property. A rating of 9 is given to the United States.

All forms of exchange controls were abolished in the U.K. in 1979. Currently the U.K. has no exchange controls. A score of 10 is given. Similarly West Germany has no exchange controls and a score of 10 is given.

Exchange controls were substantially liberalized in Japan under the Foreign Exchange and Foreign Control Law. The limited exchange control system is operated primarily by the Ministry of Finance, the Ministry of International Trade and Industry and the Bank of Japan (acting as the agent for the government). Unrestricted non-resident accounts in yen may be opened by any non-resident with any authorized bank in Japan. Both residents and non-residents may acquire foreign currency deposits with authorized banks in Japan and the freely exportable limit is 5 million yen. Overseas deposits by resident individuals up to the equivalent of 10 million yen are subject to automatic approval by the Bank of Japan. Capital transactions are in principle free unless required to follow certain procedures. For example, foreign loans by banks are legally subject to prior notice with a waiting period but in a large number of cases they can be made upon notification. Because of these restrictions a rating of 7 is given to Japan.

Exchange controls exist in France and are administered by the Bank of France. In March, 1989, they were liberalized. Now holders of French francs are able to lend them freely abroad. All inward and outward payments must be made through approved banking intermediaries by bank transfer. However individuals may not hold a foreign bank account or have a foreign currency account in France. It is expected that these controls will disappear by the end of next year. France is awarded a score of 4.

(ii) Can foreigners invest freely in the domestic economy?

There are a number of restrictions on foreign investment into Canada. There are specific restrictions in the financial, broadcasting and uranium sectors. For example, foreign schedule B banks are limited to 16% of the market.[29] Inward direct investment is governed by the Investment Canada Act. Under the terms of this act, new foreign investments are in general subject to notification requirements but not to review.[30] Direct acquisition of businesses with assets over $5 million and indirect acquisitions for business exceeding $50 million are subject to review. Acquisitions below these limits and investments in new businesses in "culturally sensitive" sectors may also be reviewed.[31] Investment subject to a review must be shown to yield net benefit to Canada. There is a large amount of subjectivity in this test. Under this rule the Canadian government can either encourage or discourage foreign investment. Although investment controls in Canada in the 80s are substantially more liberal than they were in the 70s, Canada still has in place extensive controls over foreign investment. A score of 4 is given to Canada.

In the U.S. investments in banks are subject to federal and state banking regulations. Ownership of U.S. agricultural land by foreigners (or by U.S. corporations which is more than 5% foreign owned) must be reported to the U.S. Department of Agriculture. Also certain states impose restrictions on purchase of land by foreign nationals. The Trade Bill of 1988 required review of certain foreign takeovers of American firms and allowed the President to oppose takeovers in industries which would endanger national security. National security is interpreted to include among others the oil, natural resources and defence sectors. By March of 1989 the Pentagon was reviewing 35 proposed takeovers and was under pressure to even be more active in this field. National security may become the catch-all category in the U.S. just as culturally sensitive industries play the same role in Canada. Nevertheless the U.S. has less stringent foreign investment controls than Canada. I rated the U.S. a score of 7.

There are no general restrictions on foreign ownership in the U.K. With the exception of South Africa, both direct and portfolio investments may be made by foreigners. However, the foreign takeovers of companies that by their size or nature constitute a vital part of British industry may be subject to considerations under the Fair Trading Act of 1973. Also the government has the power under the Industry Act of 1975 to prevent or undo undesirable takeovers of important manufacturing undertakings. In 1988 the British government imposed a 15% ceiling on non-British shareholdings in Rolls-Royce (the aero-engine maker privitized in 1987). As can be seen the British government has discretionary power to oppose any significant foreign takeover. The power exists, whether the current government chooses to use it or not. The U.K. gets a score of 5.

Table 2. Economic Freedom Rating

U.S.	U.K.	Japan	Germany	France	Canada	Weighting Factor
(a) *Regulation of the Central Bank*						
(i) Is the power of the central bank to print money restricted?						
5	4	4	6	3	4	5%
(ii) Has the central bank succeeded in providing a stable monetary environment?						
7	6	9	9	5	7	20%
(b) *Regulation of Commercial Banks*						
(i) Is there free entry into the commercial banking business?						
6	8	4	8	2	8	5%
(ii) Are deposits insured by a government agency?						
5	6	5	8	5	5	5%
(iii) Are there reserve requirements on the banks?						
5	5	5	5	5	5	5%
(iv) Are there interest rate ceilings on what the banks can pay on deposits?						
9	9	3	9	3	9	5%
(v) Can banks enter the security business?						
4	9	6	10	8	9	5%
(c) *Regulation of Capital Flows*						
(i) Are there exchange controls?						
9	10	7	10	4	10	12.5%
(ii) Can foreigners invest freely in the domestic economy?						
7	5	2	9	3	4	12.5%

Table 2. Economic Freedom Rating

U.S.	U.K.	Japan	Germany	France	Canada	Weighting Factor
(d) Regulation of the Stock Market						
(i) Are there fixed commissions on stock transactions?						
10	10	2	2	2	10	5%
(ii) Are there restrictions against insider trading?						
2	3	7	9	5	4	10%
(iii) Is there a securities regulator?						
3	4	2	8	5	5	10%
Overall Rating						
6.1	6.3	5.3	8.3	4.3	6.6	100%

In Japan the Foreign Exchange and Foreign Trade Control Law governs inward investment. The foreign investor must make a report to the Minister of Finance. The establishment of branch operations, acquisition of a major equity interest, the acquisition of shares in unlisted companies, the acquisition of 10% or more of shares in a listed company and any change in the business objectives of a company more than 33% foreign owned all come under direct investment regulations. These regulations empower requests or orders for suspension or modification of any aspect of the transaction that the minister deems to adversely affect Japanese national security, public order, public safety, the activity of Japanese enterprises in related lines of activity, the general performance of the economy or for the maintenance of mutual equality of treatment of direct investment with other countries. It will be noted that the Minister can disallow foreign investment because the foreign competition harms domestic firms. The provisions place very stringent controls on foreign investment.

In addition the government restricts foreign investment (and private investment) in water supplies, the postal service, telephone service, telex and telegram, tobacco, industrial alcohol and salt. Also certain corporations are listed as "protected corporations" and have a limit on total foreign ownership in them. Japan gets a score of 2.

West Germany has very little in the way of controls on foreign investment. Nonresident direct investment, purchases of real estate in Germany for investment or personal use and purchases of German or foreign equities do not require approval. The only industry wholly closed to private enterprise is the post office. In all industries except banking and insurance 100% foreign ownership is permitted. West Germany gets a score of 9 on freedom of investment controls.

The French government requires prior approval for foreign direct investment in a large number of industries. Direct investments are generally considered those which acquire 20% or more of outstanding shares. The Treasury is entitled to issue a finding within 1 month to forbid the foreign investment should such investment be deemed to jeopardize public health, order, security or defence. In addition there are restrictions to foreign investment in a large number of industries. French governments have traditionally intervened to protect French industry from international competition.[32] The powers of the Ministers in France are not as all pervasive as those in Japan. France receives a rating of 3.

(d) Regulation of the Stock Market

(i) *Are there fixed commissions on stock transactions?*

Fixed commissions on stock exchanges is indicative of a broker's cartel in stock trading. In Canada stock commissions are subject to individual negotiations. The Securities Act Amendments of 1975 in the U.S. instructed the Securities and Exchange Commission to outlaw fixed brokerage rates on the NYSE. The Big Bang in London brought about freely negotiated brokerage rates. Each of these countries score 10.

In Japan brokerage fees are charged according to a rigid non-negotiable schedule set by the Tokyo Stock Exchange and approved by the Ministry of Finance. Brokerage fees are generally more expensive for large transactions than in other countries but cheaper for small transactions.[33] Japan gets a rating of 2. Germany and France also have fixed commissions. They also receive a rating of 2.

(ii) *Are there restrictions against insider trading?*

Insider trading laws are perhaps the most debated in deciding their effect on economic freedom. There are those who believe that insider trading represents a violation of a fundamental trust. On the other side it is argued that insider trading laws prevent individuals from acquiring information which is important in stock evaluation. Without the free flow of information, the whole efficiency of the stock market can be threatened. I would argue that the market itself can punish any abuse of privileged position.[34] The threat to the free flow of information imposed by insider trading rules represents a fundamental threat to the efficiency of the stock market and to fundamental economic freedom. The right to acquire information and act on that information is a fundamental economic right.

The Companies Act of 1952 in Canada makes it an offense for a director to speculate in any of the company's securities. The main problem was uncertainty over the meaning of speculation (generally the term only referred to short sales). The securities act of 1966 required directors to disclose dealings in their own company shares and stated that if a director made use of confidential information for his own benefit which if known publicly would affect the price of shares, the director is liable for compensation to any person or companies for losses suffered.

In 1988 new insider trading rules were introduced in Ontario which gave the Ontario Securities Commission (OSC) a much wider latitude in introducing circumstantial evidence. The use of circumstantial evidence in criminal prosecutions cannot be considered as one which accords with the basic principles of justice. Also the definition of an insider was widened to include so-called tipees—any investor who receives confidential information not available to the marketplace in order to make trading profits. This definition would seem to include any entrepreneur who invests resources to uncover valuable information. Is it desirable to forbid company executives, lawyers, secretaries, analysts, arbitrageurs, investment bankers, shop-floor workers and middle managers from trading in company stock? Calling these people insiders will certainly discourage the collection of valuable information. In addition insider trading penalties were increased from a $2,000 fine and/or a 6-month jail term to a fine up to 3 times the insider trading profits and/or two years in jail.[35] Given Canada's extensive insider trading regulations (although there have been very few prosecutions) a rating of 4 is given to Canada.[36]

Insider trading prosecutions have been very frequent in the U.S. and very rare in Canada. At the end of 1988, President Reagan signed a bill increasing insider trading penalties and making companies potentially liable for insider trading by their employees. Maximum criminal penalties are now 10 years and the maximum fine is $1 million for individuals and $2.5 million for corporations. This bill allows the SEC to seek civil fines against companies if they "knowingly or recklessly" fail to detect and prevent insider trading by their employees. Because of the large number of prosecutions, a rating of 2 is given to the U.S.

The Companies Act of 1985 in the U.K. defines the circumstances where directors are not allowed to deal in shares of the company: when there are price sensitive matters under discussion and 2 months prior to the announcement of results and dividends. The Financial Services Act of 1986 gave the Secretary of State the power to appoint inspectors to investigate possible insider trading. A legal problem in the definition of an insider revolved around the meaning of the word "obtained." The trial judge in the Fisher case (a London barrister and businessman charged with insider trading) acquitted Fisher because he ruled Fisher was given the information and did not actively seek it. The Law lords recently ruled on appeal that people who deal in shares on the basis of what they know to be unpublished price-sensitive information are guilty of insider trading no matter how the information came into their possession. At the time of this ruling in April of 1989 the Department of Trade and Industry had 45 cases of insider trading under various stages of investigation. In the U.K. insider trading is a criminal offence punishable with jail terms up to 7 years. A rating of 3 is given to the U.K.

Insider trading is illegal in Japan but the definition of an insider is fuzzy and it is not clear what constitutes inside information. Violations of the insider trading law are not subject to criminal penalties. As a result, up to now, insider trading has not been taken too seriously in Japan. In May of 1988 Japan introduced a tougher new insider trading regulatory code. It is not clear whether this is an effective code. A rating of 7 is given to Japan.

West Germany has no legislation concerning insider trading. As such a rating of 9 is given.

Since 1967 the "Commission des Operations de Bourse" has imposed criminal sanctions for insider trading and the spreading of false or misleading information. In addition directors and certain designated employees are required to disclose stock exchange transactions in their company's stock. French authorities have a reputation for lax enforcement of insider trading rules. As a consequence France receives a rating of 5.

(iii) Is there a securities regulator?

Here as in all questions of regulation there are the two opposing theories of regulation. One would be that securities regulation is in the public interest ensuring a well-run securities market and protecting the consumer of security services. The other theory of regulation would argue that this regulation is protectionist and favours private interests. We will take this latter interpretation and assume that over-all the securities regulator infringes on economic freedom.

In Canada securities regulation is a provincial matter. There is no federal regulator. Canada does have active provincial regulators. The fact that there are 10 separate regulators does provide some competition in the regulatory market. This impinges on the ability of regulators to control the market. Too stringent regulation may cause firms to move to other provinces. As such a rating of 5 is given to Canada.

The U.S. does have a very active federal securities regulatory. The Securities and Exchange Commission (SEC) regulates almost every aspect of the securities industry. The U.S. receives a rating of 3.

The Big Bang in London brought about a new system of regulation of the investment business. This new system has been described as a 'structure of self-regulation within a statutory framework.' Regulation depends on the specific rules established by the Securities and Investment Board (SIB - consists of 18 members appointed by the Secretary of State and the Governor of the Bank of England),[37] the various Self Regulatory Organizations (SRO's), Recognized Investment Exchanges (RIE's) and Recognized Professional Bodies (RPB's).

It should be noted that the SIB has similar authority to the SEC. However because of the existence of competing regulatory bodies a rating of 4 is given to the U.K.

In Japan the 1948 Securities Exchange Law created a Securities and Exchange Commission but it was abolished in 1952. The Department of Securities administers security regulation under the direction of the Finance Minister. Hence the Finance Minister is the chief securities regulator. This sytem is inferior to an SEC system because there is no independence of the regulator from the government. The government is the regulator itself. Such a system has the potential of involving more rent seeking activity than a SEC system. A score of 2 is given to Japan.

The securities market in Germany is basically self regulatory. There is no securities act comparable to the U.S. or Canada. There is no regulatory agency like the SEC. The self governing stock exchanges (of which there are 8) make their own rules concerning the trading of securities. A score of 8 is given to West Germany.

The Commission des Operations des Bourse (COB) was created in 1967. It supervises the public insurance and trading of securities similar to the SEC. However unlike the SEC, the COB cannot prosecute offenders, has a small budget and only about 13 investigators. France gets a rating of 5.

Overall Rating and Conclusions

There is no easy way to arrive at an overall rating for each country. Twelve ratings have been given to each country in four categories. I propose to give each category a weighting of 25%. Within each category the weighting scheme is shown in Table 2. The provision of a stable monetary environment is considered to be essential to the freedom of contract. This gets a weight of 20%. The five questions on regulation of banks each get equal weight of 5% and the two questions on regulation of capital flows get equal weight of 12.5%. In the regulation of the stock market the question of fixed commissions gets a weight of 5% and the other two questions get a weight of 10%.

West Germany with a rating of 8.3 ranks number 1 in terms of economic freedom in money and capital markets. Canada, U.S. and the U.K. are for all practical purposes tied for second place with ratings between 6.1 and 6.6. Japan ranks next with a rating of 5.3 and the worse performance is recorded by France with a rating of 4.3.

Notes

[1] It should be noted that a particular data set is used to define money. One would need another data set to test the proposition that money influences prices.

[2] One could debate for a long time which definition of national income to choose. Regardless of the definition, one would want to define income as permanent income.

[3] Also see Rothbard (1988).

[4] This is consistent with the view of Milton Friedman that although monopoly can exist in the short-run it cannot exist in the long-run (unless it is fully protected by government).

[5] It should be noted that the 1933 prohibition of interest on demand deposits was not repealed. However banks were allowed to issue negotiable order of withdrawal (NOW) accounts which were in effect a way of issuing interest-bearing demand deposits.

[6] Deregulation of the London security market in October 1986 was known as the Big Bang.

[7] A similar story could be told about transportation deregulation. Airline deregulation in the U.S. forced similar deregulation in Canada. A large part of the Canadian population have easy access to U.S. airports. Similarly, U.S. trucking and train deregulation forced Canadian deregulation. Goods going from Vancouver to Montreal could just as easily use U.S. routes as Canadian routes.

[8] One may ask why it was necessary for the government to force the LSE to change its rule. Why didn't the LSE change the rules by itself. A possible answer to this question is that not all brokers would be hurt by international competition. Those brokers dealing in securities which were listed solely on the LSE would not be hurt by international deregulation. Clearly, international competition would reduce political support for fixed minimum commissions and with reduced political support such a policy was no longer politically viable.

[9] This example traces British deregulation to U.S. deregulation. Commissions on the NYSE were deregulated in the mid-1970s. One can ask what started this whole process off. Why did the NYSE deregulate commissions. A possible answer is that financial institutions were accounting for a larger and larger share of trading volume of the NYSE. The development of computers allowed large institutions to trade blocks of share off the NYSE. To be competitive, the NYSE had to reduce commission fees for their customers. Hence this example also illustrates the importance of substitute products in eroding monopoly positions.

[10] The modern attack on this view started with Klein (1974). For a complete analysis of the free banking position see Selgin (1988).

[11] The description of the activities of the central banks is taken from Fair (1979).

[12] See Revell (1973).

[13] It should be noted that the Federal Reserve is not adverse to making such requests. However, with the large number of U.S. banks such a request is bound to be ineffective.

[14] These foreign banks are known as Schedule B banks. They are restricted in their ability to branch and on the share of the market they are allowed. The recent Canada-U.S. Free Trade Agreement has freed U.S. Schedule B banks from these restrictions.

[15] From 1983 to 1987 interest rate margins fell by about .4 of a per cent.

[16] Not one Canadian bank failed during the Great Depression but there were bank failures after deposit insurance was introduced in 1967.

[17] Building societies have their own scheme.

[18] Foreign banks can be exempted if they have their own scheme in their home country.

[19] The Bank of Canada is proposing a complete abolishment of reserve requirements for the Canadian banking system.

[20] This was a bitter lesson that U.S. banks discovered during the Great Depression.

[21] This data is taken from Brock (1989). It is interesting to note that many Latin American and African countries have both high reserve requirements and high inflation rates. For Latin American countries reserve requirements are in the 30 to 40% range.

[22] See Euromoney, February 1988, p. 37. It should be noted that these interest rate controls exist in Japan in spite of attempts at deregulation. In addition, it should be noted that some observers claim that Japanese banks do in fact get around some of the interest rate controls. If this is the case the estimate of the subsidy will be on the high side.

[23] Part of this is due to the desire of regulators to restrict the riskiness of banks' portfolios in a regime of non-risk rated deposit insurance.

[24] In Canada, no one can own more than 10% of a chartered bank. The rationale for this restriction is to prevent the bank from self-dealing (e.g. making loans to its major shareholder). Such restrictions prevent the exis-

tence of major shareholders and this may very well prevent significant shareholder monitoring of management because of the free rider problem.

[25] As of September 30, 1986 there were 6,550 bank holding companies in the U.S. Through this form of organization U.S. banks have been able to avoid some of the anti-branching restrictions and some of the product line restrictions imposed on them.

[26] This rule is known as Article 65 and dates back to the time of U.S. occupation. Essentially Article 65 is importation by the occupation administrators of Glass-Steagall into Japan.

[27] The year of Le Petit Bang. The monopoly existed from the time of Napoléon.

[28] The monopoly was broken primarily because of the development of substitutes. It was estimated that at the height of the bull market, the LSE traded 25 to 30% of the shares of the top quarter of French companies. See International Management, January 1989, p.18.

[29] Under the Free Trade Agreement, U.S. banks are exempt from this restriction.

[30] For U.S. companies, the Free Trade Agreement has modified these terms.

[31] As one can imagine industries try to convince the government that they are culturally sensitive in order to receive protection from foreign competition.

[32] Sometimes the French government has prevented takeovers by increasing the cost to the foreign firm of the takeover. Such actions as asking for guarantees to keep the management French and to ensure all French nationals keep their jobs are typical examples.

[33] As would be expected average commissions on the TSE are higher than those charged on the NYSE. With more and more international competition, this differential may be difficult to maintain.

[34] If a firm deems that trading by certain individuals could be harmful to its owners, then employment contracts can have clauses which prevent such trading.

[35] It should be noted that after the Boesky case in the U.S., the OSC spent almost 2 years and $1 million investigating insider trading. As a result of this investigation, 3 individuals face losing their rights to trade stock for using information to make trading profits.

[36] Canada has had one high profile insider trading case and the government (of British Columbia) lost this case; the case of the former Premier

of British Columbia (William Bennett, Jr.) trading in the shares of Doman Industries Ltd.

[37] The SIB is the overall regulatory agency under the Act. It can investigate and prosecute. The SIB has the power to withdraw or suspend authorization to carry on an investment business if a firm fails the 'fit and proper test.'

References

P. Brock, "Reserve Requirements and the Inflation Tax," *Journal of Money, Credit and Banking*, February 1989.

S. Bronte, *Japanese Finance: Markets and Institutions*, Euromoney Publications: London, 1982.

J. Carr and F. Mathewson, "Unlimited Liability as a Barrier to Entry," *Journal of Political Economy*, August, 1988.

_____, "The Effect of Deposit Insurance on Financial Institutions," Working Paper Series No. 8903, University of Toronto, 1989.

D. Fair, "The Independence of the Central Banks", *The Banker*, October 1979.

M. Friedman and A. Schwartz, "Has the Government any Role in Money?" *Journal of Monetary Economics*, January 1986.

_____, *A Monetary History of the United States 1867-1960*, Princeton University Press, 1963.

International Monetary Fund, *Annual Report Exchange Arrangements and Exchange Restrictions*, Washington, D.C., 1988.

B. Klein, "The Competitive Supply of Money," *Journal of Money, Credit and Banking*, November 1974.

Price Waterhouse, *Doing Business in France*, Price Waterhouse Center for Transnational Taxation: France, 1985.

_____, *Doing Business in Germany*, Price Waterhouse: Frankfurt am Main, 1988.

_____, *Doing Business in Japan*, Price Waterhouse Center for Transnational Taxation: Osaka, 1983.

_____, *Doing Business in the United Kingdom*, Price Waterhouse: London, 1987.

_____, *Doing Business in the United States*, Price Waterhouse: New York, 1988.

G. Penn, *Banking Supervision: Regulation of the U.K. Banking Sector under the Banking Act 1987*, Butterworths: London, 1989.

L. Pressnell (ed.), *Money and Banking in Japan*, MacMillan: 1973 (first published in Japan, 1969).

J. Revell, *The British Financial System*, MacMillan: London, 1973.

M. Rothbard, "The Myth of Free Banking in Scotland" in *The Review of Austrian Economics*, vol. 2, edited by Rothbard, M. and Block, W.

J. Sasseen, "Can Paris Clean Up the Bourse," *International Management*, January 1989.

Schneider, et al., *The German Banking System*, 4th ed., F. Knapp: Frankfurt am Main, 1986.

G. Selgin, *Theory of Free Banking: Money Supply under Competitive Note Issue*, Totowa, N.J.: Rowman and Littlefield, 1988.

Y. Suzuki, ed. *The Japanese Financial System*, Clarendon Press: Oxford, 1987.

M. Tatsura, *Securities Regulation in Japan*, University of Tokyo Press: Tokyo, 1970.

U.S. Department of Commerce, *Foreign Economic Trends and Their Implications for the U.S.: Canada*, Washington, D.C., June 1989.

_____, *Foreign Economic Trends and Their Implications for the U.S.: United Kingdom*, Washington, D.C., February 1987.

_____, *Foreign Economic Trends and Their Implications for the U.S.: Federal Republic of Germany*, Washington, D.C., April 1989.

_____, *Foreign Economic Trends and Their Implications for the U.S.: Japan*, Washington, D.C., October 1988.

_____, *Foreign Economic Trends and Their Implications for the U.S.: France*, Washington, D.C., February 1989.

M. Walker, ed. *Freedom, Democracy and Economic Welfare*, Vancouver: The Fraser Institute, 1988.

L. White, *Free Banking in Britain: Theory, Experience and Debate, 1800-1845*, Cambridge University Press, 1984.

Discussion

Tom DiLorenzo suggested that there is over $100 billion per year allocation of U.S. government loans, loan guarantees, and government sponsored enterprises like Fanny-May and Ginny-May and off budget items that crowds out private allocations for which some sort of measure should be made. Walter Block liked the table at the end and felt that the weights were reasonable, but would change the rating on the U.S. for insider trading to a 2 rather than a 5. He also saw no difference between government deposit insurance and government house insurance, and thus felt it should be privatized from the perspective of economic freedom. Portfolio regulation on insurance companies is also an abridgement of freedom. Similarly stock market regulation is also a restriction on economic liberty. It is a restriction on a private company, the stock exchange, who agree on the rules for whoever wants to play. The fractional reserve system seems to require the government to intervene in the face of banking bankruptcy, and Block saw no economic justification for such a stance as it prevents bankruptcy from playing its role in the economic system. Milton Friedman asked Walter Block whether government provisions for bankruptcy reduce economic freedom, to which Block responded, "yes." Friedman pointed out that bankruptcy is a legal arrangement by which bad debts are allocated, and may not qualify as a restriction. Bernard Siegan indicated that bankruptcy provisions were considered by Justice Marshall in 1827 as a violation of the obligation of contract clause of the Constitution unless both parties agreed. But more to the point of the paper, he did not see a consistent thread of a maximization of economic liberty through the absence of coercion. Carr replied that in the paper he looked at how restrictions affected economic well-being. If there are restrictions that are meaningful, then they have to be judged by some standard. If they reduce freedom to transact in financial markets, then they reduce economic well-being.

Edward Crane did not like the 5 given to the U.S. for deposit insurance which he feels should be private—if at all. This in turn would give rise to a demand for a market accounting of financial institutions' portfolios. Carr argued that the ranking reflected relative levels. Canada and the U.S. are the same so both get a 5. Milton Friedman argued that there may be some occasions when government interventions are justified. For example, deposit insurance, established in 1934, laid the foundation for recovery from the Depression. Today there is no justification for such an intervention. Going back to the bankruptcy issue, he asked Siegan to suggest what Marshall would have done as an alternative to bankruptcy legislation. Siegan said suit would be brought against the offender as in any other failure to pay a contract. Friedman pointed out that the issue is not an argument of principle since there is government intervention in both potential processes. The question is which is the most effective way of enforcing this type of contract. Block maintained that there is a violation of economic liberty, regardless of economic efficiency. The bankrupt should be treated as a thief. Clifford Lewis wondered whether market failure was a good argument for intervention in this context. Friedman remarked that he, too, was skeptical of many examples of market failure, but in some cases, you have to choose among alternatives, both of which may be coercive and lead to a choice that balances among the levels of coerciveness and efficiency.

Carr, responding to the argument that portfolio regulation reduces economic freedom, suggested that when we observe ubiquitous legislated rules governing insurance companies portfolios, and we are unable to see who this benefits in the industry, it may be that it protects freedom. For example, if the public wants to be protected from a one-time shift in portfolios by insurance companies, and the least costly way of doing so is through legislation, then the companies themselves may acquiesce happily. We cannot just dismiss the rules as freedom reducing. Furthermore, Canada went through the Depression with fractional reserve banking, no deposit insurance and no bank failures. The only failures have been recent during the period in which deposit insurance has been in force. There is no incentive to monitor portfolios now, and the response is clear.

Ed Crane wanted Milton Friedman to reconsider his approach to market failure. Look at the $200 billion in liabilities to S&L's the deposit insurance system has caused, he requested, and consider the problem as a matter of principle. Tax withholding is another issue that reduces freedom. Friedman responded that on the tax withholding point, he had supported it as a measure taken in the midst of the Second World War, but there was little justification for it in peace time. On the more general point, he agreed that the government's action causes incentives that may not be desirable, but in certain cases, at particular times, the actions are justified. If it needs the money to fight a war, it is hard to stand on principle in the face of necessity. Gerald Scully maintained that Friedman trivialized the difference between contract and bankruptcy. Bankruptcy is an ordered allocation of assets, while enforcement of contract law means rendering a judgment which may mean payment of more than is currently available and must be paid over time. Bankruptcy reduces freedom from this perspective. Friedman wondered whether driving on the right side of the road reduces freedom. In Block's sense, yes, he suggested, but since we need some mechanism to decide certain issues, he viewed bankruptcy as one set of rules. Siegan pointed out that the penalty for the contract may affect the kinds of contracts into which one enters. Bankruptcy is one set of rules, while the law of contract is another. Friedman argued that in principle, since some decision must be made about the rules of the contract, bankruptcy is just one set of rules like any other. Carr suggested that bankruptcy does not prevent contracts. It is for residual claimants. Some way of allocating assets and settling contracts is needed.

Alan Reynolds felt that changes in economic progress can be related to economic freedom even though Carr does remark that the levels of economic progress are very different and may not be related directly to levels of economic freedom. DiLorenzo felt that the production function does not reflect the effects of economic freedom. Carr responded that the production function is just a method for organizing our thoughts about these issues. If one wants to do the simple correlation between economic freedom and GNP, fine, but economic freedom can also be included as an input. Walter Block was unhappy with identifying economic freedom with economic welfare such as GNP. Carr responded that if you accept the production function in which economic freedom is another factor, then the next step is to try to get an empirical measure of the inputs. When one tries to get an empirical counterpart to the theoretical measure, there are problems—the usual problems. In any production function analysis some method is needed for deciding what is the "best" definition in the context of some specific problem. There is no absolute definition of economic freedom. Using a problem to identify a characterization of economic freedom is the only way to proceed. There may be better ways to proceed, but he did not see them on the table.

The Measure of Economic Freedom

Measuring Economic Freedom

**James Gwartney,
Florida State University,
Walter Block,
College of the Holy Cross,
and Robert Lawson,
Florida State University**

Introduction

ECONOMIC FREEDOM IS HETEROGENEOUS AND extremely complex. No doubt, many believe that it is impossible to quantify. In a sense, this is clearly true—there are so many facets of economic freedom that it is an impossible task to quantify fully all of its dimensions. However, we believe that important ingredients of economic freedom can be quantified. The purpose of this paper is to construct an index which will provide valuable information on the status of economic freedom across countries and time periods.

The paper is divided into five sections. Part I briefly discusses our concept of economic freedom. Part II analyzes how one might measure economic freedom in four major areas: (1) time-dimension exchange, (2) size of government and freedom of domestic exchange, (3) "takings" and discriminatory taxation, and (4) freedom of international exchange. Part III briefly explains the construction of an index of economic freedom which we calculated for 79 countries. Part IV presents our results for 1975, 1980, 1985, and 1988-89. Finally, the concluding section considers some of the limitations of the index.

What is Economic Freedom?

A short reasonably accurate definition of economic freedom is that it exists when persons, and their rightfully-owned property (that is, "things" acquired without the use of force, fraud, or theft) are protected from assault by others. An individual's private ownership right includes the right to trade or give rightfully-acquired property to another. Thus, protection from invasion by others and freedom of exchange are the cornerstones of economic freedom.[1]

Of course, short definitions often raise questions. Some may ask, "What constitutes an assault?" "Who are the others who qualify for such a role?" "Does private ownership mean that you can use your property to do anything you want?" Briefly, we will seek to clarify these points.

What constitutes an assault, or a trespass, or a violation of private property? The most important property right possessed by a human being is the right to one's person. This right is violated when others invade or infringe upon one's person without consent. Thus, murder, kidnapping, assault and battery, and rape are violations of one's property right to his or her person. In like manner, violations of one's property right to physical objects takes place when others, without consent, invade or otherwise infringe upon an individual's passive use of his or her property. Therefore, actions such as theft, arson, and trespass are violations of private ownership rights. So, too, are restrictions upon the sale or use of one's property, as long as the use of the property is compatible with the rights of others.

The "others" who can qualify for a role as a denigrator of economic freedom must be human beings. If private property rights are destroyed as the result of storm, lightening, wild animals, or "acts of God," this is not a violation of economic freedom. Similarly, if people are poor because of ignorance (the cave men), their unhappy state cannot be characterized as a violation of economic freedom. Rather, they can properly be seen as lacking in wealth. Only purposeful human beings can deny economic freedom to other people.

The economic freedom of an individual is violated as the result of both "takings" by private criminals and "takings" via the political process. Discriminatory taxation—that is, taxation for the purpose of providing goods and transfer payments *to others*—is a taking, just as stealing is a taking (Epstein, 1985). It makes no difference that we refer to one as a "transfer" and the other as "theft." In terms of economic freedom, the impact on the victim is the same. In both cases, goods are taken from one individual without compensation and transferred to another. Similarly, regulatory activities such as price controls, property-use restrictions, and trade restrictions often involve the taking from one group with the intent of providing benefits to another. Like private criminal activity, these, too, are a violation of economic freedom.

Does this mean that individuals are free to use their private property in any way that they would like? No, the use rights of a private owner are limited by the ownership rights of other private owners. Owner A cannot use his property in a manner that invades or infringes upon the property rights of B. If A's violation of B's property right damages B, A is liable for the damage. Sometimes these issues are quite complex. If an airplane flies 20 feet over your roof, bursting your eardrums and shaking your dwelling to bits, this is clearly a private property right violation; but if it flies overhead at 20,000 feet, it is clearly not. You will probably not even be aware of it.[2] Similarly, a light shined on your house with the power of one lumen is invisible to the naked eye, and constitutes no violation of your rights. In contrast, a super powerful beam focused on your house could incinerate it and everything within.[3] In the former case, your private rights were not violated, but in the latter case they clearly were abridged. The proper boundary of private property rights is somewhere between these two extremes. One of the most important functions of a legal system is the determination of precisely where the boundary line should be drawn in the difficult cases. However, the presence of difficult cases does not negate the general principle: private property provides individuals with the freedom to act as long as they do not invade or infringe upon the private property of others.

Economic freedom can also be viewed within the framework of negative rights and positive rights. Negative rights protect people against others who would invade and/or take what does not belong to them. Since negative rights are nonaggression rights, all citizens can simultaneously possess negative rights.[4] In order to maintain negative rights, all people have to do is to refrain from initiating aggression against others and their property. In contrast, positive rights, such as a "right" to food, clothing, medical services, housing, or a minimal income level impose "forced labor" requirements on others. If A has a right to housing, for example, this would imply that A has a right to force others to provide the housing. But A has no right to the labor of others. Thus, A cannot possibly have a right to housing and other things that can only be supplied if they are provided by other people. Forced (slave) labor is the other side of positive rights. If a positive right is going to be achieved, some people will have to give up their possessions to others. In reality, positive rights are disguised demands for the forced transfers of income and wealth from some to others. Since positive rights force some to provide labor to others, they are clearly inconsistent with economic freedom.

It would be an impossible task to acquire detailed information for various countries that fully reflects the dimensions and complexity of economic freedom. However, the core of economic freedom is (a) the protection of private ownership rights (including one's property right to his or her own labor) to things acquired without the use of force, fraud, and theft, (b) freedom of personal choice with regard to the use of one's resources, and (c) freedom of exchange. It is possible to identify major areas and quantify important indicators of economic freedom in these areas. This is precisely what we seek to do in this paper.

Quantifying Economic Freedom in Four Major Areas

Recognizing that the protection of private property, freedom of exchange, and freedom of choice are the core of economic freedom, we have sought to quantify economic freedom in four major areas: (1) time-dimension exchange, (2) voluntary market exchange, (3) takings and discriminatory taxation, and (4) exchange across national boundaries. Of course, this list of components of economic freedom is not exhaustive. In some cases, data limitations precluded our inclusion of other categories. In other instances, the availability of data has influenced our choice of variables used to quantify an element of economic freedom.[5] However, we do believe that the four major components included in our analysis capture important dimensions of economic freedom. We also believe that the variables utilized to measure the components are reasonably good indicators of the presence or absence of economic freedom across countries within the four major categories. Let us now turn to the major components of our index and the variables used as indicators of economic freedom in each area.

Restraint of Time Dimension Exchange—Instability of Money and Prices

Monetary instability inhibits freedom of exchange involving time-dimension contracting (for example, bonds, mortgages, and credit purchases) and thereby reduces economic freedom. Unexpected changes in the money supply (and price level) alter the terms of time-dimension contracts. Thus, monetary instability increases the risk accompanying time-dimension contracts. Potential gains from exchange are lost as the result of this risk.[6]

The following variables were used to quantify monetary stability: (a) the standard deviation of the annual growth rate of the money supply during the last five years, and (b) the standard deviation of the annual inflation rate during the last five years. Of course, monetary stability and price stability are linked—variability in money growth creates variability in the inflation rate. However, some countries use price controls which may temporarily reduce the *measured* rate of inflation. Thus, we include both a price stability measure, as well as a monetary stability measure. In principle, a country could have a rapid increase in the money supply *and* the price level without having much variation in the inflation rate or growth rate of the money supply. In reality, however, that is seldom the case. Countries with low rates of money growth and inflation also tend to have more stability in these variables. Correspondingly, countries with high rates of money growth and inflation tend to exhibit substantially more variability. Thus, while our measures focus on variability, monetary stability (and price stability) is highly correlated with low rates of monetary growth (and low rates of inflation).

Each country will be ranked on a scale ranging from 0 to 10 for this component, as well as for all other components of our index. Countries with stable monetary policies and stable inflation rates are rated high (near the 10 end of the scale). In contrast, countries with unstable money and inflation are given low ratings (near the zero end of the scale).

Size of government—the proportion of resources allocated via coercion rather than market exchange

Milton Friedman consistently reminds us that government expenditures are a better measure of the size (and cost) of government than tax revenues. The real cost of government—the proportion of output allocated by politicians and other central planners rather than by those who earn it—stems from government spending, not just taxes. There are two broad functions of government that are consistent with economic freedom. First, there is the protective function of government. Government expenditures that protect the "life, liberty, and property" of individuals against the invasion of intruders, both domestic and foreign, are perfectly consistent with economic freedom. Second, the theory of public goods explains why certain types of activities (those for which it is difficult to restrict consumption to those who pay for the good) cannot easily be provided through market transactions. Thus, government provision of public goods may also be consistent with economic freedom. These two functions correspond to what James Buchanan (1975) conceptualizes as the protective and productive state.

When government moves beyond these protective and productive functions into the provision of private goods, it restricts consumer choice and economic freedom. Most modern governments are heavily involved in the rechannelling of income toward the production of some commodities and away from others, operation of businesses, the protection of government businesses from the discipline of competition, the forcing of some to pay for goods that benefit others, the imposition of price controls, and numerous other expenditures and regulatory activities that have nothing to do with either the protection of property rights nor the provision of public goods.

Given the breadth and magnitude of these activities, precise quantification of these activities is an impossible task. However, we have obtained data on three important indicators of economic freedom in this area. First, data on total government expenditures (including both central and local governments) are available. In general, as government expenditures rise relative to GNP, governments become more heavily involved in activities that do violence to economic freedom—activities beyond the protective and productive functions of government. Therefore, when total government expenditures of a country are large (and market expenditures small) as a share of GNP, the country is given a low rating. Similarly, countries with small government expenditures (and a relatively large market sector) are rated high.

Second, we have also assembled data on (a) the number of nonfinancial central government enterprises and (b) the representation of central government enterprises in 10 major industries (for example, steel, hotels, oil refinery, and airlines) where the argument for government production is weak. Countries with only a small number of government enterprises are rated highly. Similarly, countries with only a few government enterprises in the ten industries where the case for government provision is weak are given a high rating. In contrast, countries with a large number of government enterprises and government enterprises in many industries where markets work quite well are given a low rating.

The inclusion of the government enterprise data helps to correct a major deficiency of government expenditures as a measure of the size of government. The government expenditure variable substantially understates the size of government when government-operated enterprises are widespread. To the extent that the expenditures of government enterprises are covered by sales revenue, they generally do not appear in the government budget. The sales of the enterprises contribute to private consumption in the national income accounts. Only the subsidy (or revenue surplus) enters into the government's financial accounts. Given this methodology, government enterprises exert little impact on budgetary expenditures. Thus, since government enterprises generally operate in a protected, noncompetitive environment, it is vitally important to include a variable that will, at least partially, capture the contribution of government enterprises to the size of the government.

Third, price controls are an important regulatory area where some data are available (for the late 1980s). When the prices of goods and service are determined almost exclusively by market forces, a country is given a high rating. In contrast, countries with widespread use of price controls are rated low.

Denial of the right to private ownership—takings and discriminatory taxes

Governments can (and should) protect individuals against intruders who would take items that belong to others. However, governments themselves are often used as a vehicle for plunder. Often governments tax some in order to provide transfers or subsidies to others. They sometimes levy high marginal tax rates which deny individuals the fruits of their labor. Conscription is sometimes used to deny directly various segments of the population the property right to their labor. Such takings and discriminatory taxes are inconsistent with economic freedom.

Economically free people are permitted to reap the fruits of their labor. Income transfers, whether from rich to poor (or as is often the case from poor to rich), from men to women, or from one race group to another, are per se violations.[7] From an aesthetic point of view, it may make some difference whether funds are taken from people in order to give them to the poor rather than to the rich. However, from the perspective of economic freedom, it makes not one whit of difference. In essence, the use of force to take someone else's property is theft. It makes no difference what the thief intends to do with the stolen goods. Neither does it matter whether the theft takes place via the ballot box, or more directly as in the style of an armed robber. Thievery is thievery, regardless of motive or method; and it is a clear violation of economic freedom.

High marginal tax rates are also a form of taking. They take most of the labor and other earnings of people without even the pretense of providing them with proportional compensation (for example, government services) in return. To the extent that they raise revenue, they force some people to pay for services provided to others. Generally, however, high marginal tax rates are a very inefficient form of raising government revenue, since people will often reduce their work effort when a large proportion of their earnings is taxed away. Thus, high marginal tax rates impose an additional cost (and an additional loss of economic freedom) over and above the revenues transferred to the government. Perhaps the following example will help illustrate this point. Suppose that the government threw everyone who earned more than $100,000 per year in jail for six months. In essence, this is a form of a high marginal tax rate. A tax scheme like this would substantially reduce economic freedom over and above the revenue it generated for the government. In fact, it probably would not raise much revenue. Nonetheless, the impact on economic freedom would be substantial. So it is with high marginal tax rates—they impose a discriminatory cost on people over and above the cost of the revenue that they generate.

Conscription is perhaps the single most discriminatory tax that is widely used by modern governments. Some persons are drafted in order to provide labor services used to supply a government-produced good—national defense—that benefits all. Of course, protection of the "lives, liberties, and property" of citizens is a central function of government. But the cost of this protection should be imposed on all citizens. Singling out a specific group (for example, young men or young women) to pay for something that benefits all is a clear "taking." The military draft falls into this category and, as such, it is a clear violation of economic freedom.

In an effort to quantify the magnitude of takings and discriminatory taxes, we developed three variables: (a) income transfers and business subsidies as a percent of GNP, (b) the maximum marginal tax rate and the income threshold at which it is applied, and (c) the number of military conscriptees per 1000 population. Countries with a small transfer/subsidy sector, low marginal tax rates (and/or high income thresholds for the top marginal rate), and a voluntary military force (or only a small number of conscriptees per 1000 population) are awarded high ratings in each of these categories. In contrast, a large transfer/subsidy sector, high marginal tax rates (that take effect at a low income threshold), and a large proportion of military conscriptees results in a low rating.

Restraint of International Trade

Numerous policies ranging from tariffs and quotas to exchange rate controls and limitations on foreign investments reduce the economic freedom of citizens to exchange with trading partners in another country. Tariff rates retard exchange across national boundaries. The higher the tariff rate the greater the restraint of trade. Non-tariff barriers are also an important source of restraint on international trade. Unfortunately, the non-tariff trade restraints are numerous, complex, and heterogeneous. Given the current state of the data, direct measurement of these non-tariff barriers is virtually an impossible task.

We developed two variables that provide some insight on the magnitude of trade restrictions. First, tax revenue from tariffs and export taxes were derived. These taxes on international trade can be used to derive an average (discriminatory) tax rate imposed on international trade. Countries with a low average tax rate (international trade tax revenue divided by the value of exports plus imports) on international trade were given a high rating. In contrast, when the average international trade tax rate was high, the country was assigned a low rating.

Second, we developed a variable designed to provide an indirect measure of the extent that non-tariff barriers restrain international trade. We utilized the following equation to derive an expected size of the trade sector for each country:

$$T_c = f\,(GNP_c, Pop_c, t_c)$$

where

T_c — represents the expected size of the trade sector (one-half of exports plus imports divided by GNP; all variables were measured in the domestic currency of each country),

GNP_c — is the country's real GNP per capita measured in U. S. dollars,

Pop_c — is the logarithm of the country's population, and

t_c — indicates the country's average tax rate on imports and exports.

If a country is using quotas, exchange rate controls, tariffs so high that they exclude entry of certain goods, and other regulatory devises to retard international trade, one would expect that the actual size of the country's trade sector would be small *relative to other countries of similar size, income level, and average tariff rate*. Therefore, if the actual size of a country's trade sector is small relative to the expected size (given the country's population, GNP, and average tariff rate), this is indirect evidence that the non-tariff trade barriers of the country are high. Such countries are rated low on our one to ten rating scale. On the other hand, countries with low non-tariff trade barriers will tend to have a large actual trade sector relative to what would be expected. When this is the case, the country is given a high rating.

Construction of the Index of Economic Freedom

Table 1 summarizes the data included in the construction of our indexes. We constructed indexes for 1975, 1980, 1985, and the late 1980s. As Table 1 illustrates, we were able to obtain the required data for only ten of the eleven variables in 1975, 1980, and 1985 (the data for the price control variable were unavailable during these years). All eleven variables were included in the 1988-89 index. Appendix 1 describes each of the eleven variables and indicates the data source used for their derivation.[8]

The actual data for each variable in 1985 was arranged from the highest (most consistent with economic freedom) to lowest and divided into eleven intervals of equal size. Therefore, the 9.09 percent of the countries with the most favorable rating were assigned a rating of ten. The next 9.09 percent of the countries were assigned a nine, and so on. Thus, the number of countries receiving any given numerical rating (0 to 10) was roughly equal in 1985.[9]

Using the 1985 base year data, the intervals of the actual data that corresponded to each of the zero to ten ratings were also derived. These intervals were then used to assign the appropriate rating for each variable during the other years. Thus, the countries in aggregate can either improve (or regress), depending on how their ratings in other years compared with the 1985 base year.

After the actual data for each variable were converted to a zero to ten scale, we had to decide how the variable would be weighted in the calculation of a summary index. Table 1 indicates the weight that we utilized for the major categories (and subcategories) in our calculations. When the price control data were unavailable during 1975, 1980, and 1985; the other sub-components in the "size of government" category were given proportionally larger weights. Thus, when constructing the summary index in 1975, 1980, and 1985, the "total government expenditures" variable was

**Table 1: Tabular Presentation of the Components of the Index
1975, 1980, 1985, and Late 1980s**

Basic Weight	Variable Included In Index	Year (X indicates data were available during the year)			
		1975	1980	1985	Late 1980s
22.5%	I. Money and Prices				
(11.25)	A. Standard deviation of the Annual Growth Rate of the Money Supply (last five years)	X	X	X	X
(11.25)	B. Standard deviation of the Annual Inflation Rate (last five years)	X	X	X	X
30.0%	II. Size of Government				
(10.0)	A. Total Government Expenditures as a Percent of GNP	X	X	X	X
(10.0)	B. Nonfinancial Central Government Enterprises				
(5.0)	i. Total Number	X	X	X	X
(5.0)	ii. Government Enterprise in Designated Industries[a]	X	X	X	X
(10.0)	C. Price Controls-Portion of Economy Subject to Price Controls				X
25.0%	III. Takings and Discriminary Taxation				
(8.33)	A. Transfers and Subsidies as a Percent of GNP	X	X	X	X
(8.33)	B. Top Marginal Tax Rate (and Income Threshold at which it applies)	X	X	X	X
(8.33)	C. Conscripts per 1,000 Population	X	X	X	X

Basic Weight	Variable Included In Index	Year (X indicates data were available during the year)			
		1975	1980	1985	Late 1980s
22.5%	IV. Restraint of International Trade				
(11.25)	A. Taxes on International Trade as a Percent of Exports and Imports	X	X	X	X
	B. Actual Size of the Trade Sector Compared to the Expected Size	X	X	X	X

Table 1: Tabular Presentation of the Components of the Index 1975, 1980, 1985, and Late 1980s

[a]The ten designated industries were agriculture, airlines, radio and television broadcasting, construction material manufacture (e.g., steel or aluminium), chemicals and fertilizers, fishing or mining, hotels and/or theaters, energy production, pharmaceuticals, and real estate (including housing).

given a 15 percent weight (rather than 10 percent) and each of the two nonfinancial central government business enterprise variables were given a weight of 7.5 percent (rather than 5 percent) so that the total weight assigned to the size of government category would remain at 30 percent. If a country's data *for a major category* were unavailable during a year, the country was not rated during that year.

Presentation of Results

Table 2 presents the summary index rating and the rating for each of the four major components that comprise the summary index. Several interesting points are observable from the data of Table 2. First, the data allows one to pinpoint the areas of strength and weakness for each country. In some cases, they are quite revealing. For example, consider the data on monetary and price stability (I) and trade restrictions (IV) for Austria, Belgium, Germany, Netherlands, and the United Kingdom. In general, these countries ranked quite high (usually 8 or better) in the areas of monetary/price stability and free trade. However, the domestic economies of these countries are generally characterized by large government expenditures, high taxes, large transfer sectors, and use of price controls. Thus, they ranked low with regard to size of government (II) and takings and discriminatory taxation (III).

In contrast with most developed countries of Europe, many less developed countries ranked quite well in the areas of size of government (II) and takings and discriminatory taxation (III), but low in the areas of monetary stability and free trade. Costa Rica, Guatemala, Haiti, Honduras, Uruguay, Bangladesh, and Ghana illustrate this pattern.

Table 2 also illustrates why the summary index is low for Latin countries, including Argentina, Brazil, Mexico, Peru, and Venezuela. The economies of these countries are characterized by monetary instability, large government expenditures, numerous government enterprises, price controls, and trade restrictions. Across the board, the policies of these countries are in conflict with economic freedom.

Finally, it is comforting to note that countries such as the United States, Germany, Switzerland, and Japan (particularly in recent years) that have a reputation for monetary stability rank quite high in this area. In contrast, countries such as Argentina, Bolivia, Brazil, Peru, Israel, and Mexico (in the 1980s) rank at the very bottom in the area of monetary stability.

What impact does economic freedom have on the growth rate of GNP? Comprehensive analysis of the issue is a topic for another paper. However, we will briefly address the issue. Table 3a presents data on the growth rate of per capita GNP during the 1975-1980 period for the fifteen countries which had highest (and lowest) economic freedom ratings during this period. Several of the fifteen lowest rated countries—for example, Italy, Iceland, Chile, and Egypt—had impressive growth rates during the late 1970s. On the other hand, several countries with a high economic freedom rating had unimpressive growth rates. Nonetheless, the average annual growth rate of the fifteen top-rated countries was 3.74 percent, compared to 1.33 percent for the bottom-rated countries.

Table 2: Index Ratings by Major Category and Summary Rating, 1975, 1980, 1985, 1988-89.

Country	#	Year	I. (22.5%)	II. (30.0%)	III. (25.0%)	IV (22.5%)	Summary Rating
UNITED STATES	1	1975	9.0	6.5	5.0	7.0	68.00
UNITED STATES	1	1980	10.0	6.5	4.7	6.5	68.29
UNITED STATES	1	1985	8.5	6.5	6.3	6.5	69.08
UNITED STATES	1	1988	8.5	7.0	7.3	7.0	74.21
CANADA	2	1975	5.5	3.8	6.7	6.0	53.79
CANADA	2	1980	8.5	3.8	6.3	6.0	59.71
CANADA	2	1985	4.5	3.3	5.3	6.5	47.83
CANADA	2	1988	6.5	5.0	6.3	6.5	60.08
AUSTRALIA	3	1975	4.0	6.0	5.7	3.5	49.04
AUSTRALIA	3	1980	8.0	6.0	5.3	3.5	57.21
AUSTRALIA	3	1985	8.0	4.8	5.0	3.5	52.63
AUSTRALIA	3	1988	6.5	5.0	5.7	3.5	51.67
JAPAN	4	1975	3.5	7.3	7.0	6.5	61.75
JAPAN	4	1980	8.0	6.8	7.0	6.0	69.25
JAPAN	4	1985	9.5	7.0	7.3	6.0	74.21
JAPAN	4	1988	10.0	6.7	7.3	5.5	73.21
NEW ZEALAND	5	1975	4.0	5.0	5.3	4.0	46.33
NEW ZEALAND	5	1980	6.0	5.0	4.0	4.0	47.50
NEW ZEALAND	5	1985	6.5	4.5	3.3	4.5	46.58
NEW ZEALAND	5	1988	3.5	5.7	5.3	3.5	46.08
AUSTRIA	6	1975	8.0	1.5	4.3	6.0	46.83
AUSTRIA	6	1980	8.5	1.5	4.0	6.5	48.25
AUSTRIA	6	1985	9.0	1.5	2.7	7.0	47.17
AUSTRIA	6	1988	10.0	2.7	4.0	6.5	55.13
BELGIUM	7	1975	7.0	5.3	1.7	9.5	57.04
BELGIUM	7	1980	9.0	4.3	2.7	9.5	61.04
BELGIUM	7	1985	10.0	4.3	2.0	10.0	62.75

Table 2: Index Ratings by Major Category and Summary Rating, 1975, 1980, 1985, 1988-89.

Country	#	Year	I. (22.5%)	II. (30.0%)	III. (25.0%)	IV (22.5%)	Summary Rating
BELGIUM	7	1988	9.5	3.5	2.7	9.5	59.92
DENMARK	8	1975	5.5	2.0	2.7	5.5	37.42
DENMARK	8	1980	9.5	2.5	4.0	5.5	51.25
DENMARK	8	1985	5.0	2.5	4.0	6.5	43.38
DENMARK	8	1988	6.0	4.2	4.0	5.5	48.38
FINLAND	9	1975	4.5	4.0	2.7	4.5	38.92
FINLAND	9	1980	6.5	4.3	2.0	5.0	43.63
FINLAND	9	1985	8.5	4.0	2.3	4.5	47.08
FINLAND	9	1988	7.0	4.2	2.3	4.5	44.21
FRANCE	10	1975	8.5	3.0	3.0	7.0	51.38
FRANCE	10	1980	10.0	5.5	2.7	7.0	61.42
FRANCE	10	1985	7.5	5.0	1.7	7.0	51.79
FRANCE	10	1988	7.5	5.2	2.7	7.0	54.79
GERMANY	11	1975	8.5	3.3	4.0	8.5	58.00
GERMANY	11	1980	8.5	3.3	4.3	8.5	58.83
GERMANY	11	1985	10.0	2.5	3.0	9.0	57.75
GERMANY	11	1988	10.0	4.8	4.0	9.0	67.25
ICELAND	12	1975	3.5	3.8	6.5	1.5	38.75
ICELAND	12	1980	2.0	4.3	6.5	2.0	38.00
ICELAND	12	1985	1.0	3.8	5.5	2.5	32.88
ICELAND	12	1988	3.0	4.3	10.0	0.0	44.50
IRELAND	13	1975	5.0	3.5	4.0	6.5	46.38
IRELAND	13	1980	5.0	3.3	4.3	7.5	48.71
IRELAND	13	1985	6.0	2.8	3.3	8.5	49.21
IRELAND	13	1988	8.5	4.2	3.7	7.5	57.67
ITALY	14	1975	5.5	1.0	3.3	7.0	39.46
ITALY	14	1980	8.0	1.0	3.3	6.5	43.96

Table 2: Index Ratings by Major Category and Summary Rating, 1975, 1980, 1985, 1988-89.

Country	#	Year	I. (22.5%)	II. (30.0%)	III. (25.0%)	IV (22.5%)	Summary Rating
ITALY	14	1985	7.5	0.8	2.0	7.0	39.88
ITALY	14	1988	9.0	2.2	3.7	6.0	49.42
NETHERLANDS	15	1975	6.5	4.5	2.7	8.5	53.92
NETHERLANDS	15	1980	8.5	4.0	2.3	9.5	58.33
NETHERLANDS	15	1985	8.5	3.5	2.3	10.0	57.96
NETHERLANDS	15	1988	5.5	4.7	2.0	9.5	52.75
NORWAY	16	1975	9.0	1.5	1.3	7.5	44.96
NORWAY	16	1980	7.5	2.0	0.7	8.0	42.54
NORWAY	16	1985	6.0	1.0	1.7	7.5	37.54
NORWAY	16	1988	5.0	2.0	2.0	6.5	36.88
SPAIN	17	1975	7.5	4.0	4.0	4.0	47.88
SPAIN	17	1980	6.5	2.5	2.7	4.0	37.79
SPAIN	17	1985	9.0	1.5	2.0	5.0	41.00
SPAIN	17	1988	8.5	3.0	3.0	5.0	46.88
SWEDEN	18	1975	8.5	2.0	2.0	5.5	42.50
SWEDEN	18	1980	8.0	1.5	1.0	5.5	37.38
SWEDEN	18	1985	5.0	1.0	0.7	6.5	30.54
SWEDEN	18	1988	8.5	2.7	0.7	6.0	42.29
SWITZERLAND	19	1975	8.0	7.0	5.0	5.0	62.75
SWITZERLAND	19	1980	6.5	7.0	5.3	6.5	63.58
SWITZERLAND	19	1985	8.5	6.5	6.3	6.0	67.96
SWITZERLAND	19	1988	9.0	7.0	6.7	6.0	71.42
UNITED KINGDOM	20	1975	4.5	3.5	6.7	8.0	55.29
UNITED KINGDOM	20	1980	6.5	4.0	4.3	7.5	54.33
UNITED KINGDOM	20	1985	8.0	3.3	4.7	8.5	58.54
UNITED KINGDOM	20	1988	9.5	5.3	6.0	8.0	70.38
ARGENTINA	21	1975	0.0	6.0	3.3	1.5	29.71

<table>
<thead>
<tr><th colspan="8">Table 2: Index Ratings by Major Category and Summary Rating,
1975, 1980, 1985, 1988-89.</th></tr>
<tr><th>Country</th><th>#</th><th>Year</th><th>I.
(22.5%)</th><th>II.
(30.0%)</th><th>III.
(25.0%)</th><th>IV
(22.5%)</th><th>Summary
Rating</th></tr>
</thead>
<tbody>
<tr><td>ARGENTINA</td><td>21</td><td>1980</td><td>0.0</td><td>5.0</td><td>4.0</td><td>2.0</td><td>29.50</td></tr>
<tr><td>ARGENTINA</td><td>21</td><td>1985</td><td>0.0</td><td>2.8</td><td>3.7</td><td>1.5</td><td>20.79</td></tr>
<tr><td>ARGENTINA</td><td>21</td><td>1988</td><td>0.0</td><td>2.7</td><td>7.0</td><td>1.5</td><td>28.88</td></tr>
<tr><td>BOLIVIA</td><td>22</td><td>1975</td><td>1.5</td><td>10.0</td><td>7.0</td><td>3.5</td><td>58.75</td></tr>
<tr><td>BOLIVIA</td><td>22</td><td>1980</td><td>2.0</td><td>7.5</td><td>6.0</td><td>1.0</td><td>44.25</td></tr>
<tr><td>BOLIVIA</td><td>22</td><td>1985</td><td>0.0</td><td>5.3</td><td>6.7</td><td>5.0</td><td>43.67</td></tr>
<tr><td>BOLIVIA</td><td>22</td><td>1988</td><td>0.0</td><td>5.8</td><td>9.0</td><td>5.0</td><td>51.00</td></tr>
<tr><td>BRAZIL</td><td>23</td><td>1975</td><td>5.0</td><td>4.8</td><td>5.7</td><td>6.0</td><td>53.17</td></tr>
<tr><td>BRAZIL</td><td>23</td><td>1980</td><td>1.0</td><td>4.8</td><td>5.7</td><td>5.5</td><td>43.04</td></tr>
<tr><td>BRAZIL</td><td>23</td><td>1985</td><td>0.0</td><td>2.0</td><td>4.7</td><td>6.0</td><td>31.17</td></tr>
<tr><td>BRAZIL</td><td>23</td><td>1988</td><td>0.0</td><td>0.7</td><td>7.3</td><td>5.5</td><td>32.71</td></tr>
<tr><td>CHILE</td><td>24</td><td>1975</td><td>0.0</td><td>6.3</td><td>1.7</td><td>4.5</td><td>33.04</td></tr>
<tr><td>CHILE</td><td>24</td><td>1980</td><td>0.0</td><td>7.5</td><td>4.3</td><td>4.0</td><td>42.33</td></tr>
<tr><td>CHILE</td><td>24</td><td>1985</td><td>4.0</td><td>6.0</td><td>3.3</td><td>4.5</td><td>45.46</td></tr>
<tr><td>CHILE</td><td>24</td><td>1988</td><td>3.0</td><td>7.0</td><td>4.3</td><td>5.5</td><td>50.96</td></tr>
<tr><td>COLOMBIA</td><td>25</td><td>1975</td><td>4.0</td><td>6.8</td><td>7.0</td><td>2.5</td><td>52.38</td></tr>
<tr><td>COLOMBIA</td><td>25</td><td>1980</td><td>7.0</td><td>6.8</td><td>5.7</td><td>2.0</td><td>54.67</td></tr>
<tr><td>COLOMBIA</td><td>25</td><td>1985</td><td>7.5</td><td>6.5</td><td>7.0</td><td>2.0</td><td>58.38</td></tr>
<tr><td>COLOMBIA</td><td>25</td><td>1988</td><td>5.5</td><td>6.3</td><td>8.3</td><td>2.5</td><td>57.83</td></tr>
<tr><td>COSTA RICA</td><td>26</td><td>1975</td><td>3.5</td><td>9.3</td><td>7.3</td><td>3.5</td><td>61.83</td></tr>
<tr><td>COSTA RICA</td><td>26</td><td>1980</td><td>4.0</td><td>7.0</td><td>6.7</td><td>3.0</td><td>53.42</td></tr>
<tr><td>COSTA RICA</td><td>26</td><td>1985</td><td>1.0</td><td>6.8</td><td>6.0</td><td>2.5</td><td>43.13</td></tr>
<tr><td>COSTA RICA</td><td>26</td><td>1988</td><td>0.5</td><td>6.3</td><td>7.7</td><td>3.0</td><td>45.79</td></tr>
<tr><td>DOM REP</td><td>27</td><td>1975</td><td>2.5</td><td>7.0</td><td>7.0</td><td>3.5</td><td>52.00</td></tr>
<tr><td>DOM REP</td><td>27</td><td>1980</td><td>3.0</td><td>7.0</td><td>9.5</td><td>1.0</td><td>53.75</td></tr>
<tr><td>DOM REP</td><td>27</td><td>1985</td><td>1.5</td><td>7.3</td><td>6.7</td><td>3.5</td><td>49.67</td></tr>
<tr><td>DOM REP</td><td>27</td><td>1988</td><td>1.5</td><td>4.5</td><td>6.3</td><td>3.5</td><td>40.58</td></tr>
</tbody>
</table>

Table 2: Index Ratings by Major Category and Summary Rating, 1975, 1980, 1985, 1988-89.

Country	#	Year	I. (22.5%)	II. (30.0%)	III. (25.0%)	IV (22.5%)	Summary Rating
ECUADOR	28	1975	1.5	8.3	6.7	3.5	52.67
ECUADOR	28	1980	4.0	7.0	6.0	2.5	50.63
ECUADOR	28	1985	3.0	7.5	4.7	3.0	47.67
ECUADOR	28	1988	2.0	5.0	5.0	4.0	41.00
EL SALVADOR	29	1975	5.0	9.8	7.3	5.0	70.08
EL SALVADOR	29	1980	2.0	9.3	6.7	3.5	56.79
EL SALVADOR	29	1985	3.5	8.8	4.7	1.5	49.17
EL SALVADOR	29	1988	2.5	9.3	4.3	2.0	48.71
GUATEMALA	30	1975	4.0	9.5	9.0	2.5	65.63
GUATEMALA	30	1980	3.5	9.3	9.0	1.5	61.50
GUATEMALA	30	1985	2.5	9.5	6.7	2.5	56.42
GUATEMALA	30	1988	1.0	8.3	6.3	1.5	46.46
HAITI	31	1975	3.5	9.0	10.0	1.0	62.13
HAITI	31	1980	2.0	8.8	10.0	1.5	59.13
HAITI	31	1985	4.5	6.3	7.5	1.5	51.00
HAITI	31	1988	3.0	5.5	10.0	1.5	51.63
HONDURAS	32	1975	4.5	9.0	10.0	4.5	72.25
HONDURAS	32	1980	4.5	9.3	9.5	5.0	72.88
HONDURAS	32	1985	8.5	9.3	7.0	2.0	68.88
HONDURAS	32	1988	8.0	9.3	7.0	2.0	67.75
JAMAICA	33	1975	3.5	4.0	4.5	5.0	42.38
JAMAICA	33	1980	3.0	3.3	0.0	7.0	32.25
JAMAICA	33	1985	4.0	2.8	1.0	10.0	42.25
JAMAICA	33	1988	1.0	2.5	8.0	9.0	50.00
MEXICO	34	1975	4.5	5.3	5.3	2.5	44.83
MEXICO	34	1980	7.0	4.8	5.3	3.5	51.21
MEXICO	34	1985	1.5	4.3	5.7	4.5	40.42

Table 2: Index Ratings by Major Category and Summary Rating, 1975, 1980, 1985, 1988-89.

Country	#	Year	I. (22.5%)	II. (30.0%)	III. (25.0%)	IV (22.5%)	Summary Rating
MEXICO	34	1988	0.5	2.8	7.3	3.0	34.71
NICARAGUA	35	1975	1.5	9.3	8.0	3.5	59.00
NICARAGUA	35	1980	1.0	7.3	7.0	2.0	46.00
NICARAGUA	35	1985	0.5	0.0	3.3	3.0	16.21
NICARAGUA	35	1988	0.0	4.5	2.0	4.0	27.50
PANAMA	36	1975	4.0	7.3	7.3	6.5	63.71
PANAMA	36	1980	7.5	6.5	7.0	5.5	66.25
PANAMA	36	1985	5.0	5.5	6.3	4.0	52.58
PANAMA	36	1988	9.0	4.7	6.3	3.0	56.83
PARAGUAY	37	1975	3.0	9.5	6.0	0.5	51.38
PARAGUAY	37	1980	4.5	9.5	6.0	2.0	58.13
PARAGUAY	37	1985	2.0	9.0	7.3	3.5	57.71
PARAGUAY	37	1988	4.0	8.0	7.0	3.5	58.38
PERU	38	1975	3.0	5.0	6.0	2.0	41.25
PERU	38	1980	1.0	5.3	5.7	3.0	38.92
PERU	38	1985	0.0	6.3	5.0	2.0	35.75
PERU	38	1988	0.0	5.5	6.0	1.0	33.75
URUGUAY	39	1975	1.5	6.8	6.7	3.0	47.04
URUGUAY	39	1980	1.5	7.3	8.0	0.5	46.25
URUGUAY	39	1985	1.0	7.3	8.0	2.0	48.50
URUGUAY	39	1988	2.0	6.5	7.7	1.0	45.42
VENEZUELA	40	1975	1.5	4.5	8.0	4.5	47.00
VENEZUELA	40	1980	4.0	6.3	7.7	4.0	55.92
VENEZUELA	40	1985	4.0	4.5	7.7	2.5	47.29
VENEZUELA	40	1988	1.5	4.7	8.3	3.0	44.96
CYPRUS	41	1975	5.5	6.3	3.5	4.0	48.88
CYPRUS	41	1980	6.5	6.8	2.0	5.0	51.13

Table 2: Index Ratings by Major Category and Summary Rating, 1975, 1980, 1985, 1988-89.

Country	#	Year	I. (22.5%)	II. (30.0%)	III. (25.0%)	IV (22.5%)	Summary Rating
CYPRUS	41	1985	4.0	6.5	2.0	5.5	45.88
CYPRUS	41	1988	8.0	4.7	1.7	4.0	45.17
EGYPT	42	1975	5.0	1.3	1.0	4.5	27.63
EGYPT	42	1980	3.0	2.5	1.3	4.5	27.71
EGYPT	42	1985	6.0	1.5	2.7	4.5	34.79
EGYPT	42	1988	6.0	2.7	3.0	4.0	38.00
GREECE	43	1975	6.5	6.8	4.3	3.5	53.58
GREECE	43	1980	8.5	4.8	2.3	3.5	47.08
GREECE	43	1985	8.5	3.0	1.3	5.0	42.71
GREECE	43	1988	8.5	2.3	2.3	5.0	43.21
ISRAEL	44	1975	0.0	1.0	0.5	4.5	14.38
ISRAEL	44	1980	0.0	1.3	0.7	7.0	21.17
ISRAEL	44	1985	0.0	0.8	1.3	6.5	20.21
ISRAEL	44	1988	0.0	0.5	2.0	6.5	21.13
MALTA	45	1975	7.5	2.0	6.5	7.0	54.88
MALTA	45	1980	7.5	4.0	4.3	7.5	56.58
MALTA	45	1985	6.5	2.5	4.3	7.0	48.71
MALTA	45	1988	9.0	2.0	4.3	7.0	52.83
PORTUGAL	46	1975	3.5	5.0	1.0	4.0	34.38
PORTUGAL	46	1980	6.0	2.3	1.3	6.0	37.08
PORTUGAL	46	1985	6.0	1.8	2.3	7.5	41.46
PORTUGAL	46	1988	3.0	2.3	3.7	7.0	38.67
SYRIA	47	1975	2.0	3.8	5.0	3.5	36.13
SYRIA	47	1980	5.0	7.5	5.0	2.5	51.88
SYRIA	47	1985	6.0	1.0	1.0	1.0	21.25
SYRIA	47	1988	4.0	3.8	4.0	3.0	37.00
TURKEY	48	1975	6.5	6.8	3.0	2.5	48.00

Country	#	Year	I. (22.5%)	II. (30.0%)	III. (25.0%)	IV (22.5%)	Summary Rating
TURKEY	48	1980	1.0	5.8	2.7	2.5	31.79
TURKEY	48	1985	2.5	5.8	2.7	5.5	41.92
TURKEY	48	1988	1.5	7.2	3.7	5.5	46.42
BANGLADESH	49	1975	1.0	7.8	10.0	2.5	56.13
BANGLADESH	49	1980	3.0	7.3	5.5	3.0	49.00
BANGLADESH	49	1985	3.5	7.5	10.0	4.0	64.38
BANGLADESH	49	1988	3.5	7.5	10.0	3.5	63.25
FIJI	50	1975	4.5	8.0	6.0	3.0	55.88
FIJI	50	1980	6.0	7.5	5.0	4.0	57.50
FIJI	50	1985	5.0	6.8	6.3	2.5	52.96
FIJI	50	1988	4.0	7.8	6.3	2.0	52.58
HONG KONG	51	1975	3.5	10.0	9.7	9.0	82.29
HONG KONG	51	1980	6.0	10.0	9.0	9.5	87.38
HONG KONG	51	1985	5.5	9.0	9.0	9.5	83.25
HONG KONG	51	1988	5.0	9.5	8.7	9.5	82.79
INDIA	52	1975	6.5	4.8	6.7	4.5	55.67
INDIA	52	1980	5.5	4.0	6.7	4.5	51.17
INDIA	52	1985	10.0	3.5	6.0	5.0	59.25
INDIA	52	1988	10.0	3.2	7.3	5.0	61.58
INDONESIA	53	1975	3.0	5.3	7.0	7.0	55.75
INDONESIA	53	1980	2.5	4.8	6.0	7.0	50.63
INDONESIA	53	1985	5.0	4.3	7.7	7.5	60.04
INDONESIA	53	1988	7.5	4.5	6.7	7.5	63.92
KOREA	54	1975	3.0	6.3	4.5	7.0	52.50
KOREA	54	1980	4.5	7.0	3.0	7.5	55.50
KOREA	54	1985	2.5	7.3	3.7	7.5	53.42
KOREA	54	1988	7.5	5.8	4.3	7.5	62.08

Table 2: Index Ratings by Major Category and Summary Rating, 1975, 1980, 1985, 1988-89.

Country	#	Year	I. (22.5%)	II. (30.0%)	III. (25.0%)	IV (22.5%)	Summary Rating
MALAYSIA	55	1975	2.5	6.0	6.3	5.5	51.83
MALAYSIA	55	1980	8.0	6.0	6.0	6.0	64.50
MALAYSIA	55	1985	8.0	4.5	8.0	7.5	68.38
MALAYSIA	55	1988	6.5	4.5	7.7	8.0	65.29
MAURITIUS	56	1975	1.0	7.5	7.5	5.0	54.75
MAURITIUS	56	1980	3.5	7.3	6.0	4.0	53.63
MAURITIUS	56	1985	8.5	6.8	7.0	5.0	68.13
MAURITIUS	56	1988	9.5	7.0	7.7	5.5	73.92
PAKISTAN	57	1975	3.5	4.5	3.3	4.5	39.83
PAKISTAN	57	1980	7.5	3.5	6.7	4.0	53.04
PAKISTAN	57	1985	7.0	5.0	7.0	4.0	57.25
PAKISTAN	57	1988	6.5	4.5	7.7	4.5	57.42
PHILIPPINES	58	1975	3.5	7.5	7.7	4.5	59.67
PHILIPPINES	58	1980	6.0	7.5	6.3	4.5	61.96
PHILIPPINES	58	1985	1.5	7.5	7.0	4.5	53.50
PHILIPPINES	58	1988	2.5	6.2	8.7	4.5	55.92
SINGAPORE	59	1975	3.5	6.5	5.0	9.0	60.13
SINGAPORE	59	1980	7.0	6.5	5.3	9.0	68.83
SINGAPORE	59	1985	6.5	5.0	6.7	9.5	67.67
SINGAPORE	59	1988	8.5	6.0	6.0	9.5	73.50
SRI LANKA	60	1975	5.0	4.3	7.5	4.5	52.88
SRI LANKA	60	1980	4.5	1.8	5.0	4.5	38.00
SRI LANKA	60	1985	3.5	2.3	8.0	4.5	44.75
SRI LANKA	60	1988	4.0	2.8	8.0	4.5	47.38
TAIWAN	61	1975	1.5	6.0	4.0	7.0	47.13
TAIWAN	61	1980	3.0	5.5	4.0	7.5	50.13
TAIWAN	61	1985	6.0	8.0	3.7	8.0	64.67

Table 2: Index Ratings by Major Category and Summary Rating, 1975, 1980, 1985, 1988-89.

Table 2: Index Ratings by Major Category and Summary Rating, 1975, 1980, 1985, 1988-89.

Country	#	Year	I. (22.5%)	II. (30.0%)	III. (25.0%)	IV (22.5%)	Summary Rating
TAIWAN	61	1988	5.5	7.5	4.0	8.0	62.88
THAILAND	62	1975	4.0	5.8	5.7	4.5	50.54
THAILAND	62	1980	7.5	6.0	5.7	5.0	60.29
THAILAND	62	1985	7.0	5.8	5.0	5.5	57.88
THAILAND	62	1988	5.5	5.3	5.7	6.0	56.04
BOTSWANA	63	1975	3.0	6.3	6.0	5.0	51.75
BOTSWANA	63	1980	2.0	5.5	5.3	4.5	44.46
BOTSWANA	63	1985	3.5	5.5	5.3	5.5	50.08
BOTSWANA	63	1988	3.0	5.0	5.7	7.0	51.67
CAMEROON	64	1975	3.5	9.0	10.0	3.0	66.63
CAMEROON	64	1980	6.0	8.8	10.0	3.0	71.50
CAMEROON	64	1985	6.5	5.8	7.3	4.0	59.21
CAMEROON	64	1988	6.0	5.3	6.3	1.5	48.46
COTE D'IVOIRE	65	1975	2.5	6.0	9.0	8.0	64.13
COTE D'IVOIRE	65	1980	1.0	4.3	7.0	4.5	42.63
COTE D'IVOIRE	65	1985	4.5	4.5	9.0	5.0	57.38
COTE D'IVOIRE	65	1988	4.5	4.0	9.0	7.0	60.38
GABON	66	1975	1.0	5.0			
GABON	66	1980	1.5	7.0	10.0		
GABON	66	1985	4.5	6.5	8.5	5.5	63.25
GABON	66	1988	5.0	3.3	10.0	9.0	66.25
GHANA	67	1975	2.0	6.3	5.7	3.5	45.29
GHANA	67	1980	1.0	6.8	6.3	0.5	39.46
GHANA	67	1985	1.0	6.5	6.7	1.5	41.79
GHANA	67	1988	3.5	6.5	10.0	3.0	59.13
KENYA	68	1975	4.5	5.3	6.0	6.0	54.38
KENYA	68	1980	2.5	4.3	6.3	5.5	46.58

Table 2: Index Ratings by Major Category and Summary Rating, 1975, 1980, 1985, 1988-89.

Country	#	Year	I. (22.5%)	II. (30.0%)	III. (25.0%)	IV (22.5%)	Summary Rating
KENYA	68	1985	8.0	3.8	5.7	4.5	53.54
KENYA	68	1988	5.5	3.2	7.3	4.0	49.21
MALAWI	69	1975	3.0	6.8	8.7	5.5	61.04
MALAWI	69	1980	2.0	5.3	8.0	4.0	49.25
MALAWI	69	1985	6.5	7.0	7.7	2.0	59.29
MALAWI	69	1988	3.0	5.3	7.7	3.0	48.67
MALI	70	1975	2.0	9.5	9.0	1.5	58.88
MALI	70	1980	8.5	5.5	8.5	3.5	64.75
MALI	70	1985	4.5	4.0	8.5	5.5	55.75
MALI	70	1988	4.5	4.5	9.5	2.5	53.00
MOROCCO	71	1975	4.5	4.5	6.3	4.5	49.58
MOROCCO	71	1980	6.0	4.5	4.7	3.5	46.54
MOROCCO	71	1985	8.5	4.0	2.7	6.0	51.29
MOROCCO	71	1988	7.5	3.0	3.0	5.5	45.75
NIGERIA	72	1975	1.0	7.0	6.0	5.5	50.63
NIGERIA	72	1980	5.0	3.5	7.0	6.0	52.75
NIGERIA	72	1985	6.0	6.0	7.7	4.0	59.67
NIGERIA	72	1988	2.0	5.5	7.0	8.0	56.50
SOUTH AFRICA	73	1975	2.0	7.8	5.3	7.0	56.83
SOUTH AFRICA	73	1980	5.0	6.0	5.7	7.0	59.17
SOUTH AFRICA	73	1985	8.0	5.3	5.7	7.0	63.67
SOUTH AFRICA	73	1988	7.0	4.2	6.5	6.0	58.00
SENEGAL	74	1975	2.5	6.5	8.5	4.5	56.50
SENEGAL	74	1980	5.5	5.3	8.0	3.5	56.00
SENEGAL	74	1985	6.0	4.5	6.3	7.0	58.58
SENEGAL	74	1988	5.0	4.3	6.5	4.0	49.25
TANZANIA	75	1975	5.5	2.5	6.7	4.0	45.54

Table 2: **Index Ratings by Major Category and Summary Rating,**
1975, 1980, 1985, 1988-89.

Country	#	Year	I. (22.5%)	II. (30.0%)	III. (25.0%)	IV (22.5%)	Summary Rating
TANZANIA	75	1980	2.5	3.3	10.0	2.0	44.88
TANZANIA	75	1985	3.5	3.5	5.7	2.0	37.04
TANZANIA	75	1988	3.0	3.0	6.0	6.0	44.25
TUNISIA	76	1975	5.0	7.0	4.5	4.0	52.50
TUNISIA	76	1980	6.0	6.8	6.3	4.5	59.71
TUNISIA	76	1985	5.0	2.0	6.5	4.0	42.50
TUNISIA	76	1988	7.0	2.5	5.5	4.5	47.13
ZAIRE	77	1975	3.0	2.5	7.3	4.0	41.58
ZAIRE	77	1980	1.0	5.0	7.0	4.0	43.75
ZAIRE	77	1985	1.0	5.0	5.5	5.5	43.38
ZAIRE	77	1988	1.0	4.5	5.5	5.5	41.88
ZAMBIA	78	1975	3.0	2.5	5.0	8.0	44.75
ZAMBIA	78	1980	3.0	2.5	4.7	7.0	41.67
ZAMBIA	78	1985	2.0	2.3	5.3	5.0	35.83
ZAMBIA	78	1988	1.0	1.2	5.0	5.5	30.63
ZIMBABWE	79	1975	2.0	4.0	7.0	5.0	45.25
ZIMBABWE	79	1980	4.0	3.0	5.0	6.0	44.00
ZIMBABWE	79	1985	5.0	2.0	4.7	2.5	34.54
ZIMBABWE	79	1988	5.0	0.5	2.3	2.5	24.21

Table 3a: The 1975-1980 average annual growth rate of per capita GNP for the top 15 and bottom 15 rated countries during the 1975-1980 period.

Country	1975 Summary Rating	1980 Summary Rating	1975-80 Growth Rate
Top 15 Countries:			
HONG KONG	82.29	87.38	9.40%
HONDURAS	72.25	72.88	2.93%
CAMEROON	66.63	71.50	7.49%
UNITED STATES	68.00	68.29	2.30%
JAPAN	61.75	69.25	4.07%
PANAMA	63.71	66.25	2.86%
SINGAPORE	60.13	68.83	6.11%
GUATEMALA	65.63	61.50	3.04%
EL SALVADOR	70.08	56.79	-0.97%
SWITZERLAND	62.75	63.58	1.94%
MALI	58.88	64.75	3.39%
PHILIPPINES	59.67	61.96	3.50%
HAITI	62.13	59.13	3.83%
BELGIUM	57.04	61.04	2.74%
GERMANY	58.00	58.83	3.46%
AVERAGE	64.59	66.13	3.74%
Bottom 15 Countries:			
SPAIN	47.88	37.79	0.60%
ZAIRE	41.58	43.75	-3.97%
GHANA	45.29	39.46	-0.32%
ITALY	39.46	43.96	3.81%
FINLAND	38.92	43.63	2.69%
PERU	41.25	38.92	-0.97%
SWEDEN	42.50	37.38	-0.04%
TURKEY	48.00	31.79	0.57%
ICELAND	38.75	38.00	5.44%
CHILE	33.04	42.33	5.72%
JAMAICA	42.38	32.25	-6.11%
PORTUGAL	34.38	37.08	3.64%
ARGENTINA	29.71	29.50	0.87%
EGYPT	27.63	27.71	6.28%
ISRAEL	14.38	21.17	1.70%
AVERAGE	37.68	36.31	1.33%

Table 3b: The 1980-1988 average annual growth rate of per capita GNP for the top 15 and bottom 15 rated countries during the 1985-1988 period.

Country	1985 Summary Rating	1988 Summary Rating	1980-88 Growth Rate
Top 15 Countries:			
HONG KONG	83.25	82.79	8.82%
JAPAN	74.21	73.21	3.54%
UNITED STATES	69.08	74.21	1.98%
MAURITIUS	68.13	73.92	5.14%
SINGAPORE	67.67	73.50	6.35%
SWITZERLAND	67.96	71.42	1.67%
HONDURAS	68.88	67.75	-1.25%
MALAYSIA	68.38	65.29	2.21%
GABON	63.25	66.25	-3.48%
UNITED KINGDOM	58.54	70.38	2.65%
BANGLADESH	64.38	63.25	1.01%
TAIWAN	64.67	62.88	1.57%
GERMANY	57.75	67.25	1.82%
INDONESIA	60.04	63.92	1.38%
BELGIUM	62.75	59.92	1.36%
AVERAGE	66.59	69.06	2.32%
Bottom 15 Countries:			
TANZANIA	37.04	44.25	-2.12%
PORTUGAL	41.46	38.67	2.09%
ICELAND	32.88	44.50	1.69%
MEXICO	40.42	34.71	-1.28%
NORWAY	37.54	36.88	3.12%
SWEDEN	30.54	42.29	1.90%
EGYPT	34.79	38.00	2.92%
PERU	35.75	33.75	-1.57%
ZAMBIA	35.83	30.63	-2.40%
BRAZIL	31.17	32.71	0.03%
ZIMBABWE	34.54	24.21	2.36%
SYRIA	21.25	37.00	-2.05%
ARGENTINA	20.79	28.88	-2.87%
NICARAGUA	16.21	27.50	-3.13%
ISRAEL	20.21	21.13	1.40%
AVERAGE	31.36	34.34	0.01%

Table 4a: The 1975-1980 average annual growth rate of per capita GNP for the top 10 and bottom 10 rated developing countries during the 1975-1980 period.

Country	1975 Summary Rating	1980 Summary Rating	1975-80 Growth Rate
Top 10 Countries:			
HONG KONG	82.29	87.38	9.40%
HONDURAS	72.25	72.88	2.93%
CAMEROON	66.63	71.50	7.49%
PANAMA	63.71	66.25	2.86%
SINGAPORE	60.13	68.83	6.11%
GUATEMALA	65.63	61.50	3.04%
EL SALVADOR	70.08	56.79	-0.97%
MALI	58.88	64.75	3.39%
PHILIPPINES	59.67	61.96	3.50%
HAITI	62.13	59.13	3.83%
AVERAGE	66.14	67.10	4.16%
Bottom 10 Countries:			
ZAIRE	41.58	43.75	-3.97%
GHANA	45.29	39.46	-0.32%
PERU	41.25	38.92	-0.97%
TURKEY	48.00	31.79	0.57%
CHILE	33.04	42.33	5.72%
JAMAICA	42.38	32.25	-6.11%
PORTUGAL	34.38	37.08	3.64%
ARGENTINA	29.71	29.50	0.87%
EGYPT	27.63	27.71	6.28%
ISRAEL	14.38	21.17	1.70%
AVERAGE	35.76	34.40	0.74%

Table 4b: The 1980-1988 average annual growth rate of per capita GNP for the top 10 and bottom 10 rated developing countries during the 1985-1988 period.

Country	1985 Summary Rating	1988 Summary Rating	1980-88 Growth Rate
Top 10 Countries:			
HONG KONG	83.25	82.79	8.82%
MAURITIUS	68.13	73.92	5.14%
SINGAPORE	67.67	73.50	6.35%
HONDURAS	68.88	67.75	-1.25%
MALAYSIA	68.38	65.29	2.21%
GABON	63.25	66.25	-3.48%
BANGLADESH	64.38	63.25	1.01%
TAIWAN	64.67	62.88	1.57%
INDONESIA	60.04	63.92	1.38%
SOUTH AFRICA	63.67	58.00	-0.32%
AVERAGE	67.23	67.75	2.14%
Bottom 10 Countries:			
MEXICO	40.42	34.71	-1.28%
EGYPT	34.79	38.00	2.92%
PERU	35.75	33.75	-1.57%
ZAMBIA	35.83	30.63	-2.40%
BRAZIL	31.17	32.71	0.03%
ZIMBABWE	34.54	24.21	2.36%
SYRIA	21.25	37.00	-2.05%
ARGENTINA	20.79	28.88	-2.87%
NICARAGUA	16.21	27.50	-3.13%
ISRAEL	20.21	21.13	1.40%
AVERAGE	29.10	30.85	-0.66%

Table 3b presents parallel growth rate data during the 1980s for countries with high and low economic freedom ratings in 1985 and 1988. During the 1980-88 period, the average growth rate of the fifteen top-rated countries was 2.32 percent, compared to 0.01 percent for the bottom-rated countries. Only two of the top-rated countries—Honduras, and Gabon—experienced negative growth rates during the 1980s, compared to seven of the bottom-rated countries. Interestingly, only three of the bottom-rated countries (Norway, Egypt, and Zimbabwe) were able to achieve the average growth rate of the fifteen top rated countries.

Some might argue that the concept of economic freedom has less relevance for developing countries. Others may feel that it is improper to make comparisons between industrial nations and developing countries. Tables 4a and 4b present growth rate data for the top ten and bottom ten *less developed countries.* Twenty-one, high-income industrial countries were excluded from this analysis. During the 1975-1980 period, the average growth rate of the ten highest rated developing countries was 4.16 percent, compared to 0.74 percent for the bottom ten countries. Among the ten top-rated countries only the war-torn country of El Salvador experienced a negative growth in per capita real GNP during the period.

Table 4b presents similar data for the 1980s. Once again, the annual growth rate of the top-rated countries (2.14 percent) was well above the average growth rate for the bottom-rated countries (-0.66).

Clearly, one would not expect a close relationship between economic freedom at a point in time and the economic growth in the immediate past. If a nation moves toward economic freedom, it will take time to convince decision-makers that the change is permanent, rather than temporary. Thus, there will generally be a lag, perhaps a lag of several years between improvements in economic freedom and substantial increases in economic growth. In addition, political instability will cause people to "discount" the current conditions. When fear of dramatic future change is present, an index that reflects current conditions may be a misleading indicator. Given these deficiencies it is particularly interesting to note that countries with more economic freedom have, on average, experienced more rapid rates of economic growth than those with less freedom.

Has economic freedom changed substantially in some countries? How do *changes* in economic freedom affect economic growth? Exhibit 5 sheds light on these questions. Between 1975 and 1988, twelve countries experienced an increase of ten units or more in our summary index of economic freedom. Some of these counties (Chile, Pakistan, and Ireland, for example) moved from a very low rating into the middle rating category. Others, such as Mauritius, Singapore, and Japan, were initially in the middle category and they moved into upper-middle and top-rating categories. Except for Ghana and Chile (which experienced a positive growth rate for the entire 1975-1988 period), countries that improved their economic freedom rating also experienced economic growth during both 1975-1988 and 1980-1988. The twelve countries with a 10 unit or more increase in our index of economic freedom achieved an average growth rate in per capita GNP of 2.88 percent.

Table 5 also presents data for the fourteen countries for which the summary index of economic freedom declined by 10 units or more during the 1975-1988 period. A few of the countries (for example, El Salvador, Cameroon, and Guatemala) had pretty good ratings in 1975. Others had low rates at the beginning of the period and they sank even lower. The outcome for countries experiencing a decline in economic freedom was quite different from those experiencing an increase. Only one (Cameroon) of these fourteen countries was able to achieve a growth rate of per capita GNP in excess of 1.4 percent during the 1975-1988 period. On average, the per capita GNP of these countries was unchanged during 1975-1988, and it *declined* at an annual rate of 0.69 percent during the 1980s. In fact, only five of the fourteen countries were able to achieve a positive growth rate during the 1980s. Only one (Zimbabwe was just barely able to do so) of the 14 countries was able to achieve the *average* growth rate of per capita GNP for the 12 countries experiencing an increase in economic freedom.

Concluding Thoughts

We would like to conclude with a few words of caution. First, it is important to distinguish between economic freedom and political freedom. Milton Friedman, among others has argued that it will be difficult to maintain political freedom in the absence of economic freedom. With regard to extended time periods, this is probably true. However, we do observe countries with substantial economic freedom—freedom of exchange, protection of private property, freedom of resource use, and consumer

Table 5: The 1980-88 and 1975-88 average annual growth rates of per capita GNP for those countries that experienced substantial changes (10 units or more) in in the Summary Rating.

Country	1975 Summary Rating	1988 Summary Rating	Summary Rating Change	1980-88 Growth Rate	1975-88 Growth Rate
Countries with Substantial Increases in the Rating					
MAURITIUS	54.75	73.92	19.17	5.14%	3.84%
CHILE	33.04	50.96	17.92	-0.37%	1.93%
PAKISTAN	39.83	57.42	17.58	3.24%	3.15%
TAIWAN	47.13	62.88	15.75	1.57%	3.53%
UNITED KINGDOM	55.29	70.38	15.08	2.65%	2.29%
GHANA	45.29	59.13	13.83	-1.92%	-1.31%
MALAYSIA	51.83	65.29	13.46	2.21%	3.69%
SINGAPORE	60.13	73.50	13.38	6.35%	6.25%
JAPAN	61.75	73.21	11.46	3.54%	3.74%
IRELAND	46.38	57.67	11.29	1.01%	1.49%
DENMARK	37.42	48.38	10.96	1.66%	1.75%
EGYPT	27.63	38.00	10.38	2.92%	4.20%
AVERAGE	46.70	60.89	14.19	2.33%	2.88%
Countries with Substantial Decreases in the Rating					
MEXICO	44.83	34.71	-10.13	-1.28%	0.75%
GREECE	53.58	43.21	-10.38	0.22%	1.29%
HAITI	62.13	51.63	-10.50	-2.20%	0.08%
DOM REP	52.00	40.58	-11.42	-0.82%	0.42%
ECUADOR	52.67	41.00	-11.67	-0.07%	1.09%
MALAWI	61.04	48.67	-12.38	1.12%	0.64%
ZAMBIA	44.75	30.63	-14.13	-2.40%	-2.50%
COSTA RICA	61.83	45.79	-16.04	-0.73%	0.43%
CAMEROON	66.63	48.46	-18.17	2.03%	4.10%
GUATEMALA	65.63	46.46	-19.17	-2.79%	-0.59%
BRAZIL	53.17	32.71	-20.46	0.03%	1.36%
ZIMBABWE	45.25	24.21	-21.04	2.36%	-0.89%
EL SALVADOR	70.08	48.71	-21.38	-2.01%	-1.61%
NICARAGUA	59.00	27.50	-31.50	-3.13%	-4.55%
AVERAGE	56.61	40.30	-16.31	-0.69%	0.00%

choice—even though political freedom is limited. Hong Kong and Singapore illustrate this point. On the other hand, there are countries with substantial political freedom—free elections, competitive political parties, and relatively free access to the mass communications media—that nonetheless impose substantial limitations on economic freedom. Israel illustrates this case. Clearly, at any point in time the linkage between economic and political freedom is far from perfect. This is one reason why it is important to quantify both.

Second, the index in this paper is designed to measure economic freedom at a point in time. It is not forward looking. Ominous clouds with regard to the future of freedom may already be present. For example, the enemies of economic freedom may already occupy influential positions in both the media and the government. Political corruption may be a problem. Civil unrest may be widespread. As currently devised, however, our indexes of current economic freedom will fail to register these elements and their implications for the future of economic freedom.

Finally, inability to develop a reasonable indicator for government regulatory activities that are inconsistent with economic freedom is a major shortcoming of our measures. Government regulations are a substitute for government expenditures. Rather than taxing and spending, some countries rely more heavily on mandates and regulations. For example, while some countries levy taxes to fund unemployment benefits, others may mandate that employers provide terminated workers with severance benefits for lengthy periods of time. Both are interferences with the freedom of contract, but our indexes will only register the former. Similarly, governments often institute business and occupational licensing and property-use regulations which, in effect, prohibit transactions among parties. Simultaneously, other regulations may require a potential buyer or seller to deal only with various segments of the population (for example, government workers, the military, or favored groups). Such regulations are highly inconsistent with economic freedom. Unfortunately, our index, as currently structured, generally fails to capture the presence of such regulations.

In our judgement, the index of this paper is a start. We will continue to seek improvements and, perhaps more importantly, we hope that others will also be challenged to pursue improvements in this area.

Notes

[1] A full discussion of the concept of economic freedom is beyond the scope of this paper. For additional information on this issue, see D. Friedman (1989), M. Friedman (1962, 1981, 1983), Rothbard (1970, 1973, 1982), Rabushka (1991), Nozick (1974), Hayek (1944, 1973, 1989), Buchanan and Tullock (1971), and Hoppe (1989).

[2] Milton Friedman made this point very forcefully at an address to the San Francisco Conference of the International Society of Individual Liberty, August 1990.

[3] We owe this example to Leon Loew, who used it in an address to the San Francisco Conference of the International Society of Individual Liberty, August 1990.

[4] See Roger Pilon (1988) for additional analysis of this topic.

[5] We had hoped that we would be able to include a variable on land ownership (percent of the land owned by the government). However, we have been unable to develop this variable for more than a handful of countries.

We also anticipated including a variable on union membership. However, unions are difficult to analyze in that they are associated with two completely different kinds of actions. Their legitimate role is to organize (or threaten) quits en masse unless the terms of employment are improved. Early labor union legislation prohibited this on the grounds of criminal conspiracy. But this is nonsense, since workers do not lose their right to quit merely because others choose to exercise it at the same time. People who do not have the right to quit are called slaves, and slavery is certainly incompatible with economic liberty.

But unions often also seek to prevent employers from hiring replacements for striking workers who are refusing to work at the terms of employment affirmed by the employer. They argue that the jobs "belong" to the workers. But an employment contract is an agreement between two parties; any rights must command mutual, not unilateral support. The union which goes out on strike and demands the right to prevent "scabs" from acting as replacement workers is like a husband who demands the right to leave his wife, and also wants to prevent her from dating other people. Given our inability to develop a unionism variable which is unequivocally associated with denigration of economic freedom, we chose not to include a variable in this area.

[6] Several reviewers of this paper have argued that monetary instability is not a violation of economic freedom as long as individuals are free to conduct transactions in gold or in currencies other than the one issued by their government. We are sympathetic to this position. However, most all modern governments required the payment of taxes in domestic currency units. Countries with legal tender laws require that their currency be accepted domestically as means of payments. In addition, governments often interfere with currency exchanges and establish restrictions which make it difficult to conduct business with alternative currencies (or gold). Thus, in most countries it will be difficult to do business without the use of the domestic currency. Given these practical obstacles to the use of alternative currencies in most countries, the authors feel that it is appropriate to include a monetary instability component in the index.

[7] If economic freedom consists of not interfering with owners in the use of their private property, then forcibly taking some of their wealth, with the sole purpose of giving it to others, is a clear violation of economic freedom (Epstein, 1985). The only possible exception to this rule is transfers of income or wealth in order to return stolen property. But here, the money must be returned to those who can show that they were the victims (or heirs) of the theft, and the wealth must be taken from those who were responsible for the stealing (or from their heirs).

[8] An Appendix (2) in the extended version of the paper presents the actual data by country and year for each of the eleven variables used in the index, and the corresponding zero to ten index rating. These data are available from the Fraser Institute or the authors for a limited period of time.

[9] An alternative methodology was used for the following three variables: nonfinancial government enterprises in key industries (IIB), price controls (IIC), and marginal tax rates (IIIB). Appendix I describes the procedures used to develop the zero to ten rating scale for these variables.

Appendix 1: The Methods and Data Sources
Used to Construct the Indexes

The purpose of this appendix is to explain how each component of the index was constructed and indicate the data sources used in the construction of the index.

(IA) Fluctuations in the Money Supply and (IB) the Inflation Rate

The money supply and GNP deflator data for each country were assembled for the 1971-1988 period. The money supply data are from the IMF, *International Financial Statistics Yearbook*, while the GNP deflator data are from the World Bank, *World Tables 1989-1990*. Utilizing these data, the standard deviation for both in the annual money supply growth and the annual rate of inflation during the last 5 years was derived for 1975, 1980, 1985, and 1988. The standard deviation data for 1985 were used to allocate an equal number of countries into each of eleven ratings ranging from zero to ten. The standard deviation intervals from the 1985 base year were derived and then used to rate each country in the other years. Countries with the most stability in the growth rates of the money supply and inflation rate were given the highest ratings.

(IIA) Total Government Expenditures as a Percent of GNP

Data on total government expenditures and GNP were obtained by country for 1975, 1980, 1985, and 1988. Both of these variables were measured in the country's domestic currency units. Using the 1985 data, countries were placed into each of the eleven ratings and the interval for each of the ratings was derived. The intervals from the 1985 ratings were then used to rate each country in the other years. Countries with the lowest government expenditure/GNP ratio were given the highest ratings.

(IIBi) Total Number of Central Government Enterprises

Since 1977 the International Monetary Fund has provided a list of the Nonfinancial Government Enterprises of the central governments for most countries. It was necessary to utilize 1977 data in our 1975 index and 1979 data in our 1980 index. The total number of government enterprises was tabulated for each year. As for most other variables, the intervals for each of the 11 ratings were derived in 1985 and these base year intervals were then used to rate the countries in the other years.

(IIBii) Government Enterprises in Designated Industries

The International Monetary Fund data also indicate the industry (or business activity) of government nonfinancial enterprises. These data were used to determine whether a government enterprise was operating in the following areas: (1) agriculture products, (2) airlines, (3) radio and television broadcasting, (4) steel, aluminum, and/or cement manufacturing, (5) chemicals and fertilizers, (6) fishing or mining (7) hotels and/or theaters, (8) petroleum, gas and/or coal, (9) pharmaceuticals, and (10) real estate and/or housing. Countries which did not have a government enterprise in any of these areas were given a rating of ten for this variable. One point was subtracted for each of the ten areas in which the country was operating a government enterprise. Thus, a country would receive a rating of zero if the central government of the country was operating an enterprise in all ten of the areas. Since this procedure places each country on a zero to ten scale, no further adjustments were necessary for this variable.

(IIC) Price Controls

The *World Competitiveness Report 1989* (p. 95) contains survey data indicating the "extent to which companies can set their prices freely: 0 = not at all, to 100 = very much so." Thirty-two countries were surveyed. Since this is the most comprehensive quantifiable indicator of the presence or absence of price controls which we could find, we used it to rate these 32 countries. These countries were rated as follows:

Percent Indicating Companies Can
Set Prices Freely (countries in the
category are indicated in parenthesis)   *Rating of Country*

More than 90% (Hong Kong)	10
85% to 90% (Germany, New Zealand)	9
80% to 85% (Canada, Turkey, U.K., U.S., Singapore)	8
75% to 80% (Ireland, Netherlands, Switzerland)	7
70% to 75% (Australia, Denmark, Taiwan, Finland, France, Japan, Spain, Sweden, Indonesia)	6
65% to 70% (Austria, Italy, Norway, Malaysia)	5
60% to 65% (Portugal, Thailand)	4
55% to 60% (India, Korea)	3
50% to 55% (Belgium)	2
45% to 50% (None in this range)	1
Less than 45% (Greece, Brazil, Mexico)	0

In addition, Price Waterhouse (*Doing Business in [various countries]*) provides a verbal description on the presence or absence of price controls for several countries. This verbal description was used to place countries into the following categories and ratings:

Category	*Rating*
No Price Controls or Marketing boards	10
Only a few items (primarily agricultural goods) are subject to price controls	8
Price controls on some items; however, the price of most commodities is determined by market forces	6
Price controls on most stable goods (e.g. foods, clothing, and housing), but the price of most other goods is determined by market forces	5
Price controls on a significant number of both agricultural and manufactured goods	3
Widespread use of price controls	0

This zero to ten scale was used directly to rate each country. The data on the price control variable were available only for the "late 1980s."

(IIIA) Transfers and Subsidies As A Percent of GNP

Data on "subsidies and other current transfers" were available from the International Monetary Fund. The transfer data were divided by GNP. Both were measured in the domestic currency units of each country. If this variable was unavailable, data on the central government expenditures on "Housing, amenities, social security, and welfare" (from the *World Development Report*) as a percent of GNP were used to estimate the size of the transfer sector. As in prior cases, the 1985 data on transfers and subsidies as a percent of GNP were arranged from lowest to highest and used to allocate an equal number of countries into each of the zero to ten ratings in 1985. The intervals for each rating for 1985 were then derived and used to rate each country during the other years.

(IIIB) Marginal Tax Rates

Data on the top marginal tax rate and the income threshold at which the top rate takes effect were available for 1974, 1979, 1984, and 1989 from Price Waterhouse. These years were used to calculate the 1975, 1980, 1985, and 1988 indexes, respectively. The exchange rate at year end was used to convert to U.S. dollars. Finally, the U.S. Consumer Price Index was used to convert the income threshold for each year into 1982-1984 dollars.

The following conversion table was used to rate the marginal tax rate/income threshold of each country:

Top Marginal Tax Rate	Income Threshold Level (1982-1984 U.S. dollars)				
	Less than 25,000	25,000 to 50,000	50,000 to 100,000	100,000 to 250,000	More than 250,000
15% or less	10	10	10	10	10
16 to 20	9	10	10	10	10
21 to 25	8	9	10	10	10
26 to 30	7	8	9	10	10
31 to 35	6	7	8	9	10
36 to 40	5	6	7	8	9
41 to 45	4	5	6	7	8
46 to 50	3	4	5	6	7
51 to 55	2	3	4	5	6
56 to 60	1	2	3	4	5
61 to 65	0	1	2	3	4
66 to 70	0	0	1	2	3
71 to 75	0	0	0	1	2
76 to 80	0	0	0	0	1
More than 80	0	0	0	0	0

When there was a range of top marginal tax rates within a country, as was sometimes the case under federal systems of government, the midpoint of the top rates for the country was used to derive the rating for this variable.

(IIIC) Conscription

Data on conscription and the number of conscriptees per 1000 population were obtained from the International Institute for Strategic Studies, *The Military Balance* for each year. (Note: It was necessary to use the 1978-1979 data in the construction of the 1980 index.) Countries with a voluntary military service were given a rating of 10. If a country uses conscription to obtain military personal, the number of conscriptees (or the number in the armed forces if the number of conscriptees was unavailable) per 1000 population was derived. This data for 1985 was then used to derive the intervals for each country. In turn, the 1985 interval data were used to rate countries in the other years. Countries with the most conscriptees per 1000 population were given the lowest ratings.

(IVA) Taxes on International Trade

Data on "Taxes—International Trade Transactions" were obtained for each country from the International Monetary Fund. This number was divided by the sum of imports plus exports to derive an average tax rate for international trade transaction. This average tax rate was then used to allocate countries into the 11 rating intervals for 1985. The 1985 intervals for each rating were derived and used to rate each country for the other years. The larger the ratio of taxes on international trade relative to the size of the nation's trade sector (imports plus exports), the lower the rating of the country.

(IVB) Actual Size of Trade Sector Compared to the Expected Size.

The size of trade sector as a percent of GNP is influenced by size of country and income. Small countries tend to have smaller domestic markets and therefore larger trade sectors. Similarly, the size of the trade sector tends to increase with per capita income. The necessary data were obtained to estimate the following regression equation:

$$T_c \quad = \quad F\ (Pop_c, GNP_c, t_c)$$

where

T_c = is expected size of trade sector as a percent of GNP,
Pop_c = is the logarithm of the population of the country,
GNP_c = is the country's real income in U.S. dollars, and
t_c = is the country's average tax rate on international trade.

Dummy variables were included to indicate the year in the estimated equation. The estimate equation for the expected size of the trade sector is presented below:

Variable	Coefficient	t-ratio
Constant	.5622	16.6
Population	-.0742	-10.6
Per Capita GNP	-.3268	-1.0
Average Trade Tax	-.5470	-4.1
1980 (dummy)	.0423	1.5
1985 (dummy)	.0343	1.2
1987 (dummy)	.0279	1.0

$R^2 = .33$
$n = 314$

This regression equation was used to estimate the expected size of the trade sector for each country. The actual size of the trade sector of each country was then compared with its estimated expected size. If a country has substantial nontax trade restraints, one would expect that the actual size of the trade sector would be smaller than the expected size. When the actual size of a country's trade sector is small relative to expected size the country is given a low rating.

The following table summarizes the data sources used for the development of each component of our index.

The Primary Data Source For Variables	
Variables	**Primary Data Source[a]**
IA. Money Supply	International Monetary Fund, *International Financial Statistics Yearbook, 1989*
IB. GNP Deflator	World Bank, *World Tables 1989-90*
IIA. Total Government Expenditures	International Monetary Fund, *Government Finance Statistics Yearbook*, (various years)
IIB. Nonfinancial Government Enterprises (both the total and number in key industries)	International Monetary Fund, *Government Finance Statistics Yearbook*, (various years)
IIIA. Transfer Expenditures as a Percent of GNP	International Monetary Fund, *Government Finance Statistics Yearbook*, (various years)
IVA. International Trade Taxes	International Monetary Fund, *Government Finance Statistics Yearbook*, (various years).
IIC. Price Controls	World Economic Forum, *The World Competitiveness Report, 1989* and Price Waterhouse, *Doing Business in* (name of country)
IIIB. Marginal Tax Rates (and Income Thresholds)	Price Waterhouse, *Invidivual Tax Rates*, (various issues)
IIIC. Conscripts Per 100 Population	International Institute for Strategic Studies, *The Military Balance* (annual-various issues)
IVA. and IVB. Exports, Imports, Population and GNP (in both domestic currency and U.S. dollars)	World Bank, *World Tables 1989-90*

[a] In addition, the following data sources were also used when data were unavailable from primary sources: The World Bank, *World Development Report* (annual); James W. Wilkie (ed.), *Statistical Abstract of Latin America*, (Los Angeles: UCLA Latin American Center Publications, (various issues); Directorate-General of the Budget-Republic of China, *Statistical Yearbook of the Republic of China*, (various issues); Government Information Services, Hong Kong, *Hong Kong 1989*, (and other years).

Appendix 2: IA—The standard deviation of the annual growth rate of the money supply for the previous five years

Country	#	1975		1980		1985		1988	
UNITED STATES	1	0.0177	10	0.0071	10	0.0234	10	0.0513	7
CANADA	2	0.0573	6	0.0396	8	0.0994	3	0.0990	3
AUSTRALIA	3	0.0854	3	0.0399	8	0.0514	7	0.0929	3
JAPAN	4	0.0733	4	0.0467	7	0.0336	9	0.0262	10
NEW ZEALAND	5	0.1002	3	0.0756	4	0.0403	8	0.1394	2
AUSTRIA	6	0.0544	6	0.0452	7	0.0342	9	0.0283	10
BELGIUM	7	0.0388	8	0.0297	9	0.0278	10	0.0249	10
DENMARK	8	0.0887	3	0.0331	9	0.1012	3	0.1099	2
FINLAND	9	0.0606	5	0.0816	4	0.0336	9	0.0629	5
FRANCE	10	0.0208	10	0.0220	10	0.0519	7	0.0569	6
GERMANY	11	0.0468	7	0.0494	7	0.0235	10	0.0198	10
ICELAND	12	0.0652	5	0.1161	2	0.2843	1	0.3048	1
IRELAND	13	0.0528	6	0.0669	5	0.0362	8	0.0332	9
ITALY	14	0.0488	7	0.0431	8	0.0235	10	0.0193	10
NETHERLANDS	15	0.0691	5	0.0363	8	0.0357	9	0.2390	1
NORWAY	16	0.0219	10	0.0358	9	0.0482	7	0.1501	2
SPAIN	17	0.0289	10	0.0455	7	0.0349	9	0.0340	9
SWEDEN	18	0.0257	10	0.0160	10	0.4763	0	0.0445	7
SWITZERLAND	19	0.0587	6	0.0899	3	0.0324	9	0.0362	8
UNITED KINGDOM	20	0.0457	7	0.0581	6	0.0302	9	0.0330	9
ARGENTINA	21	0.6729	0	0.6275	0	1.7982	0	1.9508	0
BOLIVIA	22	0.1151	2	0.1167	2	18.2952	0	18.7233	0
BRAZIL	23	0.0485	7	0.1746	1	0.9999	0		
CHILE	24	0.7625	0	0.6272	0	0.0575	6		
COLOMBIA	25	0.0655	5	0.0328	9	0.0529	6	0.0672	5
COSTA RICA	26	0.0703	5	0.0721	4	0.2234	1	0.1870	1
DOMINICAN REP	27	0.1222	2	0.1160	2	0.1489	2	0.1282	2
ECUADOR	28	0.1491	2	0.0729	4	0.0784	4	0.1200	2
EL SALVADOR	29	0.0565	6	0.1286	2	0.0926	3	0.0891	3
GUATEMALA	30	0.0667	5	0.1268	2	0.2054	1	0.1788	1
HAITI	31	0.0822	4	0.1621	1	0.1034	3	0.2047	1
HONDURAS	32	0.0748	4	0.0949	3	0.0501	7	0.0584	6
JAMAICA	33	0.0688	5	0.1198	2	0.0572	6	0.1724	1
MEXICO	34	0.0559	6	0.0155	10	0.1119	2	0.2371	1

Appendix 2: IA—The standard deviation of the annual growth rate of the money supply for the previous five years

Country	#	1975		1980		1985		1988	
NICARAGUA	35	0.1750	1	0.2515	1	0.1560	1		
PANAMA	36	0.1527	2	0.0452	7	3.0642	0		
PARAGUAY	37	0.0804	4	0.0649	5	0.1275	2	0.0992	3
PERU	38	0.1075	3	0.1886	1	0.9005	0	0.7810	0
URUGUAY	39	0.1363	2	0.1906	1	0.3629	1	0.2038	1
VENEZUELA	40	0.1216	2	0.0542	6	0.0730	4	0.1135	2
CYPRUS	41	0.0606	5	0.0798	4	0.0613	5	0.0480	7
EGYPT	42	0.0616	5	0.1338	2	0.0442	7	0.0301	9
GREECE	43	0.0259	10	0.0281	10	0.0283	10	0.0355	9
ISRAEL	44	1.5557	0	0.6360	0	1.0188	0	1.2572	0
MALTA	45	0.0536	6	0.0354	9	0.0447	7	0.0361	8
PORTUGAL	46	0.1087	3	0.0600	6	0.0701	5	0.1024	3
SYRIA	47	0.1255	2	0.0632	5	0.0401	8	0.0553	6
TURKEY	48	0.0392	8	0.1423	2	0.0925	3	0.1633	1
BANGLADESH	49			0.0748	4	0.1340	2	0.1137	2
FIJI	50	0.0471	7	0.0316	9	0.0667	5	0.2305	1
HONG KONG	51	0.1520	2	0.0430	8	0.0788	4	0.1164	2
INDIA	52	0.0262	10	0.0475	7	0.0250	10	0.0283	10
INDONESIA	53	0.0699	5	0.1015	3	0.0790	4	0.0283	10
KOREA	54	0.1044	3	0.0850	3	0.1596	1	0.0673	5
MALAYSIA	55	0.1270	2	0.0197	10	0.0475	7	0.0546	6
MAURITIUS	56	0.1889	1	0.0680	5	0.0423	8	0.0307	9
PAKISTAN	57	0.0664	5	0.0593	6	0.0563	6	0.0536	6
PHILIPPINES	58	0.0632	5	0.0447	7	0.1402	2	0.0733	4
SINGAPORE	59	0.0950	3	0.0310	9	0.0638	5	0.0460	7
SRI LANKA	60	0.0393	8	0.0839	4	0.0608	5	0.0630	5
TAIWAN	61	0.1274	2	0.1020	3	0.0301	9	0.1583	1
THAILAND	62	0.0543	6	0.0399	8	0.0413	8	0.0834	4
BOTSWANA	63			0.1356	2	0.0810	4	0.0761	4
CAMEROON	64	0.0942	3	0.0739	4	0.0864	3	0.0456	7
COTE D'IVOIRE	65	0.1062	3	0.2038	1	0.0554	6	0.0543	6
GABON	66	0.1962	1	0.2773	1	0.0583	6	0.0412	8
GHANA	67	0.1507	2	0.2231	1	0.1439	2	0.0677	5
KENYA	68	0.0622	5	0.1314	2	0.0464	7	0.1270	2

Appendix 2: IA—The standard deviation of the annual growth rate of the money supply for the previous five years

Country	#	1975		1980		1985		1988	
MALAWI	69	0.1440	2	0.1337	2	0.0670	5	0.1301	2
MALI	70	0.1688	1	0.0500	7	0.1063	3	0.1068	3
MOROCCO	71	0.0469	7	0.0387	8	0.0441	7	0.0382	8
NIGERIA	72	0.3097	1	0.1678	1	0.0306	9	0.1439	2
SOUTH AFRICA	73	4.1912	0	0.0503	7	0.0238	10	0.0604	5
SENEGAL	74	0.1803	1	0.0700	5	0.0802	4	0.0640	5
TANZANIA	75	0.0422	8	0.1502	2	0.0790	4	0.1425	2
TUNISIA	76	0.0437	8	0.0477	7	0.0648	5	0.0636	5
ZAIRE	77	0.1142	2	0.2373	1	0.1812	1	0.3350	1
ZAMBIA	78	0.1500	2	0.1236	2	0.1211	2	0.2584	1
ZIMBABWE	79			0.1105	2	0.0522	6	0.0754	4
AVERAGE		0.1768	4.5	0.1075	4.8	0.4080	5.1	0.3950	4.5

Appendix 2: IB—The standard deviation of the annual growth rate of the price level for the previous five years

Country	#	1975		1980		1985		1988	
UNITED STATES	1	0.0193	8	0.0109	10	0.0244	7	0.0038	10
CANADA	2	0.0386	5	0.0190	9	0.0319	6	0.0080	10
AUSTRALIA	3	0.0430	5	0.0221	8	0.0186	9	0.0101	10
JAPAN	4	0.0574	3	0.0145	9	0.0083	10	0.0063	10
NEW ZEALAND	5	0.0340	5	0.0194	8	0.0394	5	0.0340	5
AUSTRIA	6	0.0120	10	0.0062	10	0.0131	9	0.0101	10
BELGIUM	7	0.0304	6	0.0171	9	0.0078	10	0.0169	9
DENMARK	8	0.0204	8	0.0084	10	0.0242	7	0.0043	10
FINLAND	9	0.0529	4	0.0180	9	0.0200	8	0.0146	9
FRANCE	10	0.0261	7	0.0080	10	0.0229	8	0.0168	9
GERMANY	11	0.0095	10	0.0041	10	0.0095	10	0.0053	10
ICELAND	12	0.1121	2	0.0746	2	0.1850	1	0.0367	5
IRELAND	13	0.0527	4	0.0347	5	0.0484	4	0.0193	8
ITALY	14	0.0513	4	0.0220	8	0.0357	5	0.0203	8
NETHERLANDS	15	0.0203	8	0.0164	9	0.0201	8	0.0060	10
NORWAY	16	0.0205	8	0.0308	6	0.0331	5	0.0193	8
SPAIN	17	0.0369	5	0.0321	6	0.0169	9	0.0230	8
SWEDEN	18	0.0248	7	0.0310	6	0.0124	10	0.0076	10
SWITZERLAND	19	0.0108	10	0.0115	10	0.0205	8	0.0046	10
UNITED KINGDOM	20	0.0750	2	0.0265	7	0.0245	7	0.0104	10
ARGENTINA	21	0.6002	0	1.1778	0	2.3715	0	2.5465	0
BOLIVIA	22	0.2066	1	0.1095	2	44.4849	0	44.7047	0
BRAZIL	23	0.0689	3	0.1788	1	0.5584	0	1.9621	0
CHILE	24	2.5116	0	0.8160	0	0.0830	2	0.0610	3
COLOMBIA	25	0.0571	3	0.0420	5	0.0165	9	0.0284	6
COSTA RICA	26	0.0881	2	0.0443	4	0.2415	1	4.1930	0
DOMINICAN REP	27	0.0658	3	0.0466	4	0.1316	1	0.1344	1
ECUADOR	28	0.1452	1	0.0437	4	0.1023	2	0.1000	2
EL SALVADOR	29	0.0442	4	0.0745	2	0.0492	4	0.0905	2
GUATEMALA	30	0.0648	3	0.0360	5	0.0530	4	0.1318	1
HAITI	31	0.0585	3	0.0654	3	0.0308	6	0.0417	5
HONDURAS	32	0.0417	5	0.0297	6	0.0117	10	0.0114	10
JAMAICA	33	0.0992	2	0.0514	4	0.0995	2	0.2197	1
MEXICO	34	0.0611	3	0.0495	4	0.2042	1	0.3122	0
NICARAGUA	35	0.0905	2	0.1378	1	0.5989	0	1.5771	0
PANAMA	36	0.0314	6	0.0227	8	0.0128	10	0.0135	9
PARAGUAY	37	0.0749	2	0.0524	4	0.0747	2	0.0332	5
PERU	38	0.0575	3	0.1695	1	0.3633	0	2.1504	0

Appendix 2: IB—The standard deviation of the annual growth rate of the price level for the previous five years

Country	#	1975		1980		1985		1988	
URUGUAY	39	0.2736	1	0.1038	2	0.2233	1	0.0667	3
VENEZUELA	40	0.1503	1	0.0742	2	0.0518	4	0.1333	1
CYPRUS	41	0.0323	6	0.0172	9	0.0653	3	0.0161	9
EGYPT	42	0.0404	5	0.0475	4	0.0339	5	0.0653	3
GREECE	43	0.0719	3	0.0237	7	0.0266	7	0.0197	8
ISRAEL	44	4.0173	0	0.3299	0	1.0218	0	1.5022	0
MALTA	45	0.0169	9	0.0298	6	0.0293	6	0.0128	10
PORTUGAL	46	0.0521	4	0.0327	6	0.0251	7	0.0555	3
SYRIA	47	0.0885	2	0.0425	5	0.0527	4	0.1174	2
TURKEY	48	0.0424	5	0.3138	0	0.0848	2	0.1164	2
BANGLADESH	49	0.2754	1	0.0948	2	0.0402	5	0.0375	5
FIJI	50	0.0907	2	0.0568	3	0.0384	5	0.0248	7
HONG KONG	51	0.0353	5	0.0542	4	0.0240	7	0.0230	8
INDIA	52	0.0643	3	0.0475	4	0.0119	10	0.0048	10
INDONESIA	53	0.1600	1	0.1022	2	0.0283	6	0.0418	5
KOREA	54	0.0712	3	0.0327	6	0.0489	4	0.0060	10
MALAYSIA	55	0.0710	3	0.0303	6	0.0180	9	0.0235	7
MAURITIUS	56	0.2018	1	0.0799	2	0.0135	9	0.0105	10
PAKISTAN	57	0.0855	2	0.0159	9	0.0229	8	0.0263	7
PHILIPPINES	58	0.0873	2	0.0338	5	0.1548	1	0.1733	1
SINGAPORE	59	0.0482	4	0.0374	5	0.0218	8	0.0113	10
SRI LANKA	60	0.0778	2	0.0360	5	0.0780	2	0.0682	3
TAIWAN	61	0.1717	1	0.0561	3	0.0618	3	0.0044	10
THAILAND	62	0.0799	2	0.0279	7	0.0300	6	0.0253	7
BOTSWANA	63	0.0679	3	0.0828	2	0.0601	3	0.0796	2
CAMEROON	64	0.0519	4	0.0191	8	0.0111	10	0.0411	5
COTE D'IVORE	65	0.0915	2	0.1345	1	0.0577	3	0.0613	3
GABON	66	0.2368	1	0.1149	2	0.0652	3	0.0899	2
GHANA	67	0.0886	2	0.1715	1	0.3811	0	0.0725	2
KENYA	68	0.0497	4	0.0617	3	0.0177	9	0.0142	9
MALAWI	69	0.0531	4	0.0801	2	0.0212	8	0.0473	4
MALI	70	0.0566	3	0.0127	10	0.0329	6	0.0298	6
MOROCCO	71	0.0839	2	0.0454	4	0.0092	10	0.0239	7
NIGERIA	72	0.1633	1	0.0180	9	0.0694	3	0.1195	2
SOUTH AFRICA	73	0.0530	4	0.0602	3	0.0312	6	0.0151	9
SENEGAL	74	0.0531	4	0.0287	6	0.0225	8	0.0412	5
TANZANIA	75	0.0563	3	0.0564	3	0.0603	3	0.0548	4
TUNISIA	76	0.0768	2	0.0345	5	0.0379	5	0.0171	9
ZAIRE	77	0.0519	4	0.2549	1	0.2246	1	0.2248	1

Country	#	1975		1980		1985		1988	
Appendix 2: IB—The standard deviation of the annual growth rate of the price level for the previous five years									
ZAMBIA	78	0.0541	4	0.0432	4	0.1262	2	0.2063	1
ZIMBABWE	79	0.1075	2	0.0283	6	0.0447	4	0.0310	6
AVERAGE		0.1622	3.6	0.0828	5	0.6783	5.1	0.7892	5.6

Appendix 2: IIA—Total government expenditures as a share of GNP

Country	#	1975		1980		1985		1987	
UNITED STATES	1	35.00	4	34.90	4	37.40	4	36.90	4
CANADA	2	43.00	3	42.00	3	47.30	1	44.50	2
AUSTRALIA	3	34.00	5	33.00	5	39.80	3	39.30	3
JAPAN	4	20.87	9	24.98	7	26.91	7	27.10	7
NEW ZEALAND	5	40.30	3	42.43	3	42.90	3	46.60	2
AUSTRIA	6	48.10	1	50.60	1	53.00	1	53.30	1
BELGIUM	7	46.49	2	55.40	0	59.60	0	55.60	0
DENMARK	8	43.52	2	57.90	0	56.49	0	54.70	1
FINLAND	9	41.20	3	41.50	3	43.30	3	44.40	2
FRANCE	10	42.70	3	44.10	2	50.20	1	49.10	1
GERMANY	11	48.60	1	49.50	1	48.90	1	48.20	1
ICELAND	12	38.50	3	32.20	5	34.30	4	36.60	4
IRELAND	13	49.30	1	53.40	1	57.00	0	55.40	0
ITALY	14	51.00	1	48.40	1	48.80	1	53.20	1
NETHERLANDS	15	52.30	1	57.60	0	59.00	0	63.30	0
NORWAY	16	57.50	0	54.50	1	50.10	1	55.40	0
SPAIN	17	24.15	7	31.20	5	39.90	3	38.80	3
SWEDEN	18	52.20	1	63.20	0	64.80	0	59.20	0
SWITZERLAND	19	35.40	4	37.00	4	38.00	3	37.70	4
UNITED KINGDOM	20	50.70	1	46.80	2	45.50	2	42.10	3
ARGENTINA	21	30.30	6	35.30	4	38.00	3	33.40	5
BOLIVIA	22	11.60	10	13.80	10	22.70	8		
BRAZIL	23	28.80	6	30.40	6	45.70	2	54.90	0
CHILE	24	32.70	5	28.10	7	33.30	5	30.10	6
COLOMBIA	25	14.30	9	16.50	9	16.13	9	16.40	9
COSTA RICA	26	21.00	9	25.80	7	23.50	8	25.00	7
DOM REP	27	17.55	9	16.92	9	12.70	10		
ECUADOR	28	20.94	9	23.73	8	21.39	9	17.90	9
EL SALVADOR	29	14.10	10	16.20	9	15.40	9	12.30	10
GUATEMALA	30	9.80	10	15.80	9	9.70	10	11.20	10
HAITI	31	18.64	9	17.60	9	24.60	7		
HONDURAS	32	17.40	9	14.54	9	17.00	9	20.70	9
JAMAICA	33	35.60	4	43.20	3	40.40	3	47.50	1
MEXICO	34	20.60	9	22.20	8	26.90	7	26.10	7
NICARAGUA	35	20.40	9	32.20	5	63.10	0	58.00	0
PANAMA	36	33.60	5	33.30	5	33.90	5	33.70	5
PARAGUAY	37	11.80	10	11.30	10	11.80	10	12.70	10
PERU	38	24.30	7	26.70	7	23.70	8	17.80	9
URUGUAY	39	24.90	7	24.30	7	24.36	7	27.80	7
VENEZUELA	40	34.40	4	24.05	7	28.77	6	31.00	5
CYPRUS	41	34.50	4	32.10	5	30.80	5	30.20	6

Appendix 2: IIA—Total government expenditures as a share of GNP

Country	#	1975		1980		1985		1987	
EGYPT	42	61.50	0	53.50	1	50.70	1	46.50	2
GREECE	43	31.50	5	36.80	4	43.76	2	38.30	3
ISRAEL	44	67.80	0	64.40	0	68.30	0	62.90	0
MALTA	45	56.20	0	35.50	4	45.40	2	41.10	3
PORTUGAL	46	33.96	5	37.90	4	46.00	2	44.20	2
SYRIA	47	46.79	2	18.18	9			28.10	7
TURKEY	48	21.10	9	25.20	7	25.00	7	21.90	9
BANGLADESH	49	8.50	10	11.70	10	12.10	10	12.20	10
FIJI	50			25.80	7	28.59	6		
HONG KONG	51	13.50	10	10.10	10	15.00	9	14.60	9
INDIA	52	23.00	8	25.40	7	28.80	6	30.50	6
INDONESIA	53	21.30	9	24.00	8	22.70	8	26.80	7
KOREA	54	19.30	9	20.70	9	21.20	9	20.30	9
MALAYSIA	55	36.80	4	38.70	3	43.50	2	35.90	4
MAURITIUS	56	26.23	7	30.10	6	28.30	6	25.20	7
PAKISTAN	57	27.80	7	31.50	5	22.90	8	25.10	7
PHILIPPINES	58	17.60	9	14.66	9	13.40	10	17.33	9
SINGAPORE	59	23.90	8	23.30	8	36.00	4	34.40	4
SRI LANKA	60	26.40	7	43.20	3	34.80	4	31.20	5
TAIWAN	61	21.40	9	23.20	8	22.80	8	20.50	9
THAILAND	62	16.40	9	20.50	9	22.50	8	20.40	9
BOTSWANA	63	30.00	6	34.00	5	31.20	5	37.30	4
CAMEROON	64	16.11	9	13.66	10	21.20	9	23.40	8
COTE D'IVOIRE	65	24.10	7	33.60	5	31.60	5		
GABON	66	42.26	3					45.90	2
GHANA	67	21.90	9	13.40	10	13.50	10	14.10	10
KENYA	68	26.90	7	31.10	5	29.70	6	31.50	5
MALAWI	69	27.00	7	39.80	3	28.10	7	30.10	6
MALI	70			24.43	7	34.88	4	35.50	4
MOROCCO	71	35.40	4	35.20	4	33.20	5	30.30	6
NIGERIA	72	24.10	7			12.90	10	23.60	8
SOUTH AFRICA	73	18.78	9	29.50	6	34.10	5	34.30	4
SENEGAL	74	20.30	9	24.35	7	30.76	6		
TANZANIA	75	34.71	4	30.87	5	26.00	7	20.90	9
TUNISIA	76	31.40	5	35.50	4	40.40	3	36.10	4
ZAIRE	77	36.80	4	29.00	6	29.50	6	31.90	5
ZAMBIA	78	42.80	3	37.00	4	34.90	4	40.30	3
ZIMBABWE	79	37.60	4	42.80	3	47.20	2	47.30	1
AVERAGE		30.81	5.7	32.12	5.4	34.00	5.0	34.63	4.8

Appendix 2: IIB—The total number of non-financial government enterprises with corresponding index

Country	#	'77		'79		'85		'89		'77	'79	'85	'89
		Total number of enterprises...								Designated areas...			
UNITED STATES	1	15	9	15	9	15	9	15	9	9	9	9	9
CANADA	2	35	6	31	6	35	6	39	5	3	3	5	5
AUSTRALIA	3	23	8	23	8	30	7	33	6	6	6	6	6
JAPAN	4	40	5	34	6	30	7	30	7	6	7	7	7
NEW ZEALAND	5	25	8	25	8	22	9	22	9	6	6	3	3
AUSTRIA	6	77	3	82	3	84	2	84	2	1	1	2	2
BELGIUM	7	13	10	13	10	12	10	12	10	7	7	7	7
DENMARK	8			35	6	34	6	30	7		4	4	4
FINLAND	9	30	7	30	7	30	7	34	6	3	4	3	3
FRANCE	10			8	10	7	10	12	10		8	8	7
GERMANY	11	51	4	51	4	56	3	54	4	7	7	5	5
ICELAND	12	33	6	47	4	46	4	38	6	3	3	3	3
IRELAND	13	23	8	26	7	25	8	25	8	4	4	3	3
ITALY	14					380	0	375	0			1	1
NETHERLANDS	15	12	10	12	10	25	8	25	8	6	6	6	6
NORWAY	16	48	4	48	4	120	1	120	1	2	2	1	1
SPAIN	17	120	1	163	0	210	0	316	0				
SWEDEN	18	51	4	51	4	90	2	91	2	2	2	2	2
SWITZERLAND	19	7	10	8	10	6	10	6	10	10	10	10	10
UNITED KINGDOM	20	24	8	26	7	46	4	49	4	4	5	5	6
ARGENTINA	21			23	8	49	4	43	5		4	1	1
BOLIVIA	22			33	6	58	3	30	7		4	2	4
BRAZIL	23	49	4	49	4	92	2	88	2	3	3	2	2
CHILE	24	19	9	9	10	20	9	20	9	6	6	5	5
COLOMBIA	25	33	6	32	6	41	5	39	5	3	3	3	3
COSTA RICA	26	8	10	25	8	29	7	29	7	9	6	4	4
DOMINICAN REP	27	43	5	39	5	43	5	41	5	5	5	4	4
ECUADOR	28	19	9	23	8	24	8	25	8	6	4	4	4
EL SALVADOR	29	7	10	8	10	11	10	11	10	9	9	7	7
GUATEMALA	30	10	10	9	10	13	10	12	10	8	9	8	8
HAITI	31			13	10	24	8	23	8		7	3	3
HONDURAS	32	10	10	11	10	11	10	11	10	8	9	9	9
JAMAICA	33			70	3	92	2	107	1		4	3	2
MEXICO	34	287	0	287	0	248	0	175	0	3	3	3	3
NICARAGUA	35	9	10	9	10			11	10	9	9	8	
PANAMA	36	11	10	20	9	36	6	35	6	9	7	6	6

Appendix 2: IIB—The total number of non-financial government enterprises with corresponding index

Country	#	'77		'79		'85		'89		'77	'79	'85	'89
		Total number of enterprises...								Designated areas...			
PARAGUAY	37	12	10	13	10	14	9	14	9	8	8	7	7
PERU	38	39	5	40	5	37	6	37	6	1	2	3	3
URUGUAY	39	18	9	18	9	15	9	15	9	4	6	6	6
VENEZUELA	40	32	6	32	6	60	3	57	3	4	5	3	3
CYPRUS	41	7	10	8	10	12	10	12	10	7	7	6	6
EGYPT	42	49	4	49	4	51	4	66	3	1		0	3
GREECE	43	19	9	36	6	40	5	40	5	8	5	3	3
ISRAEL	44	133	1	107	1	144	1	127	1	3	4	2	2
MALTA	45	50	4	43	5	65	3	66	3	4	3	3	3
PORTUGAL	46			196	0	106	1	122	1		1	2	1
SYRIA	47	24	8	24	8	97	2	102	1	3	4	0	0
TURKEY	48	31	6	31	6	31	6	31	6	3	3	3	3
BANGLADESH	49	31	6	41	5	37	6	37	6	5	4	4	4
FIJI	50	11	10	12	10	14	9	14	9	6	6	6	6
HONG KONG	51												
INDIA	52	146	1	153	0	190	0	205	0	2	2	2	1
INDONESIA	53	110	1	115	1	158	0	161	0	2	2	1	1
KOREA	54	54	4	31	6	27	7	27	7	3	4	4	4
MALAYSIA	55	14	9	13	10	25	8	41	5	7	8	6	4
MAURITIUS	56	15	9	13	10	24	8	29	7	7	7	7	7
PAKISTAN	57	93	2	84	2	85	2	94	2	2	2	2	2
PHILIPPINES	58	26	7	26	7	42	5	50	4	5	5	5	3
SINGAPORE	59	35	6	35	6	28	7	28	7	4	4	5	5
SRI LANKA	60	78	3	120	1	120	1	110	1	0	0	0	0
TAIWAN	61	76	3	76	3					3	3		
THAILAND	62	62	3	61	3	55	4	56	3	2	3	3	3
BOTSWANA	63	29	7	31	6	44	5	45	4	6	6	7	6
CAMEROON	64			21	9	58	3	58	3		6	2	2
COTE D'IVOIRE	65	37	6	47	4	42	5	47	4	4	3	3	4
GABON	66	16	9	20	9	20	9	32	6	5	5	4	3
GHANA	67	49	4	47	4	48	4	50	4	3	3	2	2
KENYA	68	61	3	62	3	128	1	112	1	4	4	2	2
MALAWI	69	27	7	21	9	24	8	24	8	6	6	6	6
MALI	70	7	10	31	6	31	6	28	7	9	2	2	3
MOROCCO	71	35	6	36	6	70	3	70	3	4	4	3	3
NIGERIA	72			55	4	84	2	80	3		3	2	2
SOUTH AFRICA	73	19	9	25	8	29	7	29	7	4	4	4	4

Appendix 2: IIB—The total number of non-financial government enterprises with corresponding index

Country	#	'77		'79		'85		'89		'77	'79	'85	'89
		Total number of enterprises...								Designated areas...			
SENEGAL	74	41	5	46	4	51	4	47	4	3	3	2	3
TANZANIA	75	116	1	86	2	150	0	178	0	1	1	0	0
TUNISIA	76	8	10	6	10	98	2	100	2	8	9	0	0
ZAIRE	77	153	0	50	4	40	5	40	5	2	4	3	3
ZAMBIA	78	51	4	103	1	133	1	146	1	0	1	0	0
ZIMBABWE	79												
AVERAGE		44.0	6.3	45.4	6.1	61.6	5.1	62.3	5.1	4.7	4.7	3.8	3.8

Appendix 2: IIC—Index ranking of price controls in the economy						
Country	#	1989	Country	#	1989	
UNITED STATES	1	8	CYPRUS	41	0	
CANADA	2	8	EGYPT	42	3	
AUSTRALIA	3	6	GREECE	43	0	
JAPAN	4	6	ISRAEL	44	0	
NEW ZEALAND	5	9	MALTA	45	0	
AUSTRIA	6	5	PORTUGAL	46	4	
BELGIUM	7	2	SYRIA	47		
DENMARK	8	6	TURKEY	48	8	
FINLAND	9	6	BANGLADESH	49		
FRANCE	10	6	FIJI	50	8	
GERMANY	11	9	HONG KONG	51	10	
ICELAND	12		INDIA	52	3	
IRELAND	13	7	INDONESIA	53	6	
ITALY	14	5	KOREA	54	3	
NETHERLANDS	15	7	MALAYSIA	55	5	
NORWAY	16	5	MAURITIUS	56		
SPAIN	17	6	PAKISTAN	57		
SWEDEN	18	6	PHILIPPINES	58	6	
SWITZERLAND	19	7	SINGAPORE	59	8	
UNITED KINGDOM	20	8	SRI LANKA	60		
ARGENTINA	21	0	TAIWAN	61	6	
BOLIVIA	22	6	THAILAND	62	4	
BRAZIL	23	0	BOTSWANA	63	6	
CHILE	24	8	CAMEROON	64		
COLOMBIA	25	6	COTE D' IVOIRE	65		
COSTA RICA	26		GABON	66		
DOMINICAN REPUBLIC	27		GHANA	67		
ECUADOR	28	0	KENYA	68	3	
EL SALVADOR	29		MALAWI	69	3	
GUATEMALA	30	6	MALI	70		
HAITI	31		MOROCCO	71	0	
HONDURAS	32		NIGERIA	72	6	
JAMAICA	33	5	SOUTH AFRICA	73	3	
MEXICO	34	0	SENEGAL	74	5	
NICARAGUA	35		TANZANIA	75	0	
PANAMA	36	3	TUNISIA	76		
PARAGUAY	37	6	ZAIRE	77		
PERU	38	3	ZAMBIA	78	0	
URUGUAY	39	5	ZIMBABWE	79	0	
VENEZUELA	40	6	AVERAGE		4.6	

Appendix 2: IIIA—Transfers and subsidies as a share of GNP with corresponding index.

Country	#	1975		1980		1985		1987	
UNITED STATES	1	9.42%	4	9.38%	4	10.13%	4	9.86%	4
CANADA	2	9.27%	4	9.68%	4	10.50%	3	10.22%	4
AUSTRALIA	3	7.34%	5	8.96%	4	11.08%	3	10.28%	4
JAPAN	4	1.73%	9	1.97%	9	1.70%	9	1.52%	9
NEW ZEALAND	5	11.13%	3	21.99%	0	22.20%	0	23.80%	0
AUSTRIA	6	17.49%	2	18.92%	1	19.99%	1	20.84%	1
BELGIUM	7	23.54%	0	25.89%	0	26.98%	0	26.00%	0
DENMARK	8	7.20%	5	8.27%	4	9.36%	4	9.45%	4
FINLAND	9	13.25%	3	13.27%	3	14.26%	3	14.83%	3
FRANCE	10	22.00%	0	21.87%	0	26.31%	0	26.21%	0
GERMANY	11	14.63%	3	15.15%	3	15.63%	2	15.51%	2
ICELAND	12	12.94%	3	10.55%	3	20.53%	1		
IRELAND	13	16.33%	2	17.33%	2	23.19%	0	22.87%	0
ITALY	14	15.92%	2	14.77%	3	19.14%	1	19.10%	1
NETHERLANDS	15	22.01%	0	25.40%	0	25.00%	0	25.90%	0
NORWAY	16	19.44%	1	21.48%	0	19.61%	1	21.94%	0
SPAIN	17	7.37%	5	12.17%	3	16.32%	2	14.10%	3
SWEDEN	18	14.29%	3	21.82%	0	24.40%	0	25.78%	0
SWITZERLAND	19	9.41%	4	10.68%	3	10.07%	4	10.20%	4
UNITED KINGDOM	20	13.72%	3	14.55%	3	16.04%	2	15.01%	3
ARGENTINA	21	10.71%	3	16.57%	2	15.21%	3	8.09%	5
BOLIVIA	22	1.14%	10	1.56%	9	2.15%	8	1.00%	10
BRAZIL	23	8.23%	4	10.83%	3	8.18%	4	6.56%	5
CHILE	24	10.52%	3	13.13%	3	17.20%	2	15.46%	2
COLOMBIA	25			2.57%	8	3.04%	7	2.74%	8
COSTA RICA	26	4.20%	7	6.25%	5	7.85%	5	7.60%	5
DOMINCAN REP	27	1.51%	9	2.01%	9	2.58%	8	2.12%	8
ECUADOR	28	3.50%	7	5.13%	6	3.90%	7		
EL SALVADOR	29	2.55%	8	2.73%	8	2.08%	9	1.47%	9
GUATEMALA	30	0.78%	10	1.13%	10	1.33%	9	2.06%	9

Appendix 2: IIIA—Transfers and subsidies as a share of GNP with corresponding index.

Country	#	1975		1980		1985		1987	
HAITI	31					7.35%	5		
HONDURAS	32	0.47%	10						
JAMAICA	33	3.40%	7						
MEXICO	34	3.98%	7	4.38%	7	5.34%	6	2.40%	8
NICARAGUA	35	2.37%	8	4.16%	7	6.91%	5		
PANAMA	36	3.67%	7	4.92%	6	5.51%	5	5.73%	5
PARAGUAY	37	1.77%	9	1.16%	10	2.20%	8	5.30%	6
PERU	38	2.65%	8	2.64%	8	1.82%	9	2.86%	8
URAGUAY	39	12.10%	3	9.48%	4	9.76%	4	11.80%	3
VENEZUELA	40	2.33%	8	1.95%	9	4.70%	6	2.26%	8
CYPRUS	41	10.17%	4	6.78%	5	8.10%	5	7.61%	5
EGYPT	42	25.50%	0	18.37%	2	15.40%	2	11.85%	3
GREECE	43	3.04%	7	11.77%	3	18.16%	2	15.80%	2
ISRAEL	44	18.78%	1	20.99%	1	20.00%	1	16.94%	2
MALTA	45	13.25%	3	11.33%	3	14.48%	3	15.13%	3
PORTUGAL	46	14.63%	3	16.72%	2	20.67%	1	17.43%	2
SYRIA	47	0.00%	10	0.00%	10			2.50%	8
TURKEY	48	6.40%	5	5.39%	6	10.62%	3	6.77%	5
BANGLADESH	49							1.20%	10
FIJI	50	1.93%	9	2.51%	8	4.66%	6	4.65%	6
HONG KONG	51	2.11%	9	2.98%	7	1.46%	9	2.63%	8
INDIA	52	1.19%	10	1.74%	9	2.81%	8	1.00%	10
INDONESIA	53	1.53%	9	3.48%	7	2.71%	8	4.87%	6
KOREA	54	1.57%	9	2.04%	9	2.38%	8	2.03%	9
MALAYSIA	55	6.62%	5	4.94%	6	3.20%	7	3.30%	7
MAURITIUS	56	6.52%	5	6.55%	5	5.45%	5	4.23%	7
PAKISTAN	57	3.06%	7	2.21%	8	0.68%	10	0.78%	10
PHILIPPINES	58	0.84%	10	0.24%	10	0.17%	10	0.41%	10
SINGAPORE	59	1.36%	9	1.15%	10	1.23%	10	2.41%	8
SRI LANKA	60	8.13%	5	8.22%	4	5.30%	6	5.37%	6

Appendix 2: IIIA—Transfers and subsidies as a share of GNP with corresponding index.									
Country	#	1975		1980		1985		1987	
TAIWAN	61	2.15%	8	2.56%	8	3.57%	7	4.08%	7
THAILAND	62	0.60%	10	0.67%	10	1.23%	9	1.12%	10
BOTSWANA	63	2.50%	8	5.32%	6	9.28%	4	8.21%	4
CAMEROON	64			0.83%	10	0.00%	10	2.80%	8
COTE D' IVOIRE	65			4.36%	7				
GABON	66					3.23%	7		
GHANA	67	3.17%	7	2.43%	8	1.34%	9	0.12%	10
KENYA	68	2.77%	8	2.28%	8	3.00%	7	1.98%	9
MALAWI	69	0.89%	10	0.54%	10	0.19%	10	0.22%	10
MALI	70			2.28%	8	2.81%	8	1.11%	10
MOROCCO	71	7.15%	5	5.33%	6	5.35%	6	3.83%	7
NIGERIA	72	2.87%	8	0.40%	10	1.20%	10	1.99%	9
SOUTH AFRICA	73	3.44%	7	3.21%	7	4.82%	6		
SENEGAL	74	2.72%	8	4.34%	7	0.88%	10		
TANZANIA	75	0.12%	10	0.04%	10	4.28%	7		
TUNISIA	76	8.31%	4	4.41%	7	7.14%	5	7.57%	5
ZAIRE	77	1.00%	10	0.61%	10				
ZAMBIA	78	7.56%	5	9.40%	4	4.91%	6	5.94%	5
ZIMBABWE	79	8.15%	4	21.46%	0	9.78%	4	13.28%	3
AVERAGE		7.28%	5.8	8.01%	5.6	8.91%	5.2	8.66%	5.4

Appendix 2: IIIB—Top marginal tax rates, the threshold at which they apply, and the corresponding index ratings.

COUNTRY	#	1975 Rate	1975 Level		1980 Rate	1980 Level		1984 Rate	1984 Level		1989 Rate	1989 Level	
UNITED STATES	1	70-75	185,000	1	70-75	82,645	0	50-59	156,300	5	33-42	58,937	8
CANADA	2	43-61	130,109	6	47-62	115,840	5	49-60	43,100	3	42-47	35,888	5
AUSTRALIA	3	64	74,348	2	62	51,928	2	60	28,400	2	49	23,555	3
JAPAN	4	68	185,000	2	75	546,694	2	70	305,500	3	65	178,000	3
NEW ZEALAND	5	60	83,642	3	60	31,818	2	66	17,200	0	33	15,194	6
AUSTRIA	6	54	185,000	5	62	153,581	3	62	65,350	2	50	42,728	4
BELGIUM	7	64	185,000	3	76	187,879	0	76	60,600	0	55-65	46,379	2
DENMARK	8	63	37,174	1	66	37,052	0	73	21,400	0	68	24,802	0
FINLAND	9	61-68	111,522	3	65-71	88,843	1	64-70	59,300	1	63-69	47,128	0
FRANCE	10	48	130,109	6	60	126,722	4	65	30,700	1	53	29,929	3
WEST GERMANY	11	56	167,283	4	56	193,939	4	56	39,650	2	56	114,764	4
ICELAND	12												
IRELAND	13	80	46,468	0	60	19,559	1	65	19,000	0	58	20,214	1
ITALY	14	48	185,000	6	72	819,559	2	81	248,200	0	50	180,906	6
NETHERLANDS	15	46	185,000	6	72	127,548	1	72	59,100	0	72	90,675	0
NORWAY	16	74	111,522	1	75	82,645	0	64	32,600	1	54	28,117	3
SPAIN	17	55	185,000	5	66	195,592	2	66	67,700	1	56	57,114	3

Appendix 2: IIIB—Top marginal tax rates, the threshold at which they apply, and the corresponding index ratings.

COUNTRY	#	1975 Rate	1975 Level	Index	1980 Rate	1980 Level	Index	1984 Rate	1984 Level	Index	1989 Rate	1989 Level	Index
SWEDEN	18	70	74,348	1	87	53,306	0	80	38,100	0	72	24,346	0
SWITZERLAND	19	38-42	111,522	8	31-44	76,171	6	33-46	145,300	8	26-32	299,428	10
UNITED KINGDOM	20	41	185,000	7	83	66,942	0	60	40,100	2	40	24,700	5
ARGENTINA	21	51	65,055	4	45	101,515	7	62	65,400	2	35	40,465	7
BOLIVIA	22				48	15,152	3	30	45	8	10	1	10
BRAZIL	23	50	65,055	5	55	105,234	5	60	10,400	1	25	1,434	8
CHILE	24	80	185,000	0	60	42,424	2	57	3,600	1	50	3,709	3
COLOMBIA	25	41	111,522	7	56	36,501	2	49	55,400	5	30	32,822	8
COSTA RICA	26	50	83,642	5	50	56,061	5	50	2,200	3	25	9,843	8
DOMINICAN REPUBLIC	27	49	185,000	6				73.1	497,238	2	73	183,000	1
ECUADOR	28	50	148,696	6	50	150,000	6	58	27,800	2	40	21,787	5
EL SALVADOR	29	55	185,000	5	60	137,741	4	48	11,700	3	60	39,370	2
GUATEMALA	30	34	185,000	9	40	688,705	9	48	324,350	7	34	3,791	6
HAITI	31										30	193,000	10
HONDURAS	32	27	185,000	10	40	688,705	9	46	476,400	7	46	393,701	7
JAMAICA	33	60	27,881	2	80	23,967	0	58	2,400	1	33	1,489	6
MEXICO	34	47	83,642	5	55	90,634	4	55	59,300	4	40	8,900	5

214 Rating Global Economic Freedom

Appendix 2: IIIB—Top marginal tax rates, the threshold at which they apply, and the corresponding index ratings.

COUNTRY	#	1975 Rate	1975 Level	1975 Rating	1980 Rate	1980 Level	1980 Rating	1984 Rate	1984 Level	1984 Rating	1989 Rate	1989 Level	1989 Rating
NICARAGUA	35	21	185,000	10	50	275,482	7	50	67,600	5			4
PANAMA	36	52	185,000	5	56	275,482	5	56	192,500	4	56	157,480	7
PARAGUAY	37							30	8,200	7	30	3,822	4
PERU	38	51	55,761	4	65	53,719	2	65	40	0	45	12,558	
URUGUAY	39	41	185,000	7	0		10	0	40	10	0	10	8
VENEZUELA	40	20	185,000	10	45	1,350,000	8	45	1,110,000	8	45	234,000	0
CYPRUS	41	54	37,174	3	60	19,146	1	60	20,900	1	62	18,547	2
EGYPT	42				80	196,832	0	65	148,000	3	65	61,750	4
GREECE	43	52	130,109	5	60	113,223	4	63	36,500	1	50	28,594	4
ISRAEL	44				66	70,000	1	60	55,000	3	51	82,000	0
MALTA	45				65	18,000	0	65	10,000	0	65	3,030	0
PORTUGAL	46	82	167,283	0	84	28,788	0	69	39,900	0	40	16,171	5
SYRIA	47												
TURKEY	48				75	60,000	0	60	53,800	3	50	32,800	4
BANGLADESH	49				60	10,000	1						
FIJI	50	53	27,000	3	53	13,774	2	50	16,650	3	50	21,872	3
HONG KONG	51	15	27,881	10	15	28,512	10	25	4,900	8	25	7,066	8

Appendix 2: IIIB—Top marginal tax rates, the threshold at which they apply, and the corresponding index ratings.

COUNTRY	#	1975 Rate	1975 Level		1980 Rate	1980 Level		1984 Rate	1984 Level		1989 Rate	1989 Level	
INDIA	52	77	13,940	0	60	16,529	1	62	7,700	0	53	5,194	2
INDONESIA	53	48	37,174	4	50	21,212	3	35	44,750	7	35	22,731	6
SOUTH KOREA	54				89	238,567	0	65	69,600	2	60	110,000	4
MALAYSIA	55	50	46,468	4	60	47,383	2	45	117,300	7	45	90,161	6
MAURITIUS	56				50	20,000	3	35	10,000	6	35	2,750	6
PAKISTAN	57	61	27,881	1	55	6,887	2	60	6,500	1	50	8,394	3
PHILIPPINES	58	56	167,000	4	70	94,353	1	60	24,350	1	35	18,031	6
SINGAPORE	59	55	83,642	4	55	255,096	6	40	325,000	9	33	161,850	9
SRI LANKA	60				60.5	3,500	1						
TAIWAN	61	60	111,522	4	60	110,000	4	60	100,000	4	50	97,658	5
THAILAND	62	60	111,522	4	60	68,871	3	65	70,700	2	55	62,270	4
BOTSWANA	63	75	83,642	0	75	66,116	0	60	34,300	2	50	16,472	3
CAMEROON	64							60	30,000	2	60	20,600	1
COTE D'IVOIRE	65				45	38,500	5						
GABON	66												
GHANA	67	70	22,000	0	60	700	1	60	400	1			
KENYA	68	70	46,468	0	65	27,500	1	65	9,900	0	50	400	3

Appendix 2: IIIB—Top marginal tax rates, the threshold at which they apply, and the corresponding index ratings.

COUNTRY	#	1975 Rate	1975 Level		1980 Rate	1980 Level		1984 Rate	1984 Level		1989 Rate	1989 Level	
MALAWI	69	38	27,881	6	45	20,937	4	50	13,500	3	50	7,194	3
MALI	70												
MOROCCO	71	39	185,000	8	64	261,570	4	87	75,500	0	87	28,699	0
NIGERIA	72	75	74,348	0	70	62,000	1	55	40,000	3	55	4,200	2
SOUTH AFRICA	73	66	83,642	1	60	45,868	2	50	19,250	3	45	26,456	5
SENEGAL	74							65	38,232	1	48	31,000	4
TANZANIA	75	80	74,000	0				95	19,293	0	50	1,200	3
TUNISIA	76				62.3	300,000	4						
ZAIRE	77	60	37,174	2	60	8,540	1	60	1,350	1	60	854	1
ZAMBIA	78	70	37,174	0	70	22,452	0	80	10,700	0	75	2,375	0
ZIMBABWE	79				45	34,435	5	63	22,200	0	60	13,287	1

Appendix 2: IIIC—Conscripts per 1000 population with corresponding index ratings								
Country	#	74-75		78-79		84-85		89-90	
UNITED STATES	1	0.00	10	0.00	10	0.00	10	0.00	10
CANADA	2	0.00	10	0.00	10	0.00	10	0.00	10
AUSTRALIA	3	0.00	10	0.00	10	0.00	10	0.00	10
JAPAN	4	0.00	10	0.00	10	0.00	10	0.00	10
NEW ZEALAND	5	0.00	10	0.00	10	0.00	10	0.00	10
AUSTRIA	6	3.31	6	2.53	8	4.27	5	2.71	7
BELGIUM	7	9.15	2	2.62	8	3.22	6	3.69	6
DENMARK	8	7.33	2	2.42	8	1.84	8	1.79	8
FINLAND	9	5.99	2	6.71	2	5.17	3	4.76	4
FRANCE	10	5.22	3	4.94	4	4.49	4	4.30	5
GERMANY	11	3.86	5	3.72	6	3.75	5	3.63	6
ICELAND	12	0.00	10	0.00	10	0.00	10	0.00	10
IRELAND	13	0.00	10	0.00	10	0.00	10	0.00	10
ITALY	14	7.64	2	3.98	5	4.12	5	4.73	4
NETHERLANDS	15	8.44	2	3.52	6	3.20	7	3.35	6
NORWAY	16	5.73	2	6.93	2	5.43	3	5.18	3
SPAIN	17	8.06	2	5.21	3	5.52	3	5.35	3
SWEDEN	18	6.58	2	5.61	3	5.71	2	5.84	2
SWITZERLAND	19	5.47	3	2.87	7	3.08	7	3.26	6
UNITED KINGDOM	20	0.00	10	0.00	10	0.00	10	0.00	10
ARGENTINA	21	5.48	3	5.04	3	3.66	6	1.21	9
BOLIVIA	22	4.40	4	3.69	6	4.42	4	2.72	7
BRAZIL	23	1.99	8	0.98	9	1.02	9	0.99	9
CHILE	24	5.75	2	1.95	8	2.75	7	2.57	8
COLOMBIA	25	2.64	7	2.80	7	1.01	9	1.32	9
COSTA RICA	26	0.00	10	0.00	10	0.00	10	0.00	10
DOM. REP.	27	3.47	6	0.00	10	0.00	10	0.00	10
ECUADOR	28	3.20	7	3.25	6	4.05	5	4.05	5
EL SALVADOR	29	1.30	9	1.60	8	7.86	2	9.45	2
GUATEMALA	30	1.99	8	2.26	8	4.88	4	4.80	4

Appendix 2: IIIC—Conscripts per 1000 population with corresponding index ratings									
Country	#	74-75		78-79		84-85		89-90	
HAITI	31	0.00	10	0.00	10	0.00	10	0.00	10
HONDURAS	32			0.00	10	2.88	7	2.69	7
JAMAICA	33							0.00	10
MEXICO	34	4.43	4	3.74	5	3.21	7	0.71	9
NICARAGUA	35	3.36	6	2.98	7	19.31	0	8.10	2
PANAMA	36	0.00	10	0.00	10	0.00	10	0.00	10
PARAGUAY	37	5.40	3	5.92	2	3.03	7	2.38	8
PERU	38	3.51	6	2.87	7	3.59	6	3.66	6
URAGUAY	39	0.00	10	0.00	10	0.00	10	0.00	10
VENEZUELA	40	3.37	6	3.36	6	0.64	9	0.94	9
CYPRUS	41			16.08	0	15.06	0	18.73	0
EGYPT	42	8.83	2	9.93	2	5.40	3	4.62	4
GREECE	43	12.49	1	16.06	0	13.43	1	14.20	1
ISRAEL	44	34.36	0	32.98	0	23.40	0	24.22	0
MALTA	45	0.00	10	0.00	10	0.00	10	0.00	10
PORTUGAL	46	23.59	0	6.97	2	3.70	6	4.55	4
SYRIA	47	19.28	0	28.05	0	11.54	1	34.50	0
TURKEY	48	11.63	1	8.57	2	11.19	2	10.37	2
BANGLADESH	49	0.00	10	0.00	10	0.00	10	0.00	10
FIJI	50					0.00	10	0.00	10
HONG KONG	51	0.00	10	0.00	10	0.00	10	0.00	10
INDIA	52	0.00	10	0.00	10	0.00	10	0.00	10
INDONESIA	53	2.13	8	1.77	8	1.78	8	1.62	8
KOREA	54	18.52	0	17.86	0	14.95	1	15.10	0
MALAYSIA	55	0.00	10	0.00	10	0.00	10	0.00	10
MAURITIUS	56	0.00	10	0.00	10	0.00	10	0.00	10
PAKISTAN	57	6.67	2	0.00	10	0.00	10	0.00	10
PHILIPPINES	58	1.33	9	2.12	8	0.00	10	0.00	10
SINGAPORE	59	9.73	2	15.16	0	13.65	1	13.09	1
SRI LANKA	60	0.00	10	0.00	10	0.00	10	0.00	10

Appendix 2: IIIC—Conscripts per 1000 population with corresponding index ratings									
Country	#	74-75		78-79		84-85		89-90	
TAIWAN	61	30.69	0	26.89	0	24.69	0	19.34	0
THAILAND	62	5.07	3	4.57	4	4.64	4	5.18	3
BOTSWANA	63	0.00	10	0.00	10	0.00	10	0.00	10
CAMEROON	64	0.00	10	0.00	10	0.00	10	0.00	10
COTE D' IVOIRE	65	0.73	9	0.94	9	1.23	9	0.64	9
GABON	66			0.00	10	0.00	10	0.00	10
GHANA	67	0.00	10	0.00	10	0.00	10	0.00	10
KENYA	68	0.00	10	0.00	10	0.00	10	0.00	10
MALAWI	69	0.00	10	0.00	10	0.00	10	0.00	10
MALI	70	0.67	9	0.68	9	0.64	9	0.80	9
MOROCCO	71	3.33	6	4.79	4	6.17	2	8.01	2
NIGERIA	72	0.00	10	0.00	10	0.00	10	0.00	10
SOUTH AFRICA	73	2.00	8	2.50	8	2.50	8	1.81	8
SENEGAL	74	1.37	9	1.38	9	1.54	8	1.36	9
TANZANIA	75	0.00	10	0.00	10	0.00	10	0.82	9
TUNISIA	76	3.77	5	2.08	8	1.86	8	3.46	6
ZAIRE	77	0.00	10	0.00	10	0.00	10	0.00	10
ZAMBIA	78	0.00	10	0.00	10	0.00	10	0.00	10
ZIMBABWE	79	0.00	10	0.00	10	0.00	10	5.20	3
AVERAGE		4.37	6.4	3.78	7.1	3.45	7.1	3.57	7.1

Appendix 2: IVA—Taxes on international trade as a share of the trade sector with corresponding index

Country	#	1975		1980		1985		1987	
UNITED STATES	1	2.990%	8	2.269%	8	3.016%	8	3.136%	8
CANADA	2	7.344%	6	4.768%	7	3.340%	7	3.112%	8
AUSTRALIA	3	8.768%	6	7.263%	6	7.563%	6	7.177%	6
JAPAN	4	1.871%	8	1.781%	8	1.448%	8	1.704%	8
NEW ZEALAND	5	4.860%	7	3.589%	7	4.069%	7	4.720%	7
AUSTRIA	6	3.292%	7	1.426%	8	1.199%	8	1.461%	8
BELGIUM	7	0.019%	10	0.005%	10	0.003%	10	0.031%	10
DENMARK	8	0.142%	9	0.099%	9	0.077%	9	0.080%	9
FINLAND	9	3.229%	8	1.619%	8	0.831%	8	1.038%	8
FRANCE	10	0.092%	9	0.097%	9	0.054%	9	0.055%	9
GERMANY	11	0.031%	10	0.019%	10	0.010%	10	0.012%	10
ICELAND	12	16.113%	2	13.060%	4	9.077%	5		
IRELAND	13	9.636%	5	6.361%	6	5.083%	7	5.834%	6
ITALY	14	0.515%	9	0.075%	9	0.045%	10	0.052%	9
NETHERLANDS	15	2.660%	8	0.006%	10	0.000%	10	0.000%	10
NORWAY	16	1.023%	8	0.601%	9	0.501%	9	0.748%	9
SPAIN	17	12.210%	4	8.667%	6	5.857%	6	4.197%	7
SWEDEN	18	2.131%	8	1.325%	8	0.650%	9	0.669%	9
SWITZERLAND	19	6.994%	6	4.835%	7	3.896%	7	4.249%	7
UNITED KINGDOM	20	0.768%	9	0.083%	9	0.008%	10	0.144%	9
ARGENTINA	21	20.870%	1	23.778%	0	24.923%	0	19.170%	1
BOLIVIA	22	17.241%	2	15.652%	2	0.013%	10	0.008%	10
BRAZIL	23	0.011%	10	0.015%	10	0.006%	10	0.007%	10
CHILE	24	11.123%	4	5.572%	7	11.389%	4	9.090%	5
COLOMBIA	25	14.799%	2	15.518%	2	13.841%	3	15.699%	2
COSTA RICA	26	11.745%	4	10.509%	5	13.606%	3	14.802%	2
DOMINCAN REP	27	32.233%	0	19.497%	1	13.697%	3	19.635%	1
ECUADOR	28	17.767%	1	15.581%	2	12.419%	4	9.650%	5
EL SALVADOR	29	12.795%	4	12.479%	4	14.264%	2	13.290%	3
GUATEMALA	30	11.241%	4	14.381%	2	9.649%	5	19.533%	1

Appendix 2: IVA—Taxes on international trade as a share of the trade sector with corresponding index

Country	#	1975		1980		1985		1987	
HAITI	31			19.711%	1	16.068%	2	13.647%	3
HONDURAS	32	10.645%	5	13.438%	3	16.700%	2	14.200%	2
JAMAICA	33	7.979%	6	1.864%	8				
MEXICO	34	15.517%	2	34.901%	0	5.112%	7	12.889%	4
NICARAGUA	35	9.764%	5	17.400%	1	10.524%	5	2.828%	8
PANAMA	36	6.789%	6	6.039%	6	8.439%	6	9.769%	5
PARAGUAY	37	17.622%	1	12.083%	4	4.255%	7	4.395%	7
PERU	38	18.891%	1	20.752%	1	17.646%	1	18.274%	1
URUGUAY	39	6.828%	6	17.745%	1	11.465%	4	14.897%	2
VENEZUELA	40	7.651%	6	5.969%	6	17.947%	1	24.928%	0
CYPRUS	41	6.908%	6	7.999%	6	8.841%	6	9.319%	5
EGYPT	42	33.427%	0	26.152%	0	24.120%	0	23.073%	0
GREECE	43	6.873%	6	6.459%	6	0.664%	9	0.180%	9
ISRAEL	44	13.333%	3	4.000%	7	5.769%	6	4.861%	7
MALTA	45	9.185%	5	9.741%	5	8.912%	5	9.148%	5
PORTUGAL	46	9.216%	5	4.228%	7	2.505%	8	1.901%	8
SYRIA	47	16.950%	2	14.242%	2			6.788%	6
TURKEY	48	28.800%	0	12.652%	4	5.924%	6	6.203%	6
BANGLADESH	49	21.859%	1	26.823%	0	35.764%	0	27.331%	0
FIJI	50	13.251%	3	11.552%	4	15.748%	2	15.345%	2
HONG KONG	51	1.458%	8	0.699%	9	0.643%	9	0.764%	9
INDIA	52	29.544%	0	31.040%	0	48.478%	0	55.837%	0
INDONESIA	53	7.997%	6	5.782%	6	3.170%	8	7.253%	6
KOREA	54	6.134%	6	7.114%	6	7.190%	6	7.895%	6
MALAYSIA	55	14.083%	2	15.422%	2	10.752%	5	7.085%	6
MAURITIUS	56	14.128%	2	21.732%	1	19.283%	1	17.008%	2
PAKISTAN	57	30.636%	0	30.571%	0	30.019%	0	32.471%	0
PHILIPPINES	58	26.770%	0	13.509%	3	13.834%	3	15.326%	2
SINGAPORE	59	1.486%	8	0.942%	8	0.724%	9	0.549%	9
SRI LANKA	60	22.265%	1	23.434%	0	21.172%	1	21.665%	1

Appendix 2: IVA—Taxes on international trade as a share of the trade sector with corresponding index									
Country	#	1975		1980		1985		1987	
TAIWAN	61	9.669%	5	7.196%	6	5.713%	7	4.564%	7
THAILAND	62	16.563%	2	13.756%	3	12.967%	4	11.074%	4
BOTSWANA	63	20.787%	1	25.500%	0	15.221%	2	11.081%	4
CAMEROON	64	26.874%	0	21.997%	1	12.181%	4	18.690%	1
COTE D' IVOIRE	65	0.027%	10	25.559%	0	19.402%	1		
GABON	66					13.482%	3		
GHANA	67	42.685%	0	34.538%	0	38.084%	0	26.146%	0
KENYA	68	10.935%	5	12.126%	4	13.758%	3	16.281%	2
MALAWI	69	7.504%	6	13.154%	4	17.751%	1	12.530%	4
MALI	70	28.180%	0	7.615%	6	9.654%	5	17.060%	2
MOROCCO	71	15.025%	2	21.361%	1	12.779%	4	12.072%	4
NIGERIA	72	13.279%	3	8.900%	5	10.345%	5	3.965%	7
SOUTH AFRICA	73	4.050%	7	2.420%	8	2.792%	8	3.619%	7
SENEGAL	74	33.329%	0	22.832%	0				
TANZANIA	75	14.652%	2	15.442%	2	12.491%	4		
TUNISIA	76	21.394%	1	17.986%	1	26.608%	0	21.809%	1
ZAIRE	77	37.694%	0	20.527%	1	17.017%	2	16.664%	2
ZAMBIA	78	5.223%	7	4.784%	7	13.675%	3	16.943%	2
ZIMBABWE	79			3.335%	7	16.064%	2	17.772%	1
AVERAGE		12.610%	4.4	11.461%	4.6	10.555%	5.1	10.348%	5.0

Appendix 2: IVB—Actual trade sector size minus predicted trade sector size with corresponding index								
Country	#	1975		1980		1985		1987	
UNITED STATES	1	-2.07%	6	-2.72%	5	-2.90%	5	-1.30%	6
CANADA	2	-1.80%	6	-2.74%	5	-2.47%	6	-3.20%	5
AUSTRALIA	3	-14.14%	1	-15.67%	1	-13.62%	1	-14.15%	1
JAPAN	4	-4.35%	5	-5.56%	4	-5.89%	4	-7.87%	3
NEW ZEALAND	5	-15.81%	1	-15.49%	1	-11.81%	2	-18.76%	0
AUSTRIA	6	-5.48%	5	-3.28%	5	-1.01%	6	-5.07%	5
BELGIUM	7	9.31%	9	19.78%	9	30.60%	10	22.28%	9
DENMARK	8	-10.05%	2	-9.89%	2	-6.55%	4	-11.50%	2
FINLAND	9	-13.30%	1	-10.76%	2	-15.36%	1	-17.47%	1
FRANCE	10	-5.47%	5	-4.90%	5	-3.64%	5	-5.13%	5
GERMANY	11	2.45%	7	3.04%	7	6.57%	8	3.78%	8
ICELAND	12	-15.30%	1	-22.04%	0	-19.04%	0	-20.11%	0
IRELAND	13	4.52%	8	8.59%	9	22.55%	10	18.16%	9
ITALY	14	-5.40%	5	-6.18%	4	-5.58%	4	-8.01%	3
NETHERLANDS	15	15.71%	9	16.03%	9	23.78%	10	14.43%	9
NORWAY	16	3.53%	7	0.31%	7	-1.52%	6	-6.45%	4
SPAIN	17	-6.22%	4	-9.95%	2	-5.70%	4	-7.92%	3
SWEDEN	18	-7.37%	3	-8.36%	3	-5.51%	4	-6.80%	3
SWITZERLAND	19	-5.80%	4	-1.41%	6	-2.86%	5	-4.30%	5
UNITED KINGDOM	20	2.38%	7	-1.78%	6	0.77%	7	-0.10%	7
ARGENTINA	21	-11.54%	2	-5.93%	4	-6.70%	3	-11.59%	2
BOLIVIA	22	-3.97%	5	-19.80%	0	-31.36%	0	-24.70%	0
BRAZIL	23	-11.06%	2	-15.83%	1	-12.45%	2	-14.25%	1
CHILE	24	-5.07%	5	-13.18%	1	-3.41%	5	-0.71%	6
COLOMBIA	25	-9.20%	3	-11.44%	2	-13.34%	1	-8.21%	3
COSTA RICA	26	-8.74%	3	-14.77%	1	-9.99%	2	-5.94%	4
DOMINICAN REPUBLIC	27	2.62%	7	-13.81%	1	-6.31%	4	-0.50%	6
ECUADOR	28	-1.66%	6	-9.37%	3	-10.19%	2	-7.46%	3
EL SALVADOR	29	-2.32%	6	-7.97%	3	-12.98%	1	-16.79%	1

Appendix 2: IVB—Actual trade sector size minus predicted trade sector size with corresponding index

Country	#	1975		1980		1985		1987	
GUATEMALA	30	-13.41%	1	-14.09%	1	-18.77%	0	-12.60%	2
HAITI	31	-16.91%	1	-10.70%	2	-18.10%	1	-21.06%	0
HONDURAS	32	-5.75%	4	0.07%	7	-9.49%	2	-12.43%	2
JAMAICA	33	-5.93%	4	-1.99%	6	28.49%	10	18.01%	9
MEXICO	34	-8.81%	3	3.18%	7	-10.35%	2	-12.41%	2
NICARAGUA	35	-10.40%	2	-8.98%	3	-18.05%	1	-28.57%	0
PANAMA	36	3.36%	7	-2.80%	5	-10.89%	2	-13.98%	1
PARAGUAY	37	-22.90%	0	-23.07%	0	-21.45%	0	-21.01%	0
PERU	38	-8.57%	3	-4.24%	5	-9.30%	3	-15.90%	1
URUGUAY	39	-25.99%	0	-23.87%	0	-21.27%	0	-21.84%	0
VENEZUELA	40	-6.80%	3	-10.56%	2	-6.19%	4	-0.56%	6
CYPRUS	41	-9.86%	2	-5.57%	4	-3.48%	5	-9.32%	3
EGYPT	42	20.40%	9	21.00%	9	11.21%	9	5.54%	8
GREECE	43	-13.74%	1	-15.85%	1	-14.16%	1	-14.85%	1
ISRAEL	44	-0.39%	6	0.84%	7	2.72%	7	-0.79%	6
MALTA	45	21.92%	9	25.35%	10	12.84%	9	17.07%	9
PORTUGAL	46	-7.22%	3	-3.07%	5	0.79%	7	-1.87%	6
SYRIA	47	-3.99%	5	-9.23%	3	-14.66%	1	-21.63%	0
TURKEY	48	-3.01%	5	-14.42%	1	-4.27%	5	-3.68%	5
BANGLADESH	49	-6.25%	4	-0.24%	6	5.54%	8	0.79%	7
FIJI	50	-8.80%	3	-5.93%	4	-6.91%	3	-10.20%	2
HONG KONG	51	58.82%	10	64.84%	10	59.02%	10	74.21%	10
INDIA	52	14.45%	9	13.38%	9	23.76%	10	29.05%	10
INDONESIA	53	7.08%	8	7.63%	8	2.94%	7	9.18%	9
KOREA	54	6.56%	8	9.85%	9	9.64%	9	15.32%	9
MALAYSIA	55	15.26%	9	26.40%	10	23.57%	10	27.62%	10
MAURITIUS	56	6.83%	8	1.39%	7	8.20%	9	20.11%	9
PAKISTAN	57	8.92%	9	7.64%	8	7.52%	8	10.12%	9
PHILIPPINES	58	8.56%	9	-0.79%	6	-2.42%	6	2.61%	7
SINGAPORE	59	69.89%	10	139.92%	10	83.54%	10	99.01%	10

Appendix 2: IVB—Actual trade sector size minus predicted trade sector size with corresponding index

Country	#	1975		1980		1985		1987	
SRI LANKA	60	6.87%	8	16.22%	9	5.21%	8	4.81%	8
TAIWAN	61	11.42%	9	18.75%	9	13.58%	9	16.00%	9
THAILAND	62	1.44%	7	3.47%	7	2.96%	7	6.36%	8
BOTSWANA	63	17.40%	9	14.37%	9	18.14%	9	35.22%	10
CAMEROON	64	-0.28%	6	-3.90%	5	-6.16%	4	-11.97%	2
COTE D'IVOIRE	65	-1.92%	6	8.80%	9	11.86%	9	1.07%	7
GABON	66					5.14%	8	11.50%	9
GHANA	67	3.27%	7	-14.95%	1	-7.52%	3	-1.71%	6
KENYA	68	2.78%	7	2.67%	7	-2.14%	6	-2.42%	6
MALAWI	69	-2.80%	5	-5.51%	4	-7.14%	3	-10.38%	2
MALI	70	-6.67%	3	-16.81%	1	-1.08%	6	-8.68%	3
MOROCCO	71	1.60%	7	-1.74%	6	4.35%	8	0.09%	7
NIGERIA	72	4.04%	8	0.13%	7	-6.74%	3	8.64%	9
SOUTH AFRICA	73	0.20%	7	-0.56%	6	-1.73%	6	-4.18%	5
SENEGAL	74	14.42%	9	2.50%	7	2.20%	7	-5.79%	4
TANZANIA	75	-1.48%	6	-10.35%	2	-19.23%	0	-0.47%	6
TUNISIA	76	3.00%	7	7.64%	8	7.05%	8	5.43%	8
ZAIRE	77	3.75%	8	0.57%	7	22.44%	9	14.04%	9
ZAMBIA	78	8.54%	9	2.11%	7	1.52%	7	12.29%	9
ZIMBABWE	79	-3.33%	5	-4.41%	5	-6.80%	3	-6.18%	4
AVERAGE		0.00%	5.4	0.00%	5.0	0.00%	5.1	0.00%	5.0

References

Block, Walter, ed., *Economic Freedom: Toward a Theory of Measurement*, Vancouver: The Fraser Institute, 1991.

Buchanan, James M., and Gordon Tullock, *The Calculus of Consent: Logical Foundations of Constitutional Democracy*, Ann Arbor: University of Michigan, 1971.

Buchanan, James M., *The Limits of Liberty*, Chicago: University of Chicago Press, 1975.

Directorate-General of the Budget, Republic of China, *Statistical Yearbook of the Republic of China*, Taipei, Taiwan: Republic of China, various issues.

Epstein, Richard A., *Takings: Private Property and the Power of Eminent Domain*, Cambridge, Massachusetts and London, England: Harvard University Press, 1985.

Friedman, David, *The Machinery of Freedom*, Chicago: Open Court, 1989.

Friedman, Milton, *Capitalism and Freedom*, Chicago and London: The University of Chicago Press, 1962.

Friedman, Milton and Rose Friedman, *Free to Choose*, New York: Avon Books, 1981.

Friedman, Milton and Rose Friedman, *Tyranny of the Status Quo*, San Diego/New York/London: Harcourt Brace Jovanovich, 1983.

Government Information Services, Hong Kong, Hong Kong 1989, various years.

Hayek, Friedrich A., *The Road To Serfdom*, Chicago: The University of Chicago Press, 1944.

Hayek, Friedrich A., *Law, Legislation and Liberty*, Chicago: The University of Chicago Press, 1973.

Hayek, Friedrick A., *The Fatal Conceit : The Errors of Socialism*, Chicago: The University of Chicago Press, 1989.

Hoppe, Hans-Hermann, *A Theory of Socialism and Capitalism*, Boston: Kluwer, 1989.

International Institute for Strategic Studies, *The Military Balance*, annual, various issues.

International Monetary Fund, *Government Finance Statistics Yearbook*, Washington, D.C.: International Monetary Fund, various years.

International Monetary Fund, *International Financial Statistics Yearbook, 1989*, Washington, D.C: International Monetary Fund, 1989.

Nozick, Robert, *Anarchy State and Utopia*, New York: Basic Books, 1974.

Pilon, Roger, "Property Rights, Takings, and a Free Society," in *Public Choice and Constitutional Economics*, edited by James Gwartney and Richard Wagner. Greenwich, CT: JAI Press, 1988.

Price Waterhouse, *Doing Business in [name of country]*, various issues.

Price Waterhouse, *Individual Tax Rates*, various issues.

Rabushka, Alvin, "Taxation, Economic Growth, and Liberty, *Cato Journal*, Spring/Summer, 1987.

Rabushka, Alvin, "Rating Economic Freedom," in Walter Block, ed., *Economic Freedom: Toward a Theory of Measurement*, Vancouver: The Fraser Institute, 1991.

Reynolds, Alan, "Some International Comparisons of Supply-Side Tax Policy," *Cato Journal*, Fall, 1985.

Reynolds, Alan, "International Comparisons of Taxes and Government Spending" (this volume).

Rothbard, Murray N., *Power and Market: Government and the Economy*, Menlo Park, California: Institute for Humane Studies, 1970.

Rothbard, Murray N., *Man, Economy and State*, Los Angeles: Nash, 1970.

Rothbard, Murray N., *For a New Liberty*, New York: Macmillan, 1973.

Rothbard, Murray N., *The Ethics of Liberty*, Atlantic Highlands, N.J.: Humanities Press, 1982.

Walker, Michael A., ed., *Freedom, Democracy and Economic Welfare*, Vancouver: The Fraser Institute, 1988.

Wilkie, James W., ed., *Statistical Abstract of Latin America*, Los Angeles: UCLA Latin American Center Publications, various issues.

The World Bank, *World Tables, 1989-90*, Baltimore and London: The Johns Hopkins University Press, 1990.

The World Bank, *World Development Report*, Oxford: Oxford University Press, annual.

World Economic Forum, *The World Competitiveness Report, 1989*.

Discussion

Milton Friedman argued that money and prices should not be in the index. Insofar as inflation is a tax on money it is being counted twice as it is counted as social expenditures. Insofar as instability of money is being regarded as economic freedom, then the standard deviation or some measure of price change should be there. (This was done in the revised version of the paper presented in this volume.) He did not think that growth rates of money or inflation should be there. Although it is true on average that high rates of inflation are associated with more variability of inflation, it is not direct enough to be useful in this context. Friedman remarked that he did not know what to define as a monetary system consistent with complete economic freedom. Clearly there is no such system in modern times. What should be the baseline? Is monetary freedom a contribution to economic freedom or a contribution to wealth?

Ronald Jones continued this theme by pointing out that if the government does something that changes relative prices, then you get gains and losses. Should that be counted as a loss in freedom? Referring to the analysis in his paper with Alan Stockman he concludes a loss occurs only if the markets are impeded. If, as Gwartney, Block and Lawson argue, the price level changes due to government action which alters the nature of contracts, so long as contract formation is not impeded, this is not a loss in freedom.

Juan Bendfeldt felt that when the value of money is destroyed it does reduce economic freedom, and that right now the U.S. dollar functions as a world money. But Milton Friedman argued that this still does not help us establish a norm for monetary systems. Alan Stockman suggested that we may still want to measure the way in which resources are extracted from the economy as some may lead to greater violations of economic freedom than others, for instance, different types of taxation. But there is another issue which is one of regulation. Can you enforce, in courts, contracts written in various currencies. Does government money compete with private money? John Chant remarked that although the time dimension for contracts is dealt with in the paper, he did not recall seeing measures of interest rate control—usury laws and the like, or other measures of the regulation of financial intermediation.

Walter Block felt that there was some double counting but that it was not too serious as some losses were probably missed. A measure of standard deviation would be an acceptable measure. His view was that the best system from the point of view of economic freedom was the gold standard. Richard Stroup suggested that the budget does capture losses in freedom except when there is a restriction of alternatives. If gold is not forbidden, then it is not clear what the restriction on freedom is beyond the budget itself. Zane Spindler made the point that only a part of the inflation tax would show up in government expenditures in a fractional reserve banking system.

Arthur Densau suggested that there are more subtle issues having to do with government credibility associated with particular monetary regimes and policies. Michael Walker drew an analogy to the imposition of rent control policies which, even when removed, were always remembered as a potential instrument of intervention. Milton Friedman interpreted the discussion to parallel the debate about what goes into a constitution. A country that has certain guarantees of economic freedom will be freer than if that guarantee is left to current legislation. Spindler noted that this may just increase the cost of rent-seeking as now rent-seekers will have to go for constitutional reform rather than simple legislative changes. Block thought that although integral to the idea of economic freedom, we may not have the ability to quantify the economic freedom potential at different levels of the political process.

Alan Stockman wondered about the use of the term discriminatory taxation in the paper. What isn't? Just count all taxes as contributing to the loss in economic freedom. Similarly, the discussion of taxation for public goods must be mirrored by a discussion of public bads. James Gwartney tried to clarify that the concept of discriminatory taxation is that the amount of tax is in no way tied to the amount of benefit you receive from direct government spending or through the provision of public goods. A better term might be a disproportionate tax.

In a more general reaction to the comments, Gwartney liked the idea of a variance measure of inflation, but felt that growth, economic freedom and credibility were very difficult issues.

Prospecting for the "Homework" Measures of Economic Freedom: A Summary

Z. A. Spindler and J. F. Miyake,[1]
Simon Fraser University

"If it is worth doing, it is worth doing imperfectly."
—W. Block [2]

Introduction

WE STARTED OUR PAPER ENTITLED "The 'Homework' Measures of Economic Freedom," which was prepared for the "Rating Economic Freedom IV Symposium" with the aphorism given above. It was gleaned from Walter Block's remarks at the end of the "Rating Economic Freedom

II Symposium." In those remarks, Block listed the freedom measures that are the subject of this paper. These diverse measures were suggested by various Symposium II participants as part of their "homework" assigned in an earlier session. This aphorism and historical note were intended to explain our paper's title and subsequent designation of the freedom measures contained within, as well as our meta-methodological perspective.

Our task for the Fourth Symposium was to explore whether the measures listed had statistical analogues in data collected or processed by others. In our explorations, we neither searched for nor obtained perfection. Instead, what we did was a rather exhaustive (or at least exhausting!) search of existing literature and data sources for measures which at least approximated the (sometimes fuzzy) "Homework Measure of Freedom" desiderata. We then used that data to make a first stab at providing ratings for each measure when ratings were not given by the original source. We also tried to be more or less methodical about marking our path and providing some commentary on the problems of, and reasons for, treading it.

Further, in an attempt to make some sense of these fairly diverse measures, we separated them into documentation, discussion, and presentation sections. In order, these sections were government size, tax measures, government regulation, indirect measures and civil rights measures.

Where possible, we also calculated Spearman Rank Correlations between measures within sections and across sections. These correlations suggested that a few alternative measures within sections, and even across sections, were sometimes reasonably close substitutes in terms of measuring the extent of freedom in any given country. That in turn suggested that our resources might be better devoted to developing to a higher state of perfection fewer key indicators.

Since our original paper was very long, we have chosen to incorporate only the essential elements from our data explorations into a summary section giving a "concordance" between the original descriptions given in Block's listing and our versions of the "homework" measures along with our sources and rating scheme. Our original discussions, rationales and source data can be found in our original paper which, for a limited time, will be available from the authors or The Fraser Institute. We have also included our summary statistics, and, of course, our summary table of country economic freedom ratings.

Table 1. Basic Data Matrix

Category	1	2	3	5	6	7	8f	9a	9b	10	11	12	14	15	16	17	18	19	20	21	22	23	24
Year	88	80	81	85	81	85	*	85	87	75	87	80	60	85	80	89	87	80	88	80-84	88	80	81
Afghanistan							2																
Albania				5																			
Algeria			1		1		5				5	2	1	3	3	5		3	1				
Argentina		3	2	4	1		1	3			3	5	3	3	3	3		2					
Australia	2	2	1	4	1	4							2	3	1			5	1	5	1		
Austria	1	5	1	4	1	5			2	3		1	2							2	2		1
Bahamas						3						4	2		3								
Bahrain				1							5	2	2	2	4		2						
Bangladesh			2		2		1	2			5	2	3										
Barbados								3			5	1	3	2	2	5	5						
Belgium	2	5	1	5	1	5	1	3	2	4	5	5	5		2	5	4	1				1	2
Benin			2	5	1																		1
Bolivia		2	1	5	1		5	1			4	2				3	5	1	5	5		2	1
Botswana			1		1	5		5	1		5	3								2			
Brazil			1	4	1	3	1	1			3	3					5	3	2	4	5		1
Brunei				5	5																		
Bulgaria			5	3			1																4
Burkina Faso						2	4	2										1	5	2			
Burma							2	2					4							1			
Burundi				4	4	3		3			5	4					5		2	2		1	
Cameroon			2	3		3	1				4	4	2	2	1	1			4	2		1	1
Canada	2	2	1	5	1	5		2		3		4		2		2		4	1	2	1	4	1

Table 1. Basic Data Matrix

Category	1	2	3	5	6	7	8f	9a	9b	10	11	12	14	15	16	17	18	19	20	21	22	23	24
Year	88	80	81	85	81	85	*	85	87	75	87	80	60	85	80	89	87	80	88	80-84	88	80	81
C. African Rep.				5			1				5									2			
Chile		3	2	3	2		1	3			3	3	3				5	2		3	5		5
China			4	5	4		3	3	5		5						5			1			2
Colombia			1	2	4		1				4	2					2	1		3	3		1
Congo				5			1				5						5			2			
Costa Rica		3	1	5	1		1	3			4	3					3	2		3	2		1
Cuba			5	5	1	4									1								4
Cypress																							
Cyprus				3	2			3			5							3		2		2	
Czechoslavakia	1			5	1				1	3					1	3				2	4		4
Denmark		4	1	5	1			5	1			5	1	2	3			5	1	2	4	5	1
Dominica											5												
Dominica R.			1	2	1		1	2					3			1		1	3	3			1
Ecuador		3	2	3	1		1	2			4	2					2		4	2	2		1
Egypt			4	1	2		1	5			4	2					5	5	4	2	5	3	1
El Salvador				4		2	4	2			4	2					5			2	2		
Ethiopia				5	5		2	3			5	2	3					2		2			4
Fiji				1		4		3	5		3		3			1	5			2			
Finland	1	4	1		1	4		3		3		5	2	5	1	3	3	4	1	2	5	5	1
France	1	3	1	5	1			4		3		5	2	3	5		4	4	1	2	4	3	1
Gabon											5		5				5			2			
Gambia											5		5					3		2			

Table 1. Basic Data Matrix

Category	1	2	3	5	6	7	8f	9a	9b	10	11	12	14	15	16	17	18	19	20	21	22	23	24
Year	88	80	81	85	81	85	*	85	87	75	87	80	60	85	80	89	87	80	88	80-84	88	80	81
Germany W.	2		1		1	4			1	3		5	1	4			4	4	1	2	2	4	1
Germany E.			5	5	2										3								2
Ghana			2		1	2	5	2			4								4	4			1
Greece	1		1	5	1	5	1	3			3	3	4	4			4	3	1	3	2		1
Grenada				5							5							2		2			
Guam																							
Guatamala				4			1				3	2					2	1		2	2	1	
Guinea											5												
Guyana		3		5				5			5												
Haiti			2	1	4		1	3			5	2	4				3			2	2		2
Hong Kong			1	1	1		1					2	4				3			2	2		1
Honduras		3		5			1	2	1		4	2	3				4	1		2	2		
Hungary			2		1	3		5			5	2	3	2						2			4
Iceland	5					3		3					4		1			5	2	3		4	
India			1		1	4	2	2			5	2	4		2			3	5	2	2	1	1
Indonesia			2		4	3	1	3			4	2	4				3	2	5	2	2		1
Iran					5	3	5						3					3		3			
Iraq			4	5																			
Ireland	2	4	1	1	1	5		4	1	4		4	2			5		5	2	2	2	3	2
Israel		4	1		2	4		2				3	2			3		5	1	4	3		1
Italy	1	5	1	4	1			3	1	5		3	4	2	1	3	5		1	3	2	3	1
Ivory Coast	1			2			1			5		4							5				

Table 1. Basic Data Matrix

Category	1	2	3	5	6	7	8f	9a	9b	10	11	12	14	15	16	17	18	19	20	21	22	23	24
Year	88	80	81	85	81	85	*	85	87	75	87	80	60	85	80	89	87	80	88	80-84	88	80	81
Jamaica			1	1	1		2	3		3	4		3		5	2	5			3		3	1
Japan	1	5	1	2	1			2	2			4	2		1	2	5		1	1		2	1
Jordan				1				3			5							5	5	2			
Kenya			2	1	2	3	1	3	1		4	3	4			3	5	5	2	2	5	2	1
Korea (S)			2	2	2		2	2	3		4	3	4		1	1	5	3	2	2	5	2	1
Korea (N)			5		5	5																	4
Kuwait			2	4	1	5	1	5										3	1	2			2
Laos				5							5												
Lebanon				1							5												
Liberia			4	5	2	4	1	3			5						4		5	2		2	2
Libya			2		2		3																4
Luxembourg	2	5				4			1			4	4		5	4	4	4		2	4	3	
Madagascar								2			5	3	4				5	3		3			
Malawi							3	3			5	2	4				5			2			
Malaysia			2	3	1		1	3	1		4						3		2	2	2		1
Mali											5	3							2	2			
Malta	3			3		4		5			5				1		3	3		2		3	
Mauritania							2				5									2			
Mauritius			1	1		3	1	3	1		4		4			2	4		4	3			
Mexico				5	1		1	2	2		4		4		1	2	5	2	2	3	2		1
Mongolia				5																			
Morocco			4	1	2	4	1	3			4	3					4			2			1

Table 1. Basic Data Matrix

Category	1	2	3	5	6	7	8f	9a	9b	10	11	12	14	15	16	17	18	19	20	21	22	23	24
Year	88	80	81	85	81	85	*	85	87	75	87	80	60	85	80	89	87	80	88	80-84	88	80	81
Mozambique			4	5	4		5																1
Nepal		3	1	1	1	2	1				5								3	2			
Netherlands	1	3	1	5	1			5	1	3		5	3		2	4	5	5	1	2	1	3	1
New Zealand	2	2		1	1	5		4	1					1	5	3	4	4	2	2	2	5	1
Nicaragua		3		4			5				5									3	2		
Niger				3			1				3									2			
Nigeria	1		1				3		2		4	4			2	2	2	5	1		1		1
Norway		4	1	1	1	4		5		4		5	2	4	2			3	1	2	1	5	1
Oman							1	5			5							3	1			3	
Pakistan			2	4	2		1	2			4	2	4				2	3	5	2	2		1
Panama		3	1		1	4	1				5	2					4	3	1	2	2		1
Papau N.G.			1		1			3					4						3	2			1
Paraguay		3	2	3	1		2	1	1		4	3	4			3	3	1	2	2			1
Peru			1	2	2	2	1	2			4	2					4		4	4	5		1
Philippines			1	5	4		1	2			3	2	4				2			3	3	2	1
Poland			4	5	2							2	4		1				2	3			2
Portugal	3		1		1		1				4	3		4	1					3	3	2	1
Qatar				1																			
Romania			5	5	2						5							4		2			5
Rwanda				1	2		2				5									2			
Saudia Arabia			4	2	2		1										5			1	1		1
Senegal			1		1		1				4	3								2		1	1

Table 1. Basic Data Matrix

Category	1	2	3	5	6	7	8f	9a	9b	10	11	12	14	15	16	17	18	19	20	21	22	23	24
Year	88	80	81	85	81	85	*	85	87	75	87	80	60	85	80	89	87	80	88	80-84	88	80	81
Seychelles				5							5				4			3		2			
Sierra Leone			1		2	1		2			5		5						4	3			1
Singapore			2	3	1	3	1	3	2							1	3	2	1	2	2	3	1
Somalia				5							5									3		3	
South Africa	1	3	5		5		1	2	3				2			4	2	2		2	2	1	2
Soviet Union			5	5	4								4	4									4
Spain	2		1	4	1	3				2		3	4	4	1			3	2	2	2	3	1
Sri Lanka			1		1	4	2	3			4	1	4					4	4	3		2	1
St Lucia											5									2		3	
St. Vincent				1							5												
Sudan				2			2				4		4		1			4		3		1	1
Suriname				3														4					
Swaziland											5							2		2		2	
Sweden	1	4	1	5	1	5		5	1	4			2	4	5	5	1	5	1	2	5	5	1
Switzerland	1	3	1	2	1	4	1	1	1				2	5		1	2	3	1	2	5	3	1
Syria			4		2						5				4					2			2
Taiwan			4		4		5										5				5		1
Tanzania			4	3	2	3	1	2			4	3	4	4		1	5			3		1	4
Thailand			1	3			1		3		3		4				5	2	4	2	2	2	1
Togo				3			1				5								4	2		1	
Trinidad			1		1						5							3	5				1
Tunisia			2		1			4			5	3	4					3	5	2			1

Table 1. Basic Data Matrix

Category	1	2	3	5	6	7	8f	9a	9b	10	11	12	14	15	16	17	18	19	20	21	22	23	24
Year	88	80	81	85	81	85	*	85	87	75	87	80	60	85	80	89	87	80	88	80-84	88	80	81
Turkey	2		4	5	1		2	2	1		4		3				3		2	3	2		1
Uganda							5				5		5						1			1	
United Arab Em.						2															1		
United Kingdom	1	3	1	5	1	5		4	1	3		4	2	3	2	3	4	4	1	2	2	5	1
United States	1	2	1	4	1	5		3	1	3		4	2	2	2	2	2	3	1	2	1	4	1
Uruguay		2				3	1	3			4	3						2	5	3			
Vanuatu											5									2			
Venezuela		2	1	5	1	3	1	3			4	3	3		2		3	2	2	2	2		1
Vietnam			4	5	4																		5
Yemen Arab Rep.											5							4					
Yugoslavia	5		1	5	1	3	3				2	3					5	3	3	3			5
Zaire			4		4		1				5		5				5	2	4	3			2
Zambia			4	1	4		2		3		4	3				2			2	2		2	1
Zimbabwe			4		2	4	3				5	3						4	4	2		1	1

* Twenty-five year averages used to make rations

Concordance: Measures of "Homework" Measures of Economic Freedom

In this section we give the abbreviated code which appears in our "Summary Rating Table," the associated original description of the variable from Block's list, a) the associated proxy we have found for that variable, b) the source(s) of our proxy, c) the date(s) of the data, and d) the verbal or numerical basis for our ratings, where appropriate. When we have not provided an equivalent measure for a specific measure on the original list, it is either because that measure is approximately the same as one we have provided or because we have not been able to find anything approximating the requested measure.[3]

HMF 1 "Restrictions on International Trade"
   a) Per capita cost of Restrictions on International Trade
   b) Easton, Stephen (1989) *Rating Economic Freedom: International Trade and Financial Arrangements.* (Mimeo) LF-FI Conference. International Monetary Fund (1989) *International Financial Statistics.* Washington, D.C.
   c) 1989
   d) Ratings (based on the ratio of per capita cost of trade and capital restrictions to per capita GDP)

0	< rank 1	0.05
0.05	< rank 2	0.1
0.10	< rank 3	0.15
0.15	< rank 4	0.20
0.20	< rank 5	

HMF 2 "Restrictions on Immigration"
   a) Permanent Immigration Requirements
   b) United Nations (1982) *International Migration Policies and Programmes: A World Survey.* Dept. of International Economic and Social Affairs. Population Studies, No. 80.
   c) 1980

d) Rating:

  1 = No restrictions
  2 = Quota or weighted system
  3 = Skilled labor or professionals only
  4 = Entry restricted to a given ethnic or religious group only
  5 = No permanent immigration

HMF 3 "Restrictions on Emigration"
  a) Freedom of immigration
  b) Humana, C. (1986) *World Human Rights (The Economist)*. London: Hobber & Stroughton.
  c) Early 80's
  d) Rating (derived from Humana's four point rating)
    1 = Respect for this freedom
    2 = Some violation or infringement
    4 = Substantial oppression, violation or restriction
    5 = Continuous violation or total denial

HMF 4 "Government Spending /GNP by Selected Categories"
  a) Major Categories of Government Spending/GNP ratios
  b) International Monetary Fund (1987) *Government Finance Statistic Yearbook*: Washington, D.C.
  c) 1980
  d) Aggregation of categories of Government spending produces the Government spending /GNP ratio, see HMF 19 for rating.

HMF 5 "Education - Whatever the State Monopolizes"
  a) Education - What the state does not monopolize
  b) UNESCO (1987) *UNESCO Statistical Yearbook*. London.
  c) 1985
  d) Rating (based on percentages not monopolized)
    100% ≥ rating 1 ≥ 80%
    80%   ≥ rating 2 ≥ 60%
    60%   ≥ rating 3 ≥ 40%
    40%   ≥ rating 4 ≥ 20%
    20%   ≥ rating 5 ≥ 0%

HMF 6 Freedom of Travel, Freedom to Relocate One's Domicile, Absence of Internal Passports"
   a)   Freedom of internal migration
   b)   Humana, C. (1986) *World Human Rights (The Economist)*. London: Hobber & Stroughton.
   c)   Early 80's
   d)   Rating (derived from Humana's four point rating)

1	=	Respect for this freedom
2	=	Some violation or infringement
4	=	Substantial oppression, violation or restriction
5	=	Continuous violation or total denial

HMF 7 "Total Government Spending/(Net National Product + Transfer Payments)"
   a)   As above
   b)   United Nations (1986) *National Account Statistics: Main Aggregates and Detailed Tables Part I & II*, New York. International Monetary Fund (1985) *Government Finance Statistics Yearbook*, Washington, D.C.
   c)   1985
   d)   Rating (based on numerical value of HMF 7 ratios)

$$0.0 \leq 1 \quad <0.1$$
$$0.1 \leq 2 \quad <0.2$$
$$0.2 \leq 3 \quad <0.3$$
$$0.3 \leq 4 \quad <0.4$$
$$0.4 \leq 5$$

HMF 8f "Official Price Level/Blackmarket Price Level"
   a)   Real Average Official Exchange rate/Real Average Blackmarket Exchange rate
   b)   Wood, A. (1988) *Global Trends in Real Exchange Rates 1960 to 1984*. World Bank Discussion Paper No. 35
   c)   1960 to 1984

d) Ratings (based on HMF 8f ratios)

0.00	≤	1	<0.25
0.25	≤	2	<0.50
0.50	≤	3	<0.75
0.75	≤	4	<1.00
1.00	≤	5	

HMF 9a "Aggregate Tax Rate"

a) As above

b) International Monetary Fund (1989) *International Financial Statistics Yearbook.* Washington, D.C.Price Waterhouse (1988) *Individual Taxes: A Worldwide Summary.* London.

c) 1985

d) Rating (based on HMF 9a rates)

0.0 ≤	1	<0.1
0.1 ≤	2	<0.2
0.2 ≤	3	<0.3
0.3 ≤	4	<0.4
0.4 ≤	5	

HMF 9b "Ratio of the Top Marginal Income Tax Rate to the Average Income Tax Rate"

a) As above

b) International Monetary Fund (1989) *International Financial Statistics Yearbook.* Washington, D.C. Price Waterhouse (1988) *Individual Taxes: A Worldwide Summary.* London.

c) 1987

d) Rating (based on HMF 9b ratios)

0	≤	1	< 3
3	≤	2	< 6
6	≤	3	< 9
9	≤	4	<12
12	≤	5	

HMF 10 "Reaction Index = (Government Deficit + the Underground Economy)/GNP"

a) As above
b) Frey, B.S. & Weck-Hannemann, H. (1985) "The Hidden Economy as an 'Unobserved' Variable." *European Economic Review.*
c) 1975
d) Rating (based on numerical value of HMF 10)

0	$\le$	1	<0.05
0.05	$\le$	2	<0.10
0.10	$\le$	3	<0.15
0.15	$\le$	4	<0.20
0.20	$\le$	5	

HMF 11 "Ratio of Total Government Debt to Total Debt Outstanding"

a) External Government Debt/External Total Debt (Data on internal debt is not available except for a few countries)
b) World Bank. (1988) *World Debt Tables - External Debt of Less Developed Countries.* Washington, D.C.
c) 1980
d) Ratings (based on numerical value of HMF 11 ratio)

0.00		1	<0.25
0.26	$\le$	2	<0.50
0.51	$\le$	3	<0.75
0.76	$\le$	4	<1.00
1.0	$\le$	5	

HMF 12 "Ratio of the Exchange Adjusted Price of a Standard Basket of Commodities in the Domestic Economy to the World Price of Those Same Commodities"

a) Real Exchange Rate
b) United Nations. (1986) *World Comparison of Purchasing Power and Real Product for 1980.* New York. United Nations. (1987) *World Comparisons of Purchasing Power and Real Product for 1980.* New York.
c) 1980

d) Rating (based on numerical value of HMF 12 ratio)

$$0.0 \leq 1 \quad <0.1$$
$$0.1 \leq 2 \quad <0.2$$
$$0.2 \leq 3 \quad <0.3$$
$$0.3 \leq 4 \quad <0.4$$
$$0.4 \leq 5$$

HMF 13 "Price Relative as a Measure of Regulatory Restriction"
No appropriate proxy found

HMF 14 "Fraction of Total Income Devoted to Various Expenditures by the Median Household"
a) Non-Discretionary Expeniture/Income
b) United Nations (1980) *Compendium of Social Statistics - 1977*. New York.
c) 60's.
d) Rating (based on HMF 14 percentages)

$$40\% \leq 1 \quad <50\%$$
$$50\% \leq 2 \quad <60\%$$
$$60\% \leq 3 \quad <70\%$$
$$70\% \leq 4 \quad <80\%$$
$$80\% \leq 5$$

HMF 15 "Fraction of Total Agricultural Output Marketed by Government Agencies"
a) 15-1 Average Level of Agricultural Protection; 15-2 Social Cost of Price Distortions
b) Gulbrandsen, O. & Lindbeck, A. (1973) The Economics of the Agricultural Sector. Almquist & Wicksell: Stockholm. Peterson, W.L. (1979) "International Farm Prices and the Social Cost of Cheap Food Policy. American Journal of Agricultural Economics. 61: 12-21.
c) Mid 60's and 1969.
d) Rankings (based on HMF 15 Percentages)

$$0\% \leq 1$$
$$1\% \leq 2 \quad <25\%$$
$$26\% \leq 3 \quad <50\%$$
$$51\% \leq 4 \quad <75\%$$
$$76\% \leq 5 \quad <100\%$$

HMF 16 "Emigration Rate as a Ratio to the Birth Rate"
  a)   Emigration Rate/Birth Rate ratio
  b)   United Nation (1985) *Demographic Yearbook*. New York.
  c)   1980
  d)   Rating (based on HMF 16 ratios)

0.00	≤	1	<0.25
0.25	≤	2	<0.50
0.50	≤	3	<0.75
0.75	≤	4	<1.00
1.00	≤	5	

HMF 17 *"Marginal Tax Rate of a Person with an Income Twice the Mean"*
  a)   As above
  b)   International Monetary Fund (1990) *International Financial Statistics Yearbook*. Washington, D.C. Price Waterhouse (1988) *Individual Taxes: A Worldwide Summary*. London.
  c)   1989
  d)   Rating (based on HMF 17 rates)

0.0	≤	1	<0.1
0.1	≤	2	<0.2
0.2	≤	3	<0.3
0.3	≤	4	<0.4
0.4	≤	5	

HMF 18 *"Highest Marginal Tax Rate Minus the Base Marginal Tax Rate"*
  a)   As above
  b)   International Monetary Fund (1989) *International Financial Statistics Yearbook*. Washington, D.C. Price Waterhouse (1988) *Individual Taxes: A Worldwide Summary*. London.
  c)   1989
  d)   Rating (based on HMF 18 net rates)

0.0	≤	1	<0.1
0.1	≤	2	<0.2
0.2	≤	3	<0.3
0.3	≤	4	<0.4
0.4	≤	5	

HMF 19 "Government Expenditures as a Share of GDP"
   a)   Government Expenditure/GDP ratio
   b)   International Monetary Fund (1987) *Government Finance Statistics Yearbook* : Washington, D.C.
   c)   1980 (or closest year as noted)
   d)   Rating (based on the numerical value of HMF 19 ratios)

0.10	≤	1	<0.20
0.20	≤	2	<0.30
0.30	≤	3	<0.40
0.40	≤	4	<0.50
0.50	≤	5	

HMF 20 "Tariff Revenue Divided by Total Value of Trade"
   a) Tariff Revenue/Total Trade
   b) International Monetary Fund (1988) *International Government Statistics Yearbook*. Washington D.C.
   c) 1988
   d) Ratings (based on numerical value of HMF 20)

0.00	≤	1	<0.05
0.05	≤	2	<0.10
0.10	≤	3	<0.15
0.15	≤	4	<0.20
0.20	≤	5	

HMF 21 "Inflation Rate during Last Five Years"
   a) Five-year Average Inflation Rate
   b) International Monetary Fund. (1987) *Financial Statistic Yearbook - 1987*. Washington, D.C.
   c) 1980
   d) Rating (based on HMF 21 percentages)

0%	≤	1	< 4%
4%	≤	2	< 16%
16%	≤	3	< 64%
64%	≤	4	<256%
256%	≤	5	

HMF 22 "Share of Aggregate Output Subject to Price Controls"

    a) As above

    b) Business International Corporation. (1990) *Investing, Licensing & Trading Conditions Abroad.* New York.U.S. Dept. of Commerce (1990) *Marketing Pamphlets.*

    c) 1989

    d) Rating (detailed definition given by source)

1	=	No price controls
2	=	Price controls - limited market coverage
3	=	Moderate market coverage - government regulates monopolies and essential prices
4	=	Moderate plus - government also monitors all prices
5	=	Extensive market coverage - all prices controlled

HMF 23 "Government Employment as a Share of Total Employment"

    a) Government Employees per capita

    b) Heller, P.S. & Tait, A.A. (1983) *Government Employment and Pay: Some International Comparisons.* International Monetary Fund, Occasional Paper 24.

    c) 1980 (or closest as noted)

    d) Rating (based on HMF 23 percentages)

$$0.00 \leq 1 < 2.00$$
$$2.00 \leq 2 < 4.00$$
$$4.00 \leq 3 < 6.00$$
$$6.00 \leq 4 < 8.00$$
$$8.00 \leq 5$$

HMF 24 "Property Rights"

    a) Freedom of property

    b) Humana, C. (1986) *World Human Rights (The Economist).* London: Hobber & Stroughton.

    c) Early 80's

    d) Rating (derived from Humana's four point rating)

1	=	Respect for this freedom
2	=	Some violation or infringement
4	=	Substantial oppression, violation or restriction
5	=	Continuous violation or total denial

Descriptive Statistics Tables

For the purpose of interpreting the following tables, remember that **r** is significant at 0.05 for all r ≥ 0.30 for n ≥ 30.

Section A

II. Government Size

Rank correlations between all rankable Government Size categories.
n=48

HMF7	1		
HMF19	0.74	1	
HMF23	0.45	0.58	1
	HMF7	HMF19	HMF23

This table suggests that alternative measures of government size are redundant.

III. Tax Measures

Rank Correlation between all rankable Tax Measure categories.
n=48

HMF9a	1			
HMF9b	0.06	1		
HMF17	0.67	-0.22	1	
HMF18	0.45	0.47	0.14	1
	HMF9a	HMF9b	HMF17	HMF23

This table suggests that HMF 9a may redundant since HMF 17 & 18 are good substitutes for it but not for each other or for HMF 9b.

IV Government Regulations

Rank Correlation between all rankable Government Regulation categories.
n=68

HMF5	1	
HMF22	-0.14	1
	HMF5	HMF23

This table does not reveal any redundancies for measures in this category.

V. Indirect Measures of Economic Freedom

Rank Correlations between all rankable Indirect Measures categories.
n=32

HMF10	1			
HMF12	-0.23	1		
HMF16	0.04	-0.26	1	
HMF21	0.24	-0.24	0.40	1
	HMF10	HMF12	HMF16	HMF21

No important redundancies are revealed here.

VI. Civil Rights Measures

Correlations of ordinal ratings between Civil Rights Measures and Lindsay Wrights categories **Civil Freedom** (CIV) and **Political Freedom** (POL).
n=83

HMF3	1				
HMF6	0.63	1			
HMF24	0.57	0.40	1		
CIV	0.74	0.63	0.64	1	
POL	0.77	0.64	0.56	0.93	1
	HMF3	HMF6	HMF24	CIV	POL

Apparently, not much is gained by using these HMF measures as substitutes for Wright's measures. Further, these HMF measures appear to be good substitutes for each other.

Section B

Rank correlations between all rankable categories and Scully's (REF III Symposium, 1989) overall index.

HMF	1	7	9a	9b	10	12	16	17	18
corr	-0.25	-0.59	-0.26	0.41	-0.57	-0.25	-0.26	0.23	-0.30
n	26	90	68	29	16	59	29	30	56

HMF	19	20	21	23
corr	-0.30	0.58	0.23	-0.8
n	70	64	99	57

This table suggests that only a few of the HMF measures are substitutes for Scully's measure. Others may be compliments.

Section C

Rank correlations between all rankable categories.

	1	7	9	9	10	12	16	17	18	19	21	23
1	1	-0.23	0.37	-0.07	0.14	0.42	0.2	-0.24	-0.07	0.18	-0.32	0.37
7		1	0.62	-0.66	0.85	0.53	0.35	0.74	-0.37	0.72	-0.15	0.56
9			1	0.03	0.19	0.53	0.36	0.48	0.08	0.64	-0.32	0.52
9				1	0.06	0	-0.87	-0.51	0.4	-0.14	-0.02	-0.49
10					1	-0.15	0.09	0.49	0.08	0.62	0.59	0.14
12						1	0.65	0.39	0.17	0.55	-0.5	0.74
16							1	0.67	-0.31	0.24	0.35	0.44
17								1	-0.17	0.65	0.07	0.21
18									1	0.01	0.13	-0.3
19										1	-0.24	0.54
21											1	-0.39
23												1

This table shows that almost all of the HMF measures are substitutes for a number of other HMF measures with the possible exception of HMF 1.

Notes

[1] We acknowledge the assistance of L. Still in the preparation of a section of our original paper and financial support from Challenge 90.

[2] Rating Economic Freedom II Symposium, 1988, published as Walter Block, ed., *Economic Freedom: Toward a Theory of Measurement*, Vancouver: The Fraser Institute, 1991.

[3] This is especially true of item 8 of which a number of subparts are duplicated elsewhere or are impossible to find. Indeed, we have given a detailed description of only one measure—8f—in the body of the paper. A second measure—8b (or 8-2)—we have proxied by the Draft Freedom Rating originally developed by Spindler and Still (1988) and printed out that measure in the SUMMARY RATING TABLE.

Discussion

Looking at HMF19, government spending relative to income, Milton Friedman argued that it indicates that India is the freest country among eleven which he used in discussing the Gwartney et al. paper. Since we would all agree that India is not the freest economically, why did this occur? If a country has 90% of its population in agriculture, then it is impossible for the government to spend any large fraction of their income. Somehow, he argued, we must modify this ratio to account for the level of income or the fraction of the population in agriculture, to have a useful measure. This points to the limitation of a technique that ranks 169 countries about which we know relatively little and the need to use the same measures for each.

James Ahiakpor suggested that the agricultural/urban mix should be considered in any ranking. He wondered if use of government employment and government expenditures is not double counting. Alan Stockman wondered about any suggested adjustment for agriculture or any other adjustment for the government's inability to interfere with economic freedom. Why do we want to adjust. For example, suppose personal computers make it more difficult for the government to infringe on economic freedom. He did not think we would want to "adjust" for computers. There is in fact an increase in economic freedom. If taxes are hard to collect, then it interferes less. Milton Friedman responded that the ratio of government expenditure to income may not be a good measure in these circumstances. Instead, the government interferes with freedom of movement, fixing prices and the like.

Arthur Denzau pointed out that property rights are difficult to measure. He gave the example of South Africa in which the legal system works very smoothly and well, but where blacks are unable to participate in certain lines of business in any way. Gwartney mentioned that although India looks relatively free according to the G/Y measure, it is less free along the other dimensions: number of government enterprises in many sectors, or price controls. These are part of the regulation dimension. Other countries like Guatamala and Honduras rank surprisingly high, and he argued, that it is because of the absence of the regulatory dimension. Mike Walker noted that Canada has 407 quasi-governmental companies. Juan Bendfeldt argued that the underground economy and emigration are both symptoms of diminished economic freedom.

Richard Stroup argued that if entry is not prohibited, then even if the government runs the trains, it matters little in terms of economic freedom. Apart from subsidies, counting government employees is over emphasizing the problems. James Gwartney replied that government almost always uses taxes, restricts entry, or restricts competitors. He gave examples in the U.S. of the post office and public schools. Walter Block argued that the very act of taxation which underwrites government enterprises reduces freedom. Edward Hudgins emphasized that the enforcement of laws on the books is often problematic and that the measurement of the informal sector may give some guide to how constraining it is. Stephen Easton remarked that a problem with public companies is that they create an expectation of further interference. He gave as an example public bus companies that typically need to enlarge their routes as they are continually losing money on those that they have. In the process they continually reduce the activity of private companies. Arthur Denzau pointed out that expectations are always difficult to measure. Rick Stroup argued that this is the same problem that we always face with prices and the like. The government budget captures all these effects. You need a handle on government regulation. Government enterprise is not a problem except as it is a function of regulation or restriction on entry.

Alan Stockman suggested that G/Y might not be a good measure of restrictions on economic freedom. G alone is a better measure. If you have $100 worth of government spending and income that is $200 or income that is $300, then the economic freedom that is lost is still $100. Why should we adjust by wealth or income instead of measuring the number of goods the government is taking away. Ron Jones stressed that both absolute and relative measures were useful in different contexts. Easton mentioned that by using the dollar approach as was done in his papers, evaluating economic growth may be more difficult as government expenditure policies may gather increased revenue simply because of the expansion of economic activity. This leads to the conclusion that governments of expanding economies have expanded their role, while governments of contracting countries appear to improve in comparison. Similarly, cross country comparisons are difficult.

James Ahiakpor suggested that some trade taxes are for the purpose of raising revenue and are not serious impingements on international trade. Milton Friedman argued that tariff revenue has no relationship to economic freedom whatsoever. He indicated that prior to 1860 Japan had no tariff revenue, nor any trade. Further, emphasizing Ahiakpor's point, he stressed that a level of tariff equal to a general tax domestically does not interfere with trade at all. What interferes with trade is the difference between the level of tariff and domestic tax. A large country will have less trade, all else equal than a small country, so tariff revenue is simply misleading. Some acknowledgment of country size must temper the trade tax kinds of claims about economic freedom. When Easton did this, Friedman recalled, he used the full expenditure levels on the goods rather than simply the amount of the tariff.

Arthur Denzau wondered what was actually used for exchange rates in some of the countries, and further how data on black markets had been collected. Gwartney wondered about what tax rates were being counted and Spindler responded that senior government rates were collected. John Goodman said that Swedish central government tax rates were about 40%, but rates rose to 70% when other levels of government taxes were included.

Milton Friedman argued that government spending rather than the various tax rates as a measure of government activity should be used. Ratios of top tax rates to bottom rates would seem to be a very insensitive measure of what one wishes to measure. Ratio of government debt to total debt would seem to be totally inappropriate for anything in which we are interested.

In the general discussion that ensued, total government expenditures (GNP account based) were distinguished from total government spending or total government purchases which include transfers or other kinds of spending not counted in the national income accounts. The use of marginal versus total taxes was discussed with the burden of the marginal being contrasted with the effect of the redistribution of the average. Ron Jones referred to Figure 4 in the Jones and Stockman paper to argue that the loss in economic freedom will always outweigh the level of tax revenue and that loss will increase as tax rates rise even though revenues rise and then fall. Alan Stockman argued that the wedge of the tax is the marginal tax and is relevant for the consumer surplus losses calculated in both Easton, and the Jones and Stockman paper. If the tax rate is increasing, then the average tells you what the government takes. Therefore both are needed. Milton Friedman claimed that he had no difficulty in recognizing that both the average and the marginal are important components of economic freedom but that the ratio of the top marginal tax to the average tax can be foolish since the ratio will be the same if the marginal rate is 20% and the average 10% as it would be if the top marginal rate is 90% and the average is 45%. Richard Stroup stressed that there is a problem with the high marginal rates as they may apply to a very small group of people, and he wondered how one can deal with this. James Gwartney responded that they tried to use some income based measure ranking a country lower if the high rate kicked-in earlier in the tax system. Stroup responded by suggesting that the different tax rates might have to be weighted by the number of people affected.

Measuring Economic Liberty

Gerald W. Scully,
School of Management,
University of Texas-Dallas
Daniel J. Slottje,
Department of Economics,
Southern Methodist University

Introduction

MEASURING THE AMOUNT OF LIBERTY available to citizens of countries throughout the world has been in the domain of political scientists for about 30 years. Early efforts at measuring political and civil liberty were made by Banks and Textor (1963), Dahl (1971) and Claude (1976). These early studies suffered from limitations on source material, the comprehensiveness of political and civil rights measures, and the comprehensiveness of attributes that make up the indexes.

Gastil (1987) has constructed indexes annually since 1973 of political and civil rights for virtually all nations. His political rights measure ranked from 1 (the highest degree of liberty) to 7 (the lowest) is based on rankings of criteria such as the meaningfulness of elections for the executive and legislature as an expression of the will of the polity, election laws and campaigning opportunities, voting power of the electorate (electoral vote weighting), multiple political parties, evidence of political power shifting through elections, significant opposition voting, freedom from external and military control of domestic politics, minority self-determination or plural-ism, decentralization of political power, and the attempt of political agents to reach a consensus on major national issues [Gastil (1987, p.9)]. Gastil's measure of civil liberty, ranked on a similar scale, is based on rankings of criteria such as freedom of the press from political censorship, freedom of speech, freedom of assembly and peaceful demonstration, freedom to organize for political purposes, equal protection under the law, freedom from search and seizure of property, an independent judiciary, freedom from arbitrary imprisonment, freedom from State terror and abuse, free trade unions and worker associations, free business and professional asso-ciations, freedom of religion, protected social rights (including freedom of property, internal and external travel, choice of residence, marriage and family), socioeconomic rights (including freedom from dependency on landlords, bosses, union leaders, or bureaucrats), freedom from gross socioeconomic inequality, and freedom from gross government indiffer-ence or corruption [Gastil (1987, p.10)].

Humana (1984, 1986) has developed a human rights rating for nations based on conformity to the United Nations Universal Declaration of Human Rights, the International Covenant on Economic, Social and Cul-tural Rights, and the International Covenant on Civil and Political Rights. These 40 separate attributes of human rights include many of those consid-ered by Gastil, but include also freedom from compulsory work permits or conscription of labor, freedom from capital punishment and corporal pun-ishment, freedom from mail censorship or telephone-tapping, political, legal, social and economic equality for women and ethnic minorities, the right to free legal counsel, and freedom of personal rights (inter-racial marriage, equality of the sexes, use of contraception, homosexuality).

While the Gastil measures of civil and political liberty have gained widespread acceptance among scholars, they are subject to criticism, because they do not distinguish between natural or negative rights and positive or human rights. Negative rights are those that a freely constituted society reserve for themselves exclusively, denying the State any, or severely restraining rights to interfere. These are the individual rights articulated in the Virginia Bill of Rights, the original Constitution of the United States, and the Bill of Rights Amendments to the U.S. Constitution. Positive or human rights (e.g., the right to a job at a reasonable level of reward, the right to pursue a given life style without any interference or discrimination, the right to decent housing, the right to a clean environment in which to work, live, and pursue leisure activities, etc.) are those rights granted by the State to all or some individuals at the expense of other individuals. Fundamentally, positive rights interfere with and diminish negative rights. The State cannot set working hours, minimum wages, employment benefits, working conditions and regulate product markets (fair price competition, consumer product safety, licensing, etc.) without diminishing the right to freedom of contract. The State cannot define land use and license business activity without diminishing the economic right of due process. Positive rights essentially are transformations of rights to stream of income and utility. For the State to act as an agent that brokers the distribution of these positive or human rights, it must as a natural consequence interfere with negative rights. The justification for the circumspection of negative rights is that sovereignty rests with the political majority. Political scientists adhere religiously to the notion of majoritarianism as a principal of sovereignty. As a consequence individual rights are subject to the political market place in which vote maximizing politicians aggregate coalitions (special interests) to get elected and remain in office. Liberty as understood by classical liberals loses its meaning under a regime of sovereignty by majority rule.

Gastil (1982) in collaboration with Lindsay Wright, developed measures of economic liberty. Skepticism has been expressed about these measures (Walker, 1988). The aggregate measure of economic liberty is an aggregation of four sub-indices of economic freedom: (1) the right to private property (but, including attributes such as land reform and social services); (2) the right to freedom of association (including, the rights to form trade unions and to form business associations or cartels); (3) the right to freedom of internal and external travel (but, including such attributes as discrimination and socioeconomic mobility); and (4) the right to information (price controls, subsidies, minimum wage, media ownership). Freedom of association, so measured, is freedom to collude to redistribute income, which is hardly the notion that a classical liberal has of a negative or constitutional right. Although freedom of the media is an important attribute of economic (as well as civil and political) liberty (competition of ideas and policies in an open forum), freedom of information ought to be the right of economic actors to confront free market prices (see Rabushka, (1989)) for further criticism of the Gastil-Wright economic liberty measures).

Rabushka (1989) has argued that a quantitative measure of economic liberty needs to be much more comprehensive in scope and more precise in definition of the attributes that aggregate to an overall measure than are found in the Gastil-Wright measures. He would include the right to private property, including freedom of contract, the rule of law (equal protection under the law, an independent judiciary, etc.), the size of the State or the State's command of resources through taxation and non-tax revenue, public spending, economic regulation of business and labor, the monetary framework and monetary policy, and commercial policy (free versus restricted trade). In addition to the definition and scope of the attributes of economic freedom, there is the problem of weighting the attributes to construct an overall measure of economic liberty. Past measures of economic liberty have either adopted the egalitarian standard of equal weighting (a social welfare function that treats each right as of equal utility or preference) of the attributes or the researcher imposes his own standard of relative importance of the attributes (see Spindler and Still (1989) for a discussion of the weighting of the four sub-indices of economic freedom in the Gastil-Wright ratings).

The purpose of this paper is to construct some aggregate indexes of economic liberty and to demonstrate how relative rankings of liberty across countries will vary, contingent on how relative information about liberty, from individual liberty indicators, is aggregated and weighted. This paper is essentially a sensitivity analysis demonstrating how world rankings of liberty vary as we alter the way we summarize the information from several liberty indicators into one summary index.

Attributes of Economic Liberty

The objective of this paper is to measure economic liberty as comprehensively as possible with available data for as many countries as possible. A total of fifteen attributes of economic liberty were selected.[1] L1 is the Foreign Exchange Regime (available from Pick's Currency Yearbook, which has been renamed as World Currency Yearbook). The foreign currency regime is coded 1 = Free, 2 = Liberal, 3 = Strict, and 4 = Dictatorial and characterizes the degree of State control of international financial transfers and the relationship between official exchange rates and market shadow exchange rates. Since exchange rate and foreign currency restrictions are coincidental policies of trade restrictions, the measure captures the degree of openness (price competitiveness) of the economy and the right of economic actors to confront world prices. Free trade induces allocative efficiency in the economy and permits the exploitation of gains from comparative advantage. We experimented with a trade openness measure: exports plus imports divided by GDP. However, there are problems with such a measure (e.g., the European customs union arrangement yields a high degree of trade among the partners, but a modest level of trade with the world, some countries have very large domestic markets and can rationally home produce (e.g., the USA, etc.)). Moreover, the data was not complete for the large sample of economies in this study.

Attribute L2 is Military Draft Freedom, coded 1 to 5 (see Spindler and Still, 1989). Conscription is a tax and the probalistic taking of life and liberty. Attributes L3, L4, and L5 are Lindsay Wright's measures of freedom of property, freedom of movement and freedom of information. Attribute L6 is Gastil's Civil Rights index, a measure of the rule of law, coded 1 to 7. Attribute L7 is the Gastil-Wright classification of type of economic system, which ranges from capitalist inclusive = 1 to socialist non-exclusive = 9 and is a measure of the degree of individual versus State control of property and reliance on the market for the allocation of resources. Attributes L8 and L9 are the freedom of the print and broadcast media, respectively, coded 1 to 3, and represent the degree of competition in the market place for ideas (source: Gastil). Attributes L10 to L15 from Humana (1986), are coded 1 to 4, and are respectively, freedom to travel domestically, freedom to travel abroad, the right to peaceful assembly, permit not required for work, freedom from public search without a warrant, and freedom from the arbitrary seizure of property. For all of the attributes 1 is free and the highest value represents the least amount of freedom. In the next section we define the various economic liberty indexes analyzed in the paper.

Weighting the Attributes of Economic Liberty Indexes

In the construction of indexes of liberty, the current practice is to weight each attribute equally. By this egalitarian standard freedom of property, freedom to form trade unions and other collusive associations, due process of law, the military draft, capital punishment, and so on, are rights of equal preference in a citizen's utility function. Rights are logically separable and may or may not be lexicographically ranked by individuals. If it was possible to rank rights lexicographically in a social welfare function, weights based on the relative rankings of the attributes of liberty could be employed to construct an overall measure of liberty. Of course, this approach is not possible. An alternative is for the researcher to impose his own ranking on the relative importance of rights, but this is ad hoc. There are two objective methods of weighting the attributes of liberty in constructing an overall index of liberty. One method is to weight the attributes by the variances in the attributes. This is the method of principal components analysis. This technique has the feature that the normality assumptions in statistical theory are invoked. A second method is to use an instrumental variable or hedonic approach and weight by the regression coefficients. This technique has the feature that the regression coefficient of the liberty attribute on the instrumental variance (say, per capita income) measures the implicit value assigned to the attribute. These are the techniques employed here in the construction of overall indexes of economic liberty.

In the last section the individual economic freedom measures that others have used to examine economic liberty were described. In this section we present a multidimensional representation of economic liberty by combining the information from several different individual measures into a class of aggregate liberty indexes. As with the construction of any aggregate index, the critical step in combining various attributes into a single summary measure is the choice of appropriate weights. Since the index is a representation of a multidimensional view of a given country's level of economic liberty, we utilize several indexes that all represent different undimensional capsulizations. There are many ways to aggregate information into one broad index. One strategy we adopted was suggested by the social choice and income inequality literature. This body of research can be extended to our work by examining the relative ranking of economic liberty between countries. Absolute notions of liberty become meaningless when the absolute metric is based upon an index derived from a vector of characteristics that all purport to measure a different aspect of the same problem. Maasoumi and Nickelsburg (1988), Scully and Slottje (1991), Slottje et al. (1991), and Slottje (1991) have used principal component analysis to compare the quality of life between countries. This is a statistical technique which relies solely on the variation and covariation of the data matrix to construct the weights in the indexes. Griliches (1971) has suggested that if there is one attribute which we desire to analyze, but can't observe directly, like the level of economic liberty in a country, we can use a hedonic model to see how other factors affect this variable. This generally implies that we use some variable as an instrument for the latent variable and then see how other characteristics affect this instrumental variable. Frank (1985) is the leader of a new school of economists that argue that it is the relative levels that matter in the utility economic agents derive from consuming goods. We extend this argument to economic liberty by suggesting that it is relative rankings between countries given a set of liberty indicators, that have the richest information content in comparing liberty between countries.

In our study we use all of these approaches in constructing our economic liberty measures and in comparing the level of economic freedom between countries. We construct several different measures where the weights are alternatively determined by ranks of attributes, principal components of the attributes and a hedonic representation of the attributes. We then present the relative rankings for each index to serve as a sensitivity analysis of the different weighting specifications. Finally, we take the average rank for each country over all the different indexes as the final index of economic freedom.[2] These ranks can be used directly as indexes. In Table 1 (column 1), we take the average rank across all 15 attributes for each country. We then rank these averages. This is our first liberty index and we call it RINDEX1 (Rank Index 1). We can also use information about the ranks as the weighting factors as we discuss below.[3]

Table 1. Average Rankings Based Upon Index Weights Constructed By:

Country	Mean Rank of 15 Liberty Indicators	Mean Rank of Principal Component Techniques	Mean Rank of Hedonic Models	Overall Index
Afghanistan	105.3	123.5	105.8	116
Albania	112.5	140.5	135.4	142
Algeria	76.6	118.5	110.4	114
Angola	112	139.5	136.4	143
Argentina	37.7	52	36.4	42
Australia	5.3	19	15.2	14
Austria	12.9	9.5	12.6	12
Bahamas	7	13	16.2	13
Bahrain	55.3	15.5	28.4	39
Bangladesh	57	85	92.6	86
Barbados	11.5	14	10.8	10
Belgium	7.8	7.5	3.2	5
Belize	10.5	42	35.8	32
Benin	79.1	101	105.6	110
Bolivia	42.9	38	20	24
Botswana	17.333	53.5	54.8	52
Brazil	29.9	45.5	35.8	37
Bulgaria	112.5	140.5	135.4	140
Burkina Faso	63.4	92.5	99.8	98
Burma	94.6	126	126.4	130
Burundi	60.3	101.5	102.2	100
Cameroon	68	91	124.8	115
Canada	3.5	6	7.2	6
Cape Verde	62.9	95	121.8	112
Central Africa	61.6	67	81	77
Chad	74.9	97	128.6	124
Chile	59.55	69	64.2	67
China	94.2	108.5	89	99
Colombia	35.5	47	71	62
Congo	71.1	90.5	103.8	101

Table 1. Average Rankings Based Upon Index Weights Constructed By:

Country	Mean Rank of 15 Liberty Indicators	Mean Rank of Principal Component Techniques	Mean Rank of Hedonic Models	Overall Index
Costa Rica	4.6	19	20.6	15
Cuba	99.7	133	81.6	102
Cyprus	31.6	57.5	78.4	70
Czechoslovakia	105.66	136	105.2	120
Denmark	16.5	29.5	24.2	19
Dominica	5.9	23	31.2	20
Dominican Republic	17.1	35.5	39.6	34
Ecuador	33.6	49	25.6	31
Egypt	57.5	79.5	55.8	64
El Salvador	57.1	94.5	77	81
Ethiopia	106.3	131	123	131
Fiji	12.2	24	30	21
Finland	12.5	31	31.8	25
France	26	44	23.4	26
Gabon	33.4	51.5	78.2	68
Gambia	27.7	39	53.2	50
German Dem.Rep.	2.3	6	17.2	11
Germany Fed.	102.8	133	107.6	123
Great Britain	14.3	45	38.4	35
Greece	22.3	43	25.2	28
Grenada	66.8	88.5	70.8	78
Guatemala	40.4	38	78.8	65
Guinea	84.5	126.5	112.2	122
Guyana	72.1	107	128.4	126
Haiti	63.9	78	104.8	96
Hong Kong	11.9	13.5	3.6	8
Honduras	29.5	40	66.4	59
Hungary	84	121.5	73.4	92
Iceland	5.7	31.5	36.4	30
India	37.7	74	65.8	66

Table 1. Average Rankings Based Upon Index Weights
Constructed By:

Country	Mean Rank of 15 Liberty Indicators	Mean Rank of Principal Component Techniques	Mean Rank of Hedonic Models	Overall Index
Indonesia	62.2	74	107.8	97
Iran	83.1	113	93.4	104
Iraq	102.1	128.5	123.2	129
Ireland	1	1	7	1
Israel	35.4	52.5	34.2	40
Italy	19.5	54	41.4	44
Ivory Coast	43.3	54	81.6	73
Jamaica	24.9	63.5	60.4	61
Japan	4.6	19	20.6	16
Jordan	56.2	65.5	49.2	57
Kenya	40.5	72.5	94.2	83
Korea	46.7	80	99	89
North Korea	112.7	141.5	131.8	139
Kuwait	50.2	42	10	18
Laos	97.1	131.5	135.8	138
Lebanon	33.1	35	61.2	55
Liberia	57.3	52	83.2	76
Libya	81.9	115	117.2	121
Liechtenstein	1	1	7	3
Luxembourg	1	1	7	2
Madagascar	73.9	112.5	119.6	118
Malawi	66	103	106.4	108
Malaysia	37.6	55	51.2	54
Mali	67.7	85	113.2	107
Mauritania	73.1	109	137.4	132
Mauritius	8.4	26.5	30.6	22
Mexico	32.4	35	50	48
Mongolia	112.5	104.5	135.4	141
Morroco	59.7	86	78	79
Mozambique	89.5	126.5	136.2	136

Table 1. Average Rankings Based Upon Index Weights Constructed By:

Country	Mean Rank of 15 Liberty Indicators	Mean Rank of Principal Component Techniques	Mean Rank of Hedonic Models	Overall Index
Nepal	48.8	78	65.4	69
Netherlands	15.1	15	5.8	9
New Zealand	5.7	31.5	36.4	29
Niger	61.8	73	97	88
Nigeria	33.2	68.5	80.6	75
Norway	16.9	32	14.4	17
Oman	63.3	61.5	47.4	58
Pakistan	59.5	94.5	109.8	106
Panama	22.8	27.5	28.6	23
Papua New Guinea	13.5	47.5	52.4	49
Paraguay	54.1	73.5	57.8	63
Peru	41.1	73.5	74.6	74
Philippines	52.2	80	99.8	90
Poland	88.6	127	76.8	95
Portugal	26.6	62	55.6	56
Qatar	60.4	58.5	30.2	45
Romania	107.2	136.5	120.8	133
Rwanda	78.2	108.5	101.8	109
Saudi Arabia	69	68.5	68.2	72
Senegal	27.5	45	65.4	60
Seychelles	70.1	112	114	113
Sierra Leone	37.7	57	97.2	82
Singapore	52.2	52.5	47	51
Somalia	97.7	128	129	135
South Africa	97.3	126.5	87.2	105
Soviet Union	115.1	139	142.2	144
Spain	17.9	56.5	44	47
Sri Lanka	37.1	72	76.2	71
St.Lucia	11.3	45	45.6	41
St.Vincent	11.2	47	50.6	46

Table 1. Average Rankings Based Upon Index Weights Constructed By:

Country	Mean Rank of 15 Liberty Indicators	Mean Rank of Principal Component Techniques	Mean Rank of Hedonic Models	Overall Index
Sudan	61.3	100.5	129	119
Suriname	77.1	115.5	121.8	125
Swaziland	62.2	97	120.6	111
Sweden	13.9	32.5	45.2	38
Switzerland	12.8	15	1.6	7
Syria	75.7	96.5	123.6	117
Taiwan	48.7	67.5	29	43
Tanzania	88.9	122	124.4	128
Thailand	42.3	75.5	95	85
Togo	62.9	83	100.4	94
Trinidad and Tobago	17.6	54	55.2	53
Tunisia	55.1	90	78.6	80
Turkey	64.7	102	85.8	91
Uganda	79.3	123	124.4	127
United Arab E	59	53	22.2	33
United States	1	1	7	4
Vanuatu	19	25.5	45.4	36
Venezuela	17.7	32.5	29.6	27
Vietnam	110.1	140.5	129.8	137
Yemen Arab Re	75.3	111	71.2	84
Yugoslavia	76.1	113	74	87
Zaire	72.6	106	142	134
Zambia	61.3	99	105.6	103
Zimbabwe	65.3	94	94.6	93

Principal component analysis is a method whereby we analyze how much independence there is in a group of variables. This method is discussed in Scully and Slottje (1991) and Slottje (1991), and Slottje et al. (1991). In Table 1 (column 2), we present the ranks for each country based upon their respective first principal component. This is our Index 2, denoted

RINDEX2. We only consider one component because this component contains 60% of the total variation in the attribute data and the other principal components do not have a strong economic interpretation. While this is a statistical procedure, and perhaps not an economically intuitive one, it still is instructive. It tells us that if the 15 variables are reasonable indicators of liberty, they can be combined in such a way that different combinations of them create 15 new variables which contain as much information as the original 15, but without any multicollinearity problems. If we were to rely on any one of them (say the first one) then the coefficients a_{1j} represent the weights that give maximum variance. We construct one for each country and then rank them. Thus, countries like the U.S. and Luxembourg which have relatively low attribute values and low variances across all attributes, consequently will have a small first principal component, which will rank that country first. A country with a large amount of variation across attributes and large attribute values (low levels of economic freedom) will have larger component values. As we move to higher order principal components we get different ranking results since the variance is all that is left after filtering out the first principal component.

Information about the principal components can also be used directly as weights. This is done in the construction of Index 3. We call this RINDEX3 and discuss these results in the empirical section. Also, the values of the attributes were weighted by their ranks and normalized ranks ($rank_i$/max $rank_j$) and then these were weighted by the w_i's. All of these different weighting schema were highly correlated with Index 3. The average rank associated with two major principal component techniques (an average of RINDEX2 and RINDEX3) is reported as column 2 of Table 1. The other index specifications are given in Appendix Table A.1 for the interested reader. Indexes specified in these ways for each country will reflect to varying degrees the information content from each attribute relative to other countries and the country's ranking relative to other countries, as well as account for variation in the data. Again, the correlation (over 90%) between these alternative specifications of the indexes made the reporting of these alternative indexes with these various weighting specifications redundant. The other principal component-based indexes are also defined in Appendix Table A.1.

Rankings of Economic Liberty

In constructing an overall index of economic liberty, the simplest procedure is to rank the liberty indicators, average the ranks, and then rank the average of the 15 separate economic liberty indicator ranks. This procedure can be obtained from the average ranks of column 1 in Table 1. The rankings of economic liberty by this simple method yields plausible results. Nations like the United States, Luxembourg, West Germany, Canada, and Japan rank very high, the communist block countries rank at the bottom, much of Europe is in the upper quartile of rankings, and much of Africa is in the lower quantile of rankings. Index 1 also is highly correlated with some of the other economic liberty indexes (RINDEX2 and RINDEX6), but less so with some of the others (RINDEX8).

RINDEX2 is the rank of the index based on the first principal component. RINDEX3 is the rank of the index based on the weights obtained from the first principal component multiplied by the actual values of the fifteen attributes. Average rank in Table 1 (column 2) is the average of RINDEX2 and RINDEX3. The two ranks of the indexes are correlated (r = .81), but not coincident. The United States ranks first by both methods. But, there are some dramatic differences for some countries (such as Bahrain, Belize, Bolivia, Botswana, Chad, Congo, Cyprus, El Salvador, Guatemala, Haiti, Iceland, India, Italy, Jamaica, Jordan, Kuwait, Lebanon, Liberia, Mexico, Portugal, Qatar, Singapore, St. Lucia, Thailand, Trinidad and Tobago, and the United Arab Emirates).

RINDEX4 is the rank of the index based on the normalized coefficient estimates multiplied by the value of the liberty indicators for the full regression model (i.e., all 15 regressors). RINDEX5 is the same as RINDEX4, except that the normalized regression coefficients are multiplied by the rank of the liberty indicator. RINDEX6 is the same as RINDEX5 except that the liberty indicators (and RGDC) have been transformed into logarithms so that the coefficients are elasticities. RINDEX7 is the same as RINDEX5 except that the regressors have been restricted to only those that were independently statistically significant (L_1 - L_3, L_6, L_{10}, L_{11}, L_{13}). RINDEX8 is the same as RINDEX7 except that ranks rather than the values of the attributes were employed in the restricted regression. While these indexes are highly correlated with each other, several of the other indexes constructed but not discussed here, had considerably lower correlation values. The correlation values for the indexes discussed here ranged from .7 to .99, indicating some variation. For example, the United States ranks 1 by RINDEX7 and 15 by RINDEX6, Canada ranks 1 by RINDEX1 and 19, Spain ranks 22 by RINDEX6 and 53 by RINDEX4 or RINDEX5, and so on. The overall index, is highly correlated with all of the rank indexes which is of course a consequence of its construction and provides further evidence that it is a good summary statistic of the other indexes.

Conclusions

We have constructed a number of summary indexes of economic liberty based on principal component and hedonic weighting techniques. While overall these indexes are related to each other in a statistical sense, there are sufficient differences among them to conclude that choice of the weighting technique is important in the construction of an overall index of liberty. Because the liberty indicators currently available for use are fairly coarse, the differences that these weighting techniques yield in the summary liberty indexes are understated. As research on liberty yields finer measures of the liberty indicators, the choice of the weighting technique will become more crucial in defining an overall measure of economic liberty.

Notes

[1] The data for these attributes appears in an earlier version of the paper as Appendix Table A.1 and is available for a limited period from The Fraser Institute.

[2] In an earlier version of this paper, Appendix Table A.2 ranks each country from the lowest level (more liberty) to the highest level of economic freedom for each attribute.

[3] In the earlier version of this paper, all the rank indexes are available. For reasons of space limitations, only the selected average ranks rather than each RINDEX, the weighted ranks, are presented.

[4] Indexes (RINDEX2 - RINDEX8) which were selected to be representative of all the types of weighting that were possible are available in the earlier version of this paper.

[5] Spearman correlations for all these results which demonstrates how the indexes' rankings are related to each other are available in earlier verisons of this paper.

[6] A full comparison of the country by country differences in the liberty indexes by method of weighting the liberty indicators can be discerned in earlier versions of the paper.

Appendix

Table A.1. Formulas for Constructing Indexes

Index 1 = $\Sigma L_i.R_i$
Where L_i is the ith liberty indicator and R_i is the ith indicator's rank.

Index 2 = $\Sigma L_i.\{R_i/\max R_j\}$
Where $\{R_i/\max R_j\}$ is the ith indicator's rank normalized by the maximum indicator rank.

Index 3 = $\Sigma L_i.R_i.\{\lambda_i/\Sigma\lambda_j\}$
Where $\{\lambda_i/\Sigma\lambda_j\}$ is the proportion of total variance in the x matrix due to the ith eigenvalue.

**Index 4 = $\Sigma L_i.\{\lambda_i/\Sigma\lambda_j\}$
See index 1 and index 3 for definitions of variables.

Index 5 = $\Sigma \{R_i/\max R_j\}\{\lambda_i/\Sigma\lambda_j\}$
See index 2 and index 4 for definitions of variables.

Index 6 = $\Sigma R_i.\{\lambda_i/\Sigma\lambda/j\}$
See index 1 and index 4 for definitions of variables.

Index 7 = $\Sigma L_i.\{\beta_i^*/\max \beta_j^*\}$
Where $\{\beta_i^*/\max \beta_i^*\}$ is the normalized coefficient estimate from $\Psi = \beta_0 + \Sigma\beta_i L_i + \mu_i$ where Ψ is real gross domestic product per capita consumption share per country.

Index 8 = $\Sigma L_i.R_i \{\beta_i^*/\max \beta_j^*\}$
See index 1 and index 7 for definitions of variables.

Index 9 = $\Sigma \{R_i/\max R_j\}\{\beta_i^*/\max \beta_j^*\}$
See index 2 and index 7 for definitions of variables.

[**]Index 10 = $\Sigma R_i.\{\beta_i^*/\max \beta_j^*\}$
See index 1 and index 7 for definitions of variables.

[**]Index 11 = $\Sigma R_i.\{\alpha_i^*/\max \alpha_j^*\}$
The same index 7 except $Y = \alpha_0 + \Sigma\alpha_i R_i + V_i$.

[**]Index 12 = $\Sigma L_i.R_i.\{\alpha_i^*/\max \alpha_j^*\}$
See index 8 and index 11 for definitions of variables.

Index 13 = $\Sigma \{R_i/\max R_j\}.\{\alpha_i^*/\max \alpha_j^*\}$
See index 2 and index 11 for definitions of variables.

Index 14 = $\Sigma R_i.\{\alpha_i^*/\max \alpha_j^*\}$
See index 1 and index 7 for definitions of variables.

Index 15 = $\Sigma L_i.\omega_i^*$
Where ω_i^* is the elasticity from the model $\ln Y = A + \Sigma\omega_i \ln L_i + \Sigma_i$.

Index 16 = $\Sigma L_i.R_i \omega_i^*$
See index 1 and index 15 for definitions of the variables.

Index 17 = $\Sigma \{R_i/\max R_j\}.\omega_i^*$
See index 2 and index 15 for definitions of the variables.

Index 18 = $\Sigma L_i.\{\gamma_i^*/\max \gamma_j^*\}$
Where γ_i^* is the coefficient normalized from the model $Y = \gamma_0 + \gamma_1 L_1 + \gamma_2 L_2 + \gamma_3 L_3 + \gamma_6 L_6 + \gamma_{10} L_{10} + \gamma_{11} L_{11} + \gamma_{13} L_{13} + \mu$.

Index 19 = $\Sigma L_i.R_i \{\gamma_i^*/\max \gamma_j^*\}$
See index 1 and index 18 for definitions of the variables.

[**] Index 20 $= \Sigma L_i . \{\gamma_i^* / \max \gamma_j^*\} \{R_i / \max R_j\}$
See index 2 and index 18 for definitions of the variables.

Index 21 $= \Sigma R_i \{\gamma_i^* / \max \gamma_j^*\}$
See index 1 and index 18 for definitions of the variables.

Index 22 $= \Sigma L_i . R_i \{\delta_i^* / \max \delta_j^*\}$
Where δ_i^* is the normalized coefficient from the model
$Y = \delta_0 + \delta_1 L_1 + \delta_2 L_2 + \delta_3 L_3 + \delta_6 L_6 + \delta_{10} L_{10} + \delta_{11} L_{11} + d_{13} L_{13} + \mu$.

Index 23 $= \Sigma \{R_i / \max R_j\} . \{\delta_i^* / \max \delta_j^*\}$
See index 2 and index 22 for definitions of the variables.

Index 24 $= \Sigma R_i \{\delta_i^* / \max \delta_j^*\}$
See index 1 and index 22 for definitions of the variables.

Index 25 $= \Sigma L_i \{\delta_i^* / \max \delta_j^*\}$
See index 1 and index 22 for definitions of the variables.

[*] In Index 1 to 17 the summations are over 15. For indexes 18 to 21 they are over 7, and for 22 to 25 they are over 8.

[**] These indices are analyzed in the text above.

Table A.2. Coefficient Estimates of the Hedonic Models

$Y = {}^*5149 - {}^*298.95L1 + {}^*283.17L2 - {}^*320.32L3 + 200.6L4 + 51.53L5 - {}^*610.94L6$
$- 59.24L7 + 312.66L8 - 413.31L9 - {}^*461.05L10 + 348.75L11 - 58.07L12 +$
${}^*575.85L13 - 79.19L14 - .92L15$
$$R^2 = .64$$

$Y = {}^*7.65 - .002R1 + {}^*.009R2 + 0003R3 - .001R4 + .00006R5 - {}^*.01R6 - {}^*.005R7$
$+ .002R8 - .002R9 - {}^*.007R10 \quad .004R11 + .001R12 + {}^*.01R13 - .002R14$
$$R^2 = .65$$

$\ln Y = 8.3 - .11\ln L1 + .25\ln L2 + .04\ln L3 + .03\ln L4 + .003\ln L5 - .28\ln L6 - .10\ln L7$
$+ .10\ln L8 - .09\ln L9 - .31\ln L10 + .08\ln L11 + .008\ln L12 + .38\ln L13, - .38\ln L13 -$
$.08\ln L14 - .04\ln L15$
$$R^2 = .67$$

$Y = {}^*4818 - {}^*328.73L1 + {}^*307.14L2 - {}^*279.72L3 - {}^*632.87L6 - {}^*397.45L10 +$
${}^*318.86L11 + {}^*579.99L13$
$$R^2 = .62$$

$Y = {}^*3490 - {}^*6.66R1 + {}^*9.93R2 - {}^*10.82R3 - {}^*23.76R6 - {}^*8.68R9 - {}^*11.64R10 +$
${}^*11.79R11 + {}^*20.07R13$
$$R^2 = .60$$

* indicates coefficient is statistically significant at the .10 level.

Y is per capita real gross domestic product times consumption share per country.

To construct hedonic models real gross domestic product per capita (RGDP) was used as an instrumental variable. Summers and Heston constructed this series. RGDP is weighted by a country's consumption share. Many countries (e.g., oil exporting) have a high RGDP, but the State "owns" a large fraction of output that is not available for private spending. Real gross domestic consumption (RGDC) was regressed against the various attributes,

(1) $$RGDC = \beta_0 + \Sigma \beta_i L_i + \varepsilon$$

where L_i is the ith liberty attribute and β_i is the coefficient estimate of the effect of L_i on RGDC. The β_i's in normalized form were used as the weights in our indexes. This index is called RINDEX4 and corresponds to Index 10 in Table A.1. These results are discussed fully in section 4 below. In another procedure the attributes L_i were replaced by the ranks of the attributes R_i,

(2) $$RGDC = \alpha_0 + \Sigma \alpha_i R_i + \varepsilon$$

where a_i is the coefficient estimate of the effect of a country's rank on its RGDC. This can be interpreted as a method of examining whether countries with low (high freedom values) liberty have high or low RGDC relative to other countries and is denoted RINDEX5 (Index 11 in Table A.1) and is calculated by multiplying the attribute by the normalized coefficient estimate from (2). We also examine the elasticities of the attributes to see how responsive each individual countries' relative RGDC is to each countries' relative economic freedom measures. This specification is the same as (1) except the variables are in natural logs,

(3) $$RGDC = \omega_0 + \Sigma \omega_i \ln L_i + \mu$$

This gives rise to RINDEX6 and corresponds to Index 16 in Table A.1 which also includes other possible weighting schemes. For example, we weight the attribute by the normalized rank. Finally, one of the indexes is based on a hybrid hedonic procedure. The procedure is a hybrid one in that the same regressions model as in (1) and (2) was used, but a stepwise procedure was employed to only include those attributes which maximize the likelihood function, or, in other words, demonstrate that they belong in the model, subsequently implying they are the major hedonic attributes with respect to RGDC. For the Li model, these variables include economic freedom indicators 1, 2, 3, 6, 7, 8, 10, 11, 12 and 13. For the ranks (R_i) model, these factors include 1, 2, 3, 6, 8, 10, 11, 12 and 13. RINDEX7 and RINDEX8 correspond to index 20 and index 24 respectively. These are included to capture rank and normalized rank effects. While a wide spectrum of indexes were constructed for each hedonic specification, we report only the average of the hedonic indexes RINDEX4-RINDEX8 in column 3 of Table 1.[4] The underlying regression results for all of the hedonic models are given in Appendix Table A.2. All of the formulas needed to construct the various indexes are given in Appendix Table A.1. A summary was constructed by taking the average of all eight previously discussed indexes and then taking the ranking of these averages. This index is presented with all the other index rankings as a summary in the final column of Table 1.[5] We now discuss the empirical results.

References

Banks, Arthur and Robert Textor (1963), *A Cross-Polity Survey*, Cambridge, Mass.: MIT Press.

Dahl, Robert (1971), *Polyarchy: Participation and Opposition*, New Haven: Yale University Press, 1971.

Claude, Richard P., ed., *Comparative Human Rights*, Baltimore: Johns Hopkins University press, 1976.

Frank, R. (1985), *Choosing the Right Pond: Human Behavior and the Quest for Status*, Oxford: Oxford University Press.

Gastil, Raymond D. (1987), *Freedom in the World*, Westport, Conn.: Greenwood Press.

Griliches, Z. (1971), *Price Indexes and Quality Changes: Studies in New Methods of Measurement*, Cambridge: Harvard University Press.

Humana, Charles (1984), *World Human Rights Guide*, New York: Pica Press. (1986), *World Human Rights Guide*, London: Hodder and Stoughton.

Maasoumi, E. and G. Nickelsburg (1988), "Multivariate Measures of Well Being and an Analysis of Inequality," *Journal of Business and Economic Statistics*, 6, 327-334.

Rabushka, A., "Preliminary Definition of Economic Freedom," in Walter Block, ed., *Economic Freedom: Toward a Theory of Measurement*, Vancouver: The Fraser Institute, 1991.

Scully, G. and D. J. Slottje (1991), "Measuring Economic Liberty across Countries," *Public Choice*, 69, 121-152.

Slottje, D. J., G. Scully, K. Hayes and J. Hirschberg (1991), *Measuring the Quality of Life Across Countries*, Boulder: Westview Press.

Slottje, D. (1991), "Measuring the Quality of Life across Countries," *Review of Economics and Statistics* (forthcoming).

Spindler, Zane and Laurie Still, "Economic Freedom Ratings," in Walter Block, ed., *Economic Freedom: Toward a Theory of Measurement*, Vancouver: The Fraser Institute, 1991.

Summers, R. and A. Heston (1988), "A New Set of International Comparisons of Real Product and Prices," *Review of Income and Wealth*, 34, 1-27.

Walker, Michael A., ed., *Freedom, Democracy and Economic Welfare*, Vancouver: The Fraser Institute (1988).

Wright, Lindsay M. (1982), "A Comparative Survey of Economic Freedom," in Raymond D. Gastil, *Freedom in The World*, Westport, Conn.: Greenwood Press.

Discussion

Milton Friedman began the discussion by emphasizing two technical issues related to Table A1, the basis for the rest of the weighted results, and two conceptual issues. The technical issues hinge upon the problems associated with using category scores that range from 1 to 4 in most cases and 1 to 7 or 1 to 9 in others. In this case the weights assigned to the categories are implicitly different. The average score in the various categories will differ, and this will create different weights within the index. The rankings will be influenced by the size of the intervals. One possible way to handle this is that if a country appears to be in the top quartile, it could receive a score of .125, within the next quartile, .375 etc. Further, the actual scores in several of the categories appears to be highly arbitrary. For example, Hong Kong with respect to L13, Freedom to Work, is given a 3 while the United States gets a 1. What is this? In what way is Hong Kong less free than the United States?

And this led to the conceptual issue that in order to gain some feeling that the measures are capturing important differences among countries, there should be some basis or benchmark for comparison. In this way those measures which are patently at odds with our common sense can be discarded. We need test cases. The comparison between the US (ranked number 1 in terms of economic freedom) and Hong Kong (ranked number 20) is one example.

Argentina and Chile is another good test case — that Argentina ranks above Chile in economic freedom is not right. Similarly, although Hong Kong ranks above Sweden, the difference, 1.27 to 1.47 is very small. Similarly one can be suspicious of a measure that puts Switzerland (1.33) just barely more economically free than Sweden.

A second conceptual problem, Friedman suggested, is that the various measures take no account of trade arrangements or the fiscal burden. Ed Crane did not like the use of the term comprehensive in the paper since it also left the nature of government ownership versus regulation out of the measures. Richard McKenzie felt that Scully and Slottje had been overly confined by using published measures of what other people felt constituted economic freedom. Instead, he argued, we must use what is important. How it is obtained is less relevant now.

At this point Scully responded by stressing that his paper tried to illustrate the effects of different weighting techniques on the calculation of potential measures of economic freedom, and that to this end he had normalized all the categories and stuck with published indexes. To that extent he was not prepared to defend any particular score in any particular category. The sensitivity of the indexes of freedom to the different weighting schemes was the focus of the paper.

Alan Reynolds suggested that to be useful in promoting economic freedom, a paper should be simple, and that rather than striving for objectivity, the notion of economic freedom should be thought of like the scores of a diving competition: judged by expert opinion, and while not objective is nonetheless reasonably consistent. Milton Friedman responded that this was an attempt at scientific inquiry and, as such, it constitutes a search for important components of economic freedom and how they relate to other measures such as those Scully has mentioned: the GNP, quality of life, etc.

Bernard Siegan stressed that the absence or presence of the judiciary (another index) does not mean that economic freedoms are less or greater. The actual role of the judiciary, on the one hand enforcing confiscatory taxation, or on the other protecting economic liberties, is not picked-up in any measures. This led Charles Murray to wonder which of the indexes hung together, and which appeared to be measuring different things. Scully responded that perhaps eight of the indexes were independent.

Walter Block argued that the issue of weights to be put on the sub-indexes was overly detailed. He averred that using one's own introspective tastes to weight the indexes was as acceptable as some arbitrary criterion of variance weights. In contrast to the "high-tech" strategy of Scully and others, a "low-tech" strategy would be simply to add-up the indexes with equal weights. Jack Carr pointed out that the criterion for adequate weighting depended upon the purpose to which the indexes were to be put. Like the definition of money as M1 or M2, the question is not independent of use.

Carr stressed that some income maximization would appear to be both desirable and consistent with the basic perspective of economic behaviour. In this respect the hedonic weighting scheme looked better than the others. Stephen Easton then remarked that the optimal tariff raises domestic income, but according to some measures, reduces economic freedom. Carr responded that from a global perspective, there is a net income loss, and further something beyond a gut feeling is needed to establish the relevant weights in any index. He argued that a definition that maximizes economic well-being is appropriate so that greater economic freedom means greater economic benefit. James Gwartney remarked that this was the same basis for the use of GNP as a summary indicator of economic well-being. GNP tends to rise when most good things are increasing and tends to fall when times appear to be bad. As a more specific remark directed toward the paper, he wondered why inflation was not included as an indicator of the loss in economic freedom as it interrupted the execution of private contracts. Juan Bendfeldt remarked that indexes are better when used to compare one year to the next, and Scully and Slottje amalgamated data from several years into one index. Scully responded that while the desire to use a ("low-tech") counting exercise to identify indexes of economic freedom is more simple, it is also open to individual biases. A "high-tech" methodology is more useful as the methodology for the derivation of the weights is clearly apparent.

Milton and Rose Friedman's Experiment

[Editor's note: At the end of the first day of the Sea Ranch Conference (the second in the series reported in this volume), Milton and Rose Friedman proposed the following experiment. This is reported in a slightly different fashion since it was not a written document as a formal part of the series. We have tried to capture the sense of the presentation as well as the occasion without actually transcribing the proceedings.]

IN REVIEWING THE PAPERS, ROSE and I have had difficulty making sense of the different measures in the large number of countries. We have taken eleven countries about which we feel we know something and would ask you [the conference participants] to rank these countries from the most free to least free. We will tabulate the results tomorrow. One conclusion we have reached is that we are studying too many countries.

[One Day Later]

In the handout there is a tabulation which summarizes the results of the survey. In the results for the eleven countries which we know relatively well, we have provided an average, a standard deviation, the range and the maximum and minimum values of the rankings made by the 23 people at the conference. In each case 1 equals the greatest economic freedom and 11 the least. Every country was ranked by each person. In addition we have provided the rankings where possible by the indexes from Gwartney, Block and Lawson, by Easton's measures, and by Spindler and Miyake's HMF ranks. It is fascinating that there is both a great deal of agreement and considerable disagreement. The greatest agreement was on Hong Kong which everyone but one person ranked as 1 and that person ranked as 2. The United States had one 1, and three 3's and all the others ranked it as 2. Beyond that there is roughly the same amount of dispersion which is fairly moderate. The greatest dispersion is for Chile which is understandable given recent history. But if you look at the standard deviations and means, except for Hong Kong and the United States as the most economically free, and India, Israel, and Sweden as the least free, there is little to distinguish the intermediate countries.

If you look at the Gwartney ranking of his number 1, the ranking is not that different. Chile and India were a bit out of line. The right way to do this is to send surveys to people who know something about these countries, people who live there—almost everyone here is from the United States or Canada (and we should have put Canada in this). Looking at the Easton list, F1 seems way out of line as India ranks so high. The key thing to know in the cardinal approach is that what you call economic freedom or utility or whatever, is the numerical measure however you choose to construct it. You use a set of specified steps. The useful thing in the Jones-Stockman paper is the steps that they set out to define economic freedom. Many people object to the results of this kind of methodology. Indeed, as Stockman has suggested, the use of government expenditures as a fraction of income is an application of their kind of methodology, and we find that it doesn't give very good results. It is fine for the developed countries, but none of us here will accept the fact that by that measure all underdeveloped countries will be freer than developed countries. The test of whether we have a good measure is that it "works" and gives you results that you like. As I heard Fermi once say, the concept of length may be a good measure on earth, but it may be useless on the surface of the sun. The results that appear in F1 are very important from that point of view since they expose a defect. Easton's F2 is much better from this perspective. It has Japan as 1 and France as 2 and the U.S. as 3, and Sweden comes in last. Looking at the "HMF-homework" averages, the main thing that comes out is that these measures give you no discrimination. That doesn't mean that there are not some good ones among them, but as an average they are not very helpful.

Rank of the following countries in accordance with their level of economic freedom in accordance with measurements of indicted authors.
(1 = greatest economic freedom, 11 = least)

Country	GB Lint 1+2	Easton F1	Easton f2/gdp	HMF 7	HMF 10	HMF 23-2	HMF 9a	HMF 18	HMF 5	HMF 15-1	HMF 20	HMF 1	HMF 12	HMF 21	Count	Average	Rank of Average
Australia	9	6	4.5	3	3	7	5	4	5	1	8	6.5		5	13	5.15	8
Chile	7				2		6		3				8	10	6	6.00	9
France	8	3	2		5	3	8	5	6	4	3	5	6	8	13	5.08	6
Germany	5	4	4.5	4	7	4		7		5	2	6.5	7	2	12	4.83	5
Hong Kong	1							3	1				5	9	5	3.80	3
India	4	2	6.5	1	1	1	1				9		9	7	10	4.15	4
Israel	11			2	9		3				7		4	11	7	6.71	11
Japan	2	1	1		8	2	2	8	2	2	5	2	2	1	11	2.55	1
Sweden	10	8	8	7	8	8	9	1		6	4	3.5		6	12	6.46	18
United Kingdom	6	7	6.5	6	6	6	7	6	7	3	1	3.5	3	4	14	5.14	7
United States	3	5	3	5	4	5	4	2	4	2	6	1	1	3	14	3.43	2

Topics in the Measure of Economic Freedom

Politicized Prices

Arthur T. Denzau,
Center for Political Economy,
Washington University (St. Louis)

Introduction

WHEN A PRICE GOES UP, economists would normally expect that the quantity demanded would decline. But when some prices go up, people riot in the streets and overturn buses and governments. What determines the difference in responses?

Some prices are believed to have been politicized, and influenceable not only by supply and demand forces, but by activity in the political arena as well. If a part of the public believes that a price has become, or could readily be, politicized, then there is less reason to view the price as a parameter and to be a passive price-taker. Using the notion of politicized prices, we gain important insights into the political economy of the modern state in both developed countries and in the Third World.

Bates has investigated the developing economies of Western Africa, and found extensive politicization of prices in key markets. Most of these economies had developed at least one cash crop during the colonial period, and continued exporting this product after independence. However, the monopsony trading companies which had organized export in the colonial period were not just continued. In addition, they were used much more extensively as revenue sources by paying the cash crop producers less than the world price. The resulting politicization of the export price generated substantial urban-rural tensions and lackluster export performance.

De Soto has produced a remarkable book, *The Other Path*, which details the restrictions on the private sector which Peruvian governments have created. The result of the restrictions is the creation of a dual economy which is quite different from the dual economy discussed by some labor or development economists. The relatively modern formal sector of the economy exists in urban areas. It employs a small fraction of the labor force, usually unionized, at relatively high wages. Most of the formal sector consists either of State Enterprises (SEs) or of firms which are subsidized or protected by the state from foreign competition.

Large numbers of rural migrants have come to the cities, particularly to the capital of Lima, during the twentieth century. Most of these migrants are indigenous Indians, while most of the urban residents had been at least partially of European origin. To halt the in-migration, various governments passed laws and regulations restricting the economic opportunities of the migrants, making them ineligible for jobs in the formal sector and unable to own urban land. The result is a nation in which associates of de Soto have estimated that 63% of the labor force works in illegal informal economy employment. At any time, the police or other bureaucrats can harass or put the squeeze on these workers and, in fact, do so from time to time. The entire formal sector is required to adhere to detailed labor laws and other regulations to the extent that de Soto estimates (p.150) that, on average, a formal sector firm incurs costs of satisfying these regulations that are three to four times the taxes paid by the firm.

The formal firms have access to three key resources controlled by the state. Such firms can borrow from the formal sector banks, which may charge 15% to 20% interest on a loan in the face of an inflation rate that often exceeds 100% p.a. Access to such a loan means a subsidy of at least 80% of the principal loaned, and access is limited. The banks can lend money at this negative real rate since they are allowed by the government to borrow from the central bank discount window at 6% to 9%. Again, access to this source of funds is rationed, presumably by political means.

The second key resource to which formal sector firms can compete for access is foreign exchange. The Peruvian governments have maintained a heavily overvalued currency, making foreign exchange quite cheap, typically 10% to 20% of the black market price. Gaining access to foreign exchange then consists of an 80% to 90% subsidy, and access is rationed by the political authorities.

In both the foreign exchange and bank loan markets, the prices are completely politicized, bearing no serious relation to market equilibrium, other than being far away from an unpoliticizerd equilibrium. This politicization of price provides considerable resources for the political authorities to allocate at will. The negative real interest paid on savings and deposit accounts causes almost complete disintermediation in the financial sector except for those firms and organizations required by their ties to the state to keep such deposits. The major source of funds for banks to lend is the discount window, and this means that the inflation rate is a residual variable that results from the satisfying of political demands for subsidies. The foreign exchange markets are more problematic for the regime in power, as it cannot print dollars. In this case, all formal sector firms are required to sell their foreign exchange to the central bank, and holding bank accounts denominated in foreign currencies is either totally illegal or tightly regulated. In addition, all transactions by the state with foreign governments, such as aid payments, and international bodies such as the I.M.F. are used as sources of foreign exchange to give away. Through these two sources, a substantial fraction of GNP may be allocated by the state without the use of taxation, being given away to build and maintain political support by helping some friends, and buying off enemies.

The third key resource to which only the formal firms have access is the facilitation services of the state: its legal system. The informal businesses have little if any recourse to the formal legal system in Peru, as this system operates such that recourse would have negative value in almost all cases for the informals. As Douglass North has written, there is a fundamental tension between the predatory and the facilitative roles of the state, and Peru has a state that is largely predatory. The only external third party systems of enforcement available to the informal businesses involve the usual social norms of kinship systems and neighborhood control, and the informal systems that they have developed to substitute for the biased formal system. Without access to these three resources provided by the state, the informal sector of the economy is able to progress only so far, and the lackluster performance of the Peruvian economy, like that of most of Latin America, derives in large part from this cause.

In order to measure important aspects of economic freedoms, I believe that macro methods, while attractive for advertising purposes, are not now suitable as science. The ultimate aim of measuring transaction costs and the politicization of prices is to determine which factors are most clearly related to the economic failure of the typical less developed economy. This means that measures which can be compared across nations are needed, just as in the macro approach. However, I do not believe that any single number can capture the myriad of ways in which the state can be used to distort an economy, since we do not know how to make the various distortions commensurable operationally.

Rather, my approach to measurement is to find ways of measuring the politicization of the set of markets in which a firm operates. With such measures, one can go in two directions. The effects of each type of the politicization on the behavior and performance of an industry can be researched. Does the inability to obtain import licenses to buy spare parts for a modern machine mean that the technology used must be obsolete? Does the illegality of an informal sector business mean that it must avoid the use of fixed capital, since such capital represents quasi-rents that the local gendarmerie and bureaucracy can extract? I believe that these questions are best dealt with at the micro level, especially if we are to obtain theoretical and empirical results that can convince the skeptical or currently indifferent political scientist, economist or public official. Given useful measures of politicization of prices at the level of an industry, performed across a set of industries, one can begin to discuss how to measure economic freedom in a more aggregative way that would enable the measures to be compared across polities. With these measures, we can also determine what factors are related to politicization and of the different forms of politicization. But that is further down the road than what can now be accomplished, and much research is needed to get there.

This paper examines the notion of the politicized price in a single market, attempting to provide means of measuring the politicization. It begins with an examination of several different types of price controls which have been used. The actual effects of these controls vary greatly with the resources available for enforcement, and the belief of the citizenry in the validity of the price control system. The typical less-developed country has limited fiscal resources available for any sort of use, and its administrative competence is often very meager. Means of evasions and corruption are discussed in this context.

A further limitation on the ability of the state to politicize prices is economic, resulting from the endogenous behaviors of the actors in the economy. The ability of political authorities to affect prices is particularly limited for commodities in international trade and is investigated in Section B. Means of measuring factors which would hinder or allow successful politicization are provided. The ability to enter and exit the industry at will also limits the discretion of the state in politicizing prices, and is considered in the remainder of Section B.

The final substantive section, C, presents some recent examples from U.S. history of the politicization of prices. The California auto insurance regulatory system, described as relying on market forces by MacAvoy (p. 23), was changed in two key ways during the 1980s, resulting in a market that is intensely politicized. The Iraqi invasion of Kuwait on August 2, 1990, caused a substantial increase in crude oil prices and retail gasoline prices. This led inexorably to their politicization, but only to a very slight degree so far. Finally, the industrial policy debate of the early 1980s identified the semiconductor and computer industries as sunrise industries in which the United States had commanding leads. By 1986, the Japanese dominance of the computer memory chip market, called Dynamic Random Access Memories (DRAMs), was clear to all. The response of our politicians was to politicize the price of DRAMs and help make them almost inaccessible for our computer system houses in 1988. These examples suggest that while the U.S. economy may be one of the least politicized economies in the world, one can easily measure significant amounts of politicization in some sectors. While this politicization has not usually lead to riots or the toppling of governments when prices change, it does show that politicized prices are a universal phenomenon, differing largely in the degree of politicization in each market, and the pervasiveness of politicization in almost all markets.

A. A Private Firm and Controls

Consider the typical firm in the private sector. To avoid problems peculiar to specific sectors, let's assume that the firm is in a business that is not especially likely to be affected by intervention in the usual course of its business. In other words, the firm is not in a regulated industry and is not publicly owned.

How does this firm set its price? The neo-classical model of perfect competition lacks any convincing discussion of how prices are set by competitive firms. Price-setting in real markets, as opposed to perfectly competitive markets in the textbooks, occurs through a process that Popper, in a related context, describes as *conjecture and refutation*. The firm, by setting a price, has made a conjecture that this price is sustainable as an equilibrium. An equilibrium would mean that there are no net forces for change away from the situation that results. Setting a price above the competitive level would make entry profitable, representing forces for change. Entry would occur with the new firms pricing below the first firm in order to get market share, with each making a new conjecture about the equilibrium price. Each conjecture that is incorrect generates a refutation. If the price is still too high, then further entry would still be profitable with the new firms cutting price further. If the price conjecture is too low, then that firm would have many customers, sell most or all of its inventory, and be unable to replace that inventory for sale with the revenues generated. This process would result in the usual equilibrium with all firms producing somewhere near the minimum of their Long-Run Average Cost (LRAC) curves and pricing at that minimum average cost level. Such a conjecture is not refuted by market response, there are no net forces for further change, and it would be an equilibrium. This can result even if the original firm really does not know its cost curves at all, but simply can evaluate its profits and inventories.

What are the ways in which the prices of this firm might be politicized? We shall ignore the specific structure of the state, such as whether it is unitary, federalist, or so forth, and simply view all organs and levels of the state as part of an amorphous whole. That whole is motivated to avoid political problems with the citizenry, and may wish to further the interests of certain groups of people, whether its supporters or dangerous opponents, at the expense of the rest of the citizenry. We expect that it may wish to intervene in the private sector to further these goals.

The most direct form of intervention that politicizes prices is to set up a system of specific, or general, price controls. The price of each product of a firm may be controlled, with new controls generated for each product added by each firm. Any changes in a product require new limit prices and the sheer magnitude of the attempt to utilize a centralized mechanism of price-setting for all the products produced by each firm soon overwhelms any attempt to operate a control system at this level. The informational flows involved in such a system are beyond belief. As a result, actual systems usually do not attempt to operate at that level, although the Price Control Phases of the Nixon Administration attempted a self-enforced system which tried to set prices firm by firm for each and every product.

Price controls are costly to administer and can require substantial skill and administrative competence. Many states do not seem to possess these characteristics. This limits their choices to three types of price controls. Some types of price controls can be relatively self-enforcing, with one side of the transaction or the other, as well as third parties, quite willing to report attempted violations to the authorities. Alternatively, the controls can be selectively enforced, with whatever enforcement resources that exist being devoted to some small subset of the possible violations, but with no real expectation that the controls are being complied with in general. Finally, the system of controls may simply be something for the supporters of the state to point at as an exemplar that those in the know realize is simply a statement of hope.

Self-Enforcing Controls

Typical price controls on goods sold at retail or wholesale are not self-enforcing. Both parties to the transaction are desirous to make the transaction at the agreed price. The party on the short side of the market, typically the buyer, might have to engage in costly search or incur substantial costs if the transaction does not occur, and may well wish to make sure that the supplier is available for future dealings. The seller would rather receive a price above the controlled one, ignoring differences in risk involved. Neither would usually have an incentive to notify the authorities about the illicit transaction, at least based on the illegal contract alone.

Self-enforcing controls are generally of two types. When wages are controlled, and the controls are generally enforced, the employer has a financial incentive to stay within the law, particularly if the employer believes that other employers are going to comply. This is not a prisoner's dilemma game, but an assurance game. The general experience during World War II was that this seemed to be the result in most labor markets (Rockoff, p.123). A second type of control that lends itself to self-enforcement is one that makes the limit price(s) easily known or seen, and requires each seller to post its own prices, making them highly visible even to third parties. In examining a system of politicized prices, one must find out if there are posting requirements that might make the system more self-enforcing than otherwise.

Uniform Price Controls

A price system that appears simplest to administer, is one which sets uniform prices for a specific commodity for all sellers. Such uniform systems seem quite attractive until one considers the range of commodities and the enormous diversity of the types and forms in which even a "single" commodity can be produced and sold. This type of system may be adequate for those commodities for which standardized contracts such as those traded on public exchanges can be used. But there are contracts on only a few dozen such commodities in the United States, and others which have been attempted have failed, often because of the inability to define and standardize the product sufficiently so that the paper contract could be a nearly perfect substitute for the product itself.

Technology has not been kind to this simplest form of price control. The introduction of flexible manufacturing systems of the type that allowed Coleco to individualize each Cabbage Patch doll are reducing the size of production runs and allowing manufacturers to greatly widen their product lines. This proliferation of product lines makes all price control systems operate poorly, but go to the heart of a uniform price control system: how does a bureaucracy set new limit prices in an economy that produces thousands of new products each month? Obviously, such a system would slow or at least greatly stifle innovation if it attempts to control each commodity. The reality of such control systems, with their human bureaucracies, is that the introduction of new products is the easiest way to evade the controls entirely.

All U.S. price controls systems that attempt to control prices charged by manufacturers have bogged down and failed to work for products such as clothing. Once an industrial economy gets past the initial stages of mass-produced fabric manufacturing, the increasing incomes of the populace gets spent on greater diversity in styles, colors and the fabrics used in apparel making. Each year and each season sees the introduction of new products, with great rewards for those who can discern the desires of the buying public the earliest. Adding price controls and delays to the system is not only not desired generally by the public, but means substantial resources would have to be used to set prices for each of the new products that are continually being introduced. Even though a workforce 1/20 the size of the Post Office was used during World War I for the price control bureaucracy, and a force half the size of the Post Office costing 0.2% of GNP during World War II, these bureaucracies failed to be able to deal with this problem at all (Rockoff, p. 74, 125, 150-4). The apparel companies were easily able to evade any price control at will by introducing a replacement garment. The company itself was expected to determine the control price on the garment, and could expect relatively little oversight in most cases. Enforcement resources were devoted to the larger companies, and clothing with substantial numbers of smaller firms, was very hard to control.

There were attempts to introduce uniform price controls in apparel. These attempts were embodied in the formation of committees to design a standardized garment which all firms in an industry would be expected to produce. Robert Brookings pushed the Liberty Shoe project (Rockoff, p. 50) during World War I for a single design of shoe to be produced by all manufacturers. This effort was unsuccessful, but Bernard Baruch was able to get the firms to produce a more limited range of styles. During World War II, a similar effort was made with women's dresses. Stanley Marcus of Neiman-Marcus was asked to develop a standardization order which covered dresses and bathing suits (Rockoff, p. 117). Before this effort could proceed further, however, the Office of Price Administration (OPA) leadership was removed as having too many professors, and few businessmen (Rockoff, p. 94). This episode illustrates the enormous problems that any uniform price control system would have in a truly modern economy with flexible manufacturing.

The continued use of this system in less-developed economies, such as those of Latin America, illustrates its attraction, just as it may suggest its power to stifle further economic development. When a state with a weak administrative apparatus and relatively limited resources attempts to operate a price control system, it must use a system that is easy to administer, or accept the result that the price controls will be widely violated. A typical national state in Latin America can acquire about 10% of GNP in the form of tax revenues, and this greatly limits what the state can do administratively. Given such limited real resources to help build political support, the politicians try to use regulatory and other devices to give themselves more with which to acquire and maintain political power. Hence the ubiquity of controls on currency transactions, overvalued exchange rates and high rates of money growth and inflation.

Margin Controls

The earliest form of price controls in the United States were margin controls, which stated the maximum margin allowed on resale of goods purchased domestically or imported. Such controls are simpler to administer than any form of control that requires use of historical records about the prices charged by a firm in the past, or which attempt to control profit margins. In the earliest system of price controls in colonial America, each importer in Virginia was supposed to charge no more than 100% more than their delivered cost for imported goods (Rockoff, p. 16). These early systems were faced with severe administrative problems, and tended to rely on the fear of mob action rather than the direct coercive power of the state. A typical form of enforcement during the Revolution was to publish the names of violators in the local newspaper, with the expectation that the local Sons of Liberty would make the violators see the error of their ways. These schemes might have an effect on prices for a month or two, but usually broke down completely at that point as means of evasion were discovered or shortages developed.

In addition to the administrative problems in enforcement, margin controls are also relatively easy to avoid. Retailers always bundle some services with the goods that they sell. These bundled services also are the first to be adjusted when price controls are used. The physical good may even stay the same as before the controls, but fewer, and less costly, services are afterwards bundled with the commodity. Traditional discounts and courtesies are removed. The customer may have to pick up the product or arrange transportation itself. The systems in the United States during the twentieth century have allowed higher margins for firms which provide more services to their customers. This created loopholes through which firms could readily go in order to raise prices. But these firms provide the minimum services that could allow the new designation and the higher margin. In general, all bundled services become of reduced quality, and for each class of supplier, the level of services bundled is reduced.

When a manufacturer adds new goods to its output, or a retailer new lines of goods, the margin control system runs into problems. In both cases, no established margin exists on the product, and discretionary decisions must be made. Given the usual flexibility of cost accounting systems, there is some ability to shift costs across products. A supplier with several goods usually finds that some are selling quite poorly, possibly within the price controls. By shifting costs away from these goods and toward the new goods, a higher cost basis can be established for the new good and a higher price charged. Retailers can add the new lines and claim new services that must be bundled with them, and get a higher margin on the new products than on the existing products. Such flexibility gives most price control systems trouble, and the margin control systems are easily evaded by such devices.

Along with the price controls themselves, additional regulations are often imposed to improve compliance with the goals of the system. Advertising of prices is often restricted in various ways, being required or prohibited variously. Requirements of visibly posting transaction prices or legal limit prices are also used to make self-enforcement easier. These features of price politicization also need to be measured.

Avoidance and Politicization

Attempts to politicize prices are often resisted by the private sector agents on whom they are foisted. This is not always the case, as these agents may expect countervailing benefits accruing from the state as a *quid pro quo*. However, such bargains are not normally enforceable in any court of law if the political authorities change their mind and renege on the agreement. In general, we expect the private agents to use their skills to attempt to avoid or evade the politicizing actions.

One standard result we should always expect from an attempt at politicization of any sort is organizational change. The type of change varies with the opportunities and costs presented by the new environment, but some sort of change is usually forthcoming. Sometimes the politicization favors small firms, as did the Nixon price controls on oil, which focused on the largest firms. This allowed smaller firms to creatively redesignate old oil as new oil through various ruses and charge the much higher price allowed on the new oil. The converse can also occur, with larger firms being favored, as in the World War II price controls involving wage negotiations. And always, politicization means that one must reallocate efforts toward an office in the capital.

An American example can make these ideas concrete. In 1965, in the case of Williams v. Walker-Thomas Furniture Co., Judge Skelly Wright of the D.C. Circuit Court of Appeals wrote an opinion affecting credit instalment contracts. As the court he then sat on was the highest common law court of the District, this was new judge-created law of the usual sort, but does not appear to have the efficiency characteristics discussed by Posner. The furniture store defendant was selling furniture to slum-dwellers on credit, maintaining title through an instalment contract to allow it to more easily use the self-help remedy of repossession. In addition to these clauses, the contract dealt in a special way with repeat customers. A customer with an open account who bought additional furniture on credit would agree to pro-rate all payments as between all the open contracts. All open contracts would now be paid off at the same time. This provision, though cryptic, meant that all furniture not already completely paid off would be available for repossession if payment on any were in default. This obviously provided more security to the furniture store, but had a second result: in order to use the provision effectively, the furniture would normally have to carry all its own contracts. It might well borrow against them from others, but it would not sell them as auto dealers and savings banks do with their loans, as this would complicate the consolidation of all debts and rearrangement of payments whenever further purchases occurred.

The D.C. Court ruled that such a provision in an instalment contract could well be unconscionable, and thus unenforceable. Let's suppose that the provision actually became illegal and was not used any more in the District. This politicizing of credit contracts would likely generate an organizational innovation. Without the provision, there is far less reason for a furniture store to hold its own contracts. It would be more likely to sell these contracts after the court decision and help develop a secondary market in them. One would expect that this would have a standardizing effect on the contracts and on the information concerning the creditworthiness of the borrower. It is conceivable that, once organized, the cost of credit could decline with a new source of funding made available to the retail furniture stores, especially those located in slums. In any case, organizational innovation through vertical disintegration in the financing and servicing of contracts is a likely result. In the actual instance, later decisions by the same court undercut the original decision and allowed the continued use of the offending contract clause and business practice.

Politicized Hiring and Suppliers

Large formal firms in Latin America and defense firms in the United States often find it in their interest to hire former politicians and bureaucrats. These people have specialized knowledge of the procedures and machinations of the part of the state from which they came. In addition, they may have important personal and political ties to those with some power to help the firm. This is especially important in Latin America, in which court proceedings can be influenced substantially through the appearance of a military official or politician friendly to one of the parties. The formal sector in Latin America may be operating as a golden parachute retirement system for bureaucrats and military officers who have not disgraced themselves during their time in office. Such a device would be of considerable value to the polity as it would allow the state to recruit better people than otherwise and help provide the type of continuity in the political economy system that the weak party politics cannot provide.

The use of certain suppliers can be a politicized decision in any polity. In American defense contracting, a common claim is that subcontractors are chosen so as to have people working on a contract in as many congressional districts as possible. But this is a public contract, and these contracts are commonly politicized almost everywhere. For comparative differentiation, the politicization one would want to examine involves ordinary private business. An attempt by the state to influence the choice of suppliers in purely private business can become intensely political once started.

Intervention into the choice of vendors is most common with foreign versus domestic suppliers. Any Buy American policy (or Buy Missourian) policy which attempts to affect private contracts has this character. So do the continual interventions that most nations employ in trade policy. Federal law prohibits the export of Alaskan oil, effectively requiring it to be shipped to the Pacific coast, where oil spills have become a major political problem. This prohibition was part of the price paid by the domestic oil firms to get the Trans-Alaska Pipeline built, but some sort of control on export might have been required so long as crude oil price controls were in existence. This interaction of controls and trade is discussed further in Section B.1.

Effort Allocation

Perhaps the largest costs involved in the politicization of prices occur through the new incentives that they create and the reallocation of effort by private firms that these incentives call forth. These effects have been well discussed by others, including the media, although they have generated only aggregative forms of modeling efforts. Consider the time of the CEO of a large corporation in an industry in which some prices have become politicized. A substantial amount of the time of the CEO may now be devoted to dealing with politicians and regulators. The potential profitability of the firm may now depend more on what these politicians and bureaucrats do, than on what the firm itself does to improve its processes and products. With these rearranged incentives, the reallocation of effort makes profitable sense. The often-told story of the large number of Washington offices operated by corporations and the extensive use of Washington lawyers, lobbyists and public relations firms testifies to the new incentives created. The value of these efforts may be so substantial that they create a new barrier to entry for small firms in an industry. The need to have a presence in Washington becomes a cost of some minimal size that generates decreasing average costs up to a relatively large firm size. The presence of a jungle of federal regulations and regulatory bodies adds to the problem, as this clearly creates a substantial fixed cost not present before 1933. The example of Peru illustrates a near-limiting case of these problems. Almost every firm of any size at all has its headquarters in the capital city, Lima, in order to be able to deal continually with the bureaucracy. Complicating the problem in Peru is the fact that publication of regulations and bureaucratic decisions is not mandated. Thus, the 99% of laws which are produced by the administrative sector of the government can only be known by having agents talking regularly with the bureaucracy or by renting the services of such people. While this seems to be in stark contrast with U.S. federal operations under the Administrative Procedures Act, it is closer to reality in those state governments which lack a counterpart state requirement. And county and municipal regulations add layers of complication to the problem in our federal system.

Let's now consider some recent examples of the politicizing of prices in the United States to see what other factors need to be measured to evaluate the extent of politicization of the prices in a market.

B. Requirements for Effective Price Politicization

Not all markets can be politicized, and the politicization of many markets can take place only after they are insulated from similar markets outside the jurisdiction of the state which is attempting to politicize. At base, actual market contestability limits the ability of the state to affect pricing decisions, at least at the individual firm level. To the extent that the domestic market is linked to the world market, then contestability means that the ability to import or export the commodity involved reduces the ability of the state to affect industry-level results. These links with the rest of the world are often severed precisely because they reduce the power of the state to politicize prices.

International Features of a Politicized Market

The significance of market politicization is greatly weakened if it is easy for buyers to substitute imported goods and of sellers to export price-controlled goods. Consider a control consisting of a maximum price for the output of an industry, which we presume to be a single, homogeneous good for simplicity. If the commodity can be exported, and no barriers exist on imports and exports of the commodity, then this attempt to influence the price can be avoided. Trying to lower the domestic price would cause firms to export the commodity, and would quickly dry up the domestic supply. The availability of the world market generates a perfectly elastic supply curve for the commodity at the world price (for a small country in that market), and any attempt at price controls would cause substantial shortages. This occurred during the Nixon Administration price controls in the scrap copper markets (Rockoff, p. 225). The attempt to control the price domestically caused the metal to be exported to satisfy increasing world demand. Even though the United States is not a small country with respect to the copper market and it can influence world price, the controls still generated a shortage very quickly, and forced the regulators to free the price in both the virgin and scrap copper markets.

Suppose that the state attempts to force down the price of an input used by an industry. The subsequent reduction in quantity supplied would normally create a higher price in equilibrium for the products of any downstream industry. Such a result would raise the shadow price of the controlled input for the industry, and cause them to attempt to try to get around the controls. Besides various quid pro quos for access to the scarce input, imports may supply the demand. Once again, the availability of a perfect world market implies a perfectly elastic supply of the input to the industry, and would enable the firms to still get their supplies, even though at the higher import price. Competition for the controlled domestic supply would be expected to generate quasi-rents for access to it, and a variety of methods used to bid for access. But if the input commodity can be imported, then it could also be exported, and the state would have to control exports to preserve the price control. This is what occurred in the American oil market after 1973 with the systems of price control that were introduced and evolved in order to maintain control. The attempt to insulate the American market from world market phenomena required continual changes to deal with the import and export opportunities that were created by the controls. Any attempt to control the price of a product in international trade requires controls on import and export in order to have a chance of affecting monetary transaction prices. Whether the system can actually affect the "full prices" inclusive of the resources devoted to gaining access to the commodity, finding customers, or bribing the enforcement bureaucracy, is a different question which we leave to later work. One recent paper has claimed that price controls cannot change full prices. While this result is obviously wrong if multiple equilibria exist, the analysis suggests that costs incurred in the new forms of competition generated by the price controls are likely to wipe out or exceed any gains that the supposed beneficiaries of the controls may have expected to receive.

Tables 1 through 3 show some of the questions which one would like to ask concerning the international features of the markets in which a firm operates. The intended initial use for these questions is in Latin America. Several of us at Washington University are trying to measure transaction costs which limit the extent of markets, and make the use of modern production methods with substantial fixed capital a very risky proposition for a private firm. We have focused on Peru, given the study by de Soto which shows how a government can, in the name of paternalism and equity, ruin the private sector of the economy. Table 4 then shows the questions concerning price-setting that constitute the basic means of measuring the politicization of an output or input market.

Domestic Market Contestability

The contestability of the domestic market itself can greatly limit the ability of the state to influence prices. One means is the domestic counterpart of the international effects described in Section B. Suppose that a sub-jurisdiction of the state, say a state or city in the United States, tried to control prices within its jurisdiction. Its ability to do so would certainly be affected by markets outside itself. The survey just used, with appropriate changes to avoid questions involving foreign exchange or currency, would allow one to measure these features. Beyond this, how could market contestability affect the ability of a jurisdiction to politicize prices?

Table 1 International Aspects of a Politicized Market
Foreign Exchange and Inputs

1) Could some of the products that your firm uses in order to make your product(s) be purchased from firms or suppliers in other countries?

Suppose that your firm were trying to import some parts needed for equipment used by your firm. Suppose that the cost of the parts is about $100 (U.S.). If your answer would differ if the amount were much larger, say $1,000 (U.S.), then please state so and try to provide answers for that case also.

2) Is it possible to get foreign exchange legally for importing goods without approval of a governmental official?

2A) If not, how difficult is the approval process, without special influence?

> Impossible
> Almost impossible
> Very difficult
> Difficult
> Somewhat difficult
> Easy
> Automatic on application

2B) How likely is it for a bribe to be requested? Try to answer with a percentage of the time this is likely to happen.

2C) Would you have to pay the bribe? About what percentage of the time would the bribe be necessary to get approval?

2D) If a bribe were paid, about how much would you expect to pay?

3) Are there laws or regulations that affect your ability to buy the inputs you need from foreign vendors?

3A) If there are laws and regulations that would affect your buying internationally, then how easy is it to satisfy these laws? In particular, can you decide yourself whether you are complying with these laws, or must you get approval from a government agency?

3B) If you need approval from the government, must you get approval from more than one agency?

3C) Would this approval be automatic, or is it possible for the request to be rejected?

3D) How likely is such a rejection without incurring costs beyond simply making the request for approval? Try to state what percentage of such requests are likely to be rejected without your incurring additional costs.

3E) If costs would have to be incurred to gain approval, including bribes, what would you expect would be the smallest amount that would make you quite sure of approval?

Table 2 International Aspects of a Politicized Market
Industry Conditions
Exporting

1) Could the good that your firm produces be sold to buyers in other countries? If not, please go to the importing questions.

Suppose that you were contacted by a buyer from another country who wished to purchase some of your product. Suppose that the amount involved in the sale would be $100 (U.S.). If the amount were larger, say $1,000 (U.S.), would the answer be different? If so, please try to provide both the answers for a $100 sale and a $1,000 sale.

2) Are there laws or regulations that affect your ability to sell to foreign buyers?

2A) If there are laws and regulations that would affect your selling internationally, then how easy is it to satisfy these laws? In particular, can you decide yourself whether you are complying with these laws, or must you get approval from a government agency?

2B) If you need approval from the government, must you get approval from more than one agency?

2C) Would this approval be automatic, or is it possible for the request to be rejected?

2D) How likely is such a rejection without incurring costs beyond simply making the request for approval? Try to state what percentage of such requests are likely to be rejected without your incurring additional costs.

2E) If costs would have to be incurred to gain approval, including bribes, what would you expect would be the smallest amount that would make you quite sure of approval?

Table 3 International Aspects of a Politicized Market
Industry Conditions
Importing

1) Could the good that your firm produces be purchased from suppliers in other countries? If not, this is the end of the International Aspects survey.

Suppose that there were a very large increase in demand for one of your products that can be imported. Suppose further that you can buy the product at a reasonable price from a foreign firm, and that the amount involved in the purchase would be $100 (U.S.). If the amount were larger, say $1,000 (U.S.), would the answers be different? If so, please try to provide both the answers for a $100 sale and a $1,000 sale.

2) Are there laws or regulations that affect your ability to buy from foreign firms?

2A) If there are laws and regulations, other than those involving foreign exchange, that would affect your buying internationally, then how easy is it to satisfy these laws? In particular, can you decide yourself whether you are complying with these laws, or must you get approval from a government agency?

2B) If you need approval from the government, must you get approval from more than one agency?

2C) Would this approval be automatic, or is it possible for the request to be rejected?

2D) How likely is such a rejection without incurring costs beyond simply making the request for approval? Try to state what percentage of such requests are likely to be rejected without your incurring additional costs.

2E) If costs would have to be incurred to gain approval, including bribes, what would you expect would be the smallest amount that would make you quite sure of approval?

Table 4 Controls on Pricing

Suppose that you wished to raise the price on one of your products by a substantial amount.

1) Would you have to notify anyone other than people in your own firm and the firms to which you sell?

2) Do you have to post your price in some prominent place?
Or post some maximum or minimum price anywhere? If so, where?

3) Are there any price controls imposed by the government on the products that you currently make and sell? In other words, are there laws or regulations that affect your power to raise or lower the price substantially on any of your products?
If not, then go to question 10.

4) To raise a price substantially, must you get approval from some governmental office? If so, who? If not, what is the nature of the controls?
If approval need not be obtained, go to question 7.

5) Is the required approval relatively automatic, or are a substantial fraction of increases turned down?
If relatively automatic, go to question 7.

6) If your firm produces a new product and tries to sell it, must you obtain approval of the price you charge before selling it?

7) If you raised your price without notifying the appropriate officials, or without the required approval, is it likely that this would be detected by the authorities?

8) If it were detected, what type of sanction might be used against you?

9) Is it likely that a bribe would be expected by the official telling you of your violation?

10) Are there any restrictions on the prices you can pay to any of your suppliers? Describe these.
If no restrictions, go to question 14.

11) If you paid a price in violation of these restrictions, is it likely that this would be detected by the authorities?

12) If it were detected, what type of sanction might be used against you?

13) Is it likely that a bribe would be expected by the official telling you of your violation?

14) What sort of controls are there on the wages you pay your employees? Are there minimum or maximum wages set by the government?
If there are no controls, or only maximum wage controls, then end the survey.

15) When the government raises the legal minimum wage for unskilled workers, does this affect the minimum wages you are supposed to pay? If so, about what proportion of your employees are affected by such a change? State as a percentage.

16) Can you pay less than the official minimum wage, legally?

17) If you paid less than the minimum wage for a job without the required approval, is it likely that this would be detected by the authorities?

18) If it were detected, what type of sanction might be used against you?

19) Is it likely that a bribe would be expected by the official telling you of your violation?

Entry

Suppose that the state attempts to control the output price of the subject firm. Suppose that entry into the industry is easy whenever profits are being earned by incumbents, or when potential entrants believe that they could make money. If the state attempts to set a maximum price on the output of the industry, then this would not seem to induce entry, as it would reduce potential profits for the incumbents. However, entry may still occur due to imperfections in the regulatory apparatus.

The incumbents are producing output before the imposition of controls which can be compared with the post-controls output. This may, in the case of physical goods, enable the regulators to better control quality degradation. If it did, then entrants may be advantaged since they can enter with a lower quality product than the average incumbent and charge a higher effective price for that output. By suitably changing the product so that it would be sufficiently different from the incumbent output, the new entrants may be able to bypass comparisons with the output of the incumbents. While this still means that the price controls do lower the quality of the product, as we expect from theory, it would be the potential for entry that reduces the ability of the authorities to attempt to delay this change by controlling the quality of the incumbent firms.

Entry is much more of a problem when the state attempts to set a minimum price on industry output. Tullock has discussed the problems present in this case, and a literature has developed around this problem. The basic notion is that raising the price of a product without restricting the supply of that product has little long-run effect on the profits earned by incumbent firms. Even when an agreement has been reached by incumbent firms on market-sharing, such as O.P.E.C. has, this does not directly affect potential entrants, and entry can spoil the market for the incumbents and the attempt of the state to raise prices.

The common experience of agricultural programs throughout the developed market economies reflects this problem. Attempts to raise output price always require the removal of some of the output from market supply. The removal may be through state purchase, mandatory destruction of part of the output, or restrictions on the use of inputs. All have been used in American agricultural policy. But state purchase or destruction alone are not enough. They may raise the price, but give incentive to further production and new entry. Entry restrictions are commonly imposed now when any policy is employed to raise output prices. By grandfathering incumbent producers and inputs, such restrictions hinder future innovation and competitiveness. They also create perverse incentives and images that can create forces for further politicization in the future. A new minority labor-market entrant who is told she should stand on her own two feet may resent the payments made to absentee tobacco land owners by Virginia tobacco farmers. The right to grow tobacco on an acre of land can be worth several thousand dollars. The infamous taxicab medallion systems, with medallions worth over $100,000, similarly can generate demands for the politicization of other markets and prices to reduce the unfair concentration of such governmental largess.

A final type of price control involves input prices. An attempt to reduce the price of a key input, whether labor or material, to an industry so as to lower its costs normally backfires without additional constraints. The system of oil price controls in the United States after 1973 and the Nixon price controls generally reflected the problems with such approaches. Suppose that one controls the price of crude oil or the price a manufacturer charges for its output. The natural result of this control is to reduce the quantity supplied by producers. The reduced supply is all that the distribution channels and refiners have to work with, and thus the supply of refined products or the supply of goods at retail are reduced. The reduction in supply now has an obvious effect: higher prices. The upstream controls on price would not reduce downstream prices without additional and more widespread controls. The attempts to lower input prices by command simply pushes up the prices downstream. Of course, this means that somewhere between the controlled upstream source and the downstream profits there must be rents to be earned by gaining access to the reduced supply. Access to the supply is going to be rationed by some means, and additional cash payments, bundling with other commodities, non-pecuniary payments and discrimination of all forms are likely to result.

Table 5 is an attempt to measure restrictions on entry. Using the data obtained from the survey, one can ascertain the extent of the politicization of an industry, and determine to what extent that potential entry can restrict the power of the political authorities. The job of determining which types of entry restrictions are the most important is one for future research with these measures.

Table 5 Entry Controls

1) Suppose that you wished to set up a new business making and selling some particular products. Would you be able legally to set up such a business and get it going quickly, assuming that you had all the other requisites, such as financing, technical personnel, facilities, etc?

If the answer is yes, then this part of the survey is over. If the subject states some particular business to make the questions concrete, write down the business.

2) What governmental agencies would have to approve for you to operate this new business?

2A) Is this approval automatic, or are such requests often rejected?

Suppose that you did not get approval but still went ahead and set up the business.

3) Would you think it likely that someone in authority would discover that you would be operating illegally?

4) What type of sanction might be imposed on you as a violator?

5) Would the official involved typically expect a bribe to be offered?

Controls on Operation or Resources

Incumbent firms can be forced to behave somewhat differently than those in the process just described. Their operations can be affected or influenced by legal restrictions and requirements. The regulations can be directed at the market relationships in the industry, marketing methods, or production techniques used. As the public school movement gained momentum in the nineteenth century, the continuing competition from private and religious schools was viewed as irritating. Gradually increasing interventions into controlling these schools were attempted, with some states during the 1920s banning them. This ban, aimed at Catholic schools by Ku Klux Klan related politicians, was declared unconstitutional in 1925 in the case of Pierce v. Society of Sisters, but other restrictions and requirements have been maintained.

One basic means of controlling an industry so as to gain leverage over pricing exists when the government has something that firms in the industry want. This can be a license or a permit that is necessary to do business, or can be the use of eminent domain to take land or rights-of-way to put in a railroad or pipeline. The threat of no longer helping a firm by providing these services can be very powerful, as they can easily force a firm out of business or greatly reduce profits. In such circumstances, the state can usually get a lot of what it wants in terms of prices charged.

In most countries, the government owns the mineral resources and must grant permission for extraction companies to remove the minerals. Since this is often done only before the initial investment by the company, this works just like a permit would. After the nationalization of oil resources by many countries during the 1960s and 1970s, foreign oil companies were required to either bid regularly for the production rights, or to bid for the crude that had been produced. To continue to be certified as a bidder, one must follow both formal and informal requirements of the state and this provides means by which the prices charged by a firm could be influenced. Since oil is traded in competitive international markets, this has relatively little influence on export sales, but can affect the prices charged to other domestic users. In general, the existence of any inputs monopolized by the state provides substantial leverage for affecting prices in ways the political authorities want.

In other situations, a firm is not allowed to sell on an open market at all. Argentina was an economic success until around 1900, when its liberal economic policies were changed, and controls over importing and export-ing were implemented. Since then, Argentina has regularly employed export controls, using a monopsony trading company for wheat and beef exports. The result has been that this nation which had a per capita income quite close to that of the United States in 1900 has fallen far behind in the century since. The use of a monopsony trading company and insulating domestic markets from foreign competition has resulted in the politiciza-tion of key prices in this economy. The government has operated much like those of Africa which are described by Bates. The urban proletariat is provided with lower-priced food through the imposition of export controls, the monopsonization of farm sales and the cross-subsidization of urban domestic food prices paid for by the profits of the monopsonized export products. This politicizes not only the prices paid to farmers and ranchers for their output but also the retail prices paid in the urban food markets. When the state can no longer maintain the urban food prices at their below equilibrium levels, their increase tends to generate riots and can topple the government. To avoid these effects, the state may attempt to offset the effect of the increased food prices by raising wages for all urban workers at the same time, extending the system of politicized prices to the labor markets. The resulting prices become so distorted that the resource allocation result-ing from them takes on an Alice-in-Wonderland character, with resources devoted to arbitraging the domestic prices against world prices and also to gaining special licenses and privileges to buy at lower prices than the general public, or sell at higher prices. Competing for the rents created by the artificial scarcity becomes more profitable than competing by dealing with the real scarcity that exists.

Table 6 attempts to provide indicators of the politicization of the organization, operation and flexibility of a firm. In this area especially, there are many dimensions in which the state may try to influence a private firm, and a more open-ended investigation is required at the start of an empirical investigation. Once the particular means used in an industry have been discovered, then more specific questions about these means would have to be designed and asked.

Table 6 Regulations on Operations

1) Suppose that you wished to change the way that your firm produces one of your products. Would this require your notifying some governmental agency or getting their approval?

2) If you were to change the location of your business, would this require your notifying some governmental agency or getting their approval?

3) Suppose that you were operating your business as a sole proprietorship. If you then added a partner, would this require your notifying some governmental agency or getting their approval?

4) Are there any restrictions imposed by the government on who your firm can hire for a job that is unfilled? Please describe them.

5) Suppose that you wished to change one of your suppliers of products used by your firm. Can you choose to use any other supplier, or would there be problems with the government caused by such a change? Please describe.

Exit

Exit controls have effects similar to those created by entry, but with reversed signs. One additional element created by exit controls is that the firms forced to remain in an unprofitable business are sometimes viewed by a particular government as deserving of offsetting help from the state. The results can be new distortions and controls that make the economic costs even larger than the exit controls themselves would have been.

For example, a steel company may not be allowed to go out of business because this would put too many urban workers out on the street. Urban workers are much more dangerous than the rural masses because it is much easier for them to organize and to create problems for the regime in power. Avoiding urban unemployment for the organized part of the urban labor force is particularly important politically. If the firm is not allowed to go out of business, or to lay off most of its workforce, then the private owners of the firm can easily threaten to simply abandon the assets and leave the nation. Alternatively, the obvious financial drain to the private owners may be important if they can present a political threat to the regime in some manner. This can result in several possible means to defuse the pressures.

Compensated nationalization may be a way out, with the state buying out the private owners. This requires financial resources that may not be available to the state, and may create political problems if the compensation is viewed negatively by the supporters of the government. Regardless, nationalization, whether compensated or not, creates new problems and distortions. Now that the firm is a State Enterprise (SE), its operation can become intensely politicized with pricing becoming quite arbitrary. Steel plants, whether in India or in Peru, have been viewed as evidence of the modernization of the economy that the state is creating, and these SEs must be kept alive at great cost. In Peru, the state steel plant sells its output for five times the world price of steel, and is obviously insulated from foreign competition in order to do so. It also is supposed to be insulated from domestic competition. All other SEs are required to buy Peruvian, if at all possible, as are private enterprises which need help from the state.

The higher price of the nationalized steel causes all steel-using firms to have much higher costs than similar firms in foreign countries, and these firms now demand help in turn. This same process has occurred in the United States with the steel and auto firms. While the auto firms may have been negatively impacted by other federal policies, and been complacent about Japanese competition, an important cause of competitive problems for domestic auto firms in the United States has been the higher price of steel that they must pay, caused by two decades of protection for the domestic steel industry [see Denzau (1985)]. First the price of steel became politicized in 1969 with the Voluntary Export Restraint (VER) negotiated with Japan, and then the price of autos became politicized in 1981 with the Japanese automobile VER. It is also noteworthy that the federal government was a substantial investor in one of the threatened auto companies, Chrysler, at the time of the auto agreement. The VER probably saved Chrysler and Ford from bankruptcy. Both of their stocks fell in value in 1985 when President Reagan attempted to remove the VER with Japan, suggesting that investors understood the importance of politicization to the value of the firm assets.

Table 7 investigates the restrictions on exit that a state may impose. Some of the forms that these restriction may take are subtle and as with Table 6, the questions may have to be supplemented in each particular case. In addition, the means by which the state may help the industry in exchange for the exit restrictions may be quite difficult to measure without careful historical research. Open-ended questions of industry observers can provide paths to research and uncover unexpected links that depend greatly on context. For example, the payment for keeping open a business may be for a family member of the owner to get a lucrative government job. Finding such links may be very difficult for an investigator who lacks considerable background knowledge of the political economy being investigated.

Some examples of the politicization of prices can make more concrete some of the ideas suggested so far. In addition, these episodes can suggest some further data about markets to gather in order to determine how politicized a market is.

Table 7 Exit Controls

1) Suppose that you wished to close down your business entirely and fire all your workers. Would you have to notify any governmental agency in advance?

If no notification required, then end the survey.

2) If you did notify the agency, what would you expect that agency to try to do? Would they attempt to convince you to stay in business? Would they try to force you to do so? hat might they do?

3) Would you have to gain the approval of some governmental agency?

4) How easy would it be to get the approval to close the business? Would it be relatively automatic?

5) What would be required to gain the approval to close the business?

6) If being forced to stay in operation caused your firm to incur substantial losses, would you be able to go to some governmental official for help? Who could you go to?

If there is no one to go to, then end the survey.

7) What sort of help might you request, and how likely would it be that you could get it?

C. Examples of Politicizing of Prices

Recent history in the United States reveals many examples of the politicization of prices. Sometimes the means have been extremely direct and coercive, such as the seizure of the coal mines during World War II by President Roosevelt to avoid a strike, and the seizure of steel attempted by President Truman during the Korean War. The latter seizure was invalidated by the Supreme Court (Rockoff, p. 193), but the method was legal in the coal mine case. Less coercive in appearance was the jaw-boning of the steel companies by President Kennedy. It appeared that he simply requested that the price increase initiated by one of them not be followed. But the reality was much stronger, with the threat of cutting off all government contracts involving their steel actually being used. Exhortation and the velvet glove are normally ineffective as means of politicizing prices when large corporations are involved. The steel blade covered by the glove is often uncovered to make the point more cogent. On the other hand, exhortation by political authorities can be quite powerful if it so matches the mood of the public as to license vigilantes to beat up those who fail to follow it, such as small retailers. This means was used during the Revolution as part of price control schemes, and seemed effective for short periods in lowering food prices. The government in twentieth century America usually relies on legal pronouncements backed up by the full force of the federal government, if necessary.

The past four years reveal three episodes which reflect some quite diverse situations and means of politicization. These episodes are only a tiny sample of the diverse types of politicization that occurs at all levels in the world's largest market, the United States. But they do suggest additional features to measure which reflect on the politicization of prices.

Proposition 103

California used to have a regulatory system in automobile insurance that relied heavily on market forces to keep prices in line. This system was praised in the Ford Administration Papers on Regulatory Reform edited by Paul MacAvoy. The system, however, exists no longer. In November, 1988, the voters of California adopted a popular initiative, Proposition 103, by a 51%-49% margin. During the 1980s, automobile insurance rates in California had risen substantially: by 12.2% from 1982 to 1986, and by 14% in 1987 and 1988. By the time of the vote on 103, California auto insurance premiums were 40% above the national average, at $673.18 per insured auto (Zycher, p. 68).

While costs for claims had risen for the insurers, and they were earning only a 3.3% return on equity after taxes according to the California Department of Insurance, the most serious problem causing rates to rise was the state-mandated assigned risk program, the California Automobile Assigned Risk Plan (CAARP), which did seem to smell like a carp. Insurers were required to participate in this program in proportion to their market share. Drivers were eligible to buy assigned risk insurance if they were rejected by two insurers for regular coverage, and the assigned risk customers did tend to be the worst drivers. If eligible, what did one pay for coverage? By 1988, an adult male living in Watts (east Los Angeles) without the best driving record would pay $1,640 for a regular policy, but only $575 for an assigned risk policy with only slightly smaller coverage. If one were not already eligible for an assigned risk policy, it would seem to pay to get a bad driving record to qualify.

The large subsidy to bad California drivers existed because the price of assigned risk insurance had become a politicized price set by the insurance commissioner, an official appointed by the governor. More than 50% of each rate increase requested by the industry from 1983 to 1989 has been denied, with the February 1989 request of 112.3% increase totally denied. The result for the insurance companies is three-fold. They have losses of $2 for each $1 of premium collected on the assigned risk policies. These losses are a cost of doing regular insurance business in California and cause the companies to raise the rates on regular policies, resulting in the above-national rates mentioned above. Finally, CAARP creates a prisoner's dilemma situation for each company which causes the problem to grow. Any individual firm can cut its own payments of the assigned risk losses by redirecting customers from regular policies toward an assigned risk policy, as the assigned risk losses are socialized, being paid by all the firms in proportion to their market share. Even the largest auto insurer in California, State Farm, holds only 6.4% of the market. This means that 93.6% of the losses on the CAARP policies that State Farm writes are paid for by other insurers, while State Farm pays 100% of the losses on its regular policies. So long as it is earning less on its assets devoted to regular policies than those assets cost, it certainly pays an insurer to sell CAARP policies rather than regular insurance. The result has been that CAARP policies grew from 94,400 policies in 1983 to 1,233,400 by 1989.

The subsidized growth of these politicized-price products resulted in a revolt in the Proposition 103 vote which mandated a 20% reduction in auto insurance rates from the November 1987 rates. This would have been more than 30% below the November 1988 rates. This rollback did not occur but not because of the court proceedings initiated by the industry. This occurred because the law also politicized the price-setting mechanism in the auto insurance industry. Only certain criteria were to be allowed to determine rates, and geographic location is not currently allowed. The result was that the rates would not actually drop for all drivers after 103's implementation. In fact, the rates were to increase in all except four counties in the state. The increase in Modoc County was nearly 58%. The insurance Commissioner Roxani Gillespie decided that these increases were unacceptable, and disallowed the large rollbacks for Orange and San Francisco counties—only Los Angeles would be granted the 30% rollback implied by the law. Rates also were to drop in Orange, Riverside and San Francisco counties, but increase in all other counties. This result is somewhat different from the 20% rollback stated in the law, but the votes by county seem to reflect a pretty accurate understanding of the eventual results by the voters of California (Zycher, p. 74). That is why almost 50% of the voters voted against a 30% price cut.

One other feature of the initiative was that the insurance commissioner who would be setting the rates in the future was no longer to be appointed by the governor. Instead, this was to be an elected office. This is helping to further politicize auto insurance rates in California, as the campaigning for insurance commissioner has heated up. Several of the candidates are campaigning on a platform of not being fair to the insurance companies, but instead in being their worst nightmare. The ads sound more like professional wrestling promotions than competition to perform public service. Clearly, the means of getting into an office that deals with politicized prices and the means of removal affect how politicized those prices are, and need to be discovered.

Gasoline Prices and OPEC

When OPEC raised its crude oil prices in 1973 from $3 a barrel to $10, the U.S. government intervened with price controls to buffer consumer-voters from the effects of these increases. The controls continued into the Reagan Administration, costing the oil-patch states an estimated $30 billion p.a. (Kalt). While most of this system of controls was dismantled by the Reagan Administration, some parts of it are still around or could easily be revived.

The invasion of Kuwait by Iraq in August 1990 has generated calls for a new energy policy and for reinstating controls on energy prices. The only response by President Bush was a statement in mid-August asking the oil firms to avoid unnecessary price increases. Two oil firms stated publicly that they would freeze their prices for a week, but a week later operated just as the other firms had. After the process of conjectured price increase and market response as discussed above, the result was an average increase of 15 cents per gallon at retail for unleaded gasoline. The crude oil futures price in New York as of October 1990 was still $6 a barrel above the pre-invasion price, approximately 30% higher, and exceeded the before tax increase in the gasoline price. The politicization of this price has been more attenuated than in 1974.

The Kuwaiti invasion and American military response focused attention on the price of gasoline that far exceeded the attention that the eventual increases would have generated. Such media visibility are important in helping to generate demands for politicizing prices and would need to be measured in studying the process of politicization. Media events that hit the nightly news programs have far greater potential for politicization than those which are generally ignored by the media.

DRAMs and Computers

Practically all major innovations in the design, production and products of the semiconductor industry have been made by American companies. This helped create an industry which the United States dominated in 1980. But in the largest dollar volume product, the Dynamic Random Access Memory (DRAM) used as memories in computers and various other electronic equipment, the Japanese were making considerable progress. Today, this market is about $7 billion p.a., and the Japanese have over half of the global market in DRAMs. This situation has been infuriating to some American firms and they have responded in several ways. One governmental response occurred in 1984 with the adoption of copyright protection for the photographic masks used to produce integrated circuit chips. Prior to that passage, the Japanese had been photographically copying the masks from finished parts and producing copies without payments to the designers. A standard myth from that period is that Hitachi made a chip which had Texas Instruments' logo, a map of Texas, on the chip. Such obvious copying has ended and the Japanese have been making substantial royalty payments on numerous designs, as the American industry is well ahead in its ability to define marketable chips and to design them.

The mask copyright protection simply defined a set of intellectual property rights which are relatively innocuous, and are probably promotive of efficiency. The second stage of the governmental response, however, had little of this innocuous character. In 1983 and 1984, the home computer boom of the early 1980s turned into a bust as consumers told the producers that they really wanted home video game machines (which most already owned) and might buy a computer if it was like those used at the office. Between 1984 and 1986, the downturn in demand for integrated circuit chips and especially DRAMs resulted in billions of dollars of losses for American and Japanese producers. In 1985, negotiations between the U.S. Department of Commerce and the Japanese government began. The Americans were responding to complaints about the dumping of DRAM chips by the Japanese, complaints from American firms and by the trade association, the Semiconductor Industry Association (SIA).

Dumping, in terms of selling chips at below production cost, is a well-established practice in an industry like semiconductors which has very large learning curve effects. By selling output early on at below cost, a firm can increase its market share, sell and produce more product and achieve lower costs than other firms through learning effects. The American firms could complain about foreign firms selling at below cost, but they themselves regularly have done this for years. In spite of this problem, the SIA convinced the Administration that the industry needed help. By around March of 1986, an agreement in principle had been worked out and was announced in July as the Semiconductor Trade Agreement of 1986 (STA). The STA required Japanese firms to sell DRAMs at prices above their Foreign Market Value (FMV), which was to be based on historical accounting cost data and updated quarterly. The price of DRAMs had become politicized.

After indications of grey market leakage from Japan to other Asian markets was discovered, the Administration announced in March 1987 a 100% tariff on certain electronic equipment produced by the Japanese firms making DRAMs. When this leakage ended, half of the tariffs were removed, but the remainder continued. This tariff continued as the secret letter agreement which accompanied the STA had not been carried out. The secret letter, which leaked out within months of the STA, stated that American semiconductor firms should have a 20% share of the Japanese semiconductor market. The 1986 share was 10.3%, and has risen to about 14% since. The attempt at managed trade has largely been a failure, partly due to disagreements as to how to measure market share. The SIA and the Electronics Industry Association of Japan (EIAJ) have quite different numbers for the American market share, with the SIA number always being lower than the EIAJ one. After the Japanese government washed its hands of enforcing the letter, the EIAJ has attempted to help increase its members' purchases of American parts.

The STA helped prop up American prices for DRAMs, raising them to at least double the internal Japanese transfer prices charged their electronics divisions which used the parts. As only two U.S. firms still were producing DRAMs, the positive effects of these higher prices were quite small. While other firms announced their return to the DRAM market, some actually were producing a related part, the Static Random Access Memory (SRAM), and produced DRAMs in only small quantities, if at all. The higher prices hurt our globally dominant computer industry and threatened our successful software industry which writes the programs that allow the computers to do anything useful. The damage was most severe in 1988 when the prices of some types of DRAMs had tripled over their 1986 price and were practically unavailable on the open spot market. A huge grey market developed in DRAMs with some 7,000 brokers estimated to be in the business by the summer of 1988. Stories of Japanese and Korean firms offering DRAMs to American computer firms in exchange for licenses to their key proprietary technology were very common. In the spring of 1988, the SIA asked the Department of Commerce to get the Japanese government to end the DRAM production quota it had imposed on the Japanese firms, and prices slowly started falling by the winter of 1989.

The STA episode illustrates how attractive politicized prices are for firms, just as they are for consumers. Our most innovative industry, the semiconductor producers, have been sucked into the political arena and many semiconductor firms came to view their profitability almost totally determined by decisions in Washington and Tokyo. Our other most innovative industry, the computer industry, found itself a victim of the resulting politicization of DRAM prices and it too was forced to fight back with political weapons. The resulting diversion of attention and effort of the management of the firms in these industries was not helpful to efforts to improve productivity or discover new products. Prices in many industries may be politicized if insulated from external markets and the downstream impacts require defensive politicization in turn.

D. Conclusions

The politicization of prices is at the heart of myriad problems in every nation of the world, especially the lack of economic development in much of the Third World. As usual, we could wait for political scientists to take up this effort. We could wait for sociologists to start examining how economic and political variables are related to collective phenomenon such as riots. The response by these other disciplines seems only to occur when the turf of that discipline is challenged by outsiders, and we can trigger those responses.

The *explananda* include the politicization of prices itself. Economists need to look beyond their ordinary concerns and try to discern the determinants of politicization. Which prices are politicized, and how? What determines the form and timing of politicization? Given that politicization, what social outcomes does it affect? Does the form and extent of politicization, or the level and type of government involved, affect what happens when such politicized prices change? The usual normative analyses of efficiency and fairness need to be done as well, but so does a new form of normative analysis. The implications of politicization for the type of dynamic or adaptive efficiency analyzed by Pelikan also needs to be studied. Chapter 26 of my forthcoming intermediate microeconomics text includes an example of standard policy analysis which attempts to ascertain the implications of the policy for this dynamic efficiency. If Joseph Schumpeter has taught the economics profession anything useful at all, it is that an economy that is efficient dynamically may be far more valuable to be a member of than an economy which attains 100% static efficiency.

References

Bates, Robert H., *Market and States in Tropical Africa: The Political Basis of Agricultural Policies*, (Berkeley: Univ. Calif. Pr., 1981).

Denzau, Arthur T., *American Steel: Responding to Foreign Competition*, Formal Publication No. 66, Center for the Study of American Business, Washington University (St. Louis), February 1985.

_____, *Trade Protection Comes to Silicon Valley*, Formal Publication No. 86, Center for the Study of American Business, Washington University (St. Louis), August 1988.

_____, *Microeconomic Analysis*, (Homewood, IL: Irwin, 1992).

de Soto, Hernando, *The Other Path: The Invisible Revolution in the Third World*, (New York: Harper & Row, 1989).

Frey, Bruno S., "Economists Favour the Price System—Who Else Does?" *Kyklos*, 39(4) (1986), 537-63.

Kalt, Joseph P., *The Economics and Politics of Oil Price Regulation: Federal Policy in the Post-Embargo Era*, (Cambridge: MIT Pr., 1981).

MacAvoy, Paul W. (ed.), *Federal-State Regulations of the Pricing and Marketing of Insurance*, Ford Administration Papers on Regulatory Reform, (Washington: American Enterprise Institute, 1977).

North, Douglass C., "A Transaction Cost Theory of Politics," *Journal of Theoretical Politics*, (forthcoming).

Pelikan, Pavel, "Can the Imperfect Innovation Systems of Capitalism Be Outperformed?" Ch. 18 in G. Dosi et al. (eds.), *Technical Change and Economic Theory*, (London: Pinter, 1988), 370-98.

Pierce v. Society of Sisters, 268 U.S. 510 (1925).

Popper, Karl R., *Conjectures and Refutations*, (London: Routledge and Kegan Paul, 1963).

Posner, Richard A., *The Economic Analysis of Law*, (Boston: Little, Brown, 1973).

Rockoff, Hugh, *Drastic Measures: A History of Wage and Price Controls in the United States*, (Cambridge: Cambridge Univ. Press, 1984).

Tullock, Gordon, "Rent-Seeking as a Negative-Sum Game," in J.M. Buchanan, R. Tollison and G. Tullock (eds.), *Toward a Theory of the Rent-Seeking Society*, (College Station: Texas A&M Pr., 1980), 16-36.

Williams v. Walker-Thomas Furniture Co., 350 F. 2d 445 (D.C. Cir. 1965).

Zycher, Benjamin, "Automobile Insurance Regulation, Direct Democracy, and the Interests of Consumers," *Regulation: Cato Review of Business & Government*, (Summer 1990), 67-77.

Discussion

Ed Hudgins remarked that we often have government agencies intervening to insure the firms whose prices they have distorted in the first place. This leaves no incentives to change the system. This is especially true with the IMF, the World Bank and AID. Walter Block noticed that although there are fights over particular regions in British Columbia which might be used for logging, there are few fights over baseballs and hockey sticks. The problem is that there is a very unclear definition of private property. Hudgins saw that in Washington both the left and right push for controls over their prices albeit for different nominal reasons. Richard Rahn remarked that in Bulgaria they had a system for allocating foreign exchange for different firms all of which were government-owned. Many export firms do not have foreign exchange to buy imports.

Ed Hudgins suggested that politicized prices breed more politicized prices. They create a dynamic of their own. Juan Bendfeldt argued that the reason that there are riots over prices in some countries is that people know where those prices are going to be set. They are out of the usual market. Thus, quite naturally, people go under the president's balcony. In Latin America, generally speaking, even the mayor of a town has the legal right to set the prices in the local market. This is seldom exercised, but nonetheless the law is on the books. And this points out a very bad trend associated with the human rights discourse. We start linking human rights to social rights, and to environmental rights, and even to so-called economic rights. But these are really transfer or entitlement systems. It is incredible to make such linkages, and it is being developed under the auspices of the United Nations. Quotas on textiles, sugar and coffee to the U.S. cause no end of political allocations in Latin America as each government now organizes a single monopoly to meet the quota. Milton Friedman remarked that in response to a *Newsweek* column he had written that suggested that government actions often create more problems with the situation they are attempting to solve, it was suggested he call this "law" the "invisible foot of government." Should the loss created in other countries be included in our measure of economic freedom? Ron Jones suggested that the answer is, yes, as it is a consequence of the restriction.

James Ahiakpor argued that by informing people of the costs of regulated prices we can remove them since the common people actually lose through the price controls. The importance is to explain so they understand they are last in line. Ed Hudgins agreed and stressed that the media have little incentive to do so. Walter Block described the free trade debate within Canada in which although by survey 95% of economists favour free trade, on the state radio, the CBC, only two percent of the time were economists interviewed, and of these, half were for it and half against. Alan Stockman indicated that the reason for this is that the media is there as a result of market forces, and this means they attempt to create entertainment. This has to be sufficiently differentiated so as to allow many people to add their little bit to a basic story.

Returning to the theme that Ahiakpor had raised, Melanie Tammin argued that in the cases of the USSR and Eastern Europe, it is important to privatize property before liberalizing prices. Arthur Denzau agreed and pointed out that the whole process may break down to the extent you cannot do it all at once and the first owners are the biggest winners. Zane Spindler suggested that what must happen is that there will be a collapse of the security system and then, and only then, will there be a sensible allocation of property rights. Richard Rahn disagreed. Rather than a breakdown, he suggested that it must be an open process so as to be free from the taint of the "nomenclatura" who have been running things for so long. There is a "chicken and egg problem" as property rights, freer prices, and the difficult task of valuing assets must be accomplished in a proper sequence. Milton Friedman felt that speed of privitization and freedom are not incompatible. Instead, the property should be given to the people since they own it, but you must do a lot of things at once. The political process, still controlled by many of the same interests that have been in power for many years, will not let you do it, and as Spindler suggests, it will happen almost inadvertently or by breakdown—in spite of the people who are trying to run it. The political structure has no incentive to provide the kind of public good (economic freedom) that we would like to see. This, Richard Stroup suggested, is an application of Mancur Olsen's idea that there must be some kind of revolution to make significant changes in the economic structure. The old ossified government must be swept away—as happened in Japan and Germany. Juan Bendfeldt argued that in decontrolling the economy, the reformers should leave selling the assets as the last option. Those who would have money to buy would be those who have been in power which is now seen as illegitimate. If you must sell, then you soak up all the liquid assets and concentrate them in the hands of the government. Not a happy prospect. If you must sell, then collect the currency and burn it!

Labour Markets and Liberty

Thomas J. DiLorenzo, Loyola College in Maryland

Introduction

THIS PAPER SUGGESTS A WAY of thinking about one of the most important economic freedoms—the freedom to earn a living. Economic freedom may be defined generally as the freedom to trade or to engage in any consensual economic activity.[1] In the context of the labour market, economic freedom means the freedom of an employee or a group of employees to "trade" labour services in return for remuneration. Since free trade in the labour market is mutually advantageous, it benefits both parties. Moreover, labour market freedom entails many other freedoms, such as freedom of contract, of choice, and of association. To maximize their own well being, workers and employers must be free to contract with whomever they want, to associate with whomever they want to, and to have as wide a choice of labour market options as possible, as long as they don't interfere with the equal rights of others. Thus, an unregulated labour market is most conducive to individual workers' (and employers') pursuit of happiness and economic well being as they subjectively value it.

Government can play two different roles regarding the labour market. One role is to serve as a "referee" by enforcing voluntary contracts, protecting private property rights, and generally maintaining the rule of law. Government, in other words, can enforce the rules of the game without directly determining the outcome.

The second role of government is to make rules that determine the outcome by passing legislation and issuing regulations that affect wages, working conditions, and other aspects of labour markets. This second role is the predominant objective of governmental labour policy in democratic countries, and it conflicts with the objective of economic freedom. Rather than protecting private contracts and private property, government all too often attenuates the rights of both individual workers and employers.

The reason governments do a poor job of protecting these rights is the basic asymmetry in political decision making in democratic countries. Generally speaking, governments pass legislation to benefit relatively small, well-organized, and well-financed interest groups. The costs of the legislation are usually hidden and widely dispersed among the general population. To promise voters well defined and exaggerated benefits, and to hide the costs, is the route to a successful political career. Thus, labour legislation is typically (but not always) intended to improve the economic well being of one group by diminishing another's. Such laws infringe on the economic liberties of individuals and groups that are less politically effective.[2] Most labour legislation, in other words, amounts to protectionism—it tries to protect the jobs and incomes of one group of employees by restricting the opportunities of others. Like protectionist trade policies, such laws tend to impoverish an entire nation while providing benefits to a relatively small, politically-active minority.

This paper attempts to explain how labour legislation has reduced economic freedom and suggests a way of ranking countries in terms of the degree of labour market freedom. Four countries—the U.S., Canada, Great Britain, and Japan—are then tentatively ranked.

The types of legislation (and its economic effects) to be discussed are: 1) union legislation; 2) domestic labour legislation; and 3) immigration legislation. Because there are literally thousands of labour laws and regulations, the following analysis is at best a preliminary assessment of economic freedom in the labour market. Only the most severe labour market interventions are considered.

Although preliminary, such an analysis is important because labour market freedom is arguably the most important economic freedom of all. Without the freedom to earn a living, citizens are bound to become ever more subservient to the state.

Union Legislation

Much labour legislation deals with the relationships between unions and employers. From the perspective of economic freedom—particularly freedom of association—there is nothing particularly objectionable about "combinations of labour" any more than there is about any other combinations of individuals for whatever purpose, as long as the group does not interfere with the equal rights of others. A government that respects economic freedom will not restrict the rights of individuals to associate freely with one another, nor will it restrict the rights of individuals who choose *not* to be associated with any such groups.

Labour law in democratic countries contains much rhetoric about protecting freedom of association, but in reality it does a poor job of it. Governments interefere or meddle with private contractual relationships between workers (or their unions) and employers on a massive scale. Most union legislation attempts to replace private, voluntary labour contracts and agreements with governmental edicts. It in essence socializes labour relations. Furthermore, much legislation confers special privileges on labour *unions* often to the detriment of individual workers and employers.

Compulsory Unionism

One example of such legislation is laws that encourage or even mandate unionization. In the U.S., for example, labour legislation discusses the importance of freedom of association, but then it talks of such freedom in terms of freedoms "to form, join, or assist labour *organizations*" for the purpose of *collective* bargaining (emphasis added).[3] Many of the employee "rights" that are protected by U.S. labour law are ones that can be advanced only through unionization.

Thus, an important measure of labour market freedom is the degree to which labour law protects *individual workers* rather than unions as organizations. Since the interests of individual workers are quite often in conflict with the interests of union officials, a legal framework that encourages or mandates unionization diminishes individual economic freedom. Laws that mandate collective bargaining, for example, are a restriction of workers' (and employers') freedom. A worker may prefer to bargain individually and an employer may prefer to just ignore a union.

The benefits of individual, rather than collective, bargaining is clear. Research in labour economics has shown that collective bargaining tends to reduce the dispersion of wages. More specifically, more productive workers are usually paid less than they could earn had they bargained individually, whereas less productive workers often earn more, as union wages are set at something close to the median wage within a bargaining unit. Thus, if collective bargaining *imposes* an outcome on all employees, it is bound to make some of them—usually the most productive ones—worse off.

Despite the fact that some workers are made worse off, it is illegal for workers in a unionized industry in the U.S. and many other countries to bargain individually. Such bargaining is deemed an "unfair labour practice" and is a punishable offense. Thus, the ability to bargain individually is one measure of labour market freedom that will be examined. Of particular interest will be various "union security" laws which deprive workers of individual bargaining rights by compelling them to participate in union bargaining.

Yellow-Dog Contracts

With regard to employers' rights, it is illegal in many countries for an employer to refuse to bargain with a union. In the U.S. it is a *per se* violation of the National Labour Relations Act to refuse to bargain with a union, but it is not illegal for a union to refuse to bargain with an employer.[4] So-called "yellow-dog" contracts—agreements between employers and employees not to have a union—have been illegal in the U.S. and many other countries for decades.

Labour historians have found that one of the reasons for such contracts (which, it is worth stressing, were voluntary) is the desire by *workers* to avoid the work disruptions and loss of wages during strikes that characterize unionized industries.[5] Moreover, since such agreements were voluntary, they must have benefitted employers *and* employees, just as all voluntary free market agreements do. Either party was free to end the employment relationship "at will" if dissatisfied.

The only way that such agreements could persist in a free marketplace is if they were "efficient" in the sense that they enhanced the welfare of both parties—the anti-union employees and employers who must have believed that unionization would not be in their best interest. Thus, legislation that outlaws such contracts must necessarily make some workers and employers worse off. In international comparisons the existence of so-called yellow-dog contracts reflects positively on economic freedom.

Exclusivity

Another aspect of labour legislation that grants special privileges to unions at the expense of economic freedom for workers is so-called exclusive representation. Exclusivity gives a union, once it has been certified, the legal right to be the *exclusive* bargaining agent for all workers in a bargaining unit, whether they wish to be represented or not. Any attempt by employers or workers to bargain individually—even over the most mundane things—is illegal.

Exclusivity gives unions a legal monopoly in the employee representation business. It is not only illegal for workers to bargain individually with their employers; exclusive representation legislation also prohibits bargaining through another, competing union, or any other agent.[6]

Protected from competition by exclusive representation laws, unions act like all other monopolists: they restrict their "output" and raise their prices. Because unions face no competition in the employee representation business, they are less constrained than they would otherwise be to charge excessive dues and other obligations and are also likely to provide fewer services to their members. Evidence of the latter type of behavior abounds. In the U.S. unions are major participants in all sorts of political causes that are unrelated to labour relations or to the economic welfare of their members. Unions have been active in the pro-abortion movement; they have spent considerable resources in support of left-wing authoritarian governments in Central America, Africa, and elsewhere; they are part of the anti-nuclear power movement; they have lobbied for sanctions against the South African government; and they actively lobby for socialistic economic policies (i.e., price controls and nationalization of some industries) that, by hampering economic growth, are not in the best interests of the workers they represent.[7]

Exclusivity allows unions to shirk some of their basic responsibilities, such as contract administration, bargaining, and grievance handling, in order to pursue political causes that are irrelevant or even harmful to the economic welfare of workers. An indication of how far afield U.S. unions have strayed from their basic responsibilities is a recent decision by the U.S. Supreme Court that it is unconstitutional to compel workers to pay union dues to finance activities that are not directly related to bargaining, contract administration, and grievance procedures. In the case of Beck vs. Communication Workers of America, the Court found that the union spent less than 20 percent of its dues revenues on appropriate expenses. The other 80 percent was spent on politics. Other cases have found that as little as 10 percent of dues revenues are spent on legitimate purposes. The Supreme Court ruling will likely weaken the monopolistic grip that unions have over their members, but exclusivity continues to entrench much of their monopoly power.

Because of the monopoly powers granted to them by exclusivity legislation, unions may also be unresponsive to their members' demands for changes in collective bargaining strategies. There have been many cases in the U.S., for example, where workers were convinced that they would have to make concessions if they wanted to remain employed. Union officials, however, have often refused to heed the preferences of their members, sometimes causing the members to lose their jobs. Unions would be more likely to cater to their members' preferences if there were competitors in the employee representation business, but such freedom of choice is precluded by law.

Pushbutton Unionism

In a number of countries unions and businesses are given quasi-governmental powers to the extent that they are able to coerce workers to financially support or even join a union as a condition of employment. For example, in the U.S. a new automobile plant built by the Saturn Corporation, a spinoff of General Motors, has a unionized work force because before the plant opened, Saturn management agreed with the United Autoworkers union (UAW) that its employees would be represented by the UAW. No certification election was ever held where the workers would be given the opportunity to vote on whether or not they wanted to join the union. Indeed, the agreement was signed before employees were even hired.

The Saturn plant is in Tennessee, a "right-to-work" state. This means that workers cannot be compelled to join the union, although the union is still given the privilege of exclusive representation. This form of "pushbutton unionism" is not as coercive as closed shop agreements which compel union membership as a condition of employment, but it is still a diminution of labour market freedom.

Agency Shop

A further infringement on the economic liberties of workers is the so-called agency shop, whereby workers who do not belong to a union must nevertheless pay union dues. The rationale for agency shop is derived from exclusivity. Since unions are required to bargain for all workers (union and non-union) in a bargaining unit, it is supposedly necessary to compel all workers to pay for bargaining services.

In the terminology of economics, collective bargaining is said to provide workers with "public goods," and compulsory union dues are supposedly necessary to prohibit free riding. But since government created the situation where all workers are forced to submit to a single monopoly bargaining agent, a better phrase than "free riders" would probably be "forced riders." Workers are forced to accept the results of union bargaining and, where agency shop exists, are also forced to financially support the union. To workers who are worse off because of this arrangement, exclusivity creates a "public bad," not a public good: they are forced to pay dues for the "privilege" of being made worse off. Agency shop literally constitutes taxation without representation and is a serious encroachment on economic freedom.

Union Violence

The long history of union violence can be readily explained by economic theory. In order to push wages above competitive levels, unions must restrict the supply of labour services on the market. They strike or threaten to strike in order to do this, and strikes are often more effective if workers who choose not to strike can be intimidated by violence. Employers can also be subjected to violence, threats of violence, and the destruction of property unless they acquiesce in union demands.

Accordingly, another measure of economic freedom for labour is the extent to which governments protect workers and employers from union violence. Critical questions here are: How are nonunion workers treated during strikes? How well do governments protect non-striking workers from union violence? Do workers who are victims of union violence have recourse to the courts? Do employers whose property is vandalized have recourse to the courts? These questions must all be answered in order to rank countries according to this criteria.

Domestic Labour Legislation

Governments also deprive workers of economic freedom through laws and regulations that affect wages and working conditions. Although these restrictions vary greatly, they all share the common element that they substitute governmental for individual (or market) decision making. They are all carried out under the pretense that government somehow has better knowledge of the "best" wages, hours of work, types of jobs, etc. than individual workers and employers do. This type of thinking is what F.A. Hayek calls "the fatal conceit" because of the dire economic consequences it lends intellectual support to.

Minimum Wage Legislation

Most democratic countries have a minimum wage law that raises wages of low-skilled workers above going market rates. Virtually any economics text explains that mandating above-market rates causes unemployment by pricing low-skilled workers out of jobs. There is no better example of a law that hurts those whom it purports to help or which constitutes a clearer infringement on economic liberties. As Adam Smith said in *The Wealth of Nations*, "the patrimony of a poor man lies in the strength and dexterity of his hands," and to deprive him of this through restrictive labour legislation "is a manifest encroachment upon the just liberty...of the workman, and those who might...employ him."

The minimum wage law even harms workers who are not priced out of the market by it. If employers are forced to pay higher wages, they will either lay off some workers or cut back on other fringe benefits so that the total compensation package does not exceed each worker's marginal productivity. Thus, freedom of choice is diminished for workers who may prefer a different mix of wages and fringe benefits.[8]

The minimum wage law is inefficient and inequitable, but it persists for several political reasons. First, it lends itself to demagoguery better than most government policies. It is natural for politicians to claim to be able to solve social problems by simply passing a law, and what nicer law than one mandating higher wages for the poor?

A second reason is that unions want to price unskilled nonunion labour, which competes with more skilled, union labour, out of the market. In the name of compassion for the poor, unions lobby for legislation that makes the poor even poorer. The minimum wage is a device through which the poor are used as political pawns to the benefit of demagogic politicians and politically-active unions seeking protectionist legislation.

How detrimental the minimum wage law will be depends on its level compared to the market rate for unskilled labour. For example, in the U.S. the federal minimum wage in 1989 was $3.35 per hour, but in many cities entry level jobs at fast-food restaurants paid as much as $8.00 per hour. The harmful effects of the minimum wage were limited to smaller cities and rural areas where market wages for entry-level employment would be below $3.35.

For purposes of cross-country comparisons, the minimum wage in a country should be compared to some standard wage, ideally the market wage for unskilled labour, in order to rank its severity. To the extent that such data are not available, a possible substitute would be an average hourly wage. Thus, a useful standard might be the degree to which the statutory minimum wage in a country diverges from the average wage.

Maximum-Hour Legislation

Another infringement on economic liberties is maximum-hour legislation which, in general, limits the number of hours that workers can work and/or mandates that higher wages must be paid for any work hours over a specified amount. Since overtime pay provisions increase labour costs, the effect is to reduce the level of production and, consequently, the number of hours worked. Individuals who prefer to work more hours or to vary their work hours over the course of a week may be precluded from doing so.

Davis-Bacon Laws

Another related measure of labour market freedom is the existence of laws, such as the Davis-Bacon Act in the U.S., which mandate that government-specified wages be paid. In the case of Davis-Bacon, the government-specified "prevailing wage" in an area must be paid on all federally-supported construction projects, even if the federal support is less than 1 percent of the cost of the project. The "prevailing" wage is almost always the union wage, and the effect of the Act is to drive from the market lower wage, nonunion labour. Making wages artificially high restricts competition from lower-wage firms, depriving their owners, managers, and employees of economic opportunities.

Restrictions on Child and Female Labour

For over a century various countries have prohibited or limited child and female labour. The rationale behind the restrictions is that they are supposedly needed to protect women and children from being exploited by employers.

Even though this rationale for regulation is widely believed by the general public, the regulations are not likely to protect the intended beneficiaries. It is difficult to perceive that regulations prohibiting such work would benefit those individuals who *voluntarily* chose to work. If they felt they were being made worse off by their employment situation, they could simply quit.

There is evidence, moreover, that when such regulation was originally being proposed in England there was fierce opposition to it *by the women who the regulation was supposed to help*. It is likely, therefore, that such regulation may always have been designed to protect incumbent workers from competition. Thus, an examination of laws and regulations across countries that deprive these groups of employment opportunities will be another measure of labour market freedom.

Occupational Licensing Laws

Occupational licensing laws have been shown to create barriers to entry in literally hundreds of professions in the U.S. and many other countries.[9] The restrictions come in many forms, such as license fees, educational requirements, and regional or national examinations.

Licensing has been defended on the grounds that it assures professional competence and protects consumers from lower-quality products and services. These arguments may or may not have merit and they will not be discussed in detail here. But regardless of the motivation for the laws, their effect is to make it more difficult to enter regulated professions. Consequently, many individuals are deprived of employment opportunities.

This licensing-induced reduction of employment opportunities likely imposes a greater burden on lower- rather than on higher-income individuals since it often deprives the former group of valuable opportunities to accumulate human capital—opportunities they may not be able to otherwise obtain.

Again, there is much evidence that occupational licensing is often a *political* response to pressures from incumbent practitioners who want protection from competition. An anecdote will illustrate what I believe to be typical of the politics of occupational licensure.

Economist Walter Williams recently appeared on a televised debate with U.S. Congressman Charles Rangel. Williams made the point that the licensing of hairdressers in Rangel's home state of New York discriminates against blacks. It does so, said Williams, because to become certified as a hairdresser one must pass a practical exam as well as a more academic one that includes math problems. (The relationship between the ability to coif hair and the ability to do mathematics is, to say the least, dubious.) Williams pointed out that an equivalent percentage of blacks passed the practical exam as whites, but the failure rate of blacks on the academic exam was several times higher than the whites. Williams blamed the discrepancy on inferior government schools that so many black New Yorkers are compelled to attend.

Congressman Rangel, who is black, did not dispute the test results and did not deny that the system kept many of his constituents unemployed. But he nevertheless supported the licensing system. His preferred "remedy" for urban unemployment was not to eliminate the sources of unemployment, such as occupational licensing laws, but to suggest more welfare spending.

This type of behavior is readily explained by elementary public choice logic. On the "demand side," the unionized practitioners are well organized and well financed politically, and are able to use the political process to protect themselves from competition with occupational licensing regulations. Those who are harmed by the regulations are not well organized and, hence, are less politically effective.

From a "supply side" perspective, politicians can win votes from the incumbents by supporting licensing, and they can also win votes from those who are denied employment opportunities because of licensing by offering them welfare payments or government patronage jobs.

In this instance the citizens whose liberties are abridged are made effective wards of the state either as welfare recipients or by relying on another form of handout—a government job—for their livelihood. Thus, occupational licensing is yet another way in which the poor are used as mere political pawns by cynical political opportunists.

Ideally, to measure the extent to which occupational licensing restricts employment opportunities across countries one might want to know what percentage of the labour force is subjected to licensing or what proportion of all professions require formal licensing. This information is difficult, if not impossible, to obtain. Furthermore, it is difficult to discover how severe licensing restrictions are for various occupations in a country. For example, an occupation that requires only a small license fee is not as restrictive or harmful as one that requires a large fee, years of schooling, and rigorous state-sponsored examinations.

Equal Pay for Equal Work Laws

These laws are intended to protect certain groups, particularly women, from wage discrimination by mandating that employers pay equal wages for the "same" work performed by workers of different sex and race. The irony is that these laws result in reduced employment opportunities for those who are supposedly helped.

If an employer pays females less than males, for example, it is because he subjectively values female labour less highly. He may genuinely believe that his female employees are less productive and less capable, or he may simply be discriminating against them because they are women. In either case, equal-pay-for-equal-work laws will induce the employer to hire fewer female workers. If forced to pay equal wages, the employer will prefer male workers. Thus, women who are willing to work at least temporarily for lower wages in order to prove that they can do the job are denied the opportunity.

In other words, women can provide employers with *economic* incentives to hire them, despite discrimination, but are not permitted to do so because of "equal pay" laws. Thus, equal-pay-for-equal-work rules, which are supposed to reduce discrimination, actually increase it.

That these laws harm the groups they are supposed to help is made clear by the fact that in some countries, such as South Africa, there is no pretense that the laws are supposed to protect people who are discriminated against. In South Africa, white racist labour unions lobbied for "equal pay" laws for black workers because they knew the laws would protect white employees from competition by relatively less skilled black workers. Since most blacks were less experienced, forcing employers to pay them wages that exceeded their marginal productivity would price them out of jobs.[10] In other countries the motivation behind the laws may be well intentioned, but the effects are the same.

Equal-pay-for-equal-work laws reduce economic freedom, but "equal pay for work of comparable value" legislation would be even worse. This is a proposed system of governmental wage determination, whereby government bureaucrats, rather than the marketplace, would set wages. I will not say anything more about this other than it's already been tried—in the former Soviet Union, China, and Eastern Europe—and it doesn't work. History shows that such governmental control over wages is grossly inefficient and inequitable.

Employment Quotas

Most democratic governments have policies that require employers to make some of their hiring and promotional decisions solely on the basis of noneconomic factors, such as race or sex. Obviously, this denies individuals the freedom to seek employment or career advancement based on merit.

In the U.S. employment quotas were originally enacted with the promise that they would *not* be used to force employers to make decisions based solely on race. The late Senator Hubert Humphrey promised that the Civil Rights Act of 1964 "does not require an employer to achieve any kind of racial balance in his work force by giving preferential treatment to any individual or group." The phrase "affirmative action" was coined by President Kennedy in his executive order that "affirmative action" should be taken to assure that governmental contractors *do not* make employment decisions based on race, creed, color, or national origin.[11]

In practice so-called affirmative action policies do exactly the opposite of what their proponents claimed they would. They *require* that employment decisions be made specifically according to employees' race, creed, color, or national origin. Consequently, "non-preferred" individuals who may be more qualified are passed over by employers who must satisfy the *government's* preferences for discrimination in the workplace. There is mounting evidence, moreover, that even many of the "protected" minorities are denied economic opportunities because of affirmative action policies.

Economist Thomas Sowell has found that the relative economic position of "protected" minority groups in the U.S. actually *fell* after employment quotas were instituted. "In 1969, *before* the federal imposition of numerical 'goals and timetables,' Puerto Rican family income was 63 percent of the national average. By 1977, it was down to 50 percent. In 1969, Mexican American family income was 76 percent of the national average; by 1977 it was down to 73 percent. Black family income fell from 62 percent of the national average to 60 percent over the same time span."[12]

Sowell also found that blacks with less education and job experience have fallen further behind, while blacks with more education and experience have been advancing even faster than their white counterparts. He offers a clear explanation of this phenomenon: affirmative action hiring pressures make it costly to have no minority employees, but continuing affirmative action pressures at the promotion and discharge phases also make it costly to have minority employees who do not work out well. The net effect is to increase the demand for highly qualified minority employees while decreasing the demand for less qualified minority employees or for those without a sufficient track record to reassure employers. Those who are most vocal about the need for affirmative action are of course the more articulate minority members—the advantaged who speak in the name of the disadvantaged. Their position on the issue may accord with their own personal experience, as well as their own self-interest.[13] Thus, like the minimum wage and occupational licensing laws, employment quotas deny employment opportunities to those who need them the most—relatively unskilled and uneducated minorities who are "targeted" for help by the government.

In making international comparisons, one benchmark that may be useful is the number of racial "categories" the governmental authorities have created in order to enforce such policies. The more racial categories the less economic freedom. Another criteria may be the proportion of governmental budgets allocated to enforcement activities. In theory there should be a positive correlation between regulatory budgets (or regulatory employment) and enforcement activity.

Government "Jobs" Programs

All democratic governments have long been involved in employment or job training programs. Despite their popularity, however, they *reduce* economic liberties *and* employment opportunities. It is impossible for government to "create" jobs because of the law of opportunity cost. Government may "create" some jobs with such programs, but it necessarily destroys other private-sector jobs by diverting financial resources from the private sector (through either taxes, government borrowing, or inflationary money creation) to pay for the government jobs. At best, government "jobs" programs alter the *composition* of employment, but not the aggregate level.

Furthermore, many government jobs are wasteful because they do not meet legitimate consumer demands. The history of government job programs is filled with examples of "make work" jobs that seem to emphasize political patronage more than employment opportunity.[14]

The reason government jobs programs remain popular despite their failure to stimulate employment (or training, for that matter) is that the benefits are well defined—job recipients know where the jobs came from and who to thank (or vote for)—whereas the costs are hidden. Those who are unemployed because of the crowding out effect of these programs have no idea of the cause of their unemployment.

This is one way—generating unemployment—that government jobs programs diminish economic freedom. Economic freedom and opportunity is also impaired by government jobs programs because of the fact that the kind of jobs and training provided are determined by government bureaucrats, not individuals in the private sector. This allows government bureaucrats to exert a degree of control over what *kind* of jobs will exist in the economy and what kind of skills people will possess. It is likely that the types of jobs and skills that individuals may choose for themselves will differ from the type the governmental labour market "planners" will prefer.

Giving government such powers opens the door for ever-expanding governmental control of the allocation of labour. In totalitarian regimes such as the former Soviet Union there was a nearly complete domination of the labour market by government. Its "jobs programs" were so extensive that *everyone* worked for the state. The only "real" jobs in the Soviet Union were ones held by black marketeers.

In Nazi Germany, government officials were allowed to monitor and control every proposed job change, thereby directing workers into those endeavors the bureaucrats thought served "national interests" regardless of the interests of individuals who comprised the nation. Of course, modern democratic governments do not possess anything like the powers over labour markets that the Soviet Union or Nazi Germany did. But the differences are only a matter of degree (albeit a large degree). Along with extensive employment programs, all democratic countries keep extremely detailed personal information on labourers and labour markets and they use that information to shape government policy.

Goverment employment programs threaten economic freedom in a very general sense in that consumer sovereignty is replaced by bureaucratic sovereignty. In a free market the type of jobs created are those which serve the desires of consumers. Government jobs, on the other hand, are usually designed to serve the whims of the political authorities, which are often in conflict with consumers. After all, if there is a legitimate consumer demand, there is an incentive for a private entrepreneur to meet it and to hire workers to assist him in doing so. Thus, to a large extent, government jobs are created specifically to provide goods or services that consumers have either not expressed a preference for or, if they have expressed any preference at all, it was a negative one.

Where there is a clear demand for a good or service which government provides, government often competes unfairly with private-sector providers. For example, outside of national defense and a few other activities, most of what governments provide in the U.S. are purely private goods that are also supplied by the private sector. A U.S. Senate hearing once revealed that the federal government alone provides more than 11,000 different goods and services in competition with the private sector. Thus, government uses its powers of taxation, and its ability to exempt itself from regulations it imposes on its private-sector competitors, to monopolize markets for private goods and services.[15]

Since in my view nearly all government employment diminishes economic freedom (and many other freedoms as well), a possible measure of the "costs" of jobs programs in terms of economic freedom is the proportion of a nation's labour force that is employed by government in whatever capacity—as permanent employees or as participants in temporary "jobs" programs.

Mandatory Government Arbitration

All the labour market interventions discussed thus far involve government's attempt to intervene in private contractual relations between workers (or their unions) and employers by setting wages, establishing bargaining procedures, etc. In addition, governments also intervene in the *arbitration* of labour disputes. The U.S. government, for example, has a "Federal Mediation and Conciliation Service" which cajoles negotiating parties into "voluntarily" cooperating in order to end a labour dispute. The U.S. government doesn't yet have the power to mandate a settlement, but it can apply significant political pressures to achieve that end. The effect of this intervention is that disagreements between workers (or their unions) and employers are often settled according to criteria established by the Federal Mediation and Conciliation Service, not by the negotiating parties.

Even though there is no formal power to coerce such agreements in the U.S., the ability of the government to indirectly force an agreement should not be underestimated. U.S. industry is so heavily regulated, and so many corporations accept government subsidies, that government has a tremendous amount of "leverage" over the private sector. Government has a long list of "carrots and sticks" it can use to affect private bargaining outcomes. It can threaten regulation and the withdrawal of subsidies, or it can bribe the bargaining firms and unions with promises of subsidies and other governmental favors.

Thus, another measure of economic freedom is the degree to which governments can compel the settlement of labour disputes. Countries that clearly have that legal right would of course receive a lower ranking than those without it.

Occupational Safety and Health Regulation

Modern democracies also heavily regulate "occupational safety and health." This intervention gives government enormous powers over private labour relations because an argument can be made that almost any aspect of a business operation can be interpreted as at least tangentially related to safety and health. Governments have taken advantage of these broad powers to regulate everything from the construction of ladders to the shape of toilet seats.

Research has shown, however, that occupational safety and health regulation is not likely to have improved workplace safety at all, despite massive expenditures.[16] Furthermore, the regulation has interfered with market forces, which "address" the problem through compensating wage differentials. That is, in a free market, employees in more dangerous jobs will be paid higher wages, all other things equal. Employers must pay higher wages to attract workers to more dangerous jobs. This will not necessarily eliminate or even reduce the incidence of workplace accidents, but then, neither does regulation. Furthermore, reliance on compensating wage differentials, rather than regulation, would avoid the loss of jobs associated with the heavy costs of occupational safety and health regulation. It would also give workers and employers more freedom in determining how to improve workplace safety, rather than relying on bureaucratic edicts.

There is much to commend this former approach, for no one has stronger incentives to assure a safe workplace than employees themselves. Regardless of how well intentioned the safety regulators may be, they just don't have either the incentive or the detailed knowledge required.

It should be kept in mind that there are economic (and common sense) incentives to reduce workplace accidents, for accidents are costly to employers and especially to workers. And it should also be remembered that governmental "safety" regulation can provide a false sense of security. Job safety depends ultimately on how careful and responsible individual workers are. If they are told by governmental safety inspectors that their workplace is "safe," they may be less inclined to take their own precautions. The end result may very well be a *less* safe workplace.

For purposes of international comparisons, data on governmental expenditures for occupational safety and health regulation, perhaps standardized according to the size of a country's labour force, would be useful. Spending $1 billion annually is likely, for example, to be far more onerous in a country with a labour force of 10 million than in another with a labour force of 100 million.

Employer Payroll Taxes

All democratic countries have mandatory employer payroll taxes, the most significant of which are taxes for unemployment insurance and old-age pensions, or social security. A detailed examination of the economic effects of such programs is beyond the scope of this paper, but several aspects of them are particularly relevant to economic freedom.

First, these programs constitute what might be called "mandated benefits," whereby governments compel employers to finance certain benefits on behalf of their employees. One implication of this is that employees consequently have less freedom of choice to determine their own mix of wage and non-wage remuneration. Furthermore, even though the taxes are at least partly paid by employers, they are passed on to employees in the form of lower wages or other benefits, thereby constituting a hidden tax on workers. Because the tax is hidden, workers are less able to make well-informed choices regarding their own compensation mix.

Government-operated unemployment insurance and social security programs often allow governments to become monopolists in the provision of those services. There are many actual and potential substitutes for these government-controlled programs but it is difficult, if not impossible, for them to compete with government. For example, individual retirement accounts (IRAs) compete with the social security system in the U.S., but since the system drains so much income from workers through mandatory payments, there is much less available for private retirement plans.

It would also be possible for individual workers to contribute to an IRA-type account to be used as unemployment insurance, but governments usually prohibit such options. This is especially unfortunate in light of the many failures of governmental unemployment insurance, which essentially pays people not to work by offering unemployed workers "replacement income" as a percentage—sometimes close to 100 percent—of their prior wages. By reducing the cost to workers of being unemployed, unemployment insurance lengthens the duration of unemployment. It also increases unemployment by indirectly subsidizing industries that experience seasonal or cyclical variations in employment. For example, without unemployment insurance a firm with an unstable employment pattern would have to pay higher wages to attract workers. The higher wage would be necessary to compensate workers for the risk of becoming unemployed. But with unemployment insurance the *government* compensates workers for becoming unemployed. This in turn makes unstable employment more attractive to workers than it otherwise would be. The increased supply of labour in those industries will reduce wage rates, which in turn reduce the incentive for firms to do anything to reduce instability in employment. Thus, unemployment insurance encourages unstable sectors of the economy to expand, resulting in a higher overall unemployment rate.

Both unemployment insurance and social security taxes are major infringements on the economic liberties of workers and employers, because they place severe limitations on freedom of choice, freedom of exchange, freedom of contract, and freedom of association. Because government controls a significant portion of workers' income through these programs, and because the programs crowd out private-sector alternatives—if the law permits alternatives at all—individuals are denied all these freedoms.

Peter Ferrara described how the social security system infringes upon individual economic liberties. Government-controlled social security programs, writes Ferrara, force individuals to enter into contracts, exchanges, and associations with the government that they should have the right to refuse. It prohibits individuals from entering into alternative contracts, exchanges, and associations with others concerning the portion of their incomes that social security consumes. It prevents individuals from choosing courses of action other than participation in social security, although these courses of action will hurt no one. It prevents individuals from enjoying the fruits of their own labour by taking control of a major portion of each individual's income. The program prevents individuals from arranging their own affairs and controlling their own lives. It operates by the use of force and coercion against individuals rather than through voluntary consent. The social security program thus restricts individual liberty in major and significant ways, violating rights that are worthy of great respect.[17]

The same can be said for any governmental mandated benefit program. For our international comparisons, an appropriate measuring rod might be the percentage of labour income that is extracted to finance unemployment insurance and social security programs. The greater the tax burden, the lesser the degree of economic liberty.

Taxes on Labour Income

Perhaps the most important interference with an individual worker's economic freedom is the income tax. The income tax denies a worker the ability to keep the fruits of his or her own labour, and is truly a way in which workers are exploited—by government. Karl Marx's labour exploitation thesis was half right. He complained that labour was unfairly exploited because it supposedly produced *all* value—an incredibly naive and simplistic assumption—yet it received only a small part of it in the form of wages. Marx was correct about labour being exploited, but he was wrong about who the exploiters were. By blaming capitalists, he ignored the productive contributions of capital and entrepreneurs. He also ignored the fact that government is the major source of worker exploitation by expropriating income that government itself has no legitimate claim to. Ironically, Marx was a strong proponent of progressive income taxation, which exploits workers even more than proportional taxation.

Income taxation is, in effect, a form of slavery or forced labour. It forces individuals to work and to pay income taxes so that part of their income is given away to someone else—farmers, corporations, welfare recipients, defense contractors, unions, and thousands of other well-organized special-interest groups—who did nothing to earn or deserve it. H.L. Mencken's dictum that an election is an advance auction on stolen property is as trite as it is true.

Of course, not all income that is taxed is necessarily used for government-mandated income transfers. To the extent that some of it is used to finance a criminal justice system, national defense, and generally maintaining the rule of law, it enhances rather than diminishes economic freedoms. However, these functions are a relatively minor aspect of the modern welfare state. The modern state is a vast income redistribution machine that shuffles wealth around *within* the middle class.

For purposes of measurement, it would in theory be desirable to separate the amount of income tax revenue that is used for redistributive purposes and the amount used for the justice system, national defense, etc. In reality, such a task is virtually impossible. One problem is that a government that spends X billions on national defense will include in that amount some legitimate defense expenditures as well as a considerable amount of patronage payments to consultants and contractors and academicians and others who do not necessarily contribute to the national defense. The same is likely to be true for spending on the justice system and virtually every other government program. I will ignore these intractible problems and consider the percentage of wage income extracted through income taxation as another measure of the loss of economic freedom.

Employment in the Military

Another relative measure of labour market freedom will be whether or not a country raises an army through conscription or through more voluntaristic means, such as by offering competitive wages. Obviously, the existence of a military draft will count negatively against a country's standing in terms of economic freedom.

Mandating Job Security

Many countries have various laws and regulations that supposedly guarantee "job security" by restricting the flow of capital. Laws that make it more costly or prohibitive to close down a plant are examples. Such laws may be well intentioned, but they deprive workers and business owners of economic freedom and are undeniably harmful to a nation's economy. By hampering economic growth, they ultimately impoverish the workers in whose name the laws are enacted. Job security laws, in other words, reduce job security.

Advocates of such legislation usually ignore the fact that workers and employers do negotiate various types of "job security" provisions in their contracts. It must be realized that if, for example, a union wants a contract that includes severance pay in the event that the plant closes down, that provision will be "paid" for by a negotiated reduction in wages or other fringe benefits. There is no free lunch; acquiring such benefits requires tradeoffs. That's why laws that mandate job security provisions reduce economic freedom. They deprive workers of freedom of choice by forcing them to accept one particular benefit—a benefit they may not want if they know how much it cost them in terms of foregone wages. So-called job security regulation also deprives employers and business owners (i.e., shareholders) of economic freedom. It prohibits them from making the best use of their resources, which can only be impoverishing. The extent to which governments control the flow of capital through "job security" regulation is another measure of labour market freedom. Countries will be evaluated according to such criteria as whether they actually make plant closings or relocations costly or prohibitive or if they have milder restrictions, such as the plant-closing notification law that exists in the U.S.

Immigration

Freedom of migration is a basic human right that is essential if individuals are to be free from governmental oppression. The ability to change employment or to seek employment elsewhere—even in another country—is a hallmark of economic freedom. Thus, free immigration and emigration is most conducive to economic freedom and opportunity.

No country in the world has perfectly free immigration. The U.S. is generally regarded as among the most free—there are about twice as many immigrants entering the U.S. each year as there are in all the rest of the world combined. Yet the U.S. does place restrictions on immigration.

Since freedom of migration is so essential to labour market freedom generally, there are a number of criteria that can be used in combination to try to measure this aspect of economic freedom.

Overall Limits on Immigration

Since all countries place some limits on immigration, one method of comparing them is by calculating the allowable number of immigrants as a percentage of the nation's population.

Taxes on Immigration

Some countries charge immigrants fees or taxes. In such cases large statutory numbers of allowable immigrants may not be very meaningful if the charges are so high as to exclude large numbers of people. Therefore, the existence of "entrance fees" into a country is another criteria that may be used. The amount of the fee may be standardized as a percentage of average annual income in the country receiving the immigrants.

Enforcement

Many countries are concerned about illegal immigrants. From the perspective of labour market freedom, however, the more illegals the better. The fact that the U.S. claims that its enforcement of illegal immigration is weak, and that its borders are "out of control," is a plus. Consequently, another possible measure of labour market freedom is the budget of the appropriate immigration enforcement agency as a percentage of the nation's total governmental budget. The higher the budget allocation, the stronger is enforcement, and the lesser the degree of economic freedom.

Labour Market Tests

In some countries immigration laws specifically outlaw immigration if the immigration enhances rather than stifles a free market in labour. In the U.S. immigrants are required to prove that their employment will not displace a U.S. worker *and* that their presence will not cause a reduction in wages. This is clearly a protectionist law instigated by organized labour. The existence of such tests will cause a country to be ranked lower on our economic freedom scale.

Lists of "Undesirables"

Some countries limit immigration according to racial or ethnic criteria. The U.S. has a long history if discriminating against Chinese and Japanese immigrants in this way, although such discrimination was outlawed in 1965. Thus, another criteria is the existence of a list of racially or ethnically "undesirable" immigrants.

Amnesty

Granting amnesty to illegal immigrants who have over a period of years established "roots" in a country is another way in which immigration restrictions are diluted and, consequently, economic freedom is enhanced. Thus, the existence of an amnesty program will provide a country with a more favorable economic freedom rating.

Temporary Workers

Since a half a loaf is better than none, countries that allow temporary "guest workers" exhibit a higher degree of economic freedom, all other things equal, than those that don't.

Emigration

Of course, the "supply side" of immigration depends on the ability of individuals to leave. Some measure of governmental impediments to emigration is therefore essential in our measurement. One criterion is the existence of limits on emigration expressed as a percentage of the population.

Measuring Labour Market Freedom

It's worth repeating that the above template is by no means comprehensive. In many countries there are literally thousands of labour laws and regulations and the number is growing almost daily. Heldman, Bennett, and Johnson provide the following partial view of the enormity of labour law and regulation in the U.S.

> Among the standard, heavily used tools of the labour specialists' trade are (as of 1980) 250 volumes of NLRB decisions, 87 volumes of *Labour Cases*, 103 volumes of the...*Labour Relations Reference Manual*, 11 volumes of *Federal Regulation of Employment Service*, 26 volumes of various publications of the Bureau of National Affairs dealing with labour relations, 22 volumes of *Fair Employment Practice Cases*, literally untold volumes of cases and decisions emanating from state-level employment relations boards and commissions, and a virtual avalanche of materials on private and public sector arbitration decisions. It is possible that no other topic enjoys (if that is the right word for it) the massive amount of legal reference

materials as that which must be mastered if any particular party in an employment relationship is to act in accordance with the standards of behavior laid down by agencies of government.[18]

The sheer magnitude of regulation, i.e., the number of pages of regulations, might conceivably be another measure of economic freedom—the more pages the less freedom. But such a measurement would not be very enlightening because it does not distinguish between irrelevant regulations, such as a declaration of a "national farmworkers' week," and substantive regulations such as a minimum wage law.

That we have omitted many regulations—some trivial and some not so trivial—need not impair the accuracy of our rankings. It is reasonable to assume that countries with a high (or low) economic freedom rating based on the above criteria will probably also have a high (or low) rating if the myriad other regulations were included. It would seem highly unlikely that a country with a high ranking based on the major forms of labour market regulation would be ranked very differently on most of its other interventions.

The following table contains the preliminary ranking of the U.S., Canada, Great Britain, and Japan in terms of our criteria. The rankings are based on a scale of 1 to 10 for each criteria, with a 10 being the highest degree of economic freedom. Since not all criteria are "either-or" criteria, I will attempt to classify the countries in light of the above discussion. For example, a country that has statutory restrictions on immigration but which does not enforce them will receive a higher rating than a country with identical restrictions that are in fact enforced. The rankings are necessarily subjective, but I will discuss the rationales for the various *ordinal* rankings in the table. Finally, I will attempt to collapse all the individual rankings into an overall ranking for each country.

Table 1. Measuring Labour Market Freedom

Criteria	U.S.	Canada	England	Japan
Compulsory Collective Bargaining	0	0	10	0
Yellow-Dog Contracts Permitted	0	0	0	0
Exclusive Representation Laws	0	0	10	10
Pushbutton Unionism	0	3	0	10
Agency Shop	5	5	0	7
Are Strikebreakers Protected?	5	5	3	5
Can Workers Sue Unions?	3	3	10	3
Can Employers Sue Unions?	0	3	10	0
Minimum Wage	7	-	-	-
Maximum-Hour Legislation	0	0	0	0
Davis-Bacon Laws	0	0	0	0
Child and Female Labour Restrictions	7	5	5	5
Occupational Licensing	-	-	-	-
Equal Pay for Equal Work Laws	0	0	0	0
Equal Pay for "Comparable" Work	10	10	10	10
Employment Quotas	5	5	5	3
Government Employment	-	-	-	-
Mandatory Government Arbitration	5	0	0	5
Safety and Health Regulation	-	-	-	-
Employer Payroll Taxes	5	7	7	3
Taxes on Labour Income	5	7	5	7
Military Employment	10	10	10	10
Regulating Job "Security"	7	-	-	-
Immigration Limits	7	5	5	3
Taxes on Immigration	10	-	-	-
Immigration Enforcement	9	3	3	3
Labour Market Immigration Tests	0	0	0	0
List of "Undesirable" Immigrants	5	0	3	0
Amnesty for Illegal Immigrants	10	10	10	0
Are Temporary Workers Permitted?	10	10	10	3
Emigration	10	10	10	10
Overall Ranking	118	101	126	100

Analysis

I was unable to obtain all the relevant information, for example, the number of occupations with licensing regulation is particularly difficult to discern, especially across countries.[19] Thus, in the overall ranking a computation is made only if data were available for all four countries. Since not all of the criteria are "either-or" criteria, some were given an intermediate ranking on our 1-10 scale. I have provided a purely subjective ordinal ranking, but that should not bias the overall ranking as long as the same subjective criteria are applied to each country. For example, both the U.S. and Canada have agency shop agreements, but they are not universal, so each country was given a ranking of "5." I have also assigned a score of "3" for a "low" degree of economic freedom and "7" for a relatively high degree. For example, the U.S. was given a "7" for Immigration Enforcement because it does a poor job of it, thereby creating relatively free immigration. Japan was given a score of "3" because, even though it allows some immigration, it is only a trickle. I have used only these three rankings—3, 5, and 7—in cases where there is not a simple "either-or" decision. This will hopefully minimize debate over whether a country should be scored a 4 or a 5, a 7 or an 8, etc.

To determine what constitutes a "high" and "low" ranking it was sometimes necessary to choose one country as a benchmark. For example, the literature on immigration describes the U.S. as perhaps the most open country in the world. Thus, the U.S. was ranked "high," and the other three countries were ranked low because they all appeared to be considerably more restrictive.

I suppose it might be desirable to weight the criteria in some fashion, but I can think of no way of doing so that would not lead to endless debate over any type of weighting scheme. For now I have decided to weight all the criteria equally. That in itself will elicit some debate but not as much as an arbitrary weighting scheme is likely to.

The overall results tentatively rank England first, with the U.S. a close second, Canada third, and Japan last. However, these results are only intended as an example of how one might begin constructing such a ranking, not as a definitive ranking. Because of data limitations, some of the most important categories remain unranked. The minimum wage law, for example, is set by local governments in some of these countries, so data on the various levels of minimum wages are scattered. The same is true for data on occupational licensure and several other criteria. A little more digging will be rewarded with a more meaningful ranking.

Since this is only a preliminary attempt at ranking countries according to their respective degrees of labour market freedom, and since this paper is already quite lengthy, I will conclude with a few thoughts on other possible criteria not yet mentioned and some further data problems.

The Prevalence of Unions

The proportion of unionized workers to the total labour force might have been an appropriate criterion, presumably assigning an inverse relationship. The more dominant are unions, the less free are labour markets. One problem with this criterion, however, is that there is no clear way to separate out the cartel behavior of unions from other types of behavior. For example, some unions do train workers, administer grievances, and act as bargaining agents for their members, which is not necessarily a negative function in terms of economic freedom. Thus, the prevalence of unions says nothing about the actual functions of unions.

Strikes

The number of strike days lost, perhaps on a per capita basis, has also been suggested. More strike days lost can be interpreted as conducive to less economic freedom. A problem with this criteria, at least from my perspective, is that legal *prohibitions* of strike activity have historically been a hallmark of totalitarian govenments, particularly Mussolini's Italy.

Circumstances in Japan connote another problem. In that country strikes during the past several decades have been numerous, but many of them have been symbolic. Workers go on strike for one day just to make a point or to publicize their grievances, and then they go back to work. The data on Japanese strike days lost might imply a great deal of strike activity, but very little diminution of economic freedom to the extent that strikes are used to forecefully restrict the supply of (nonunion) labour, as they often are.

Union Political Power

How politically powerful the union sector is would be especially relevant to this paper, but is difficult to quantify in any meaningful way. Unions are major sponsors of restrictive labour legislation aimed at cartelizing labour markets for the benefit of their members. One problem with quantifying this effect is that much union political muscle is "in-kind" and labour intensive—voter registration drives, phone banks, house-to-house campaigning by union members, etc. Some estimates have been made of the monetary value of these political services, but they are so wide ranging (from $100 million to $350 million annually in the U.S.) that they are not yet very reliable.

It is possible that in countries such as Great Britain, where there is a formal political party controlled by unions, that union political strength would be stronger. But an argument can be made that the British Labour party has been quite impotent compared to, say, the U.S. union movement, which has had some major legislative victories in recent years. Thus, the existence of a formal political party controlled by unions may not be of much help in constructing our economic freedom index.

Government Employment

As discussed above, the role of government employment is relevant to our discussion, but it is also plagued by data problems. First, government statistics on employment are inaccurate because they omit contract employees who are not formally counted as government employees even though they perform work for governments and are paid with tax money.

Second, government employment statistics are often "cooked" so as to understate the true numbers. In the U.S., for example, thousands of federal employees are known within the bureaucracy as "twenty-five and ones."[20] They are on the federal payroll for 25 weeks, and then when U.S. Census Bureau employment statistics are gathered—every 26th week—they work as private contractors. Once the census has been taken they return to the fulltime government payroll.

Third, despite a great deal of research on the size and growth of government, we still do not have a generally accepted definition of what constitutes "government" and government employment. Off-budget enterprises are usually omitted, and there is also the problem of how to treat the so-called private, nonprofit sector.

In the U.S., more than 60 percent of the "income" of nonprofits is from federal grants. Many of these nonprofits were established to administer government programs and the literature on nonprofits often refers to them as "shadow governments." For all practical purposes, a large part of the private nonprofit sector in the U.S., which produces approximately 9 percent of GNP, is an arm of government and so their employees are government employees.[21] In short, the government sector is larger than we generally acknowledge, which hinders our ability to construct reliable estimates of government employment.

In light of these and other limitations, perhaps the main objective of this paper is to stimulate further discussion of labour market freedom and how it might be measured. Given the enormity of labour law and regulation, this seems almost as insurmountable as getting one's arms around an elephant. I have tried to embrace the labour market elephant and I hope I have persuaded others that this is a worthy task.

Notes

[1] Economic freedom requires a set of customs, moral constraints, or laws that prevent individuals or groups from committing violent or coercive acts against others. Thus, mutual consent between two burglars plotting a robbery, for example, is not an example of economic freedom in the sense we are discussing.

[2] See Bernard Siegan, *Economic Liberties and the Constitution (Chicago: Univ. of Chicago Press, 1980); Richard Epstein, Takings* (Cambridge: Harvard Univ. Press, 1985); and Terry Anderson and Peter J. Hill, *The Birth of a Transfer Society,* (Stanford, Ca.: Hoover Institution Press, 1980).

[3] See James T. Bennett, Dan Heldman, and Manuel Johnson, *Deregulating Labour Relations* (Dallas: Fisher Institute, 1981), p. 50.

[4] *Ibid.*

[5] Morgan Reynolds, *Power and Privilege: Labour Unions in America,* (New York: Universe Books, 1984), p. 98.

[6] Thomas J. DiLorenzo, "Exclusive Representation in Public Employment: A Public Choice Perspective," *Journal of Labour Research,* Fall 1984, pp. 371-90.

[7] For a detailed discussion of the political agenda of organized labour in the U.S. see James T. Bennett and Thomas J. DiLorenzo, *Destroying Democracy: How Government Funds Partisan Politics* (Washington, D.C.: Cato Institute, 1985), chapter 13.

[8] For a survey of some of the literature on the minimum wage see Thomas Rustici, "The Minimum Wage: A Public Choice Approach," *Cato Journal*, Fall 1986.

[9] For a thorough discussion of the economics of occupational licensing see S. David Young, *The Rule of Experts: Occupational Licensing in America* (Washington, D.C.: Cato Institute, 1987). Also see R.D. Blair and S. Rubin, *Regulating the Professions* (Lexington, Mass.: Lexington Books, 1980); and Timothy R. Muzondo and Bohumir Pazderka, "Occupational Licensing and Professional Incomes in Canada," *Canadian Journal of Economics*, Nov. 1980, pp. 659-67.

[10] Walter Williams, *Apartheid: South Africa's Assault on Capitalism*, (Washington, D.C.: Cato Institute, 1989).

[11] Thomas Sowell, *Civil Rights: Rhetoric or Reality?* (New York: William Morrow & Co., 1984), p. 39.

[12] *Ibid.*, p. 51.

[13] *Ibid.*, p. 53.

[14] Thomas J. DiLorenzo, "The Myth of Government Job Creation," Cato Institute *Policy Analysis*, February 1984.

[15] James T. Bennett and Thomas J. DiLorenzo, *Unfair Competition: The Profits of Nonprofits* (Lanham, MD: Madison Books, 1988), chapters 1 and 7.

[16] W. Kip Viscusi, "The Impact of Occupational Safety and Health Regulation," *Bell Journal of Economics*, Spring 1979.

[17] Peter J. Ferrara, *Social Security: The Inherent Contradiction* (Washington, D.C.: Cato Institute, 1980, p. 276.

[18] *Deregulating Labour Relations*, p. 74.

[19] Data sources included: Organization for Economic Cooperation and Development, *Social Expenditure, 1960-1990* (Washington, D.C.: OECD, 1985); OECD, *Labour Force Statistics* (Washington, D.C.: OECD, 1988); OECD, *Taxation in Developed Countries*, (Washington, D.C.: OECD, 1987); OECD, *Financial Accounting in OECD Countries* (Washington, D.C.: OECD, 1988); R. Blanpain, *International Encyclopedia for Labour Law and Industrial Relations*, (Boston: Kluwer, 1978); International Labour Organization, *Yearbook of Labor Statistics*, (Geneva: ILO, 1988); and Albert A. Blum, *International Handbook of Industrial Relations* (Westport, Conn.: Greenwood Press, 1981). Other information was obtained from country-specific books on Canadian immigration policy, Japanese immigration policy, etc.

[20] James T. Bennett and Manuel H. Johnson, *The Political Economy of Federal Government Growth: 1959-1978* (College Station, Texas: Center for Research and Education in Free Enterprise, 1980), chapter 2.

[21] James T. Bennett and Thomas J. DiLorenzo, *Unfair Competition: The Profits of Nonprofits* (Lanham, MD: Madison Books, 1988).

I wish to thank James T. Bennett and Walter Block for their helpful suggestions. The usual caveat applies.

Discussion

Ed Crane liked the rating scale and thought the scoring was at an appropriate aggregate level. He did not like the push-button unionism. He argued that employers and employees can always agree to form a union. A "right to work" law reduces freedom to voluntarily associate. Tom DiLorenzo felt that the "right to work" tended to enhance freedom. Milton Friedman responded that although freedom reducing in principle, in fact, where used they are almost always freedom enhancing. They are really second best solutions.

Alan Reynolds felt that consumption taxation is every bit as damaging as income taxation and that DiLorenzo over emphasized income taxation. Bernard Siegan wondered why zoning or other kinds of regulation that were particularly important to labour contracts were not included. DiLorenzo responded that he thought someone else would do this.

James Gwartney found two legal restraints that impact freedom that were not dealth with directly. First, there is the mandatory requirement of collective bargaining. This is what gives bite to all the other issues which would otherwise be secondary. Second, there is the prohibition of the company association. This also highlights why unions across countries are very different. For example, Japanese unions are often company organized. DiLorenzo speculated that this may account for Japanese companies' strength.

Gerald Scully looked at Table 1 and wondered what to conclude in that Canada and Japan have the least free labour markets, England has the most free, more or less like the U.S., but in general there is little to choose among them. He thought the metric was not sufficiently fine, or the measure itself was flawed. DiLorenzo argued that the use of the many categories was a first pass. Jack Carr looked at Table 1 noticing that 18% of the U.S. labour force is unionized compared to 36% in Canada. The problem here is that they both get the same weight yet Canada is more impeded than the U.S. This bears on the issue of competition among jurisdictions. Richard McKenzie felt that some measure that will evolve over time is needed. Milton Friedman wanted to have some external referent by which to judge the results in Table 1. Does Canada have more or less freedom than the U.S.? He found it absurd to suggest that among the group, Canada, the United States, England and Japan, that England has more labour freedom. If these measures lead to such a bad result, they do not appear to be very useful. Cliff Lewis wanted to look at issues such as education rather than labour markets narrowly conceived. The California university system, he asserted, is subsidized to the tune of $15,000 per capita. This would lead to a very different sense of the distortions among the different countries. James Gwartney emphasized that the scores for Britain were at variance with his knowledge of the rankings. Walter Block felt that the total rankings were roughly correct in comparing the U.S. to Canada even though Canada appeared more free than the U.S. on the degree of unionization. But clearly there were other variables that could be measured. Further, Block did not like the idea that just because we don't like the result, the identification of a loss in economic freedom may be incorrect.

Richard McKenzie suggested that the values of the categories could be weighted by the number of people to whom the legislation applied. This may make things consistent. In the case of unions, the U.S. is at 16% while Britain is 36% of the population. Similarly, the minimum wage affects 2.4% of the population in the U.S. and thus the values are weighted more appropriately. Charles Murray suggested that after subsequent analysis the raw percent of unionization may in fact act as a proxy measure for a host of other variables affecting economic freedom.

Walter Block argued that it would be very difficult to measure the costs of immigration restrictions in any way other than categorical. Milton Friedman responded that the way to do an impediments analysis is to take each impediment and to look at how much it distorts transactions. This is not the same as the effect on wealth even though it is a dollar measure—as used in Easton's paper. If there are no transactions, then there are no distortions so if we think of immigration, it means that we analyze how the flows are impeded. Walter Block argued that a flaw in the "dollarization method" proposed by Easton is that with an optimal tariff it suggests a benefit for the country imposing the tariff, even though it is undesirable from an international point of view. Since we are measuring the effects by country, it gives a spurious view of what is taking place. Easton responded that in his example of the optimal tariff, quite clearly domestic income rises even though economic freedom is reduced. There was nothing inconsistent with this method of measuring economic freedom. Milton Friedman agreed using the example of immigration in which no assertion is made about per capita income even though barring immigration will impose a loss of economic freedom.

Responding to a question by Bernard Siegan, DiLorenzo thought that creating dollar measures in labour markets would involve a book length manuscript, but that it could be done. Milton Friedman suggested that we must also be prepared to test our notions of economic freedom. We have far more confidence in our knowledge that Hong Kong is more economically free than other countries than we have in any particular set of numbers. What we need is a way to evaluate the indexes that are being produced.

International Comparisons of Taxes and Government Spending

Alan Reynolds,
The Hudson Institute

Introduction

THE SPECIFIC DETAILS OF THE structure of taxation were largely neglected before the mid-1970s—relegated to a minor branch of "microeconomics." Instead, the superstars of the economics profession battled over whether budget deficits or money supplies were the best way to manipulate private spending, and thus manage aggregate demand. In a 1960 essay, Tobin favored "restriction of consumption by [an] increase in personal income tax at all levels," in order "to bring under public decision the broad allocation of national output." In a 1971 book on taxation, Thurow stressed that "the aim of the macroeconomic policymaker is to raise or lower the demand," and that "different taxes have different effects [only] because they affect the incomes of groups with different propensities to consumer or invest." In such cases, any effect of steep tax rates in discouraging productive effort were either brushed aside with flimsy logic and surveys, or simply ignored. Taxes were only considered a device for discouraging demand, not for discouraging supply. Neglect of tax incentives was a natural outcome of the Keynesian fetish. In his classic 1937 essay on "Mr. Keynes and the Classics," Hicks writes that, "I assume that...the quantity of physical equipment of all kinds available can be taken as fixed. I assume homogeneous labor." With both physical and human capital thus assumed to be insignificant, there was no reason for Keynesian economists to worry how they might be affected by tax policies. Incentives to produce were considered less interesting than incentives to consume, since demand was thought to create its own supply.

By the mid-1970s, though, Keynesian "demand management" had been discredited by the experience of chronic stagflation, and the effects of various taxes and subsidies on human behavior and incentives began to receive considerably more attention. This was partly due to intellectual advances, such as the pioneering work of Mirrlees on the theory of optimal taxation, and the renewed emphasis on the microeconomic conditions for economic growth among "new classical" economists, such as Barro and Davies. Under the banner of "supply-side economics," a new band of unapologetic pro-capitalist politicians, led by Jack Kemp, Ronald Reagan and Margaret Thatcher, turned tax reform into a major, worldwide movement. By the end of the 1980s, over 50 countries — including *all* major industrial countries — had significantly reduced their highest marginal tax rates (see Appendix). Limited interest in similar reforms (which often encompass privatization and deregulation as well as reduced tax rates), has even spread to the Soviet Union, Poland, Hungary, China and Vietnam.

Taxes are an important part of the cost of production, as well as the cost of living. People generally have to produce more to earn more, except in cases of theft or legal "rent-seeking" (wasteful, negative-sum games involving the abuse of government power to acquire lucrative special privileges at the expense of others). It follows that a tax system which penalizes added income will also penalize added output. Aside from the unrealistic, hypothetical case of non-distorting taxes (e.g., a tax of so many dollars per person), the specific details of the tax structure have an enormous impact on behavior of individuals, and therefore of entire economies. Most taxes introduce a "wedge" between what a productive activity is worth to consumers and what the suppliers of labor and capital actually receive. Just as excise taxes on liquor and tobacco are partly designed to discourage the use of those products, taxes on earning additional personal or business income must likewise discourage the process of wealth-creation that lead to such increased income. When taxes on effort and savings are high, for example, choices are distorted in favor of additional leisure rather than additional income and in favor of current consumption rather than future consumption. The typical welfare state blend of demoralizing taxes on success and generous subsidies for failure tends to produce fewer successes and more failures.

At one extreme, the compulsion of taxation could be used to purchase *all* goods and services, which could then be distributed to individuals on the basis of various criteria, particularly political influence. Workers and investors would, in effect, endorse their entire paychecks over to government agencies, which would then decide who gets what sort of food, housing and shelter. Such a system would have enormous difficulties in motivating people to produce up to their true potential, since they would have so little choice as to how the fruits of their efforts would be used. The political marketplace, even in its most democratic forms, typically offers the electorate only an infrequent choice between two or three package deals. Voters might want some parts of the package offered by one political party, some parts of those offered by another, and many things (such as maximum individual choice) that are not offered by either. The package deals that are offered are often meaningless anyway, since political officials who get votes by offering something they do not deliver cannot be sued for fraud.

A so-called "national economy" is nothing more than the activities of individuals that involve producing and trading with one another. Not so long ago, many observers thought the extent of government control over these activities would become more and more extensive and detailed, leaving fewer and fewer economic decisions to individuals. Heilbroner, writing in 1959, expressed a view that remained common if not dominant among Anglo-American intellectuals in the first three decades of the postwar era:

> As a means of beginning the huge transformation of a society, an economic authoritarian command has every advantage over the incentives of enterprise....Taking the long perspective of the decades ahead, it is difficult to ignore the relative 'efficiency' of authoritarian over parliamentary regimes as a means of inaugurat-

ing growth....Today and over the foreseeable future, traditional capitalism throughout most of the world has been thrown on a defensive from which it is doubtful that it can ever recover.... [The] road to abundance lead subtly but surely into the society of control....[The] trend of all industrialized nations, ourselves included [is] toward some form of economic collectivism.

The confident consensus of the early postwar era — that economic liberty would be increasingly obsolete, replaced by governmental control — has been undermined by the evident stagnation or decline of living standards in countries with socialist economies. The alleged advantages of authoritarian planning have also been refuted by the vibrant success of every economy that instead moved in the direction of reducing government barriers to commerce and government disincentives to personal effort, investment and entrepreneurship. The embarrassing success of capitalist economies, most obviously in Asia, has now put socialism on a defensive from which it is doubtful that it can ever recover. One reason is the increased international mobility of capital, including human capital, and the new information technologies that make it impossible to conceal how well or how badly an economy is performing. Gordon thus notes "the restrictions capital mobility and tax competition impose on [a country's] tax policy."

Governments, like companies, must compete in producing the most value at the lowest possible cost. Countries in which the marginal cost of government is relatively high, particularly in relation to the value of government services, will find it more difficult to attract and retain physical capital, financial capital and human capital. Just as so-called "tax havens" attract investment and immigrants, countries with punitive tax systems face chronic "capital flight," and a "brain drain." When the effects of taxation on international movement of resources are considered (as in Gordon), the results can be quite different than when each country is analyzed as an isolated island.

In addition to the new concern about keeping tax expenses competitive among industrial economies, which is a key issue in the effort to integrate European economies by 1992, there is also renewed interest in "market-oriented" reforms in the Third World and Communist countries. Unfortunately, the literature on "market-oriented" reform tends to be *extremely vague*, typically calling attention to *objectives* rather than specific policies to achieve those objectives. Wilson and Gordon, of the University of

Michigan's Center for Research on Economic Development, thus define reform in such terms as "promoting the private sector" and "ending capital flight and promoting foreign investment." Within seven such empty boxes, there is virtually no mention of taxation, except to "shift taxation burden away from export sector." In rare cases when specific policies are mentioned, they are not obviously "market-oriented." For example, Wilson and Gordon suggest "ending government fixing of the exchange rate." Yet defining a weak currency in terms of a more credible currency (or gold), and making it freely convertible, has always been a necessary, though not sufficient, component of all successful plans for stopping a runaway inflation — most recently in Hong Kong, Israel and Bolivia (Bruno).

There have been relatively few systematic attempts to compare taxes and government spending between countries. The few global comparisons that have been undertaken by official agencies, such as the International Monetary Fund or U.S. State Department, typically rely on diplomatic obfuscations ("market-oriented reforms" or "outward-looking strategies") and unacceptable simplifications. One such simplification is to look at tax receipts as a percentage of gross national product (GNP) or gross domestic product (GDP). Another is to focus on one particular tax, usually the corporate profits tax. A third simplification, related to the other two, is to look only at average tax rates on existing income rather than marginal tax rates on additions to output and income.

Taxes "As a Percentage of GNP" Ignores Incentives

A recent book from the International Monetary Fund, entitled *Supply-Side Tax Policy: It's Relevance to Developing Countries* (Gandhi, pp. 27 & 46), illustrates a common confusion between marginal tax rates and average tax revenues actually collected at those rates:

> Revenues from personal income taxes in industrial countries are generally much higher than in developing countries both in relation to gross domestic product and as a share of total tax revenue. Presumably this explains why the great bulk of the literature on the incentive effects of tax regimes and of changes in marginal tax rates on labor, savings, and investment decisions pertains to the devel-

oped world....Regressions show that the ratio of income taxes to total revenue (as well as to GDP) and the growth rate of output are negatively related and that the regression coefficients are significant, but this result does not hold in all specifications.

In these remarks, the IMF economists are simply treating the amount of money collected from income taxes as equivalent to the impact of these and other taxes on incentives. Because revenues from income taxes are a tiny fraction of GDP, writes Tanzi, "it can be concluded that these taxes are much less important...in developing countries than in developed countries." Yet taxes can have extremely damaging effects on efficient economic activity without yielding significant revenues. Indeed, the more damaging the tax system is, the less revenue it will yield over time, because incomes and sales will stagnate or decline in the overtaxed sector, and more and more productive activity will disappear into the tax-free "underground economy." This is actually most obvious in developing countries, where extremely high tax rates often push *most* productive activity underground, thus yielding little or no revenue. Failure to generate revenue, though, certainly does not mean the high tax rates have no bad effects, as Tanzi and other IMF economists suggest. On the contrary, underground enterprises lose economies of scale by the necessity to stay small in order to avoid detection. They also lose efficiencies of communication, such as the ability to advertise or to efficiently recruit the best workers. Even the vital efficiencies of a monetary economy are often lost, as commerce instead resorts to primitive barter in order to avoid both explicit taxes and also to avoid the tax on cash balances due to chronic devaluation and inflation.

Ironically, the bibliography of the IMF volume cites a few of the earliest studies on the effects of changes in marginal rates in developing countries, including Reynolds, Rabushka-Bartlett and Wanniski. All of these comparative studies emphasize very clearly that steep tax rates both damage economic growth and make taxes virtually uncollectible. Since GDP grows slowly, if at all, the tax base likewise grows slowly, if at all. Far from indicating that "the incentive effects of...changes in marginal tax rates" are insignificant in developing countries, as the IMF volume repeatedly suggests, the poor revenue yield from extremely high tax rates instead indicates that marginal tax rates can be sharply reduced, with the government then collecting a smaller increment of an expanding economy rather than attempting to collect a huge percentage of zero growth.

Excessive Emphasis on Corporate Income Taxes

Another excessive simplification is to focus almost exclusively on a single category of taxes. Most of the IMF volume thus concentrates on income taxes, as though production decisions and costs were completely unaffected by Social Security taxes, sales taxes or tariffs. Even worse, many international comparisons have been limited to only the corporate income tax. A recent report for the U.S. Agency for International Development, by Frost & Sullivan Inc., ranks the "investment climate for international business" by 14 criteria, such as "labor conditions" and "regime stability." Following the State Department as the "primary source," only 2 of the 14 criteria listed by Frost and Sullivan have to do with tax policy. The only taxes that matter, in this State Department-AID view, are the "level of corporate taxes" and "investment incentives...in the form of tax holidays...and subsidies."

This quasi-official emphasis on corporate taxes and subsidies is far too narrow on both factual and theoretical grounds. At the factual level, corporations typically exert sufficient political clout to keep corporate tax rates *relatively* low, particularly for foreign corporations, and subsidies and special tax breaks relatively high. Prior to 1989 tax reforms, for example, the highest corporate tax rates were 33-35% in Mexico, Brazil and Argentina, while maximum individual tax rates were 45-50%. One reason that large multinational corporations are often able to gain preferential tax treatment, aside from their obvious importance as a source of funds for politicians, is that the employment consequences of a large company locating in a country, or leaving, are far more conspicuous than the inability of a small, local enterprise to even get started (without evading taxes and regulations).

It is not even correct to regard the corporate tax as the only relevant direct tax on the income of business enterprises, since many *domestic* businesses are not incorporated, and are thus taxed at the higher rates typically imposed on individual income. Even incorporated domestic firms do not qualify for the "tax holidays" apparently favored by State Department researchers, and instead bear higher tax rates to compensate for revenue loss of a temporary zero tax on new foreign competitors.

Corporations are not organic entities that are able to bear tax burdens, any more than their buildings can bear a tax. A tax on corporate profits must either be paid by those who invest in the company, those who work for it, or those who buy its products. But replacing any corporate profits tax with a more obvious and direct tax on a company's stockholders, workers and customers would have a similar effect in reducing the company's opportunities for profitable production, and its offers of employment.

The familiar distinction between "business taxes" and "people taxes," which is the subject of considerable corporate lobbying (sometimes disguised as "studies") is essentially irrelevant. All taxes are paid by individual producers, as suppliers of labor and capital. It is relatively insignificant, in most cases, whether taxes are direct or indirect, corporate or personal. Capital and labor bear all taxes, either through lower incomes or higher prices. Indeed any tax itself may be considered a price —the price of government —so that *all* taxes might thus be properly included in a broad concept of the "cost of living." Since accounting conventions instead count only sales taxes as part of the cost of living, substituting an income tax for a sales tax may *appear* to reduce the usual measures of consumer prices. Yet the reality of reduced purchasing power for producers would not be changed at all, even though the burden might be shifted from some people to others.

Any "consumption tax" must actually fall on producers, because consumption is the only motive for production. Moreover, the whole purpose of taxes is to divert a portion of production away from uses determined by markets toward uses determined by political authorities, so that any form of taxation *must* reduce real rewards to producers in the market economy. A proper comparison of taxation between countries must therefore attempt to include the combined effects of *all* taxes.

Spending Measures the Average, Not Marginal, Burden

Although expressing tax receipts as a percent of GNP is a wholly inadequate measure of the distortions and disincentives of a tax system, the same is not true of government *spending* as a percent of GNP (or GDP). The ratio of government spending to GNP has considerable merit as a rough measure of the *average* burden of government activities on the voluntary activities of private producers and consumers. Wolf estimates that "a 10% increase in the ratio of government spending to GDP results in an expected decrease of 1% in the average annual rate of growth in GDP" among developed countries, and a 4% decrease among low-income countries. Spending ratios, though, are incomplete, static and too aggregated.

Government purchases of goods and services (as opposed to transfer payments) represent one form of claim on society's productive resources (labor, capital and natural resources) that are allocated through political decisions rather than through markets. At reasonably full employment, resources devoted to politically-determined uses are simply unavailable for market-determined uses, regardless of whether the government's purchases are financed by taxes, borrowing or creating new money. Persons employed by the government cannot simultaneously be employed in producing what consumers choose to buy. Energy and land devoted to government offices cannot simultaneously be used to produce, say, food, clothing or shelter (which are still mainly produced and marketed by the private sector, even in most socialist economies).

Subsidies and other transfer payments are often said to be different than purchases, since they "merely" redistribute purchasing power among people in the private sector rather than deflecting resources from private to governmental uses. Yet this observation neglects incentives. The essence of most transfer payments is to take part of the rewards away from productive individuals and firms and give them to those who do not work, do not plant crops, or do not manage viable enterprises. That is, transfer payments punish success in the marketplace and reward failure (they also punish those who lack political clout and reward those who can best manipulate the political system). Because transfer payments *are* a huge burden on the *productive* portion of the private sector, they cannot be ignored. If all that government did was to transfer more and more resources from workers to non-workers, for example, the result would surely be fewer workers and more non-workers, reducing the amount of real output left to redistribute. As Gwartney and Stroup observe, "While the income transfers do not *directly* reduce total income, the substitution effect associated with the transfer will induce *both* the taxpayer-donors and the transfer recipients to reduce their work effort." For certain analytical purposes, it may indeed be legitimate to separate transfer payments from purchases, and even to further divide government purchases between capital outlays and current consumption, or between substitutes for private services (e.g., nationalized health insurance) and services that the private sector is not permitted to provide (e.g., defense, currency). But the use of *total* government spending is nonetheless almost always sufficient to capture the general burden of strictly fiscal costs of government, even though it excludes important *regulatory* costs and uncertainties.

Although government spending thus approximates the true burden of government on the private sector, the ratio of government spending to GNP only measures the *average* burden at the moment, not the *marginal* burden over time. Two countries could have the same percentage of GNP currently channeled through government and yet have enormously different *marginal* tax burdens on future additions to GNP. The country with the lower marginal penalty on added output and income would experience more rapid growth of real GNP, so that real government spending could increase just as rapidly as in the country with higher marginal tax rates and yet nonetheless become smaller over time as a percentage of GNP. For this reason, *current* government spending as a percentage of *current* GNP should not be assigned *too* high a weight in evaluating the dynamic trends toward more or less economic liberty. In many cases, a reduction in marginal tax rates can reduce the *future* ratio of government spending to GNP *by increasing private GNP*. Indeed, an econometric comparison of 63 countries, by Koester and Kormendi, estimates that "a 10% revenue neutral reduction in marginal tax rates would yield a 12.8% increase in per capita income for LDCs and a 6.1% increase...for non-LDCs."

Ratios of Public Debt to GNP

Just as the ratio of government spending to GNP can increase because of relative weakness in private GNP, rather than unusual growth of government, the ratio of government deficits or debt to GNP may likewise conceal more than it reveals. Past debts may decline as a percentage of GNP because the central bank is buying too much debt with new bank reserves or currency. Such an inflationary monetary policy inflates *nominal* GNP relative to older debt issued at fixed interest rates. Switching to a less-inflationary monetary regime, as the U.S. did in the 1980s, may therefore appear to increase debt relative to GNP. Yet the more responsible method of financing government debt is nonetheless a beneficial reduction of the "inflation tax" on those who hold cash balances and older bonds. To the extent that governments can be bound by a credible commitment to non-inflationary methods of financing their debts, they will be able to issue new debt (for emergencies or capital outlays) at lower interest rates, thus reducing interest outlays and the nominal budget deficit.

Using chronic inflation to reduce the ratio of domestic debt to GNP is often worse than futile, since it can virtually destroy the government's ability to raise funds through either taxation or additional debt, as an IMF study by Blejer and Chu points out:

> If inflation brings about a fall in the capacity to raise taxes, to collect the inflation tax on the monetary base, and to borrow abroad, it will also increase the risk of default on the public debt...As such, it may reduce the willingness of individuals to lend to the government. This attitude on the part of the public will be reinforced by the fact that the deterioration of the inflationary situation will increase the probability of adoption of adjustment programs that might include ...higher income taxes on interest incomes....When individuals receive nominal interest payments, they are taxed on the total of these payments without an adjustment for the effect of inflation. This fact, *per se*, would induce a shift from financial assets (including government bonds) toward real assets or foreign investments, since the unrealized capital gains on real assets are tax free while the foreign investments are often totally tax free.

Blejer and Chu also note that "the fiscal deficit is, under any circumstances, a crude tool for assessing the impact of fiscal policy on the economy." In a situation of high inflation, though, conventional measures of the budget deficit become virtually useless. Attempts to reduce nominal budget deficits through "adjustment programs" involving higher income taxes can prove disastrous to incentives, as well as having the adverse effects on the financial system that were emphasized by Blejer and Chu (e.g., provoking capital flight and destroying the ability of government to sell bonds rather than printing money). Despite the enormous emphasis typically given to nominal budget deficits, particularly among developing countries, this appears far less useful than a detailed investigation of the structure of taxes and expenditures, as well as the possible abuse of inflationary methods of financing deficits.

There is a somewhat better case to be made for comparing accumulated debt-to-GNP ratios between governments, rather than just current budget deficits. Those who analyze debts of developing countries often place undue emphasis on *foreign* debt, and insufficient attention to domestic debt — which is often much larger and always pays a higher rate of interest. The rationale for emphasizing foreign debt is that debts denominated in a foreign currency must be serviced from hard currency earnings, which requires either a trade surplus in excess of interest outlays on foreign debt or a net capital inflow (i.e., a reversal of "capital flight"). A large foreign debt might also appear to encourage inflation in countries like the United States, where the debt is in the debtor's own currency. For developing countries, though, the common IMF advice to repeatedly devalue currencies will raise the amount of domestic currency needed to pay the equivalent amount of dollars to creditors. That effect of devaluation increases the nominal budget deficit, which has to be financed with new money because chronic devaluation destroys the market for government bonds. Once again, the usual emphasis on *symptoms* of bad policies — namely, budget deficits and foreign debts — may actually lead to policies that make these symptoms even worse, such as chronic currency debasement and oppressive taxation. The prolonged efforts to impose "austerity" on troubled economies (which invariably means austerity for the private sector) is as flawed in concept as it has proven in practice. It is not possible to improve the creditworthiness of debtors by reducing their prospective income.

Gordon points out some other difficulties arising from excessive emphasis on foreign debt:

> Because of the tax system, governments of countries with a higher inflation rate must pay a higher *real* interest on their debt. This is necessary in equilibrium to compensate those who purchase the debt for their higher taxable income....A high inflation country could borrow in a foreign currency (for example, debt denominated in dollars), and use the funds to retire any debt issued in its own currency.

The idea of using debt-for-equity swaps to reduce the *foreign* debt of developing countries illustrates a common confusion arising from insufficient attention to domestic debt, and to the necessity of financing that debt honestly, without simply issuing new money. Aside from direct swaps of foreign debt for new shares of privatized companies, any other debt-equity swap requires providing foreign creditors with more domestic currency, such as pesos, with which to make direct or portfolio equity investments. If the added pesos are simply printed, the result is higher inflation. If new domestic bonds are instead sold to acquire the needed pesos, this merely substitutes high-cost domestic debt for foreign debt that bears a lower interest expense.

Although the ratio of overall foreign and domestic government debt to GNP may provide a rough guide to the future *average* burden on taxpayers, it must be handled with great care. Whether the debt can be financed in an inflationary or non-inflationary manner (that is, whether a viable market for fixed-income bonds can be restored) is often at least as important as the current level of debt itself, though the two issues cannot be entirely separated. Moreover, the *marginal* cost of taxation can usually be alleviated, with favorable effects on future economic expansion. A larger economy, particularly one with low inflation, can more easily service existing debts, and also finance plant and equipment with new issues of private equity instead of new government debt. In the absence of any single measure that adequately captures important marginal and dynamic elements of alternative methods of servicing past debts, it appears preferable to instead focus on minimizing government consumption expenditures and transfer payments, while reforming the tax, tariff and regulatory structure to make the marginal cost of government less damaging to productive effort and investment.

How to Compare Tax Structures

The Table, "Maximum Tax Rates," summarizes the key features of tax systems among five Latin American countries. Under the category "Individual Income Tax," we use the maximum marginal tax rate (reported for a number of countries in the Appendix) and the income level, or "threshold," at which individuals and unincorporated enterprises encounter that highest tax bracket. The thresholds are expressed in U.S. dollars (and rounded) to make them comparable, using market exchange rates at the end of 1988. Wherever key features of the tax system are automatically indexed for inflation, such as individual thresholds in Argentina, this is indicated by the word "indexed" in the appropriate category. In general, the lower the maximum tax rate and higher the threshold, the higher a country would rank in this particular tax category. A number of countries have no income tax at all, so Bolivia's new 10% flat tax (with value-added taxes deducted from it) only scores 9 on a scale of 1-to-10, rather than a "perfect 10." Bolivia's combined income-VAT rate is so low, that the low threshold (which exempts double the low minimum wage) scarcely matters.

Although Mexico's newly-reduced 40% tax rate for 1989 does not appear much worse than Argentina's reduced 35% rate, the top tax rate in Mexico is reached by people with only one-fourth the level of those in Argentina's highest bracket. Moreover, the absence of indexing in Mexico (there was some *de facto* indexing only in 1979-82) could make the difference even wider in the future. To make matters worse, moving from Mexico's 38% bracket (at an income of only about $7000 a year) to the 40% bracket at $13,000 involves subjecting *total* income to the 40% rate, not simply the marginal increase. For these reasons, Argentina (and the similar tax in El Salvador) gets a score of 5 in this category, and Mexico is downgraded to a 3. Brazil's low tax rate, cut in half for 1989, is partly offset by the low threshold and recent repeal of indexing, but still rates a 6.

The fact that Mexico's individual tax system still looks relatively harmful, despite two recent reforms cutting the tax rate to 40% from 55%, is another lesson in why tax *revenues* can be an extremely misleading guide to the importance of tax *rates*. Mexico's top tax rate was 35% in the mid-1960s, and the threshold at which top rate applied remained reasonably high well into the 1970s —about $120,000 in 1979, for example. As chronic currency devaluations and virulent inflation pushed more and more people into the highest tax brackets, though, economic activity either stopped or went underground, provoking further currency crises, etc. Mexico thus provided an extreme example of the "stagflation" that infected many countries even earlier, and for the same reasons — mainly, easy money and punitive taxation (see Reynolds, 1985). By the early 1980s, the largely tax-exempt "informal" sector was already estimated to account for 42% of Mexico's urban employment (Inter-American Development Bank, 1987). At the same time that Mexico's tax rates were at an all-time high, and thresholds reduced to one-tenth of what they were in 1979, revenues from Mexico's individual income tax have fallen dramatically in real terms.

Maximum Tax Rates: 1989				
	Argentina	Brazil	Mexico	El Salvador	Bolivia

	Argentina	Brazil	Mexico	El Salvador	Bolivia
Individual Income Tax	35% @ $51,000 indexed	25% @ $13,000	40% @ $13,000	35% @ $50,000	10% @ $100
Social Security Tax	47.5% no limit. worker deducts 10% of 16% from income tax	18-22% $581 max corp. deduction only	9-11% $600 max corp. deduction only	2-8% $277 max full deduction	12% no limit full deduction
VAT or Sales Tax	14% VAT	8-300% on goods 9-25% on services	15% VAT 20% on luxuries	selective exercises & 2-5% stamp fee	10% VAT deductible from income tax
Wealth Tax	1.5% (1.25% corp.)	none	2% on business assets w/ credit against income tax	2.5% on business — no deduction	2% on corp. net worth
Investor Taxes	zero on interest from bank deposits & govts. 0-15% on capital gains. 32% on dividends	taxed as income @ 25% with some special incentives	0-21% on interest from bank deposits & govts. 10% on dividends or 40% if no corp. tax or capital gain on stock	30% on capital gains. up to 60% interest dividend	interest & dividends taxed @ 10% zero tax on capital gain & foreign investments
Corporate Profits Tax	33% + local license	30% (6% farm) + 10% surcharge 5% local	37% (35% in '91) indexed + compulsory profit sharing 10% of profit	35% tax on corporate vehicles w/ income tax	1% + property & credit against

Source: Price Waterhouse

Expressing individual tax receipts in 1980 pesos, using the consumer price index, real revenues fell by 82% from 1982 to 1987 — from $121.2 billion to $66.6 billion (in 1980 pesos). Since real GDP also declined, revenues did not fall so badly "as a percentage of GDP," but that method of calculation ignores the bad effects of onerous taxes on GDP itself. Governments cannot pay their bills with "percentages of GDP," but instead need growth of real revenues, which ultimately must come from growth of the real tax base (mainly, private jobs and profits).

The next category in the table, Social Security, assumes that all payroll taxes are borne by workers, even if ostensibly financed by employers. Employers are indifferent between paying higher wages or higher wage-related taxes, and the sum of the two cannot exceed the workers' marginal product or the employer will go bankrupt. Social Security tax is Argentina's disaster area. The employer and employee each pay 13% of wages and salaries for state pensions. Employers also pay 4.5% for social health, and employees 3%. Employers alone pay another 9% for a family allowance fund, plus 5% for a housing fund. It all adds up to an astonishing 47.5%. The 47.5% is also the *marginal* burden since there is, as the table indicates, *no limit*, or ceiling, on the amount of income subject to these taxes. In countries where there is such a limit, the approximate maximum tax is shown. A maximum Social Security tax means the *marginal* rate on added income declines to *zero* at some income, since added income brings no added tax. Moreover, the ceiling on income subject to this tax, where it exists at all, is not terribly high within this sample, so three countries *with* such a limit gain 1 or 2 added points in our ratings.

Corporations can almost always deduct Social Security tax payments from the corporate income tax, but this is *not* always the case with individuals (even in the U.S.). In Argentina, individuals are supposed to pay 16% for Social Security and health, but only 10% (including, quite reasonably, private pension plans) can be deducted from income tax. In reality, the Social Security tax is so onerous that employers and employees have a powerful incentive to evade the tax and split the savings. In the process, they must also evade individual income taxes (which wouldn't be so bad if they were not added to huge Social Security taxes) simply in order to avoid detection. Tanzi shows that Argentina's absurd Social Security taxes collect relatively little revenue — only 3.4% of GDP, less than half of what Brazil collects. The individual income tax, when rates were much higher than they are now, collected virtually nothing — less than one-half of one percent of GDP. This illustrates, once again, why revenues are such a poor guide to the destructive nature of punitive tax *rates*.

Argentina clearly rates a score of 1 on Social Security tax, only because we're not handing out zeros. El Salvador is the best in this group, with a tax that declines to 1% on employers and employees as income rises, and then stops altogether at a modest level. To make it even better, ordinary workers can deduct their Social Security tax from income tax. Give El Salvador a 7 for this tax. Mexico and Bolivia each get a 5, for different reasons (Mexico's tax has a ceiling, Bolivia's is deductible). Brazil rates a 3 for high tax rates (albeit with a ceiling), and no deduction for individuals.

The next category is VAT or sales taxes, which would include turnover taxes and excises as well. Some of the best economies in the world, such as Japan and the U.S., have gotten along just fine with very modest sales taxes, which has to give nearly all the Latin American countries a low score. The worst, perhaps in the world, is surely Brazil. Brazil slaps a variety of sales taxes on everything, including services, with rates up to 300%. On domestic sales taxes alone, Brazil gets a score of 1. And that isn't even counting steep sales taxes on imports (which have recently been reduced a bit).

Tariffs are somewhat beyond the scope of this paper, since they are an implicit subsidy to protected industries as well as a revenue source. It is worth recalling, though, the idea of *prohibitive* tariffs — tariffs that yield little or no revenue because they make it impossible to conduct the activity being taxed. The relevance is that there are prohibitive *taxes*, as well as prohibitive tariffs, and these too yield less revenue than a lower tax would yield. Mexico, for example, found that revenues fell when tax rates were increased from 10% to 30% on minks and jewels (Gil Diaz). The sharp reduction of tariffs in Chile was followed by so much more rapid an economic expansion that the effect on overall revenues (not just the tariffs themselves) was undoubtedly positive.

Scoring other countries on sales tax, Bolivia's deductible VAT is the best, but there are still some 30-50% taxes on "sins" and "luxuries" that brings the score down to 5. El Salvador also distorts choices with selective taxes on consumer goods the government doesn't like, though these taxes are not nearly as bad as in Brazil. El Salvador's stamp tax of 2-5% on all sorts of documents is a primitive nuisance. Give El Salvador and Argentina a 4. Mexico's VAT is fairly new, introduced at a lower rate at the start of the decade, and it may be no coincidence that the economy's worst performance in history (and therefore falling real revenues from other sources) has been while the VAT has been in effect. To be generous, score Mexico a 3 on sales taxes.

Wealth tax should properly include property, gift and inheritance taxes, which are not very significant in this particular group of countries. There are, though, direct taxes on corporate net worth in four countries in our sample, and one on individual net worth. In fairness, these taxes have to be viewed in combination with the following categories — taxes on individual investors and on corporate profits. Bolivia, for example, uses a corporate net worth as a virtual alternative to a corporate profits tax, and Argentina's wealth tax on individuals is combined with fairly light taxes on interest, dividends and capital gains. But those features will result in fairly good scores in the other categories. The sheer existence of *any* wealth tax, which is quite rare among successful economies, precludes a high score. After all, individuals and corporations acquire wealth out of after-tax income (which is also true of assets left to heirs), so it is an inherently nasty double tax on the virtues of acquiring assets and keeping debts down (as opposed to spending everything on champagne and caviar, and then buying more on credit).

Brazil gets a 10 for not having a wealth tax. Mexico gets a 6 for allowing a credit against business income tax. Bolivia's score is 5, El Salvador's is 4, and Argentina's (because individuals are included, at a higher rate) is 3.

Investor taxes obviously overlap with corporate and wealth taxes, but are separated in order to convey the flavor of the ways in which the overall tax system treats income from capital relative to income from labor. This distinction is rarely neat. Social Security taxes are clearly taxes on labor, and wealth taxes invariably exclude human capital (e.g., a doctorate degree). But consumption taxes fall on consumption from either labor income or capital assets. And although wages and salaries account for 76% of the individual income tax collections in Mexico, for example (Tanzi), income from noncorporate business and capital investments is small relative to labor income, so that a 24% share means non-human capital is nonetheless quite heavily taxed by the individual income tax.

Nearly all of our sample countries, like many advanced industrial countries, tax capital gains on financial assets relatively lightly, or not at all. A purist might properly object that this distorts investments toward assets expected to appreciate, rather than yield interest or dividends. Yet no country has found a practical way to tax capital gains in ways that theorists would prefer — which would involve full deduction of capital losses (which makes it easy to avoid the tax by timing strategies), indexing for inflation (which ought to apply to old assets too, though that would lose a lot of revenue), and taxation as gain accrue rather than when realized (which is simply too difficult). Any capital gains tax is essentially voluntary, since nobody has to sell the assets they have, or to buy more of the kinds of assets subject to that tax (a high capital gains tax in the U.S., for example, may well have made interest on junk bonds more attractive than holding stocks in promising new companies that do not yet pay dividends). Indeed, the problems are so tricky, and evasion so easy, that a low tax rate on capital gains may be the best of possible worlds. Mexico's capital gains tax of zero on stocks, though, looks a bit *too* generous, since revenues foregone must be replaced with some other tax.

For our comparative ratings, it is reasonable to assume that any low tax rate is almost always preferable to a higher tax rate. A country in which all tax rates are low and investors get no special deals will always get a better overall score (closer to 10) than a country that taxes the stuffing out of, say, payrolls and sales, and then gives a big break for capital gains. Tax breaks for investors are not obviously more desirable than tax breaks for, say, working overtime or going to school. Yet nearly everyone is both a worker and investor at some point in his or her life cycle, so tax relief for investors is better than taxing everything at steep rates.

Taxes on investors are too often a device for tilting capital toward uses determined by political rather than market forces. Argentina and Mexico give investors a special break on bonds issued by the government, for example, rather than bonds issued by private companies. Capital gains on certain investments in the same countries are completely exempt (usually investments in big companies), while other gains are not. Brazil's new 25% tax is less distortionary, and thus rates the same score of 5 given to Argentina and Mexico, whose rates are sometimes lower, sometimes higher. El Salvador's tax rates are the highest in this group, and investors don't fare much better, so the country gets a 3. Bolivia tops the list again, with rates of 10% or zero deserving an 8, even though letting Bolivians pay zero only on *foreign* investments sounds like an open invitation to capital flight (Balassa).

The final category is too often the first or only tax considered, namely, the corporate profits tax. In reality, this tax is almost always lower than individual income tax rates, and much lower than the combined effect of income, payroll and sales taxes on workers. Bolivia has virtually no corporate income tax, and thus rates a 9. Argentina, Brazil and El Salvador have comparable effective rates, for a score of 5. Mexico imposes compulsory profit sharing, at 10% of taxable profit, which cuts that country's score to 4.

The Table, "A Scorecard on Tax Regimes," summarizes the ratings discussed above. The trick is to weight the relative importance of various taxes. Weightings could be based on the relative importance of various taxes as revenue sources, but some of the worst taxes yield the least revenues. The individual income tax is surely by far the most important, since virtually all activity is subject to it. Indeed, the individual tax on corporate interest, dividends and capital gains is often more significant than the corporate tax itself. Having assigned a 40% weight to the individual income tax, the rest of the weighing scheme must be regarded as a matter of rather arbitrary judgement. Actually, the most onerous tax in each country merits the highest weight, so that Social Security tax could be given a higher weight in Argentina, consumption taxes a higher weight in Brazil, and so on. This notion seems worth exploring, but this paper will nonetheless use the same weight for each country.

A Scorecard on Tax Regimes (scale of 1 to 10, where 10 is perfect)					
	Argentina	Brazil	Mexico	Salvador	Bolivia
Individual Income (40%)	5	6	3	5	9
Social Security (15%)	1	3	5	7	5
VAT or Sales (15%)	4	1	3	4	5
Wealth (5%)	3	10	6	4	5
Invest (10%)	5	5	5	3	8
Profits (15%)	5	5	4	5	9
TOTAL	4.2	4.8	3.8	4.9	7.5

The tax scorecard may be compared with two very aggregate measures often used to evaluate countries, namely budget deficits and government spending expressed as a percentage of GDP.

Central Government Spending and Budget Deficits as a Percentage of Gross Domestic Product (1987, or most recent available year)					
	Argentina	Brazil	Mexico	Salvador	Bolivia
Deficit	8.0	11.8	14.0	1.5	0.6 %
Spending	19.1	37.9	30.7	15.5	12.2

These summary measures of government spending and borrowing, relative to the overall size of the economy, happen to rank countries in ways not so different from our tax scorecard (Bolivia is still the best and Mexico the worst). Yet these conventional aggregate measures nonetheless seem more primitive and misleading than our details about the tax structure. Looking at the ratio of spending to GDP, Argentina appears to be a country in which government is relatively small and unobtrusive, but its taxes and regulations are usually worse than those of Brazil. Bolivia really does have a small government, but was nonetheless forced to finance it with hyperinflationary money creation until 1986, when the top tax rate was slashed to 10% and real revenues soared (Reynolds, 1990). Besides, these measures are largely determined by *past* policies (including monetary policies that can inflate nominal interest rates and therefore the apparent deficit). A new government which plans significant reforms to increase individual choice and opportunity ought not to be prematurely condemned because of inherited debts, or even because of spending that may look high (relative to GDP) largely because private GDP is so low.

Conclusion

Systematic comparisons of tax and spending regimes are of interest to private entrepreneurs, professionals and investors, to help them to decide where to locate their skills and capital. For similar reasons, tax comparisons are of interest to government policymakers, to help them to understand whether their tax systems are competitive, attracting or repelling productive effort and investment. Conventional measures of spending and debt as a percentage of GNP often merely measure symptoms of other problems — including oppressive taxation, capricious regulations, insecure property rights, protected and subsidized government monopolies, and money of unpredictable value.

The details of the tax structure capture one of the principal means by which statism constrains the productive actions of individuals. These details can be measured with reasonable accuracy and (unlike spending "priorities") compared with minimal subjectivity. There is no reason to isolate a particular region, as we have done in this paper, because the competition for industrious people and their capital knows no national boundaries. An iron curtain may keep people's bodies within a country, against their will, but they will scarcely be motivated to work to their potential.

Case studies of national tax and spending systems would be a useful supplement to the relatively mechanical overview of this paper. Yet existing case studies, such as Pechman or Fels & Von Furstenberg, are usually written by several different economists, with different views on what is important. As a result, they are not suitable for comparative studies. There have been a few efforts to compare overall average tax rates (Marsden), and, far better, even marginal rates (Reynolds 1985, 1989; Rabushka-Bartlett). But the methodology of calculating the combined marginal effect of numerous taxes (some with deductions and ceilings) requires courageous assumptions and some complexity, which makes the exercise relatively inaccessible to busy businessmen and politicians (Frenkel). The concept of "average marginal rates" is also no substitute for the details. A country in which half the population (employees of multinationals) faced a 90% tax bracket, while the other half (farmers and cocaine merchants) were completely exempt might be said to have an "average marginal rate" of 45%, yet the effect would be much more discouraging and distorting than a flat 45% rate.

Assigning index numbers to the various elements of the tax code, such as the 1 to 10 scale used here, holds considerable promise as a relatively clear, and therefore effective, measure of this important aspect of economic liberty.

Maximum Marginal Tax Rates on Individual Income

	1979	1989	1991
Argentina	45	35	30
Australia	62	49	47
Austria	62	50	50
Belgium	76	71	55
Bolivia	48	10	10
Botswana	75	50	40
Brazil	55	25	25
Canada (Ontario)	58	45	47
Chile	60	50	50
Colombia	56	30	30
Denmark	73	73	68
Egypt	80	65	65
Finland	71	44	39
France	60	53	53
West Germany	56	56	57
Greece	60	50	50
Guatemala	40	34	34
Hungary	60	55	50
India	60	53	50
Indonesia	50	35	35
Ireland	65	53	53
Israel	66	48	48
Italy	72	50	50
Jamaica	58	33	33
Japan	75	50	50
S. Korea	89	50	50
Malaysia	60	45	35
Mauritius	50	35	35
Mexico	55	40	35
Netherlands	72	72	60
New Zealand	60	33	33
Norway	75	54	49
Pakistan	55	45	50

Maximum Marginal Tax Rates on Individual Income			
	1979	1989	1991
Philippines	70	35	35
Portugal	84	68	40
Puerto Rico	79	43	36
Singapore	55	33	33
Spain	66	56	56
Sweden	87	75	50
Thailand	60	55	55
Trinidad & Tobago	70	53	35
Turkey	75	50	50
United Kingdom	83	40	40
United States	70	28	31

Sources: Price Waterhouse, International Bureau of Fiscal Documentation, Tax Notes, Reuters, Financial Times.

References

Balassa, Bela, *et.al.*, *Toward Renewed Growth in Latin America*, Institute for International Economics, 1986, p. 111.

Barro, Robert A., "Taxes and Transfers," in *Macroeconomics*, John Wiley, 1987.

Blejer, Mario I. & Chu, Ke-Young, "Measures of Fiscal Impact: Methodological Issues," Occasional Paper No. 59, International Monetary Fund, June 1988.

Bradford, David & Stuart, Charles, "Issues in the Measurement and Interpretation of Effective Tax Rates," *National Tax Journal*, September 1986.

Bruno, Michael, *et.al.* (eds.), *Inflation Stabilization*, MIT, 1988.

Davies, David G., *United States Tax Policy*, Cambridge Univ., 1986.

Fels, Gerhard & von Furestenberg, George (eds.), *A Supply-Side Agenda for Germany*, Springer-Verlage, Berlin, 1989.

Frenkel, Jacob A., *et al.*, "International Spillovers of Taxation" National Bureau of Economic Research, *Working Paper* No. 2927, April 1989.

Frost & Sullivan Inc., "Measurement of the Investment Climate for International Business," Report for the U.S. Agency for International Development, September 6, 1988.

Gandhi, Ved (ed.), *Supply Side Economics: It's Relevance to Developing Countries*, International Monetary Fund, 1987.

Gil Diaz, Francisco, "Some Lessons from Mexico's Tax Reform," in David Newberry & Nicholas Stern (eds.), *The Theory of Taxation for Developing Countries*, World Bank, 1987.

Gordon, Roger H., "Taxation of Investment and Savings in a World Economy," *American Economic Review*, December 1986.

Gwartney, James & Stroup, Richard, "Labor Supply and Tax Rates: A Correction of the Record," *American Economic Review*, June 1983.

Heilbroner, Robert A., *The Future as History*, Grove Press, 1959.

Hicks, John in Helm, Dieter (ed.), *The Economics of John Hicks*, Blackwell, 1984.

Inter-American Development Bank, *Economic and Social Progress in Latin America*, 1987.

Koester, Reinhard B. & Kormendi, Roger C., "Taxation, Aggregate Activity and Economic Growth: Cross-Country Evidence on Some Supply-Side Hypotheses," University of Michigan, October 1987.

Marsden, Keith, "Links between Taxation and Economics Growth" World Bank Staff *Working Paper* No. 605, 1983.

Mirrlees, J.A., "An Exploration in the Theory of Optimum Income Taxation," *Review of Economic Studies*, April 1971.

Pechman, Joseph A. (ed.), *World Tax Reform: A Progress Report*, Brookings Institution, 1988.

Rabushka, Alvin & Bartlett, Bruce, "Tax Policy and Economic Growth in Developing Nations," U.S. Agency for International Development, 1986.

Reynolds, Alan, "Some International Comparisons of Supply-Side Tax Policy," *The Cato Journal*, Fall 1985.

— "Latin American Debt: The Case for Radical Tax Reform," February 1988, in Goodman, John & Moritz-Baden, Ramona (eds.) *The War of Ideas in Latin America*, National Center for Policy Analysis, forthcoming. Also,"La Deuda Latinamericana: Por Una Reforma Fiscal Radical" *Expansion*, Mexico, August 16, 1989.

— "The IMF's Destructive Recipe of Devaluation and Austerity," *Executive Briefing*, Hudson Institute, March 1992.

Tanzi, Vito, "Quantitative Characteristics of the Tax System of Developing Countries," in Newberry & Stern, *op.cit.*

Thurow, Lester A., *The Impact of Taxes on the American Economy*, Praeger, 1971.

Tobin, James, "Growth through Taxation," *National Economic Policy*, Yale, 1966.

Wanniski, Jude, *The Way the World Works*, Basic Books, 1978; Simon & Schuster, 1983; Polyconomics Inc., 1989.

Wilson, Ernest J. & Gordon, David F., "Global Market-Oriented Economic Reform: Scope and Meaning" Conference on Market-Oriented Paths to Economic Growth, Center for International Private Enterprise, D.C., February 15, 1989.

Wolf, Charles, *Markets or Governments*, Rand Corp., 1988, Ch.7.

Discussion

Tom DiLorenzo thought that some marginal measure should be used to see how government absorbs additional income each year. Alvin Rabushka worried that Price Waterhouse figures about tax rates may often refer to foreign residents, and domestic residents may be very different. The best source of evidence on this, he suggested, is from the International Bureau of Fiscal Documentation. Milton Friedman pointed out that the measurement of taxation goes hand in hand with the attempt to measure regulation. It makes no difference if the government taxes a company to prevent pollution or requires a company to install pollution equipment. They both create the same kind of distortions. Similarly, zoning regulation is a wealth tax. Alvin Rabushka mentioned that he had been involved in developing some measures of this kind of indirect taxation and that you have to be careful not to double count. For example, an overvalued exchange rate is an indirect tax on exporters. Thus if you study this problem area by area, you may pick-up some of this in specific categories.

Jack Carr mentioned that this assumes that more taxes reduce economic freedom. Yet a country like Israel may pay more taxes to safeguard its economic freedom in the future. You need to look at the whole to see what the taxes are spent on. Milton Friedman suggested that some of Israel's tax burden is for the military safeguarding of freedom, but there is a large component of their expenditures that reduce the economic freedom they are trying to safeguard. Alvin Rabushka took issue with Jack Carr arguing that although you might want to assess expenditures as to their freedom enhancing or diminishing effects, the cost of the taxes will reduce freedom regardless of the use to which they are put. A tax is a tax is a tax.

Easton argued that Reynolds should measure both the marginal and average tax rates. The marginal shows distortions, the average helps capture a total amount of the distortion. Milton Friedman pointed out that the cost of taxation is much higher than the proceeds to the government. James Gwartney reminded the audience that there are at least two tax rates that generate the same level of tax revenue, yet one may be more onerous than the other.

Juan Bendfeldt felt that other tax measures should be taken into account. The social security taxes should be considered. Further the quality of service should be counted in any measure. Regardless of the rates of tax, it is hard to tell what you are getting. The mix of both taxation and expenditure is an important element in considering the effect on economic freedom which may be diminished both from the tax and expenditure sides of the equation. Jack Carr responded that there is a complex problem here. If there is some kind of agreement—say an original confederation—and the winners are going to compensate the losers, then we run the risk of looking at the compensation devices and claiming that they are reductions in economic freedom. We need to know the nature of the original agreements in place to evaluate the pattern of taxes and expenditures. We are assuming that benefits should equal costs for every taxpayer. Further, we need to look at the whole tax system. If one country has a tax on gasoline and another a toll for road use, we will count the first as less free even though the cost of collecting the toll may far outweigh the costs of collecting the tax on gasoline. Walter Block suggested that this would not be a problem for an index as the tolls will be picked up in the regulation section which would correspond to a lower tax rate while the tax measure would be higher in the other country which would correspond with a lower cost of regulation.